YEMEN

INTO THE TWENTY-FIRST CENTURY
Continuity and Change

YEMEN

INTO THE TWENTY-FIRST CENTURY
Continuity and Change

Edited by
Kamil A. Mahdi, Anna Würth and Helen Lackner

ITHACA PRESS

YEMEN INTO THE TWENTY-FIRST CENTURY
Continuity and Change

Published by
Ithaca Press
8 Southern Court
South Street
Reading
RG1 4QS
UK

Ithaca Press is an imprint of Garnet Publishing Limited

First Edition

ISBN 13: 978-0-86372-290-5
ISBN 10: 0-86372-290-3

British Library Cataloguing-in-Publication Data
A catalogue record for this book is available from the British Library

Typeset by Samantha Barden
Jacket design by Garnet Publishing
Cover photo used with permission of Sergio Pitamitz/Robert Harding
World Imagery/Corbis

Printed in Lebanon

Contents

PART I
STRUCTURAL ADJUSTMENT
AND THE POLITICAL ECONOMY OF YEMEN

PART II
THE LEGAL SYSTEM

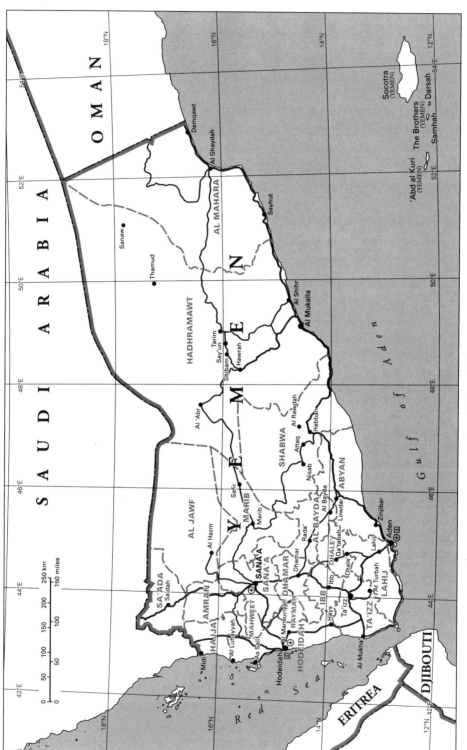

Republic of Yemen

Tables and Figures

Maps

Abbreviations

AFSED	Arab Fund for Social and Economic Development
AMF	Arab Monetary Fund
AREA	Agricultural Research and Extension Authority
CPI	Consumer Price Index
CSO	Central Statistical Organisation
EFARP	Economic, Financial and Administrative Reform Programme
ESAF	Enhanced Structural Adjustment Facility
FFYP	first five-year plan
FP	Family Planning
GIA	General Investment Authority
GPC	General People's Congress
GUYW	General Union of Yemeni Women
HD	Human Development
HDI	Human Development Index
HDR	Human Development Report
HRD	Human Resources Development
HUDP	Hodeidah Urban Development Project
HUPHC	Hodeidah Urban Primary Health Care (project)
ICD	International Cooperation for Development
IDA	International Development Agency
IFAD	International Fund for Rural Development
IILS	International Institute for Labour Studies
IMF	International Monetary Fund
IS	import substitution
MAWR	Ministry of Agriculture and Water Resources
MCH	mother and child health
MCHUP	Ministry of Housing, Planning and Urban Development
MOE	Ministry of Education
MOF	Ministry of Finance
MPD	Ministry of Planning and Development

NWRA	National Water Resources Authority
O&M	Operation and Maintenance
OECD	Organisation for Economic Cooperation and Development
PDRY	People's Democratic Republic of Yemen
PHC	primary health care
QOL	quality of life
RoY	Republic of Yemen
SFD	Social Fund for Development
SHD	Sustainable Human Development
SLRA	Survey and Land Registration Authority
SMEs	small and medium-sized (micro-) enterprises
SURDP	Southern Upland Rural Development Project
UAE	United Arab Emirates
UDP	urban development project
UNDP	United Nations Development Programme
VTE	vocational and technical education
YAR	Yemen Arab Republic
YCCA	Yemeni Centre for Conciliation and Arbitration
YD	Yemeni Dinars
YSP	Yemen Socialist Party

Acknowledgements

This volume is the result of a collaborative effort, and the editors acknowledge with much gratitude the support and encouragement received from many people at various stages of the project. The papers have been selected from a total of over forty contributions in both English and Arabic, originally presented at a conference in Exeter in 1998. Being constrained by limitations of language, book length and subject focus, we have only been able to include less than half of a very important set of research papers on contemporary Yemeni economic, social and political issues.

The present volume itself has benefited from extensive discussions by a large number of people, including the contributors, the editors and many other scholars. We especially appreciate the efforts of colleagues who reviewed papers and who made very constructive suggestions at different stages. Dr Martha Mundy was also helpful in her suggestions over the structure of the book, and she had earlier made a major contribution to convening the Exeter conference. Others whose assistance was vital in drawing together such a large group of researchers include Dr Abdul-Salam Hammad and Professor Alexander Knysh. We are especially grateful for the efforts of Dr Hussein Al-Hubaishi and Professor Hussein Al-Amri, former Yemeni Ambassador to London, who had participated in the conference and supported the project throughout. We also wish to extend our special appreciation to Dr Abdul-Kareem Al-Iryani, former Prime Minister of Yemen, who participated in the conference and engaged in extensive discussions after his keynote address. Support was also received from Dr Mutahhar Al-Saidi who was one of the scholars participating in the conference and who now represents the Republic of Yemen in London. The project is also indebted for financial support received from the Yemeni government.

We wish to thank all those who supported this project and contributed to it in different ways, and we appreciate the considerable cooperation of the contributors to this volume and the many others whose papers would have been more appropriately included in a separate volume. We wish also to thank Mrs Lindy Ayubi who has committed much of her time and her multiple skills to all stages of this project. We especially acknowledge her meticulous reading and her efforts in harmonizing the styles of different contributors. We also acknowledge the contribution of Paul Auchterlonie, Arabic subject librarian at Exeter, whose extensive knowledge of literature and sources on Yemen has been invaluable in tracing and completing references. Emma Hawker and the Ithaca Press editorial and production team deserve appreciation for their patience and thorough professionalism.

Introduction

Kamil Mahdi, Anna Würth and Helen Lackner

The first decade of the single merged Yemeni state was characterised by the process of unification of institutions of the two former states, the Yemen Arab Republic (YAR) and the People's Democratic Republic of Yemen (PDRY). After decades of tension between the two states, the 1990 unification process was not an agreement between equals. While both states had experienced deepening economic crises in the late 1980s, the PDRY with 3 million inhabitants was clearly unable to carry the same weight as the less internationally isolated YAR with 12 million. Nevertheless, the mechanism set up for the transitional period gave formal equality to the two states and their ruling parties in the new transitional institutions. So from 1990 to 1993 equal numbers of political positions were given to the Yemeni Socialist Party (YSP) which had formerly ruled the PDRY, with its capital Aden, and the General People's Congress (GPC) which had ruled the YAR, with its capital Sana'a. Although tension between the ruling elites had been building up, this system survived until the parliamentary elections of 1993. The 1993 elections resulted in a coalition government between the three major parties, the GPC, the YSP, and the Yemeni Congregation for Reform (Islah). Thereafter the disagreements about the type of united government each part of the country wanted gradually got out of control, leading to the three-month-long civil war of 1994, and a short-lived 'secession' of the southern part. The YSP leadership had been in favour of a more federal system which would have allowed them to retain their own social and economic policies, while the northerners wanted a more centralised state. In July 1994, the YSP leadership was militarily defeated, and this outcome of the civil war effectively confirmed the ascendancy of the former YAR, its institutional approach and its personnel.

After the war in 1994, the GPC continued the former coalition with the Islah party until elections in 1997, when the GPC took the majority of votes, and has ruled Yemen alone ever since. The Yemeni Socialist Party has suffered from its partial association with the 'secessionist' movement and even more so by the reassertion of power by the GPC and its leadership. The Islah party oscillated between supporting the GPC against the YSP and taking the place of the main opposition itself. Overall, the daily lives of citizens in the Southern Governorates has changed significantly in the first decade of unification, and the YSP has been unable effectively to articulate southern interests at the national level. A process of decentralisation has been taking place under external influence in recent years, and more directly under the influence of foreign aid agencies. This process, though, has been far less profound than the type of federal state that had been envisaged by the YSP or even the type of decentralisation favoured by many had the unification process taken place more smoothly.

This book discusses a number of major issues relevant to the development of Yemen in the first decade after its unification in 1990, issues which remain essential to understanding the challenges the country faces in the early decades of the twenty-first century. The book focuses on the country's internal socioeconomic developments, addressing mainly economic, social and legal issues. Most of the chapters dealing with parts of the country that were formerly in the PDRY are, in one way or another, marked by the fundamental changes in internal social and economic dynamics which were brought about by unification and in particular those taking place after 1994. These processes remain important as a subtext to current developments. The same holds true for changes in the territory of the former YAR documented in this book; developments in these governorates were, however, influenced less by the unification process and more by the socioeconomic trends of the period in general. The book brings together a selection of papers from a larger number that had earlier been delivered to a conference held at the Institute of Arab and Islamic Studies, University of Exeter, in 1998. The selection is one that is relevant to the themes addressed here and most of the papers were subsequently revised.

A number of important issues are not addressed: in particular, foreign relations, military affairs, party politics, and cultural developments, among others. Although Yemen started producing and exporting oil in the mid-1980s, the discovery of oil along the borders between the two former Yemeni states being one of the factors that accelerated the advent of unification, this is not discussed in detail here. Oil production peaked in recent years at close to 450,000 barrels per day but is already dropping, and reserves are limited. Despite the recent rise in crude prices, oil is unlikely ever to bring about the kind of bonanza Yemenis dream about, based on their awareness and experience of the situation elsewhere in the Arabian Peninsula, be it in Saudi Arabia, the UAE or even Oman. While oil revenues clearly play an important role in keeping the state solvent, they are not used in such a way as to have any direct impact on the daily lives of the population. Access to education, to health services, or to other social and economic benefits is not enhanced by the very limited employment opportunities generated and by the fact that revenues are retained centrally for purposes of power and patronage. Gas reserves have a greater potential, and in the late 1990s they raised many misplaced hopes. The state of the international gas market and the political risk associated with long-term contract agreements militated against the development of a gas export potential. However, the more significant and more rational option of using gas for domestic electricity generation has also been neglected. Hence the oil and gas sector are playing a lesser role in Yemeni society and economy than had been hoped.

International context
Similarly Yemen's international relations are not covered here. Yemen's position in the Peninsula and its former status as a major supplier of labour and migrants to other Peninsular states lead many in Yemen, ordinary citizens as well as government, to seek greater integration with the Gulf Cooperation Council states. The GCC states respond to these overtures with unsurprising reticence for a number of reasons. First, Yemen's population is alone roughly equivalent to the combined indigenous populations of all the GCC states while its Gross Domestic Product per capita is a small fraction of the GCC average and its financial positions stand in stark contrast to the positions of the GCC states. Secondly its status as a Republic, with grassroots political participation, regular elections and equal voting rights for men and women, makes it significantly different from the GCC states which are all hereditary monarchies and emirates with very limited political rights for their

population, women in particular. Whatever the flaws of Yemeni democracy, the country does adhere to the notion of a democratic system, which is not the case of the GCC states. Finally and not least importantly, the prospect of an influx of large numbers of relatively low-skilled labourers and of greater demands for financial support in a time of retrenchment are unattractive prospects for the GCC states, which generally prefer to import their labour from non-Arabic-speaking countries, rather than from among groups who can claim tribal kinship status with their own citizens, and could thus engage in an active political discourse that might resonate with their population.

On the broader regional and world scale Yemen, in this new century, is receiving more attention and aid than it had done earlier, mainly as both the EU and the US want to strengthen the state and encourage it in its efforts to control and reduce the threat of Islamic fundamentalism, regardless of the regime's own relationship to Islamic fundamentalists and its human rights record. While Yemen's former obscurity has been replaced since the mid-1990s by frequent mention and recurrent prominence in the international media as a result of its association first with kidnappings of West Europeans and, more recently, with fundamentalist Islamic groups, including some notorious individuals, the Yemeni regime has firmly aligned itself with the US and against its former ally in Iraq. The re-entry of the US as a major player in Yemen by 2000 marks an important difference from the 1990s covered in this book. There is an increasing presence of Western trainers for the military and the police, and it has even been possible for the US military to attack and deal extra-judicially against presumed fundamentalist terrorists on Yemeni territory. This is in sharp contrast with the situation at the time of the first Gulf War when Yemen lost considerable aid due to its refusal to support that first US war against Iraq in 1990–1. Current cooperation with Western security has involved training and equipping of military and security forces and has, for now, resulted in a dramatic reduction in violence against foreigners.

Unfortunately this improved security situation has not extended to ordinary Yemeni citizens who continue to suffer violence and instability in their daily lives as well as the negative features frequently associated with high levels of corruption. Although the root causes of these problems can be attributed to the rise in poverty and the lack of employment opportunities, impunity among perpetrators is a factor which affects people's confidence in the nature of the state and government, and is a bad omen for coming years unless firm measures are taken to address these issues. The attraction of fundamentalism will only disappear when its alternative, democracy, actually delivers improved living standards for the population in general, and the poor in particular.

Economic issues

Unified Yemen with a population of about 15 million in 1994 and 20 million in 2005 is one of the world's Least Developed Countries and suffers from considerable poverty. The causes of this situation and some of the policies implemented in attempting to address these problems form the core of this book. The first four chapters focus on the macroeconomic aspects and how the state is responding to its problems through a number of programmes including those sponsored by the IMF and World Bank. Nader Fergany's chapter deals with the structural adjustment programme implemented by the Government of Yemen starting in late 1994, under the auspices of the IMF and the World Bank. Fergany addresses two aspects of the programme, its impact on macroeconomic stabilisation and its consequences for Welfare and Human Development. He begins by discussing the concept of Human Development and its implications for development strategies, and proceeds to an analysis of the state of development in Yemen. Fergany develops a critique of the Economic, Financial and Administrative Reform Programme, based on the programme's failure to tackle poverty and enhance human capability, and on the doubts regarding its performance in the area of macroeconomic stabilisation. The paper concludes with a suggested policy package for poverty eradication through Human Development.

Schmitz discusses the World Bank's model of 'good governance', emphasising its limitations as a guide to the successful implementation of an economic reform and liberalisation programme in Yemen. Schmitz argues that technical measures of good governance are only held together in a programme through politics, and that therefore it is essential to address issues of politics and power in Yemen. Schmitz notes that structural economic as well as political trends during the 1990s have run counter to the liberalisation and privatisation trends advocated in reform programmes. The paper distinguishes between the absence of generally applicable principles of secure property rights and free markets and the ability of multinationals in certain fields, particularly oil, to operate with adequate risk assessment. The chapter notes that what is absent is a state and politics which guarantee stability.

Colton, through an examination of the trends in migration and in particular the return of almost one million people as a result of the first Gulf War, demonstrates that migration is unlikely in the future to regain its position as the main successful strategy for coping with poverty in the country, as circumstances in the world economy have changed and are no longer as positive for the Yemeni labour force as they were in past centuries.

Almutawakel addresses the importance and potential future role of manufacturing in providing local employment and in replacement of agriculture, whose role as the main employer is bound to continue its decline, mainly because of overexploitation of the limited natural resource base and population increase. After surveying the macroeconomy, emphasising the importance of external relations and particularly the role of remittances, he then considers the structure of the economy, focusing on recent trends of the rise in the oil industry and the earlier dominance of the service sector. His analysis of the potential of manufacturing in solving the country's economic problems is strengthened by an examination of the structure of output and employment in this sector. He identifies a number of features of the sector, discusses government economic policies and offers a taxonomy of problems and obstacles to industrial development in Yemen. Finally, the chapter advances elements of an industrial strategy which somewhat cautiously advocates the promotion of small labour-intensive industries. Given the inadequate data sets and the poor definition of Yemeni economic variables, these conclusions are tentative, but nevertheless, significant.

Legal aspects

Having outlined the basic long-term problems of Yemeni macroeconomic development and policy, the book then focuses on a set of phenomena which are directly associated with the process of establishing unified institutions in the country and the introduction of a state based on and ruled by law. Shamiry, al-Hubaishi and Würth examine the role of the legal system in creating the institutions appropriate to a modern state. Shamiry introduces the 1997 reform plan for the judiciary, and explains it by analysing the historical developments in the judicial systems of both the YAR and the PDRY. He argues for a strong role to be accorded to the Supreme Judicial Council, the Commission for Judicial Inspection, and the Supreme Court. By strengthening these institutions, at the apex of the judicial hierarchy, the successful merger between the two judicial systems will be ensured. Additionally, only strong judicial institutions can guarantee the rule of law, and an equal and thorough application of procedural and substantive law. Al-Hubaishi takes a different view. He examines the development of the commercial courts in the YAR since the 1970s and argues that strong commercial courts would create a stable investment environment which could contribute to poverty alleviation. His chapter analyses the strengths and weaknesses of the courts from a historical perspective, and argues for reforms of the commercial courts as a model for the overall reform of the legal and judicial system. Würth deals with the development of the judicial system in the former YAR, and argues that the moves towards codification and legal and judicial reform in the 1970s were part of a broader programme of political centralisation and economic integration. The increase in extra-legal institutions is discussed as a by-product of these developments. As for developments in the 1990s the author contends that, despite institutional flaws, parts of the judiciary are moving towards the rule of law, by strengthening administrative jurisprudence.

The crises in natural resource management

Natural resource management is at the core of Yemen's problems in the twenty-first century. With 70 per cent of the population still living in rural areas in 2005, the management of scarce water resources, agricultural policy and land tenure are at the heart of the nation's problems. While some of the chapters in this section address long-term problems (Ward, Tutwiler), others focus on issues which have been strongly affected by the unification process (Lackner, Alsanabani). Christopher Ward looks at the most basic aspect of the current crisis in natural resource management in Yemen, groundwater overdraft. Yemen is mining its aquifers to such an extent that serious water-related problems have emerged for both present and future generations. His chapter examines the option of groundwater mining and concludes that this is not a desirable policy choice. However, since mining of groundwater will inevitably continue, he presents the case for the development of a 'mitigation plan' that will slow the rate of depletion and give time for the economy and society to adjust. Such a plan must include local water consumers in a participatory approach, and will have to mediate the interests of rural and urban consumers.

Both Alsanabani and Lackner address the complex issue of land tenure. Alsanabani focuses on the different types of land tenure systems operating in the highlands and the impact of tenure relations on productivity and the introduction of more sustainable cultivation practices. Lackner deals with the reprivatization of state-owned land in the Southern Governorates, i.e. the former People's Democratic Republic of Yemen. She examines changes in the structural relations between the different social strata of the region and the interrelationship between social forces and political change. Her work is focused on the process of 'compensation' for the dispossessed farmers, the main implementation mechanism of which was a foreign-funded project operating from 1998 to 2004. She also discusses the effects of the process and its implications on social relations in the rural areas of the Southern Governorates and their political repercussions, in particular the extent to which political power is reflected in land tenure changes.

Having presented the main characteristics of Yemeni agriculture, Tutwiler outlines the development of the country's agricultural research agenda and examines its appropriateness in light of the severe crisis affecting agricultural production, resource use and environment. Yemen has been experiencing increasing rural poverty and decreasing food security, and Tutwiler places considerable emphasis on proposals for a research agenda that is more focused on the agricultural sectors that have potential for sustainability in the context of serious water scarcity, including rainfed agriculture and certain types of livestock husbandry. Both this chapter and the rest of the section emphasise the importance of effective resource management and appropriate policies that are based on sound knowledge. New technologies introduced through unfettered market forces have accentuated the crisis of agriculture, while the institutions and framework for policy remain weak.

Social themes, relations and policies

A major theme of the book is poverty, its emergence and main characteristics. While the topic is addressed indirectly at least by a large number of contributors (Fergany, Almutawakel, Colton, Ward, Lackner, Worm, Kangas), it is the direct focus for Hashem's paper. She discusses the social impact of development processes and policies utilising the concept of *social exclusion*, gaining importance in the 1990s. In describing poverty-reduction policies and the obstacles to their implementation, the author notes that there are difficulties with operative definitions of poverty and with identifying the processes generating poverty. She argues that quantitative economic measures need to be supplemented by dimensions emphasising *social exclusion*. The paper then proceeds to identify norms and processes of *social exclusion*, and identifies a number of 'excluded' groups in Yemen. She concludes that specific policies are required to address the problems of each of the excluded groups according to the specificity of their type of exclusion.

Poverty has many features and access to health is one of the most important. Worm's analysis of the political changes and development of the Mother and Child Health Care (MCH) policy adopted during the 1990s contributes to explaining the difficulties faced by women in their search for health care. The chapter is based on research into archival material and legislation, and on professional experience in several Mother and Child Health Care projects. After summarising the basic indicators for Mother and Child health in Yemen, the paper shows how policies in MCH became a subject of intense political competition between the major Yemeni parties which were vying for control of the Ministry of Health and its resources. Worm argues that institutional competition has helped to stifle consensus over sensitive social issues.

Contemporary and future health issues are also covered by Kangas's analysis of travel abroad by Yemeni citizens for medical treatment, mainly to Jordan, India and Germany. Interestingly her research shows that many poor families successfully make considerable financial sacrifices to take sick family members for treatment abroad, which is not always better than what they would get at home. Her paper deals with the directions of medical travel, its expense, the kinds of treatment sought, and the illnesses that necessitate treatment abroad. She argues that it is extremely important to understand the reasons for medical travel abroad and that these reasons are worthy of consideration by policy makers in the light of privatisation of the health sector.

Alongside Lackner's contribution, both Dahlgren and Pritzkat focus on time-specific issues relating to social aspects of the unification process in the Southern Governorates. While the actual events discussed in all three chapters had been completed by the beginning of the 2000s, the underlying features of social relations which they examine remain important and may come to explain events in the future. Dahlgren's contribution examines pre- and post-unification developments in the social situation of women in Aden. She argues that legal change initiated by the former South Yemeni government in the 1970s did not thoroughly change people's opinions, outlooks and normative orientations in matters conceived of as 'private'. In analysing attitudes regarding the 'ideal marriage' and 'ideal spouse', she finds that in this sphere the state-sponsored feminism of the 1970s is relevant only in the workplace, and that it is contradicted by an ideological approach that reigns supreme. Thomas Pritzkat deals with the development of the urban property market in Mukalla, the capital of Hadhramawt governorate. He demonstrates how the combination of capital inflow from returning migrants, speculators, and gaps in legislation and its enforcement have produced an urban property bonanza for some, unparalleled in the history of Hadhramawt.

The impact of externally supported development projects is an underlying issue in many papers (Ward, Lackner, Tutwiler, Worm) but is explicitly discussed by Ali Ghailan and Marina de Regt in their analysis of two projects in Hodeidah – one of the major urban centres in Yemen which has been most affected by the influx of Yemeni migrants expelled from Saudi Arabia and the Gulf in 1990 – and the levels of urban poverty that have ensued from these inflows. They examine two development projects funded by international donors, one in housing and the other a health project. The presence of expatriate administration, the involvement of the community, and the degree of improvement in the quality of life are identified as key variables responsible for the success and/or failure of the components of the respective projects.

Finally, Al-Abbasi offers an economist's analysis of the challenges facing the education system in Yemen. He identifies major relevant population variables and considers features of the labour market that govern the utilisation of human resources, particularly those with skills produced through the educational system. Al-Abbasi then surveys the status of education with respect to enrolment, drop-out rates, staffing and resources, sex and regional disparities. He considers higher education and the recent entry of the private sector to this area. All this serves as a background to a discussion of the financing of education, particularly given the government's reform programme, a major component of which is the reduction in the budget deficit. Educational expenditure is then discussed in greater detail and projections are made under different sets of assumptions. The projected levels of educational expenditure are found to be unsustainable and alternative financing and other policy options are discussed. Given the emphasis placed on education in the dominant neo-liberal development policy discourse and the limitations of practical options for a country with poor natural resources for agricultural development, this examination of education and the constraints that affect it is an appropriate note on which to conclude.

Looking into the future, the book raises a number of fundamental questions that affect the country's future development. Economically, Yemen suffers from a range of structural problems including low productivity, high unemployment, external dependence and severe imbalances across the economy. These problems are accentuated by a population level that is expected to double in the coming two decades and by an already high dependence on a natural resource base that is facing critical decline. Arguably, one of the greatest concerns is for water which has already been unsustainably exploited for decades. Urgent and effective action is needed to address this issue of extremely stark choices. As for oil, production is expected to continue dropping, thereby tending to reduce state revenues in the long run, regardless of any probable price increases. The temptation to opt for relying on natural gas exports would be a short-term palliative, and would preclude the development of a local industrial base and significant employment generation, and forgo the use of that gas as the main source of energy for both domestic and business purposes. Yemen's main coping strategy in the face of economic stress has, in the past, been out-migration: this option is unlikely to re-emerge in the coming decades both because of the restrictions in immigration imposed by most developed and GCC states and due to the fact that most Yemeni labour is low skilled. Yemen has an important potential for tourism, taking advantage of the country's architectural and historic heritage and its natural beauty, but this potential is unlikely to be in mass tourism. Other important resources and areas of advantage include fishing and the redevelopment of the country's historic position in the provision of transport and trading services. Many of these activities are contingent upon sustained security, the development of infrastructure and of appropriate policies. The book has not addressed these factors, but much of its content enhances understanding of relevant issues, and more specifically of the problems of political economy, institutional development and policy formulation.

Socially and politically, regional and class tensions have been exacerbated by poverty and economic instability. Given the economic, social, political, demographic and resource questions discussed in this volume it is more likely than not that poverty and deprivation will worsen. To what extent other causes of social tensions diminish in the future will largely depend on political factors and, in particular, on the regime's ability to respond to the population's increasing need for a deepening of the democratic process. While the early 1990s had seen pressures by international institutions and donors to encourage democratisation and the rule of law, the current 'security first' climate tends to support an illiberal 'democracy' as long as it takes part in anti-terrorism efforts. The first years of this new century have seen a gradual retreat to a form of 'one party' rule although it is formally different from that which prevailed prior to unification in each of the two parts of the country. The continuing official recognition of 'opposition' parties is not in doubt, thus providing a veneer of democracy and satisfying the requirements of donor states and institutions in this respect. However, short of major policy changes induced either by popular demand or from the current ruling group, it is unlikely that opposition parties will be allowed to play a significant role in government. As in the past, their share of the recognised vote in any election is unlikely to be fully representative of their popular support. Youth dissatisfaction is likely to continue building up a base for fundamentalist movements unless an alternative is offered through an effective democratisation process accompanied by significant improvements in the economic situation of the population at large.

PART I

STRUCTURAL ADJUSTMENT AND THE
POLITICAL ECONOMY OF YEMEN

1

Structural Adjustment versus Human Development in Yemen

Nader Fergany

Conceptual framework

The concept of Human Resources Development (HRD) had a limited content that stemmed from economic efficiency considerations. Human beings were looked upon as one factor of production that, in a genuine process of economic growth, would need to be developed through investment in human capital, as an instrument of expanding production of commodities. Education and health were recognised as the two main areas for investment in human capital.

However, with the increasing realisation of the crucial role played by institutional (social organisation) factors in the development process, HRD took on a much wider meaning in the development literature.[1] In fact HRD acquired full social-organisation ramifications well before Human Development (HD) received wide currency and visibility through its adoption by the United Nations Development Programme (UNDP), the formulation of the Human Development Index (HDI), and the publication of the annual Human Development Report (HDR).[2] Indeed, the development literature was inching towards the term 'Human Development' in the second half of the 1980s. Nowadays, the original, and limited, sense of HRD has only a historical, and much criticised, place in the development literature.

Unfortunately, HD, though widely adopted, is not fully understood. The definition and elucidation given in the first HDR (UNDP, 1990) will be sufficient here for indicating the major building-blocks of the concept. Human development is defined by UNDP as a process of enlarging people's choices or human capability in order to attain the highest level of welfare possible. The three essential capabilities are for people to lead a long and healthy life, to acquire knowledge and to have access to resources needed for a decent standard of living. Additional choices range from political, economic and social freedom to opportunities for being creative and productive, and enjoying personal self-respect and guaranteed human rights. Thus HD has two sides: the formation of human capabilities such as improved health, knowledge and skills, and the use people make of their acquired capabilities for productive purposes, such as being active in cultural, social and political affairs or leisure.

In the HD perspective poverty is not about low income, or even the failure to meet basic needs, but about human capability failure, i.e. the inability of people to generate the human capabilities required for meeting the welfare entitlement of a social entity: a person, a household or a community. It is unfortunate that the HDI became the most current component of the HD movement. The index, essentially a composition of three basic indicators (life expectancy, education and GDP per capita adjusted for purchasing power) fails to capture the infinitely rich ramifications of the concept and limits the potential for policy formulation on the basis of the index alone.[3] Luckily, however, successive issues of the HDR have attempted to make up for this deficiency by examining other important aspects of the concept. For example the second issue of the HDR (UNDP, 1991) considered the fundamental question of rights and freedoms, and was strongly criticised by governments.

To underline the significance of the institutional basis of HD, the 1993 issue of HDR dealt with the all-important issues of participation, governance and community organisation. It also advocated 'people-friendly markets' that would allow people 'to participate fully in their operations and to share equitably in their benefits. Having markets serve people rather than people serve markets.' Preconditions for such people-friendly markets would include, among other things, adequate investment in the education, health and skills of people to prepare them for the market; an equitable distribution of assets; extension of credit to the poor; access to information, particularly about the range of market opportunities; adequate physical infrastructure; adequate support for R&D; and no barriers to entry.

Accompanying conditions comprised a stable macroeconomic environment; a comprehensive incentive system, with correct price signals, a fair tax regime and adequate rewards for work and enterprise; and freedom from arbitrary government control and regulation. In addition, measures would be taken to correct for the vagaries of markets, including protection of competition and the environment, as well as consumers, workers and special groups (particularly women, children and minorities). An adequate safety net would also exist to 'look after the *temporary*[4] victims of market forces, to bring them back into the markets, primarily through human investment, worker retraining and access to credit opportunities [and] more permanent support for groups such as the disabled and the aged'.

It is important to point out that HD emphasises two basic dimensions of human capability: knowledge and health. Education, particularly formal education, is but one channel for acquiring knowledge. Other channels include socialisation inside the family and other institutions. The mass media have also come to play an extremely significant role in the acquisition of knowledge, skills and attitudes. Health as well is to be understood in the sense of absence of all types of infirmity, a state of 'positive well-being'. To stress the paramount importance of basic education and health care, the 1993 HDR maintains that 'some services should always be free: specifically primary health care and basic education'.

However, it is the institutional basis of development that furnishes the enabling environment for success. It is the arena for empowerment through effective participation and activist collective social action, as well as the guarantee of sustainability. An analysis of quality of life (QOL) indices based on a large number of development and welfare indicators in an international context concludes that investment in human capabilities plays a crucial role in the early stages of development but higher levels of welfare are characterised by material and political well-being. It is this link of the institutional aspects to investment in human capabilities and enjoying adequate material conditions that typifies any genuine notion of development, particularly HD (Fergany, 1994).

It is important, nevertheless, to be candid about the fact that the concept of HD, as presented here, with emphasis on the institutional basis, does not meet with the approval of all governments or international bodies. However, in my opinion, doing away with this basis nullifies the concept and perpetuates underdevelopment.

In preparation for the 1995 UN World Summit for Social Development, the 1994 HDR looked closely at the three interrelated problems of unemployment, poverty and social disintegration, and proposed the famous, but little heeded, 20:20 compact on HD. The compact stipulated that 20 per cent of developing country budgets and 20 per cent of industrial country aid should be allocated to human priority expenditure. The same issue of the HDR provided policy strategies for combating the three interdependent problems, including some that flew in the face of the structural adjustment paradigm, such as agrarian reform and public works programmes. The preparatory documents for the summit itself were more directly critical of structural adjustment programmes and their concomitant adverse effects on unemployment, poverty and social cohesion.

In the Copenhagen Declaration, adopted at the summit, 117 heads of state or government pledged to make 'the conquest of poverty, the goal of full employment and the fostering of stable, safe and just societies' their overriding objectives. Specific commitments, in the language of the declaration, ensured that structural adjustment programmes included social development goals, and that universal and equitable access to education and primary health care was achieved. The persistence of mass poverty in many countries of the Third World, especially under structural adjustment, pushed the issues of poverty alleviation or, if one is the hopeful type, poverty eradication and employment generation to the top of the development agenda in the 1990s.

Examination of the state of HD in Yemen reveals the need for prompt and effective action. Poverty is widespread and on the rise. Indeed, poverty eradication through building HD represents a formidable challenge. In the absence of strong commitment and sustained efforts to build HD in Yemen, the prospects for poverty eradication under structural adjustment are not bright. Capitalist restructuring under the prevailing structural adjustment paradigm aims at instituting private capital as the principal mover of economic activity. This invites favouring capital at the expense of labour. Needless to say, owners of capital represent a small minority in a poor country such as Yemen whereas earnings (income from work) are the principal source of livelihood for the vast majority of the population. Favouritism to capital, especially large capital, particularly in the context of economic recession, invariably results in widespread unemployment and widening poverty.

Moreover, the sociopolitical context of structural adjustment in a country such as Yemen ensures the worst possible results of free markets in a sea of market imperfections (barriers to entry and competition such as red tape, institutional fragility, cronyism, corruption, risk aversion). Ironically, in countries where the institutional basis of free markets is either absent or fragile, structural adjustment helps reinforce these very same market imperfections since government (and governance) reform do not score highly on the 'structural adjustment' agenda. In particular, such institutional reform runs against the interest of ruling coalitions – the 'national' side of the structural adjustment contract – and is not pursued by the international side of the contract with anything close to the fervour of insisting on macroeconomic reform, private-sector supremacy and free trade. The inevitable widening disparity in the income and wealth distribution, and hence in power, is expected to tighten the noose of poverty.

Structural adjustment, including globalisation, surely entails risks for a poor country such as Yemen. These forces can also bring forth opportunities, provided resources are utilised much more efficiently than in the past and in consonance with the requirements of the evolving 'global network society'. The character of this society makes people the ultimate resource of any nation. Hence, building HD represents the surest path to prosperity for Yemenis in the twenty-first century.

The state of development in Yemen

Information is seriously inadequate in Yemen. As simple a piece of information as the rate of population growth is not known with any accuracy: estimates vary from 3.1 to 3.7 per cent in the mid-1990s. The situation gets considerably murkier when issues such as unemployment (estimates range from 10 to 40 per cent), or the extent of poverty, are considered. All available information should be treated with caution. The information presented below, culled from a variety of often conflicting sources, and deliberately kept at the level of orders of magnitude, is no exception.

Inadequacy of information aside, Yemen is a country of limited resources, especially human and institutional ones – a situation that results in low productivity and an inadequate level of human welfare. In the mid-1990s the level of social welfare in Yemen was estimated to be quite limited. With per capita GDP estimated at less than US$300, Yemen is internationally classified as a 'low-income' country. Life expectancy at birth – a measure of the general condition of health and an indicator of the standard of living – is estimated to be lower than the average of low-income countries of 63 years (according to the World Bank classification and data).

The structure of production is weak and has not been improving significantly. This is very clear in the case of agriculture, the major sector of economic activity, which employs more than half the labour force but contributes only about one-fifth of GDP and less than 5 per cent of exports. The rate of growth of agricultural products in the last 25 or so years is estimated not to have exceeded 2 per cent per annum, roughly half the rate of population growth. Crop yields are estimated to be among the lowest in the world. The agricultural sector seems to have been transformed into a *qat*-based economy (though less labour intensive, *qat* revenue per hectare is estimated at close to 20 times that of cereals). Vegetable production has also increased rapidly, while the prime cash crops – coffee, sesame, cotton and tobacco – have registered a decline. Livestock population, steadily rising in the 1980s, seems to have begun to decrease in the 1990s, particularly in the Northern Governorates. Hence, Yemen is classified as a 'food deficit' country, and in fact is classed in the 'lower category' of the Low Income Food Deficit Countries (LIFDCs). The self-sufficiency ratio of cereals is currently estimated at about one-third only (compared to 75 per cent in 1970). For wheat, self-sufficiency is even lower (estimated at about 15 per cent of consumption). As a result, food commodities represented about 80 per cent of imports in the mid-1990s and 60 per cent of consumption needs. The weakness of productive activity also means a fragile export structure: crude oil exports accounted for 85 per cent of exports in the first half of the 1990s (94 per cent in 1995).

Population size was 15 million in 1995, but population growth is fast – though estimates vary. In addition, the age structure is young (almost half the population is less than 15 years of age). This means a high dependency ratio and a large demand on basic services such as education and health care. It also suggests a fast-growing labour force.

The size of the labour force is estimated around 3.5 million, implying a participation rate of 24 per cent. This level of participation undoubtedly underestimates the extent of effective participation in economic activity, since the mode of production in Yemen is characterised by the extensive participation of women and children, a feature that is missed by standard statistical operations.

Less than a quarter of the population lives in urban areas but the urban population grows at about double the overall rate of population growth, indicating fast rural/urban migration. This is significant, since pockets of urban poverty are characterised by extremes of deprivation. More importantly, the rural population is thinly scattered in small residential agglomerations. There are almost 30,000 villages in Yemen, which means an average size of approximately 400 persons per settlement. This wide dispersion of the population strains the provision of basic services and necessitates appropriate modes of delivery.

Human capability embodied in the population is low. Less than half the population is literate (about 24 per cent among women and 63 per cent among males). Enrolment in basic education stands at about 60 per cent of the population in the 6–14 age group, and growth in enrolment was slow in the 1990s. The gender disparity in access to education is large: the ratio of girls to boys receiving primary education is estimated at less than one-half in general and is significantly lower in the higher stages of education. Furthermore, the gender gap in enrolment is estimated to have widened in the last few years. Rural areas suffer lower enrolment ratios, especially among girls. School facilities are generally poor and the quality of education is widely assessed as being low.

As indicated earlier, the health situation is poor. Infant mortality is variously estimated at about 100 per 1,000 live births. Malnutrition and nutrition-related health problems are prevalent. Chronic undernutrition manifested in stunting (short height for age) is estimated to affect about 40 per cent of children younger than five years of age. Maternal mortality rates are estimated to be among the highest in the world. In the country-side, less than a fifth of the population has access to safe water. The ratio of beneficiaries of clean water supplies in the main cities is reported to have been declining.

Rural areas clearly suffer higher levels of deprivation of basic services. For example, there are fewer than 400 health centres and 1,200 primary health care facilities (compared to 30,000 villages). It is further estimated that about one-fifth of community-level health units are either non-functioning or inadequately staffed and equipped. Where facilities do not exist in a village, long distances and lack of transportation naturally prevent individuals from seeking health services elsewhere. The private sector has recently started providing educational and health services but these services are obviously selective of the urban rich.

Deep-seated cultural traditions restrict girls' access to education and women's participation in the social, political, administrative and economic spheres. These constraints, in addition to a preference for large families, limit women's choices and restrict their contribution to development.

Government generally suffers from weak institutional capabilities and inefficiency of personnel. Additional problems stem from the recent amalgamation of two systems of civil service, different in perspectives and modalities of action, as well as a large number of 'ghost' employees.

Governance is centralised, though recently a multiparty system was initiated, under which two elections took place. The impoverishment of outlying tribal areas militates for tension between the government and the tribes. The central government increased the extent of decentralisation through the law of local government (1991). A long and successful experience with cooperative organisations was discontinued in 1985. The democratic context in general, and civil society in particular, are judged to be rather weak and are constrained by a restrictive legal and administrative environment. The law regulating non-governmental organisations (NGOs) dates back to 1963, though new legislation is under consideration at the time of writing. By comparison, the private sector is expected to enjoy almost unregulated encouragement.

Ecology places severe constraints on development. The country's total area exceeds 55 million hectares, of which only a tiny fraction (about 2.5 per cent) is cultivable. A water crisis of unprecedented dimensions casts a dark shadow on the prospects for both agriculture and human welfare. Yemen is one of the poorest countries in water resources: renewable resources are estimated at less than 150 m^3 per capita (the world average is 7,500). Annual extraction is estimated at five times the renewable amount. Erosion of the highland terrace system has negative consequences for the overall watershed management. The crop pattern has important implications for the water situation. Due to its high water requirements, *qat* production – currently estimated to consume about 25 per cent of irrigation water – exacerbates the water scarcity and results in salinisation of aquifers. In contrast, wheat imports largely represent a form of water import embedded in grain. In addition, deforestation and desertification are real threats. Deforestation results from the increasing demand for wood burning. Estimates suggest a 5 per cent annual loss of agricultural land as a result of desertification and dune encroachment, particularly along the coastal areas. Degradation of the coastal environment threatens the country's fishery resources.

The recent history of Yemen is burdened by natural and manmade disasters. As a result the development crisis in Yemen worsened in the first half of the 1990s. Per capita GDP, in constant prices, stagnated. The consumer price index in 1995 was 537 per cent of its 1990 level, and real private consumption per capita is estimated to have declined by more than a third in the same period. Unemployment and poverty are expected to have increased significantly, and as a result, the distribution of income and wealth has probably worsened considerably. The squeeze on the resources of the poor must have placed even heavier constraints on the satisfaction of basic needs.

The embarking by Yemen on an extensive structural adjustment package has perhaps been the most consequential political economy event in recent years. Starting in late 1994, the government started a strict and wide-ranging Economic, Financial and Administrative Reform Programme (EFARP) under the auspices of the IMF and the World Bank. The programme signalled the end of Yemen's ostracism after the second Gulf War, and heralded the return of a rather grand scale of aid to Yemen from the Bretton Woods institutions as well as from their Arab counterparts.

It is claimed that EFARP achieved significant macroeconomic and financial successes in a short period, though some of the claims are dubious (favourable changes in government finance were due, in large measure, to changes in the exchange rate; the 'core' inflation rate utilised by the IMF excluded administered price rises, etc.). More important from an HD perspective was the expectation that EFARP would have wide-scale negative effects on HD. The programme instituted a reduction of government expenditure on wages (including a freeze on government employment) and started the gradual abolition of subsidies to basic commodities through administered price rises for wheat, petroleum products, electricity, communications and transport. These measures, scheduled to be deepened in the later stages of the programme, are expected to result in rises in the level of unemployment and poverty. This outcome is implicitly recognised by the programme, through its establishing of mechanisms – a 'social fund for development' and a 'public works programme' – that are aimed at alleviating unemployment and poverty through income transfers and creation of job opportunities. The experience of other countries shows that such measures are generally inadequate to counteract the negative impact of 'structural adjustment' programmes in poor countries, let alone to establish HD.

Current development strategies

Adopted by parliament, the first five-year plan (FFYP) (1996–2000) is Yemen's pre-eminent development strategy document. It is based on the indicative planning approach within the context of a market economy led by the private sector, while the government assumes the responsibility for provision of infrastructure, basic services and distributive justice.

The FFYP aims at attaining an average rate of growth in real GDP of 7.2 per cent per annum. Targeted sectoral rates of growth vary between 0.6 per cent for 'oil and gas' to more than 10 per cent in 'transport, storage and communications' and 'government services'. The set of targeted rates of growth essentially preserves the structure of GDP in the base year of the plan.

Total investment during the plan years comes to US$8.2 billion (the plan has assumed an exchange rate of 100 YR per US$1). Foreign investment in 'oil and gas' accounts for almost half of the total. Excluding investment in 'oil and gas' foreign private investment is allocated about half the remainder. Thus, almost three-quarters of total investment is allocated to foreign sources. This 'aid culture' has been prominent in Yemen. On the other hand, local investment is divided between government (US$1.2 billion) and the private sector (US$1 billion); the latter clearly belongs to the 'hoped for' category of estimates that has come to characterise 'planning' in countries undergoing structural adjustment.

From an HD point of view, the plan does not seem to provide a structure of growth and distribution that would sustain a reduction in unemployment and poverty. For example, private-sector growth is supposed to generate the vast majority of job opportunities. However, even if the local investment targets of the plan were to be realised, the parameters of employment generation embedded in the plan by the (mostly non-agricultural) 'investment' private sector could result only in a small fraction of the level of employment creation that would be sufficient to reduce unemployment by the end of the plan, taking into consideration the initial pool of unemployed persons, new additions to the labour market throughout the plan years, and expected layoffs from government service and privatised public enterprises. In addition, foreign investment in general, and in the 'oil and gas' sector in particular, cannot be relied upon for significant job creation for it tends to be highly capital intensive, labour sparse and strongly biased towards foreign manpower.

Furthermore, the rates of growth targeted by the plan were not borne out by actual economic performance in the first two years. Achieved growth was lower than the plan targets and growth scenarios had to be scaled down, resulting in the risk that both unemployment and poverty might intensify in the near future, with negative consequences for human capability and the standard of living.

Map of external assistance

External assistance in Yemen declined in the first half of the 1990s as a consequence of the stand adopted by Yemen in the (first) Gulf War. However, external assistance surged between 1995 and 1996 from a little over US$200 million to about US$425 million. The major part of the increase – 85 per cent – came from two sources: the IMF and the IDA-World Bank in conjunction with EFARP. The level of external assistance was estimated at more than US$350 million for 1997.

In 1996, multilateral sources contributed 77 per cent of external assistance. The vast majority came from the IMF (29 per cent) and IDA (22 per cent). External assistance by other multilateral sources amounted to 17 per cent. The largest of these were the Arab Fund for Social and Economic Development (8 per cent), the Arab Monetary Fund (6.4 per cent) and the European Union (2.6 per cent). Thus 1996 also witnessed the return of Arab aid to Yemen. These sources, especially the first four, are currently the prime shapers of economic, as well as social, development in the country. Bilateral sources contributed 22.5 per cent of external assistance. The Netherlands was the largest donor (8.9 per cent), followed by Germany (6.6 per cent), Japan (3.9 per cent), and France (1.1 per cent).

Differentiating between loans and grants, however, reveals that about two-thirds of external assistance in 1996 was in the form of loans. The ratio of loans rises to almost 100 per cent in the case of the largest multilateral donors: IMF, IDA, AFSED and AMF (naturally representing roughly two-thirds of all external assistance).

On examination of the fields of external assistance another disparity appears, between allocations that fall directly under HD and those related to the structural adjustment category. The majority of external assistance went to structural adjustment activities, where three fields – financial policy, macroeconomic policy and debt administration – received more than 55 per cent of all external assistance.

In contrast, direct HD fields attracted less than one-eighth of external assistance only, which was distributed on health (6 per cent) and human resources development (5.8 per cent).

Government priorities for external assistance

The document put forward by the government to the meeting of the Consultative Group for Yemen (Brussels, June 1997) reflected government priorities for external assistance. The document presented 25 projects costing YR157 billion (the FFYP contained 142 projects costing YR1112 billion). Excluding oil and gas projects, the 25 priority projects represented 37 per cent of total investment in the FFYP, and were distributed as indicated in Table 1.1.

TABLE 1.1
Government priorities for external assistance

Field of investment	Number of projects	Cost (US$ million)	Share of cost %
Agriculture	4	80	6.1
Education	3	210	16.1
Electricity	4	327	25.1
Health, population and social welfare	4	135	10.4
Transport	7	250	19.2
Water, sanitation and environment	3	300	23.0
Total	25	1,302	100.0

Source: Republic of Yemen, Ministry of Planning and Development 1997.

Table 1.1 shows that the emphasis in the priority investment programme was on infrastructure (about two-thirds of the total). Analysis of individual projects reveals that Sana'a's infrastructure benefited considerably (with one third of the total investment going to three projects for electricity, water and sewage in Sana'a, in addition to its share of road construction, airport improvement, etc.).

On the other hand, the seven projects of the 'social sectors' were allocated a little more than a quarter of total investment. Three educational projects, each costing US$70 million, for 'administration reform', 'capacity building for female education', and 'quality improvement in basic education' were to start consecutively in 1998, 1999 and 2000. The cost for 'Social Fund for Development' was put at US$80 million. The health sector was allocated US$45 million, for 'strengthening health services' and 'administrative reform'; both were to start in 1999. The 'population and children' project was allocated US$5 million, to start in 1997. Thus almost all social-sector projects would start rather late. Though details are lacking, scrutiny of these projects suggested that the investment programme in the social sector was prepared rather hastily and that it revealed a close resemblance to the World Bank sectoral priorities that will be discussed later on.

The IMF's enhanced structural adjustment facility (1997–2000)

This programme represents an extension and deepening of the first programme (EFARP), which was implemented during 1995–6 under the auspices of the IMF. Its aim is to establish a macroeconomic environment favourable to investment and growth, led by the private sector in a free and open economy, and to ensure significant improvement in 'social indicators'. The programme operates in collaboration with the World Bank and a marginal role is played by the UNDP.

The specific objectives of the programme include an average rate of growth in the non-oil sector of 6 per cent (lower than the target of FFYP), a core inflation rate (that excludes administered price rises stipulated in the programme) of less than 5 per cent, a government budget deficit of less than 2 per cent of GDP, a current account deficit of less than 2 per cent of GDP, and an increase in international reserves sufficient to maintain the present level of import cover. To improve the 'social indicators' government expenditure on education, health and social safety nets is to be increased, and the education and health sectors are to be reformed (these 'sectoral' matters fall under the purview of the World Bank). While all the specific objectives are clearly macroeconomic, the 'social indicators' issue appears as an addendum, treated essentially through financial allocations. By giving the Ministry of Finance and the Central Bank, reporting directly to the prime minister, the role of coordinating the programme, its macroeconomic and financial character is solidified.

The components of the programme that are expected to result in negative effects on HD, particularly employment and poverty, are more important for our purpose here. The programme prescribes reduction of 'unnecessary' government expenditures including the gradual abolition of subsidies (on petroleum products, electricity, water and sewage before 1999 and on wheat before 2001, to be replaced by income transfers under the Social Fund), and containing government expenditure on wages (not to exceed 8 per cent of GDP by 2000 in the context of civil service reform that is expected to reduce the number of employees by one fifth, and freeze new employment, except in education and health). The programme also calls for privatisation of public enterprises before 2000. These measures mean significant price rises that will not show in the 'core' inflation rate. As indicated earlier, given the limited capacity of the large private sector to create job opportunities, the curtailment of government employment as well as expected layoffs in privatised public enterprises translates into a significant increase in unemployment, and hence to widening poverty.

The programme does allow for income transfers to the poor through the Social Fund (allocations to the fund were supposed to rise from 0.1 per cent of GDP in 1996–7 to 1.4 per cent in 2000 – in itself an indication of the expected increase in poverty). More importantly, income transfers are not sufficient to eradicate poverty in an HD context. Even in the sense of limited, but needed, social safety nets, the efficacy of income transfers is uncertain: it is difficult adequately to cover all the poor where poverty is widespread.

The World Bank Programme (1997–2000)

At the Consultative Group meeting (Brussels, June 1997), the World Bank prepared six sectoral memoranda, for agriculture, education, health, electricity, water and transport. Each memorandum contains an analysis of the sector and a proposal to improve it. The electricity, water[5] and transport sectors are accorded the most extensive treatment, but we will focus below on education and health because of their intimate link with HD.

The objective for education was to increase enrolment in basic education giving priority to girls and deprived areas, while upgrading quality, and the proposed programme had two dimensions:

* Management reform through decentralisation and privatisation (subcontracting of the present activities of the Ministry of Education to the private sector and direct service provision by the private sector).

- A restructuring of government expenditure on education through increasing the share of recurrent expenditures, and allocating more resources to deprived areas.

Required investment was estimated at YR45 billion and current expenditures were put at YR117 billion.

The health programme was based on the following policy recommendations:

- A redefinition of the role of the Ministry of Public Health to focus on policy formulation, planning and coordination; and regulation of resources and interventions to ensure availability of public health programmes to the population. For the operation of health facilities the government should rely on the private sector and/or community-level organisations.
- Restructuring public expenditures on health to improve the utilisation of existing facilities through increasing allocations for recurrent spending, especially on medicines and equipment.
- According top priority to increasing access to primary health care, including the motivation of private-sector delivery and financing of services. The expansion of programmes to deliver preventive care (nutrition, immunisation and natal care) should also be given priority. Tertiary hospitals should be made more efficient but not increased in number. Non-public sector actors should be encouraged to deliver higher-level and longer-term services.

The strong privatisation component of the education and health programmes called for efficient mechanisms for the regulation of private-sector delivery to ensure quality and social equity.

Principal issues of human development

The principal issue of development in Yemen at the present juncture of its history is the conflict that arises between the negative impact of EFARP on HD on the one hand, and the requirements of building HD on the other. Without effective measures aimed at building HD, not just alleviating the negative impact of EFARP, poverty – seen as a human capability failure – in Yemen is bound to become considerably worse.

For a variety of reasons it is likely that this conflict will be glossed over. The results are known from the experience of other countries under similar conditions: changes in HD are not monitored closely; neither the ensuing rise in poverty nor the means of averting it is given adequate public debate; and 'palliatives' are thought of, and widely advertised, as 'cures'. If this pattern continues for a long time, the negative social side-effects of structural adjustment might intensify to a degree that would render future remedial action ineffective. From an HD perspective, the fundamental task facing Yemen is to forestall this vicious scenario, effectively to combat poverty and to work proactively to build HD.

The dynamics of poverty

Mass poverty in Yemen must be understood as a product of complex structural processes embedded in the political economy of the country. Within this complexity, a precondition for formulating an effective anti-poverty strategy is to identify the key causes of poverty.

The primary cause of poverty in Yemen can be summed up in the failure of state-led development strategies since independence, including the more recently introduced macroeconomic reforms. This failure has manifested itself in limited and inequitable access to all forms of capital: human, physical, financial and social. Being deprived of capital leads to lack of remunerative employment and poverty, while limited and inequitable access to various forms of capital is probably the most immediate cause of poverty.

Significant levels of exclusion from education and basic health care have been powerful forces of marginalisation in Yemen. Furthermore, exclusion has a profound gender aspect, with girls and women suffering disproportionately. Indications are that poor households are increasingly unable to afford the cost of basic education and health care. With widening privatisation of services, and increasing poverty, the affordability of education and health care by the poor is expected to diminish. Without human capital accumulated through education and training, the poor are doomed to open unemployment or the more sinister forms of underemployment.

Infirmity itself is one form of poverty. To be in good health is synonymous with being able to work. This is especially so in the case of the poor, who often engage in physically demanding activities. Since earnings, i.e. income from work, represent the mainstay of livelihood of the vast majority of the poor, sickness can compound poverty through depriving them of income. Sickness is thus a major road into poverty, no matter how defined.

Poverty and employment are closely linked. Remunerative employment is an essential element of human capability. For the vast majority of the poor, their work power is their most important or, indeed, their only asset. As a measure of capability failure, open unemployment defines one aspect of poverty. While the poorest of the poor cannot afford the luxury of unemployment, the employed poor pay a heavy price for being compelled to work in order to survive by low earnings, long working hours and harsh work conditions which drastically curtail their well-being. Further, an organic link between poverty and unemployment is evident if we consider the low-income dimension of invisible underemployment. The extent of poverty, on the other hand, is inextricably linked to the low productivity aspect of underemployment. Finally, poverty and unemployment become almost inseparable when the institutional aspects of employment (especially with respect to finding a good job), together with poverty as powerlessness, are considered.

The poor are by definition asset-deprived and hence have little or no collateral. As a result their access to credit, and to formal credit in particular, is seriously compromised, more so in the case of women. Lack of access to finance has often given rise to usurious practices, themselves additional components of the vicious cycle of poverty.

Structural adjustment is expected to accentuate the bias in favour of big capital, the assumption being that only big capital can afford to innovate and thus raise productivity. Thus, large investors are to be given all perks: tax holidays, land and infrastructure at concessional prices, free repatriation of profits, and so on. Their political connections sweeten the deal even more through giving them privileged access to information and markets. By comparison, the would-be entrepreneurs of small and micro-enterprises (SMEs) have to negotiate a thicket of red tape and barriers to credit. In particular, the insurmountable constraint of the collateral for credit has never been adequately relaxed.

The vast majority of the population resides in rural areas, and agriculture employs more than half the labour force. The poor are concentrated in rural areas and they are generally supported by small, marginal or landless farmers. Clearly, access to land and water is crucial to sustaining livelihoods in rural communities, but this basic right is being seriously threatened by the water crisis and soil degradation.

The poor, and women in particular, are generally denied the benefits of legal protection. The poor, and especially women, are also excluded from participation and influence in social and political institutions, ironically including even those institutions that are meant to help them overcome poverty. Marginalisation of the poor in political institutions is the ultimate deprivation because it reinforces a major cause of poverty: the powerlessness of the poor that renders them a silent majority in national and local affairs. As such, the poor are denied important citizenship rights and, therefore, key capabilities to pull themselves from poverty.

The institutional setting for poverty eradication

The consensus now is that the most effective way to eradicate poverty consists of empowering the poor to bail themselves out of poverty. But the poor have no capital other than their labour power and creative capabilities and these are suppressed by impoverishment. Empowering the poor therefore requires that the state, being the guardian of the interests of all Yemenis, should adopt policies and programmes that equip them with all types of capital: human, social, financial and physical. The most important of these types of capital is human capital, built through education, training and health care. Financial capital is essential to enable the poor to set up SMEs, since these represent one of the most effective means for job creation and income generation. In predominantly rural societies, such as Yemen, access to physical assets such as land and irrigation water is a basic requirement for a sustainable livelihood. Finally, since poverty is synonymous with powerlessness, social capital is indispensable for providing the poor with access to social and political organisations that will ensure that their voices are heard and their interests safeguarded.

That the state has the responsibility for empowering the poor through provision of capital does not, however, mean that it assumes the role of direct provision of goods and services. This has failed. Rather, the requirement is that the state guarantees the provision of different forms of capital to the poor through distributive measures. Rightly, it is feared that the evolving pattern of the supremacy of barely regulated private-sector activity is also doomed to fail in combating poverty, even if it succeeds in generating economic growth in the narrow sense (though in situations of low human capability, significant economic growth is unlikely to result). In fact, success in building HD is conditional on the evolution of a new social contract in which a synergy, not just complementarity, obtains between a revitalised and efficient government, a dynamic and socially responsible private sector, and a powerful and truly grassroots civil society.

The profit motive is, by definition, ineffective in equipping the poor with the capital necessary to combat poverty (for example, the provision of basic education or health care to the poor does not carry a profit margin to entice private-sector providers). However, means can be found to ensure that the private sector contributes to this task. Responsible payment of taxes is one way, provided the government uses such revenues to empower the poor, and donations are another. The private sector can also be persuaded to provide free services to the poor through pairing free service outlets with those operating for profit. Tax incentives could be effectively used to encourage the private sector to behave in this socially responsible manner.

However, the primary responsibility for empowering the poor will still lie with the state. Hence, to be truly representative of, and accountable to, the people, civil service reform and governance reform, including local government, will represent essential components of the new social contract.

Other than government, the most significant social actor in empowering the poor could be civil society, provided that constraints on the setting up of civil society institutions and on their activities are lifted, and that the capacity of the sector, including tribal organisation and cooperatives, is built up to make an effective contribution to Sustainable Human Development (SHD).

At the community level, a promising approach to HD combines productive, income-generating projects with service projects, such that the proceeds of the former help sustain the latter under the auspices of reformed local government or civil society. The productive projects generate jobs and incomes while the service projects develop human capabilities. Clearly, a virtuous circle in favour of HD develops between the two types of projects, which strengthens community organisation, safeguards the interests of the people, especially the poor, and ensures better chances for sustainability. This type of community organisation for building HD is more or less dictated by the pattern of population settlement in rural Yemen. The developmental dividend of this approach increases significantly if it is based on civil society organisations (including cooperatives and tribal arrangements), provided their capacities are developed in such a manner that a genuine grassroots character evolves.

On strategic priorities

In Yemen prospects for external assistance, and hence donors, have always played an important role in setting strategic priorities. This tendency has intensified with structural adjustment. To illustrate this, we discuss below two crucially important issues that, to the author, seem relatively neglected while a rather inconsequential issue receives a lot of attention.

As mentioned earlier, an HD strategy must accord central importance to rural development, the productive mainstay of which would be an improved agricultural sector. However, to deal effectively with agricultural development, several challenges and constraints need to be dealt with, including serious soil degradation; scarce water resources that depend heavily on rainfall (prolonged droughts often cause crop failure); backward technology and low-quality inputs; limited support services; the increasing share of *qat* in the irrigated area at the expense of other crops; and a weak human resource base. An agricultural development component of a human development strategy should aim at the management of natural resources, especially land and water, in a manner that will ensure their efficiency and sustainability. For achieving sustainable growth in agricultural output, the productivity of resources needs to be raised, with priority given to cereals production (which will inevitably mean reducing *qat* cultivation). But promoting agricultural production has to take place in an environment of an overall HD strategy, as outlined above.

The water crisis in Yemen needs to be addressed as an impending disaster. The situation is critical, with irrigation (and hence food security) and human consumption needs both at serious risk. Effective solutions are multifaceted and of a long-term nature. An immediate start to a societal process of rational management of water resources that will ensure sustainability is urgently required.

Yemen is considered to be facing a population problem. In addition to the population characteristics mentioned above, prevalence of contraceptive use is estimated at less than 10 per cent. Fast population growth undoubtedly compounds the burdens of development, and resources should be mobilised to help reduce population growth through the provision of widespread and efficient family planning services. However, it should be kept in mind that the provision of such services requires a considerable improvement in the provision of health care in the country, which is a major challenge in its own right. Starting from the present level of fertility and the expected decline in mortality, any significant reduction in population growth is bound to take a long time. Due to the so-called 'population momentum' phenomenon, population problems (fast growth and a young age structure) will continue to prevail, even after fertility per woman has declined. Finally, if human capabilities remain low, slower population growth will not help development.

A policy package for poverty eradication through human development[6]

The following are major policy directions for a comprehensive policy package to eradicate poverty. These directions integrate into a synergistic bundle, out of which one cannot pick and choose at will without damage to the intended collective impact on poverty.

Monitoring of poverty and employment

An efficient system for monitoring poverty and employment is badly needed. This system should allow for rapid and regular monitoring of basic parameters, as well as less frequent in-depth analyses of the character and dynamics of poverty and employment. To serve this purpose, many inputs should be integrated to constitute a significantly better and regularly updated database on human capability in the country. As a first step in this direction, an employment and standard-of-living survey needs to be undertaken as a priority.

Safety nets

The social safety net system in place in Yemen is evidently lacking in coverage and effectiveness. Two requirements of effective safety nets are clear: schemes should (1) provide for income transfers sufficient to guarantee a minimum of decent human existence to all in need, and (2) be indexed to inflation.

Poor-enabling development

A frontal attack on poverty has to be anchored in a pro-poor process of development that generates labour-intensive growth providing for productive and gainful employment opportunities. The poor, however, need to be equipped for such employment opportunities through pro-poor human capital accumulated by way of education, training and health care. More importantly, they also need to be helped to create such employment opportunities by setting up and managing SMEs. Ensuring easier access to, and firmer command of, more conventional forms of capital such as physical assets and finance, is crucial for the support of this strategy. In addition, SMEs are fragile economic entities that demand a great deal of additional support to guard against failure.

But the crux of the processes of poor-enabling development is major institutional reform, which will radically raise the share of the poor in the power structure of society. Institutional reform is the path to maximising the social capital of the poor. Such reform, rather than economic growth *per se*, constitutes the heart of poor-enabling development, and without it, growth is likely to be slow. More importantly, growth in the context of unrestrained markets is doomed grossly to favour the rich and to penalise the poor.

Pro-poor accumulation of human capital

Education and training

A pro-poor development plan should aim at universalising high-quality, market-relevant, basic education, while ensuring that the poor are not excluded on account of poverty. In some cases this means going beyond truly free education. For the poorest of the poor, some form of affirmative action providing scholarships that cover the direct and opportunity costs of education, will be necessary. Children from poor backgrounds should not be excluded from the higher stages of education through lack of material means.

Quality of education, including relevance to context-specific life skills and labour-market requirements, should be continuously improved at all stages. This is a demanding and complex societal endeavour that extends beyond the confines of the education sector.

Formal education is only one of the paths towards building human capital. More relevant to the poor, particularly in the early stages of pro-poor development, are informal channels for the acquisition of effective, market-relevant skills. This form of training would be quite relevant to those who have dropped out of the educational system altogether or who have left education with only limited skills.

Redressing the gender disparity in human capital accumulation should rank high on the agenda of pro-poor education and training strategy, while the pattern of population settlement in the country calls for appropriate channels for service provision.

Health care

The poor should not be deprived of health care because of their poverty. Special consideration should also be given to providing health care for girls and women.

Employment and productivity

Employment creation should be made an explicit policy priority. For significant increases in social welfare to result from job creation, productivity needs to be improved in such a way that real wages increase and the disparity in the distribution of income and wealth is reduced.

The job-creation strategy should have three interrelated objectives: (1) to reduce unemployment to a level near full employment; (2) to double productivity every few years; and (3) to ensure that the basic needs of the working population are adequately satisfied.

The creating of new jobs based on growth in investment, a labour-intensive growth structure and employment-intensive technology, should be expanded. With the aim of enhancing productivity, the level of the population's human capital needs to be improved by raising the quality of education, and a favourable social incentive system should be instituted, with positive rewards to education and high productivity. In addition, synergistic technological duality should be established: this involves raising the productivity of labour-intensive technologies in small and micro-enterprises, strengthening modern technologies, and reinforcing the linkages between the two types of technologies. Special consideration should also be given to the gainful employment of women.

Resources for small and micro-enterprises (SMEs)

If the small and micro-enterprises road to pro-poor development is to bear fruit, major progress will be required towards ensuring easier access to, and firmer command over physical assets (particularly land and water in rural areas). Traditional local credit systems should be promoted and made more efficient.

SMEs tend to be labour intensive, which is an obvious advantage. However, they are also notorious for high failure rates unless the economic and institutional environment in which they are set up is truly hospitable. It is also essential that they operate at reasonable, and rising, levels of productivity so that they will provide both owners and workers with adequate, and improving, earnings in real terms.

A legal and administrative context that provides credible encouragement to the creation and profitability of SMEs needs to be established, since provision of technical assistance through government channels, cooperatives and NGOs will significantly increase their chances of survival and their contribution to poverty eradication. Finally, improved access to local, national and international markets is another major requirement for the success of SMEs as an anti-poverty mechanism.

Women are prime candidates for benefits that are aimed at reinvigorating this mode of economic activity, by virtue of their higher unemployment rates and their proven ability to manage SMEs.

Sustainable rural livelihoods

In stimulating growth within the agricultural sector, a key role for the government will centre on improving rural infrastructure and farm-to-market linkages. Extension services must be improved, and agricultural research should also be reoriented towards crops that are pro-poor. Little of this potential can be captured without a rationalisation of irrigation systems. Finally, off-farm employment opportunities need to be developed for the land-poor and landless, through industrial decentralisation, micro-enterprises, and public works.

Because they represent an important mainstay of Yemen's agricultural communities, women should figure prominently in the design and implementation of rural development policies and programmes.

Institutional reform

Competitive markets

The need to reinforce competitive market mechanisms calls for more government action to regulate markets so as to ensure competitiveness through free access to information and markets. This represents the fundamental guarantee of efficiency as well as the minimisation of the harmful social impact of unrestrained capitalism.

In particular, reform of the labour market should ensure free access to information on employment opportunities and at the same time establish efficient employment exchanges. Furthermore, such reform should gradually deregulate labour markets, in order to increase flexibility within a competitive market framework while ensuring social security. This would entail (1) full rights to management, including free hire-and-fire with adequate rights of severance for employees; (2) full rights to labour, including free unions and collective bargaining tools such as slowdowns and strikes; (3) adequate inflation-indexed unemployment compensation as an integral component of a safety net; and (4) credible chances of productive employment for people, including retraining if needed.

Civil service reform

Essential economic functions remain the unique domain of government. Even so, governments in less developed countries (LDCs) are notoriously inefficient. Since the level of government efficiency has implications for economic performance at large, and for that of the private sector in particular, civil service reform therefore represents an essential component of an institutional reform package through transparent structure, adequate wages, decompression of scales, and reduction of discrepancies between various parts of the government service. Allocations for equipment and for operation and maintenance, all of which are necessary for efficient functioning, should be made available. It will also be necessary to institute sound public administration practices that will lead to higher productivity, including the basing of recruitment and advancement, as well as termination of service, on merit.

In the event of cutbacks among public service employees, remedial measures such as severance packages, redeployment and retraining, credit programmes and public works programmes need to be implemented.

In order to reduce budget deficits, the tax structure should be reformed, thereby ensuring fairness as well as raising the efficiency of tax collection, especially from the rich who generally manage to evade taxes more than the poor. Government spending needs to be rationalised.

Development of civil society

Civil society institutions, and NGOs in particular, provide a window of opportunity for contributing significantly to the eradication of poverty. However, in order for this potential to materialise, civil society institutions must develop into a social movement that is more broadly based – and hopefully more efficient – than the state. The purpose is not to replace the state, or even absolve it from its basic responsibility. Rather, the aim is to complement the faltering state. The ultimate value of such a movement lies in fostering collective social action. This is the surest way of overcoming powerlessness, which is the core of poverty.

Unfortunately, the vast majority of NGOs are top-down organisations in which the poor are at the receiving end of charity. In addition, they are weak and impoverished. As a result they are susceptible to the influence exerted by donors under the project-funding format. This mode of generous funding, which can in any case be extended only to a few privileged NGOs, creates dependency on donor funding, weakens voluntary traditions, and destroys the basis for sustainability.

Legal and administrative impediments to the creation and efficient functioning of civil society institutions must be dispensed with. But the civil society community itself needs to metamorphose into a broadly based grassroots movement of collective social action with significant potential for sustainability.

It is crucial in this respect to build on informal and culturally rooted institutions that are embedded in established traditions and that serve the poor, rather than simply trying to 'modernise' them. Informal networks allow greater opportunity for the poor to mobilise, articulate their concerns, further their interests and press them upon higher centres of power and authority. The institution of *zakat* is an important example, as is the cooperative movement which has an excellent past record in Yemen.

The empowerment of the poor through inclusion in socially effective civil society institutions would be essentially meaningless without the full integration of women.

Governance reform

Laws and administrative procedures need to be reformed to guarantee citizenship rights as well as consistency with basic human rights, particularly the rights of free expression and organisation, for all Yemenis, particularly women. The rule of law should be instituted under a positively independent judiciary.

For the poor to have their voice heard, and their interests recognised, government needs to be made truly representative and effectively accountable to the people. Genuine local government, not just decentralisation, ensures the more effective participation of people, especially the poor, in the challenging struggle against poverty. Citizenship and political rights, too, will remain highly inadequate if they are not in practice fully inclusive of women.

NOTES

1 A social 'institution' is defined in terms of systems of social relations rather than in a physical or organisational sense, since social practices that are regularly and continuously repeated are sanctioned and maintained by social norms, and have a major significance in the social structure.

2 UNDP has, however, consistently declared that the views expressed in the report 'do not necessarily reflect the views of UNDP, its Governing Council or other member governments of UNDP'.

3 The use of a small number of indicators to construct a quality of life (QOL) index, such as the HDI, has its attractions in simplicity and ease of interpretation. However, using a large number of meaningful indicators makes for a more complete understanding of levels and changes in QOL and therefore increases chances of effective social intervention to improve human welfare (Fergany, 1994). In particular, comparing HDI values over short periods of time essentially follows changes in per capita GDP because the two other components of the index change very slowly in time.

4 Emphasis added by the writer. In the case of a country such as Yemen, many victims of economic restructuring are expected to be 'out of the markets' for relatively long periods of time.

5 The sectoral memorandum on water is restricted to urban water supply. However, a document issued by the World Bank (August 1997) contains a comprehensive strategic vision for the water situation based on the work of the Multi-Donor Group for Yemen Water (whose participants are IDA, UNDP and The Netherlands). The government is in the process of formulating a water strategy.

6 The approach adopted here follows that of UNDP (1997b).

2

Politics and Economy in Yemen: Lessons from the Past

Charles Schmitz

Introduction

Yemen's extraordinary economic transformation over the last three decades has been largely driven by two sources of wealth, both located outside the state's borders. International development assistance and military assistance has supported the state(s') apparatus(es) and provided for some significant infrastructure development. Worker remittances from the Gulf states fuelled a massive expansion of consumer demand, dramatically raising the standard of living of ordinary Yemenis and transforming the economy into a commercial haven for imported goods. However, events in the last decade or so have conspired to reduce the significance of both of these sources of wealth and have forced Yemen to face the difficult task of developing domestic sources of affluence. While exports of domestic gas and oil have cushioned the economic decline of the 1990s, only the development of domestic non-oil resources appears able to generate employment for the majority of Yemenis. Growth in the domestic non-oil sectors may, however, present significant challenges to Yemen's political regime. Drawing on the experiences of market reform under the socialist as well as in the post-socialist transitional economies, this contribution will argue that domestic economic growth in Yemen, of the kind that will offer generalised growth, is contingent upon changes in the current relationship of political power to economic wealth. In other words, successful economic growth requires certain political underpinnings that are weak in Yemen today.

The relationship of the state and the market, of politics and the economy, has been a heated topic in academic and policy circles of the 1990s. After a decade of promoting a negative view of the state, posing a simple dichotomy between private 'competition' and public-sector 'rent-seeking', the World Bank recently retreated from its minimalist view and recognised some of the critical functions of the state that facilitate development of a successful market economy (World Bank 1997). However, this new view of the state still tends to ignore the political origins of institutions and of institutional change. According to Leftwich (1995: 421), it calls for 'good governance, or democratic governance, which focus on administrative, judicial or electoral good practice, entirely [missing] the point that such virtues can only be instituted and sustained by politics'. Fox also comments that 'one must take into account the nature of the political regime as a whole – the determinants of who governs and how – in order to understand that subset of state action that involves development policy' (Fox, 1995: 1–30, esp. 2). Effective economic and political institutions, and the virtuous behaviours associated with them, are not created by administrative fiat; rather such behaviours and institutions evolve out of a nexus of social, political and economic factors. In Yemen the behaviour of the state in the formulation and implementation of its reform policies is intimately related to the political strategies of the governing regime and other prominent political and economic élites, both in the country's changing institutional environment and in the international economy in the late 1990s. Some of the political strategies of the regime may, however, indirectly affect economic development in the non-petroleum sectors of the domestic economy. In particular, a certain tendency to allocate economic assets and resources for political rather than for economic goals appears related to the political strategies or means of the regime. In the light of historical experience, this type of relationship between politics and the economy may prove costly in the long run.

Origins of dependent growth

In a long view of the structural development of the Yemeni economy, the economic challenges facing Yemen at the turn of the twentieth century can be broadly characterised by a shift from a high degree of reliance upon external sources of wealth to a more domestically driven economy. From the late 1970s to the mid-1980s both the People's Democratic Republic of Yemen and the Yemen Arab Republic experienced rapid economic expansion based upon worker remittances from abroad. In the mid-1980s worker remittances declined and both economies entered a difficult period of transition that still confronts the Republic of Yemen today.

During the years of expansion both Yemeni states witnessed dramatic transformations of their political economies. From being a nation of farmers, largely insulated from world markets, Yemen rapidly became integrated into the world economy. Ordinary Yemenis saw dramatic increases in their ability to consume and their standards of living. The engine driving this economic transformation was the rapid accumulation of oil revenues in the neighbouring Gulf states, as well as the international development assistance given to the state during this period. Yemenis abandoned their fields and flocked by the millions to work in large infrastructure and construction projects in Saudi Arabia, where they were the primary labour force during this early oil boom period. Yemenis were also involved in small commerce and services in the Gulf Cooperation Council states. The remittances of these Yemeni workers precipitated an unprecedented expansion of private consumption inside both the YAR and the PDRY.

This explosion in demand for consumer products transformed the economy of the YAR into a freewheeling commercial haven. In the socialist South, the consumer boom fed an expansion of the state-owned foreign trade company. Easy import-substitution industries such as food processing, plastics and cement production also experienced a rapid expansion but industry was not, and is not, a major source of wealth in Yemen. Many of the labour-intensive agricultural terraces of the highlands fell into disrepair as Yemenis spent their new-found wealth on imported (and subsidised) wheat. A nation of subsistence farmers suddenly went shopping in world markets, opened shops and chewed *qat*.

In this initial period of Yemen's economic transformation wealth was distributed relatively evenly, since income accrued primarily to the private households of migrant workers. There were certain strategic points in the economy at which fortunes were made, such as at the financial conduits for the remittance of wages, in the commodity import firms, at the speculative frontiers of the urban explosion experienced by the major Northern cities, and in prime *qat*-growing agricultural lands. In the South these strategic economic points were occupied by the state, with the exception of the *qat*-producing economy which was located in mountainous Lahj and Yafiyya, politically significant regions for the Southern regime. But on the whole the distribution of wealth was relatively even, and directly benefited all sectors of Yemeni society.

[33]

Retrenchment and the state

The decline of world oil prices and the maturing of the economies of the Gulf states in the mid-1980s reduced the flow of worker remittances and once again radically altered the character of the economy. The marked decrease in private capital transfers from abroad and in international assistance to the state signalled the first phase of economic restructuring, with which Yemen still struggles today. In both the YAR and the PDRY, the state was prompted by a rapidly growing balance of payments deficit to regulate the economy; but plans for long-term domestic economic growth were not on the minds of state leaders. Both leaderships focused on the more short-term solution of developing domestic petroleum exports to replace the loss of worker remittances.

Economic reform programmes in the mid-1980s in both the YAR and the PDRY were aimed primarily at controlling the large and growing balance of payments deficits caused by the decline in private transfers from abroad. In both North and South Yemen the merchandise trade deficit was nearly equal to imports, meaning that neither economy generated significant exports of any kind (CSO, various years). The large deficit in the visible trade balance was offset mainly by private transfers from migrant workers. When these diminished significantly in the mid-1980s, both regimes attempted to resolve the consequent balance of payments deficits through restricting imports (see Appendix: Figures 2.2 and 2.3).

In both Yemeni states, the implementation of reform measures marked significant political shifts. In the North a new relationship was forged between the private sector and the state in which the state was clearly dominant. In the period of rapid commercial expansion, the state did little in terms of regulating the activities of the private sector. However, with the deterioration of the national economy the state began to regulate private-sector activity through import restrictions, new requirements for licensing, and restrictions on access to foreign exchange (Chaudhry 1997: 276). These restrictive measures successfully slowed the growth of deficits in the national accounts until the late 1980s when revenues from the export of domestic oil resources eased the economic crisis.

The South was less successful in adjusting to the national economic crisis. The downturn in remittances and the subsequent increase in the balance of payments deficit precipitated the political crisis of January 1986 which was, in retrospect, the mortal wound of the Southern regime. What is interesting about the 1986 crisis is that the discourse of the participants reflected quite accurately the economic aspects of the conflict. The criticisms that were levelled against the regime of Ali Nasser focused on the lack of development of domestic sources of wealth in agriculture, fisheries and industry, and on the use of expanded consumer demand to satisfy political ambitions (Qandil, 1986). However, those who remained in power after the deposing of Ali Nasser's regime and who had levelled criticisms at the previous regime were no more successful in carrying out their own economic reforms.

The post-1986 regime in the PDRY developed two strategies to quell the balance of payments problems: the first was to restrict demand for imports, as in the North, and the second was to invest with all speed in the oil sector in the hopes of bringing in oil revenues. This latter strategy was the hope of the Southern regime's Soviet backers, who were facing their own economic problems and who wished to reduce the foreign economic burdens of the Soviet empire (Halliday, 1990). Imports did decline in the two years following 1986 but by 1988 had surpassed the levels achieved prior to 1986 (CSO, 1990). Small amounts of oil were produced in the South before reunification, but not in sufficient quantities to make a dent in the rapidly deteriorating economic situation.

With the formation of the Republic of Yemen in 1990, the state essentially continued the twin strategies developed by the two former states – i.e. restricting imports and developing domestic oil – yet for the first time there were serious plans for other sectors of the economy. Economic growth was to be a major payoff for unity, a Yemeni 'peace dividend'. Thus the revival of the port of Aden played a significant part in economic agendas after unity, as did reforms designed to stimulate private investment and development of agriculture, fisheries and easy import-substitution industries, particularly in the south and with northern capital (Rais Riasit, 1991; Carapico, 1993: 9–14).

The Gulf crisis and the subsequent political crisis and war inside Yemen delayed work on the economy. The Saudis and the Americans took retribution for Yemen's neutral stance in the war by expelling hundreds of thousands of Yemeni workers. Though remittances had been in decline, the massive expulsion, coupled with a concurrent withdrawal of aid from both the Gulf States and the United States, plunged the economy into a very serious crisis. Both the YAR and the PDRY relied heavily upon foreign aid for their budgets, particularly for infrastructure investments.

Public-sector investments represented the majority of recorded gross capital formation (Chaudhry, 1997; Carapico, 1993). The cut-off of aid from the Soviet Bloc to the PDRY in 1989 was the leading impetus for the completion and implementation of the unity agreement, and the cut-off of aid in 1990 from the GCC and the US precipitated the political and economic crisis which led to war in 1994. In the years leading up to the war, economic reform was only ever alluded to in the heat of political discourse. The two regimes gave priority to building their respective political and military machinery, essentially by burning oil revenues sequestered by both sides. Between 1990 and 1994 the decline in foreign assistance to the state-caused fiscal deficits was covered by devaluing the currency. Economic problems were secondary to war efforts, and immediate economic difficulties were solved with short-term solutions like spending oil revenues off budget and printing money.

After the war of 1994, the economy again returned to the forefront of the political arena. Though political instability was by no means eliminated, significant political opposition was done away with, and after July 1994 the unified state under President Saleh was clearly in command. The biggest threat to the regime after the war was perceived to be the continued deterioration in standards of living, and not the opposition. Economic issues could be pushed aside during times of crisis and war, but not during times of 'peace'.

Thus, in spite of a decade of economic reforms and adjustment, the economy today remained based upon the revenues from development of petroleum products, remittances, and foreign aid (see Appendix, Figure 2.4). Though the days are over when remittances could finance most of Yemen's imports, they still play an important role: in 1995 they contributed almost one billion US dollars as compared to US$1.5 billion for petroleum (*The Economist*, 1998). The government recognises the importance of remittances and has cultivated good relations with the Gulf States, even attempting to join the GCC, partly with an eye to increasing the number of Yemenis working in these states, though relations remained cool till the end of the century. The level of employment in the Gulf states will never reach the level of the early 1980s, due to the changing structure of employment in these economies and the decline of construction in which most Yemenis were employed. While important to the Yemeni economy, remittances cannot be expected to carry the economy again as they did in earlier periods.

Yemen was, of course, saved from an even more severe economic deterioration during the late 1980s and early 1990s by the development of oil and gas. Petroleum revenue constitutes 80 per cent of Yemen's export earnings; in 1997 it became the largest source of government revenue as well (*The Economist*, 1998). However, by most accounts petroleum production in Yemen appears to be at or near its limits, even taking into consideration the large natural gas production due soon for development and in spite of the recent increases in revenues (*The Economist*, 1998).

Foreign aid has returned to play a significant role in Yemen, following a brief hiatus in the early 1990s. The World Bank established a permanent mission in Yemen and the Yemeni government is carrying out an ongoing reform programme negotiated with the International Monetary Fund. There are significant loans included in these reform packages. However, while foreign aid may help a budget crisis and provide for some infrastructure development (such as the World Bank's current national water resource development plan), aid only contributes to economic growth in as much as it fosters real development in the national economy; on its own, aid only delays crises. The question of domestic economic growth outside the oil sector has yet to be seriously addressed.

The future challenge

Yemen today has one of the highest population growth rates in the world: 5.0 per cent average growth over the period 1990–5 (World Bank, 1997). The expanding young population will put stress on the education system, create demands for rapid expansion of employment, and force the economy to maintain relatively high rates of growth just to maintain current standards of living. Unemployment is already estimated at very high rates, varying between 25 per cent and 40 per cent (*The Economist*, 1998). The central challenge for Yemen in the near future is to create the conditions for the kind of economic growth that will generate employment and income for a very rapidly growing population. Due to the structural transition of the Yemeni economy over the last decade or so, none of the external sources of wealth – remittances and foreign aid – hold much promise for this sort of generalised economic improvement, though the importance of both must not be minimised, particularly as a source of infrastructure investment. Although domestic sources of wealth are dominated by petroleum, the oil sector does not provide significant employment for most Yemenis, and the revenues of the oil sector accrue to the government and foreign oil producers rather than to the domestic private sector, in contrast to the remittance economy (cf. Carapico, 1998; according to *The Economist*, 1997, oil revenues surpassed other sources of state revenue for the first time in 1996). Growth and development based upon oil depends, then, upon the economic investments of the state or on the direct employment and multiplier effect of private investments in the oil sector, both of which are rather limited relative to the needs of the economy. Economic growth that will provide employment and income gains for the majority of Yemenis will come only from the development of domestic, non-oil sources of wealth. These, however, are dependent upon the functioning of domestic economic institutions which foster growth and development. The next section discusses the difficulties of cultivating such institutions.

Politics and economics: lessons from the East
The transition to a market economy in the former Socialist Bloc countries offered a real opportunity to examine hypotheses about the nature and source of economic dynamism in market economies. In the immediate rush to formulate a set of policies for transitional economies, the foundations of capitalist dynamism (and socialist stagnation) were seen as (i) private property, (ii) free markets, and (iii) competition (through liberalisation of foreign trade and decentralising economic assets by privatisation) to induce efficient production (by global standards) and stimulate innovation. However the actual experience of the transitional economies raised questions about the sources of capitalist dynamism. Some of these questions were stimulated by the unprecedented collapse (in modern terms) of the Eastern Bloc economies and the quite varied experiences of recovery or even lack thereof (World Bank, 1996). The collapse of the East Bloc against the backdrop of the stunning growth of the Chinese economy occasioned lively debate about the appropriateness of the market 'shock therapy' based on the simple model of market dynamics. In China the public sector remained large and the institution of private property was not clearly defined; yet markets under the supervision of a socialist state and with ambiguous property rights

appeared far more dynamic, at least in the short and medium term, than markets in countries of the former Soviet Union (FSU) undergoing 'shock' therapy (see Sachs and Woo, 1994 for qualifications).

On the empirical level, the comparison between the FSU and China, as well as the experiences of liberalisation in Third World and the Asian newly industrialising countries (NICs), raised questions about the role of the state in capitalist economies. In stark contrast to a view of the state as an aggregation of individual, self-serving rent-seekers sapping the scarce resources of the private sector, historical experiences of market development and rapid economic growth showed the state's importance in providing, at the minimum, the essential institutional underpinnings of a market economy (Stiglitz, 1994: 232; Moore, 1993). An effective transition to the market called for a state with strong capacity rather than an emaciated state, a fact recognised with the publication of the 1997 World Development Report on *The State in a Changing World* (World Bank, 1997).

On the theoretical level researchers questioned whether private property had the immediate importance that policy makers attached to it. In terms of labour incentives, for example, corporate ownership is diffuse and managers have significant autonomy in their decision-making over stockholders, making the relationship between effort and reward rather ambiguous. In a large corporate structure most producers are employees, not owners. Measuring the efficiency of each worker's individual contribution in large organisations is very difficult within certain boundaries of normal work standards; only the organisation as a whole is threatened by bankruptcy in a market economy. Thus, within large firms, cooperation and trust rather than cold market calculation are the dominant values for success. Nor are the incentive structures within large socialist and capitalist firms so different, as was previously assumed (Stiglitz, 1994: 233).

Similarly, in a setting more similar to that of Yemen, Oi (1992: 99–126; 1995: 1,132–49) has suggested that the critical institution which led to the rationalising economic behaviour behind rural China's extraordinary growth rates was not private property but the incentives built into the local structures of the state. At the same time, Comisso (1991: 162–88), evaluating the results of socialist market reforms in the 1970s and 1980s in Yugoslavia and Hungary, proposes that what was critical was not private property but limited sovereignty over economic decisions:

Three conditions appear to be particularly important for the efficient operation of a market economy: first, property rights must be lodged in the hands of actors with purely economic responsibilities; second, a neutral third party must enforce them; and third, policy-making authority – including the authority to specify property rights – must be placed in the hands of institutions that themselves neither exercise nor enforce them. (Comisso 1991: 162)

In Comisso's scheme there is theoretically no difference in the efficiency of public and private forms of property. Efficiency is stimulated (or inhibited) by the mechanisms of resource allocation – the market or plan – rather than in the form of ownership (see Stiglitz, 1994: 237 for qualifications). Empirically, both Stiglitz and Comisso indicate that comparison of private and public firms, which is so often made to the detriment of the latter, is based upon different standards. Public enterprises usually operate with different goals and in very different environments: 'One of the reasons that it is difficult to find convincing empirical evidence concerning the relative inefficiency of government is that, by and large, the public sector produces different goods and is engaged in different economic activities than the private' (Stiglitz 1994: 234). The major difference is not between the public and private forms of property but between these two forms and a third, which Comisso calls 'communal' or non-exclusionary. In communal property 'individuals and groups have the right freely to use property as they wish, and no one is excluded from doing so' (Comisso, 1991: 167). The fault of socialist economies was not in the form of property, i.e. public property, but in the lack of clarity of property rights, either because they were ill-defined or unenforceable:

As a consequence, even the state lacked clear title to its assets, as party officials could and often had to intervene in the actions it took to dispose of them. This was no less the case in Yugoslavia, where self-managed enterprises could and did make decisions 'as if' they had claims to the income streams generated by the assets they 'managed', but in practice found that they required the support and protection of the political leaders to exercise their rights. Because laws in general were subordinated to political priorities, property rights defined in laws necessarily suffered the same fate, regardless of who held them. (Comisso 1991: 169)

This evidence points to two apparently contrary tendencies for the state in a dynamic capitalist economy. On the one hand evidence points towards the need for a *strong state capable of facilitating development* in a market context, but on the other hand, as Comisso argues, *the strong state must also have limited sovereignty over economic actors.* As is well recognised in the literature, the state provides critical institutional foundations for capitalist economic growth, not the least of which is the promotion of 'human' capital assets (such as education, health and safety), as well as the more standard institutional assets (such as stable means of exchange, laws and courts for mediation of disputes, and police for the enforcement of judicial decisions). These demand a strong state, capable of structuring society and implementing policy at all levels. At the same time, Comisso's work specifies where the borders of the state must lie – between politics and economics – in order to establish a successful market economy: *economic decisions must be made mainly on economic grounds, not political ones.*

These findings may offer a useful perspective for market development in Yemen. For though only a small part of united Yemen is engaged in a post-socialist transition, Comisso's characterisation (above) of the problems of socialist Yugoslavia rings strikingly true for the market economy of the entire Republic of Yemen. Like the transitional economies of the former Soviet Union (FSU) countries, Yemen is today engaged in the cultivation of market institutions, in the hope that these will bring long-term economic development, not just growth, to the country. And, like socialist Yugoslavia, there are signs that this critical border between politics and economy is rather porous in Yemen.

The changing role of the state in Yemen

One of the notable structural trends in the Yemeni economy over the last decade or so has been the increasing preponderance of the state in the economy. Ironically, in an era of liberalisation, privatisation and decentralisation, the nature of structural changes in Yemen's economy has concentrated control of economic wealth in the hands of the state in the YAR and the RoY. This was principally the result of the shift in the relative importance to the economy of worker remittances and domestic petroleum resources.

As noted earlier, worker remittances accrued to private households of migrant workers. Therefore, the primary source of wealth in the period before 1986 was outside the direct control of the state. In fact the state in the YAR did little to regulate any economic activity before the balance of payment crises of the mid-1980s. In this paradise of freewheeling commercial capitalism, the state relied on two main sources of revenues for current budget and development investment, customs revenue and foreign aid. The collection of these sources of revenue does not require the sort of strong state bureaucracy required to gather detailed financial information and implement taxation on individual or business income and assets. Direct taxes not only require much greater state capacity but also critical political decisions about who should pay how much at what cost; although they contribute a large share of state revenue in most industrialised states, they contributed little to the YAR's state coffers (Chaudhry, 1997: 201; for industrialised states see Steinmo, 1993).

The second source of funds was international assistance in the form of loans and grants. These accounted for the vast majority of infrastructure investments and even gross capital formation in both the YAR and PDRY. It is perhaps one of the marks of the regime's political brilliance that Yemen's sources of foreign assistance were quite diverse and the political constraints that might have accompanied reliance on one main source of aid were mitigated. The PDRY was more tied to socialist bloc aid, but non-socialist Western and Arab aid also assisted Aden (Carapico, 1998: Ch. 2). Even today, when the collapse of cold war rivalry and bad international credit ratings have allowed the IMF and the World Bank significantly to curtail the ability of the regime to play off alternative sources of international finance, the regime continues to use petroleum contracts for exploration and production to forge varying strategic alliances with First World countries.

The downturn in remittances and international assistance reoriented the YAR's economy and expanded the role of the state within it. The import trade was strictly regulated and restricted in an attempt to stem the deterioration in the balance of payments (see Appendix, Figure 2.3). New taxes were instituted which fell upon private businesses (Chaudhry, 1997: 276). The state not only enforced new restrictions and regulations, but also entered into the import business itself. Where the state was not directly involved in importing, lucrative licences often ended up in the hands of favoured merchants allied with the state. The discovery and development of oil resources (substantial export revenues from petroleum began in 1987 but only began to have an impact on the balance of payments situation in 1989–90)[1] further concentrated economic weight in the hands of the state. Today, not only does the state own portions of the oil production and exploration of companies themselves, but taxes, royalties and concession payments also flow directly into state coffers. According to *The Economist* (1998), oil revenues surpassed all other forms of state revenue, and oil exports have accounted for the vast bulk of Yemen's exports since the late 1980s. Prior to the reassertion of state power in the economy in 1986, the state had already, by means of debt-led growth, built most of the infrastructure and much of the existing industry. The public sector accounted for two-thirds of gross capital formation in 1982 (Carapico, 1998: Ch. 2). By 1990, government services alone accounted for the largest share of GDP of any sector, contributing 23.6 per cent of GDP in 1990 (EIU, 1992–3: 47). Developments in the late 1980s combined to give the state greatly expanded power over the domestic economy.

FIGURE 2.1
Government revenue: Main components

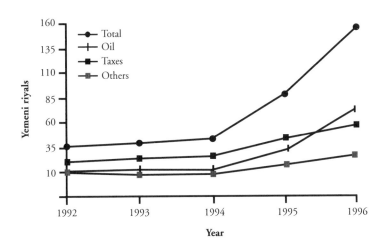

Source: CSO 1995 and Yemeni government, from *The Economist Country Report*, 1st Quarter 1997.

Comisso (1991) argues, as outlined above, that the preponderance of the state sector in the economy alone may pose no particular barrier to development, in spite of the considerable popular and academic press against public enterprise. She maintains that it is only when the boundaries of political authority and economic decision-making are not clearly divided that the large role of the state in the economy may inhibit development. This is a difficult and sensitive question, for the line between economics and politics is always vague, even in the most successful of capitalist economies. Certainly the interventionist state of the East Asian NICs mixes politics and economics, with the powerful ministries firmly guiding economic decisions in the private sector. Yet this guidance was directed towards international competitiveness and the use of international markets as discipline for export-oriented producers. Similarly, during the periods of stunning economic success, the political structure of, for example, South Korea relied upon financial transfers from the large *chaebols* to the political élite (now, with the democratic opening of Korea in the 1990s, considered 'corruption').[2] However, critical economic decisions were obviously made with economic goals in mind, as demonstrated in the tremendous growth of these economies.

In Yemen today, there are significant signs that important economic decisions are made by political means for political goals. In a report prepared by the Foreign Investment Advisory Service (attached to the World Bank) to assess foreign investment potential in Yemen and to advise the government on the measures necessary to attract such investment, the FIAS clearly placed much of the responsibility for Yemen's perceived unattractiveness to foreign investors on the state.[3] The problems of governance were identified as overlapping jurisdictions between govern-ment agencies, overregulation and discretionary application of laws and regulations, underpaid and unmotivated civil servants, lack of protection for property or enforcement of contracts, and the general weakness of the state in many rural areas (FIAS, 1997: 12). A substantial portion of these complaints relates to the nature of the state's bureaucracy. Underpaid civil servants will use vague laws or broad levels of discretion in administrative decisions to direct rents towards their own pockets (Doriye, 1992: 91).

The civil service also serves a political purpose: that of distributing income among a clientele. In a period of high unemployment and falling incomes, government employment provides welcome supplements to meagre household incomes. These government salaries, small as they often are, can provide an important means for political messages – as, for example, the raising of incomes or timely payment in critical election periods, or the threat of non-payment of salaries.[4] At the same time, as the FIAS report shows, key positions in the bureaucracy can enhance the incomes of state employees. When these sorts of practices extend into the area of production, both directly in terms of public-sector production and indirectly through the state's regulatory apparatus, then economic decision-making is in danger of being politically directed to the detriment of the economy. From this springs the concern over the extensive expansion of the state into the economy which began with the regulatory reforms of 1986 and then continued with the concentration of oil revenues in the hands of the state.

The judicial system was identified by those interviewed for the FIAS survey as the most problematic state institution:

> Whether the matter involves land ownership, commercial disputes, banks attempting to recover assets, or simply recourse to the courts to recover a rightful claim, the outcome seems to be in doubt regarding fairness, the length of time to secure a judgment, or enforcement. The lack of faith in the judicial system constitutes one of the most important constraints on direct foreign investment (FIAS, 1997: 16–17).

A conference on land registration in Yemen held at Sana'a University in April 1994 underlined the difficulties of legally defining and enforcing property rights in urban and rural land. Speaker after speaker, a large percentage of whom were members of the bureaucracies they criticised, bemoaned the lack of enforcement and clarity of land and property titles. A further problem identified by the FIAS study was the reneging on, and reopening of, tenders by the state during the period in which signed statements of intent had been in force.

All of these problems point to the 'weakness' of bureaucratic rule in Yemen. Various administrative methods of overcoming these problems, such as increased salaries for bureaucrats, technical training in their respective fields for the various branches of the bureaucracy, and campaigns against corruption, were recommended by the World Bank and the FIAS.[5] This type of recommendation was very much in line with the sort of administrative reform promoted by the World Bank as typifying practices of 'good' governance (World Bank, 1997). As other writers (Leftwich, 1995; Fox, 1995; Moore, 1993) have pointed out, the question here is whether important determinants of institutional change and development lie in the realm of politics – i.e. whether the regime's political strategies (in both domestic and international contexts) influence the state's institutional development and capacities.

There are many indications from the literature on Yemen that there exists an economic élite closely tied to the regime. An analysis of the financial sector revealed the existence of a 'financial oligarchy' (Al-Maitami, 1997). The best urban and agricultural lands are often found in the hands of important military or political supporters of the regime. Key sections of the commercial bourgeoisie rely on a close relationship with the political regime for their wealth (Chaudhry, 1997; Carapico, 1998). Military contracting and supply is a lucrative business and controls significant portions of import and wholesale trade and the granting of contracts or licences are often destined for political supporters.

There are also numerous examples of conflict between the state and economic élites in Yemen. In the financial sector powerful actors controlling workers' remittances have found themselves exiled or jailed in various periods. The southern bourgeoisie of the Taiz region have been strictly regulated by the state, for example in the case of the restriction of imports in the mid-1980s. However, the key question is not whether there is an élite that benefits from its connections with the regime, but how – in the context of changing international and domestic constraints and opportunities in the political economy – the tug and pull of the relationship between political and economic élites determines institutional outcomes. According to the FIAS report, foreign investors perceive that property rights and contracts are not respected, which suggests that the relationship between the regime and the economic élite has not contributed to the institutional development of property rights.

The popular perception in Yemen is that 'the powerful eat the weak'. In academic literature the nature of the state in Yemen and the process of politics are not well known. Though there are several excellent studies analysing aspects of state power and social structure in Yemen (Dresch, 1989; Chaudhry, 1997; Carapico, 1998), the workings of power in Yemen at all levels are little understood. Political relationships in Yemen can, in the most general and basic of terms, be characterised by two qualities: at the national level, power is concentrated and personalised; but in regional terms the state is institutionally 'weak'.

The concentration of key political and military posts in the hands of relatives and clansmen attests to the personal nature of the regime's rule, and the military is clearly an important centre of power in Yemen.

In spite of the emphasis on democratic values in the 1990s, the top political leadership is also closely related, though less so than the military. The president appoints governors and, for example, placed his half-brother in charge of the important southern province of Lahj. The ruling party, the General People's Congress, lacks the cadre training and structure that characterises political parties, being rather an amalgamation of personalities (Ilham, 1994: 176). The core leadership rules through its personal relationships with a diffuse set of powerful personalities, represented, for example, in the consultative council appointed by the regime following the 1997 elections. In the elections the president's party had removed many of the council members from power, yet these prominent personalities were graced with important roles through personal endorsements of the top leadership.

Again, concentration of power in the hands of families and rule by personalities is not directly related to lack of economic institutional development. Certainly the growth of the Indonesian economy was not initially dampened by the interlocking family relationships between political power and economic wealth (though the reforms that followed the crisis were aimed at breaking these relationships). In the Yemeni case, however, personalised rule at the top, by undermining the sovereignty of economic actors, may perhaps contribute at a more general level to the lack of institutional development of economic relations. A connection between political power at the top and economic wealth belies problems of boundaries between economic decision-making and political decisions – this is what Comisso calls 'limited sovereignty over economic actors'.

The report on investors' perceptions of Yemen also mentioned the lack of central authority in rural areas (FIAS, 1997: 18). The central government cedes large areas of territory to regional powers whose institutional power is based upon military or regional social affiliations. This lack of government authority in rural areas, particularly in the northern highlands, has been related to fundamental political processes in Yemen (Chaudhry, 1997: 193). Thus, while personalised rule and reliance on close military ties at the top are characteristic of the national leadership, regional government is characterised by diffuse ties to local leaders who are authorities on their own in rural areas. Lack of institutional authority in rural areas reveals the weakness of what Mann (1988) terms the state's *infrastructural power*. The crucial institutional support for growth highlighted in the 1997 *World Development Report*, i.e. those aspects of a strong and capable state that facilitate economic development, also appears to be weak in Yemen. Thus Yemen lacks the two qualities of a state that are emphasised by Comisso as necessary for economic development in a market context: institutional capacity, and limited sovereignty over economic actors.

The stability of property rights and contracts varies by sector (and probably very much by region). In the oil sector, for example, investors have had little hesitation in sinking their money into fixed assets in Yemen. Investments are made not only on the basis of potential profits but also, of course, on the basis of risk: nor has the threat of instability of property rights or political volatility deterred those seeking a part of the lucrative oil business. Petroleum producers have even anticipated the risk of political instability and military conflict in their physical plants. Canadian Occidental reported that after the outbreak of the 70 days war in 1994, the company's computer data was transferred via satellite to a home site in Canada. Similarly, by dispersing pumping and transport facilities, extracting plants were organised to minimise the risk of disruption.[6]

Larger commercial and industrial firms in Yemen seem to have their own ways of guaranteeing their investments. Indeed, the FIAS report (1997: 31–2) suggested that in the meantime the best strategy for foreign investors was to make alliances with the family networks within these large firms in Yemen so as to take advantage of their local knowledge and means. However for the vast majority of Yemenis, fears related to weak institutional development of property rights means that mobile assets are preferred and that fixed investments are less desirable. Fixed investments that raise the general level of productivity in the workforce are sorely needed in Yemen. While education, infrastructure and sources of finance are also needed, the roots of the future development of the non-oil sectors of Yemen's economy lie in the institutional under-pinnings of economic investment and growth. Given current political practices, this institutional edifice will be difficult to construct.

Building a market economy is a far more complex process than simply freeing markets and establishing private property; capitalist dynamism is a result of long-term institutional developments that include politics. Experiences of the post-socialist transition in Eastern Europe and the CIS have shown that the limited sovereignty of the state over economic actors is one of the institutional qualities required for growth.

At the same time, a strong state must be able to extend its capacity to regulate society in order to *create* the conditions in which markets function. A strong state is also needed to ensure that economic growth addresses the social issues of poverty and unemployment. Generalised growth in the Yemeni economy is dependent upon greater institutional capacity of the state to facilitate market development and, paradoxically, upon limited state sovereignty in the economy.

NOTES

1 Substantial export revenues from petroleum began in 1987 but started to have an impact on the balance of payments situation only in 1989–90.
2 The state also structured domestic markets to achieve social goals such as employment and income distribution.
3 This was, in part, because the report is policy-oriented, focusing on the actions that the state could take to strengthen foreign investment in Yemen.
4 As occurred at times in the south when the Northern and Southern leaderships were feuding between 1990 and 1994.
5 Newspapers at this time were full of reports of public campaigns by the Yemeni regime to root out corruption.
6 For a report on moves by Canadian Occidental Petroleum Ltd, see 'CanOxy Recounts Smooth Pullout from Yemen', *Oil and Gas Journal*, 1994, Vol. 92, No. 34 and Vol. 28, No. 3.

APPENDIX

FIGURE 2.2
Trade and remittances – PDRY

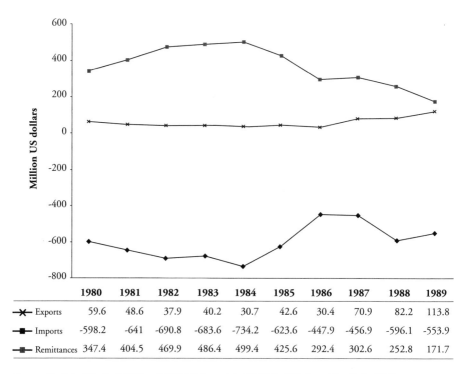

	1980	1981	1982	1983	1984	1985	1986	1987	1988	1989
Exports	59.6	48.6	37.9	40.2	30.7	42.6	30.4	70.9	82.2	113.8
Imports	-598.2	-641	-690.8	-683.6	-734.2	-623.6	-447.9	-456.9	-596.1	-553.9
Remittances	347.4	404.5	469.9	486.4	499.4	425.6	292.4	302.6	252.8	171.7

Source: *Statistical Yearbook 1992* and *SYB-CD* [copyright ©], United Nations, New York, 1995.

FIGURE 2.3
Trade and remittances – YAR

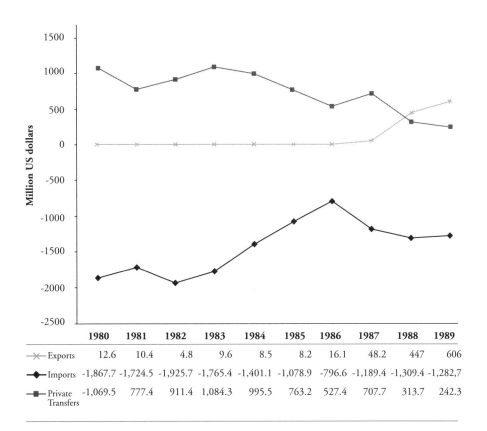

	1980	1981	1982	1983	1984	1985	1986	1987	1988	1989
Exports	12.6	10.4	4.8	9.6	8.5	8.2	16.1	48.2	447	606
Imports	-1,867.7	-1,724.5	-1,925.7	-1,765.4	-1,401.1	-1,078.9	-796.6	-1,189.4	-1,309.4	-1,282,7
Private Transfers	-1,069.5	777.4	911.4	1,084.3	995.5	763.2	527.4	707.7	313.7	242.3

Source: *Statistical Yearbook 1992* and *SYB-CD* [copyright ©], United Nations, New York, 1995.

FIGURE 2.4
Trade and remittances 1990–5 – RoY

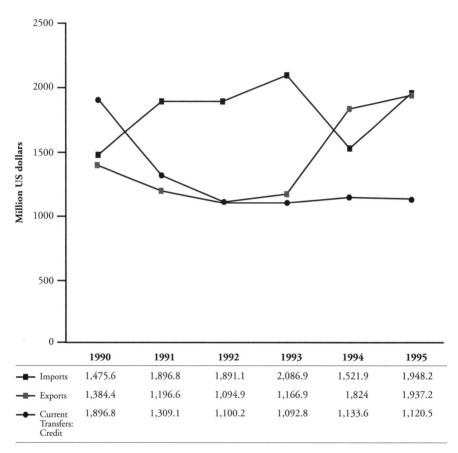

	1990	1991	1992	1993	1994	1995
■ Imports	1,475.6	1,896.8	1,891.1	2,086.9	1,521.9	1,948.2
■ Exports	1,384.4	1,196.6	1,094.9	1,166.9	1,824	1,937.2
● Current Transfers: Credit	1,896.8	1,309.1	1,100.2	1,092.8	1,133.6	1,120.5

Source: *Balance of Payments Statistics Yearbook 1997.*

3

Political and Economic Realities of Labour Migration in Yemen

―――――

Nora Ann Colton

Introduction

Since the days when the caravan routes crossed Yemen on their way to and from Europe, the country has been at the crossroads of international trade and migration. The British reinforced this importance when they set up their coaling station at Aden in the 1800s, and Yemen was again made a significant part of international trade and migration during the 1970s because of its strategic location among the Middle East oil regions.

This contribution will argue that in order to understand international labour migration from Yemen, it is crucial to analyse the 'push forces' – the diminishing opportunities in the home country that exert a compulsive pressure on an individual to leave. It is hoped that by examining these forces as important causes of out-migration, it will also be possible to appreciate their relationship to the Yemeni economy. The current rapid population growth is likely to exacerbate Yemen's growing GDP (gross domestic product), and economic adjustments need to take into account the important role that migration has played in structuring the Yemeni economy.

The first part of this contribution reviews the history of Yemeni migration prior to 1990 in an attempt not only to show that out-migration from Yemen has been a phenomenon with much historical relevance, but also to illustrate that it has been driven mainly by economic considerations. The second part examines the structural changes that have taken place in the Yemeni economy due to migration. This section will demonstrate that decades of migration have created a rentier economic system ill-prepared to sustain itself without external sources of financing. The final part looks specifically at the period after the Gulf Crisis, and attempts to understand the significance of the structural changes that took place particularly during the migration boom of the 1970s and 1980s in light of the mass return of migrants in the 1990s. It also highlights the fact that a large number of returnees from the Gulf have never been reintegrated into the Yemeni socioeconomic system. Much of the information on these returnees comes from in-depth interviews conducted by the author in three returnee camps in August 1995. Lastly it examines Yemen's attempt to revitalise its economy in the mid-1990s under the direction of the International Monetary Fund. Here the question raised is whether or not the reforms are addressing the legacy of structural changes that have resulted from external migration.

The historical roots of Yemeni migration

Yemen, as two states prior to unification in 1990, was recognised as one of the countries most dependent for its income on international labour migration. Even during the two decades that the South, the People's Democratic Republic of Yemen (PDRY), was pursuing socialism, the two states remained dependent on labour migration. Prior to the Gulf War, both North and South Yemen appeared to be using remittances to buy rather than to produce what they needed, behaviour which is not, however, new for South Arabia. The most famous legend of a mass exodus from Yemen dates back to the destruction of the Marib Dam in 575 AD. This was a migration caused by inadequate resources in Yemen – a theme that has continued to emerge as a main reason why Yemenis are forced abroad. In fact, emigration from Yemen has also been cited throughout the nineteenth and twentieth centuries (cf. Swanson, 1979)

However, whereas earlier emigration involved permanent relocation of large segments of the population, a distinguishing feature of twentieth-century migration is that it is labour-oriented: individuals migrate rather than communities and usually work abroad for relatively short periods. The Yemeni economy in the early twentieth century was a pre-capitalist economy and this condition was a leading factor in Yemeni migration during that period. Writing in 1915 about the port of Mocha, Wyman Bury noted that 'Mokha is a dead-alive, mouldering town, whose trade as a port for coffee and hides has been killed by excessive taxation in the past and its proximity to Aden' (Bury, 1915: 24). One important reason for the substantial decline in coffee exports was the expanding of world markets, which now offered alternatives to Mocha coffee. But even if demand had remained high, inadequate roads and transportation methods would have seriously hindered any expansion of cash crops. Under Imam Yahya (1918–48), North Yemen trade declined further and continued to do so into the reign of his son Ahmad ibn Yahya (1948–62). Coffee exports were estimated to be approximately 12,000 tons in 1945, but reached only 5,000 tons in 1962 (Halliday, 1974: 88).

The entry of the British into Aden in 1839 is also significant in the history of Yemeni migration. The British made the port of Aden into a coaling station for ships passing through the area, but as time passed Aden became much more than a mere coaling port. From the time of its seizure by the British, Yemeni labourers were drawn to Aden, and the port benefited greatly from the flow of migrants. As a duty-free port, it also came into active commercial rivalry with the Yemeni ports of Mocha and Hodeidah. Furthermore, Britain's occupation of South Yemen prevented the Yemenis from unifying into a single state and subsequently from integrating into the modern economy that was developing in the British Protectorate. The result was lopsided development, with most of Yemen existing on subsistence agriculture while the smaller part became a trade-based economy. It is estimated that some 80 to 85 per cent of the North Yemen population was involved in agricultural production well into the 1950s.

Although there was an affluent land-owning class, most of the land was distributed between farmers in small and medium-sized plots, except in the Tihama where most of the population were sharecroppers who worked on the estates of land-owning merchants, secular notables, or Zaydi *sayyids*. Notwithstanding the fact that most of the land was held in small plots, thereby enabling most families to undertake subsistence cultivation, famine was frequent. Among the main causes were a shortage of transport, deficient water conservation and cultivation techniques, and a lack of security for farmers. For example, in 1943 there was famine in the North, and hungry peasants trudged from village to village begging for food. The Imam is said to have refused to provide money or release grain from his stores to assist the needy (Al-Masodi, 1987). Hundreds died of starvation and thousands escaped death only by emigrating abroad or migrating to Aden.

In the immediate post-World War II period, and as a result of the general upsurge in world trade, Aden's economic activity expanded greatly, thereby helping many Aden-based North Yemeni merchants to attain a high standard of living. From the port of Aden they expanded their commercial activities to the Red Sea ports, where they built successful businesses. Indeed, Yemeni merchants were to become known as the most important group of Asian aliens in French Somaliland (Thompson and Adloff, 1968: 215–16). The port also served as a starting-point for poorer and less skilled migrants to other destinations.

Villagers from the North were drawn to the port not only during periods of famine, but also on occasions when the Imam and his regime were particularly brutal. Such episodes included the annual assessments and collection of tax, when individual villages were obliged to accommodate and feed the soldiers and officials sent on the Imam's behalf. William Brown (1963: 351) puts forward the commonly held view that assessment was made by cursory observation of the size of the crop, though it was also common practice to bribe the assessor. The average tax was approximately 25 per cent of the crop plus bribes and other imposed expenses. Villages that failed to pay their taxes were usually penalised by being required to house troops until full payment was made. In Yemen it is not unusual to hear stories from men who were forced to migrate because of their inability to meet tax obligations. Asked why he migrated during Imam Yahya's time, an informant from a Shafi'i area gave the following account:

> The Imam's soldiers came to my house and demanded I pay my taxes. The harvest had been bad so I couldn't pay; then the soldiers told me to kill my chickens to feed them; when I refused they began to beat me. I escaped and went by foot to the port; there I got on a boat.

His journey led him to Ethiopia where he remained until the Ethiopian revolution in 1974.

Most accounts of the economy under Imam Yahya give a gloomy picture of a poverty-stricken country with few means to improve its environment, making it ripe for external migration. The Imam's rule, which was characterised by a weak economy tied to imports and by the heavy burden imposed by his taxation system, prompted a large number of Yemenis to emigrate; they established themselves in France, Britain, the US, Ethiopia, Djibouti, Indonesia and Kenya.

In the Southern Protectorates, life was not much better. The region of Wadi Hadhramawt, the biggest *wadi* (valley) in the Arabian Peninsula, is well known for its out-migration to the far-off lands of Indonesia and

Malaysia. Although it is fertile, with groundwater available all year, its size and the fact that it is surrounded by deserts has enabled it to support only a limited population. Out-migration, which increased in years of political turmoil or drought, thus served as a safety valve for the region. Before the British extended their control to Wadi Hadhramawt, the region had been divided for almost a century, with the border lying between the Qu'aiti and Kathiri sultanates, a division that was coupled with much warring between the different tribes. Consequently, much of the earlier migration in this region was due to the lack of adequate means of survival, and to political repression and turmoil. In fact, for many migrants their destination was of less importance than the actual act of leaving.

Many migrants, especially those who travelled great distances, became increasingly absorbed by issues in the host country. After all, their political and economic existence was at stake. Christopher Gandy (1971: 351) notes that although emigrants did not cut themselves off from their homeland, many remained permanently abroad. On the other hand, migrants who worked in Aden seemed to maintain a keener interest in Yemeni affairs. Migration to Aden brought them into contact with a political system offering a wide range of freedoms, and also introduced them to such services as hospitals, schools, electricity, paved roads, pumped water and a host of consumer goods.

The wish of many North Yemenis to overthrow Imam Ahmad, the son of Yahya, is attributed to their being exposed to political freedoms in Aden. Upon Yahya's death, his son Al-Badr had claimed the Imamate. A coup engineered by a group of army officers successfully deposed Al-Badr on 26 September 1962, and as a result eight years of civil war ensued. The war exhausted the country's limited resources, and no major economic steps were taken toward modernisation until the early 1970s. Meanwhile South Yemen was liberated in 1967 from the British, who turned it over to the indigenous population. After the departure of the British, a group of socialists came to power with the goal of restructuring the economy according to Marxist principles.

Thus it is clear that the push factors of poverty, unemployment, taxation, uncertainty with regard to the economy, and in particular the political environment drove Yemenis abroad in the early part of the twentieth century. The pull factors seem to have been secondary to the push factors; however, geography, employment, and a more stable society in the host country appeared to have been factored into the eventual destinations. Moreover, during this early period Yemen was little more than a conduit for international trade and migration. The ports of Aden, Hodeidah and Mocha provided a constant flow of imports, and a means for migrants to abandon their homeland for the seas and destinations of unknown lands. Consequently, Yemen's strategic location in terms of sea routes, coupled with its inability to structure its economy in a way that would allow it to produce what it needed, continued to leave its citizens very vulnerable to the world at large.

The oil era

The 1970s marked a turning-point for Yemen. As the countries of the Gulf region began a rapid expansion of their economies due to their oil riches, a new source of wealth and work was to be found. The lack of an adequate indigenous labour force in Saudi Arabia to provide manpower for its development initiatives caused a huge labour shortage, and because demand for labour far exceeded supply, there was a rapid increase in wage rates. This need for labour led the Saudis to welcome the short-term migrants from Yemen who filled a significant gap in their labour market.

Saudi Arabia's economic growth reached unprecedented levels in 1972 when its GNP rose at a rate of almost 20 per cent per annum at current prices. Oil production rose by 25 per cent and oil income reached an estimated US$2.5 billion (Central Bank of Yemen, 1973: 21). As a result of the substantial gains in oil revenues, Saudi monetary reserves amounted to US$3,087 million in February 1973, compared with US$1,496 million in 1972. In terms of migration, this increased development translated into a labour requirement of 9,728,000 in the Gulf and 1,968,000 in Saudi Arabia. The higher wage rates and employment opportunities that were offered in the Gulf region were, of course, the major pull factors for Yemenis, but push factors were also relevant. The push factors of an economy unable to provide jobs and a minimum standard of living for its citizenry caused a mass male migration from Yemen to the Gulf. As many as 1.2 million North Yemenis were said to be working in the Gulf by 1975 (Central Planning Organisation, 1987: 37).

The North

The civil war in the North ended in 1970, after which North Yemen launched itself into a programme of structuring new state institutions.

Most modern institutions in North Yemen were either established in, or started functioning during, the 1970s. The physical infrastructure was greatly expanded, with roads, electricity and pumped water extended to many places in the country. In 1973 the government launched a three-year plan outlining considerable improvements for the country. In 1970/1 total imports amounted to YR174.6 million, 47.7 per cent of which was for foodstuffs, while exports amounted to YR13.5 million (Central Planning Organisation, 1987: 102, 105). The lack of an export market meant that much of the initial development was financed from capital inflows from abroad – first from foreign aid and secondly from a combination of aid and remittances. However, this situation turned out-migration into a necessity. As more North Yemenis worked abroad, those at home demanded more imports.

Because the state dominated all channels to revenues in order to fund a growing debt, the small indigenous private sector was capital-poor. Significant increases in government expenditure on infrastructure, social services and defence led to a rising budget deficit that was financed by the central bank. *In 1983 this deficit spending reached a peak, representing 26 per cent of GDP.*

Imports rose from US$87 million in 1971 to US$730 million in 1976, and it is believed that the level of imports would have been even higher had it not been for the limited size of North Yemeni ports (El Mallakh, 1986: 76). It was reported that ships often had to wait up to 180 days before being able to unload their cargo. Thus, while labour was being exported, capital goods were being imported. This cycle of trade in goods and labour created a situation in which increased out-migration became more important to national development than national development was to sustaining growth for the society and economy.

The South

In the post-independence South, the regimes that followed issued a host of reforms that were based on two premises: first that the trading economy established under the British was responsible for much of the under-development of the economy; and second that the best way to achieve rapid development was by way of a Marxist model. The British, accused of focusing on the port of Aden, had left the hinterland unchanged during the colonial period, which created income inequality that had to be alleviated. At the same time an industrial sector needed to be created for balanced development. These two goals constituted the focus of the Marxist approach in South Yemen.

From the time the socialists came to power, skilled and educated South Yemenis fled abroad. The push and pull factors for these skilled Southerners were: (1) the departure of the British, who reneged on their aid commitments; (2) the closure of the Suez Canal in June 1967, which resulted in a fall of about 75 per cent in the port of Aden's trade; (3) an anti-bourgeoisie movement initiated by the regime; and lastly (4) a major pull factor, namely the lucrative labour markets of the oil-rich Gulf countries.

This created a severe brain drain for the South. Indeed, a survey made by the Yemeni Central Statistical Organisation after the Gulf Crisis (CSO, 1991) confirmed the significance of the skill level of Southerners versus Northerners who had gone abroad. The largest employment category for pre-migration was agriculture, with 44.6 per cent of those from the North stating that they were farmers prior to migration compared to 16.73 per cent of Southerners (CSO, 1991). Furthermore, a significant number of South Yemenis were office clerks, soldiers and teachers before migrating. It is interesting to note the difference in skill level of migrants from the North and South prior to migration and during migration. Thirty-two per cent of the North Yemenis were unskilled labourers or construction workers while only 14 per cent of the South Yemenis abroad were in these occupations. However, 30.5 per cent of South Yemenis were either involved in retailing or office clerks while only 14 per cent of the North Yemenis worked in such areas (CSO, 1991). The difference in skill levels has to do with the fact that many more of the Southerners were skilled prior to migration.

The Southern government tried to address the brain drain problem of out-migration, but there was no way they could direct the local economy and compete with the wage levels and opportunities offered in the Gulf. In 1973 the government prohibited out-migration in an attempt to stop any further loss of the skilled and educated segments of the labour force, but although this prohibition slowed migration, it did not stem the flow completely.

In spite of propaganda suggesting the contrary, the South too was involved in an exchange of labour for goods. Indeed, many laws were passed to allow migrants to import goods as a way of encouraging them to produce goods and services in the home economy (Colton,

1993 personal communications). Imports rose from 62,143,000 Yemeni Dinars in 1975 to YD241,155,000 in 1985.[1] Although exports rose in the same period from YD2,920,000 in 1975 to YD12,768,000 in 1985, they failed to keep pace with imports, thereby causing an increasing trade balance problem. Due to the need to finance its import bill, the South encouraged remittance transfers, along with special accounts in foreign currencies for migrants. By 1985 remittances had risen to YD140.3 million from the 1970 figure of YD21.7 million (Colton, 1993). During the 1980s, the South Yemeni government even took to sending delegations of officials abroad to make contact with Southerners who had migrated, in the hope of convincing them either to return to Yemen or to send home their remittances as a way of investing in the domestic economy.

Structural changes to the Yemeni economy caused by the migration boom

The relationship between migration and the Yemeni economy created a number of structural changes. For example, Yemen's services/informal sector grew while its industry stagnated: in 1970 the percentage shares of GDP in North and South Yemen for services and industry respectively were 39.4 per cent and 10.0 per cent for the North, and 58.2 per cent and 23.6 per cent in the South. By 1980 these numbers had changed to 55.5 per cent and 16.2 per cent in the North and 83.0 per cent and 6.7 per cent in the South (cf. CPO and CSO, various). Unlike many developing countries which have experienced rapid urbanisation that outpaces industrial development, thereby leading to the absorption of this excess labour in the informal/service sector, Yemen was suffering from a lack of labour and urbanisation. This situation had come about as a result of the international labour migration in the 1970s and 1980s, which had absorbed much of the Yemeni labour force.

Yemen certainly saw the rise of rural-urban migration for employment reasons, but this migration was to urban centres abroad, a phenomenon that disrupted the Yemeni economy in many ways. Unlike other developing countries, where a large migration to the urban areas brought wages down or kept them just above subsistence in the modern sector or in urban centres, Yemen saw wages rise in the modern sector during the 1970s and 1980s due to the international nature of its migration. In other words, external migration produced various kinds of labour shortages in Yemen.

Development theory suggests that in a country initiating develop-ment, agriculture's share of per capita income decreases, regardless of whether the migration is internal or external (cf. on development theory, Chenery and Taylor, 1968: 391–416). However, the share of per capita income for industry and services is definitely influenced by the type of migration taking place. In the case of Yemen, high wages and the lack of an adequate labour force brought on by international migration stifled industrial development in both the North and the South. Production costs were forced up, making imports more attractive. Due to the narrow profit margins resulting from high production costs, manufacturers were unable to accumulate capital, which in turn made investment in industry more difficult. These higher costs and poor returns also deterred potential investors (returned migrants) from investing in industrial developments. In addition, the lack of investment opportunities in industry created many small-scale, individually owned establishments as migrants searched for opportunities. Therefore, as with other developing countries, this has resulted in the emergence of a large informal sector providing services and activities that do not necessarily correlate with demand (Ofer, 1967: 40–3).

In the case of Yemen the area that gained the most through external migration was the informal sector, in which some similarities with other developing countries can be seen. Even so, the large informal sector is not necessarily caused by the modern/industrial sector being unable to keep pace with industrialisation – rather it is due to the total lack of industrialisation, which causes labourers to search for other employment opportunities in this sector (cf. Todaro, 1969: 138–48). Although industrial development was stifled by high wages and an inadequate labour force in urban areas, incomes continued to rise as migrants to external urban centres remitted portions of their income to the home country or returned with their earnings. These rising incomes created demand for a sophisticated banking system, a transportation system, and a communication system to support the linkages between the home country and the external urban centres.

As long as wages were higher in the external urban centre, migration continued, but once the wage levels between the two countries began to equalise in the late 1980s migrants started trickling home. Agricultural employment did not benefit from such a scenario since the wage rate in the modern sector was so much higher than the subsistence wage labourers would receive in agriculture. Consequently, this decrease in external migration led to a further swelling of the informal sector. Attention can be drawn to the impact of these structural changes by focusing on some specific sectoral changes.

The agricultural sector

Before and during the early 1970s, Yemen had a subsistence economy. In 1973, it was estimated that some 80 to 85 per cent of the North Yemen labour force worked in agriculture. In the South in 1973, 67 per cent of the population lived in rural areas or were nomadic with agriculture providing direct employment to approximately 47 per cent of the labour force (World Bank, 1976: 1; World Bank, 1979b: 80–2).

As already noted, labourers were induced to go to urban centres abroad, and urban wages rates were bid up so as to exceed the subsistence money wage rates. These wage increases created a further movement of labourers; i.e. those who were not enticed to the external urban centres were now enticed to the internal urban centres. This second movement of labour, coupled with the ability of the external markets to absorb such large numbers of workers, caused a labour shortage in the rural areas. Not only did this affect the wage rates (in the past two decades average rural wage rates had been roughly 11 times the wage rates of 1972–3), but it also altered the entire structure of the agriculture sector (World Bank, 1979a: 14).

Changes in the types of crops produced

The most important change in agriculture was in the types of crops produced, and was caused by the high production costs associated with increased wages. The situation prompted farmers to produce crops that yielded a high price and that were not labour intensive. In North Yemen, as a result, the cultivation and consumption of *qat*, a mildly narcotic plant which requires very little cultivation and which is in great demand throughout the country, rose to an unprecedented level (Kennedy, 1987; Weir, 1985). Although official data concerning the cultivation and consumption of *qat* is almost non-existent, a visitor to Yemen cannot help but be impressed by the sophisticated levels of the production and distribution of this crop. Owing to the nature of the plant and the eventual effect desired, *qat* must be transported and sold within a few days of being picked. Yet this fact does not prevent a wide variety and quantity of *qat* from reaching the most remote parts of Yemen.

John Kennedy quotes a study where 50 per cent of the 61.4 per cent of GDP that was attributed to agriculture in 1973–4 could be attributed to the growing and trading of *qat* (Kennedy, 1987: 78). Weir reckoned that *qat* production in North Yemen at least doubled during the 1970s, and that this production increase was led by demand (Weir, 1985: 86). Kennedy estimated that 50 to 60 per cent of women and 80 to 85 per cent of men chewed *qat* more than once a week, and that much of this consumption had occurred in the previous two decades or so, a period during which discretionary income increased due to labour migration. Weir notes that *qat* went from being something that was consumed only by the élite of society to something that is consumed by all.

Although there has been much discussion by Yemenis and foreign researchers as to whether *qat* production has been at the expense of other crops, such as coffee, the crop that seems to have suffered most because of *qat* cultivation is grain. Ramam Revri (quoted by Kennedy, 1987: 162) remarked that in some areas where irrigation facilities were available, *qat* had replaced the less profitable practice of cereal cultivation. Grain is now produced mainly for household use, being much more labour intensive and less profitable. Weir, however, argued that *qat* was not necessarily replacing grain but was actually making grain production possible, since many of those who were able to grow sorghum could afford the high wage costs because of revenue from *qat*. Evidence as to whether or not *qat* was directly to blame for the diminishing level of grain production is inconclusive. What is certain is that high-cost labour and cheap foreign grain products during the 1970s and 1980s helped undermine the grain market.

Another crop that went through rapid change in the 1970s and 1980s in North Yemen is cotton. Cotton production provides an interesting example of how higher wages lead to higher prices, thus causing the competitiveness of the crop to diminish. In 1972 cotton was reported to have become the main cash crop for North Yemen, with production increasing in the three preceding seasons, and was seen at that time as a great export opportunity for Yemeni agriculture (Central Bank of Yemen, 1973). In 1972 the International Development Agency and the Kuwait Fund for Arab Economic Development granted loans to Yemen to finance a Tihama development project intended to increase cotton production by 8,000 tons annually. The Central Bank of Yemen also attempted to persuade commercial banks to assist in financing the increased production.

Even so, the production of cotton, which was still considered the main export crop for Yemen, had slowed down by 1975, and reached only 13.9 thousand tons during 1975/6. In the same year cotton textiles decreased by 1.7 million yards due to the scarcity of labour, and in 1981 cotton production decreased further, to only 5,000 tons in North Yemen. Despite the ambitious plans outlined in North Yemen's Second Five-Year Plan to bring output of cotton to 20,800 tons by 1986, cotton production continued to stagnate. Indeed, cotton disappeared completely from the list of export crops in the late 1970s/ early 1980s because of the high production costs associated with labour scarcity, and because of its lack of competitiveness in international as well as in local markets (Central Bank of Yemen, 1986: 138).

In the South, agriculture has always been limited: however, as part of its goal of self-sufficiency, the government attempted to promote agricultural development. This led the area under grain production to be increased, frequently at the expense of coffee; even so, grain productivity declined. This can be attributed to a perception by public farm workers that there were few incentives to increase production on land where price controls and state ownership had been imposed. Lackner (1985: 170) examined the amount of cultivated land that was cropped by the private sector in an average year. She found that while the private sector worked an area that was about a third of what was cropped by state farms and cooperatives, its agricultural production, by comparison, was over 50 per cent. Assuming that individual holdings were very small and did not contribute either to the introduction of mechanisation or to economics of scale, this percentage is high.

In addition, the private sector began to engage in *qat* production as an important crop. As wages in the private sector were higher than on state farms, *qat* provided the same advantages in the South as in the North – a high-yield, low labour-intensive cash crop. Lackner (1985: 170) also noted that, as a result of the migration of young males, labour shortages developed in the rural areas, leading to wage inflation. This was particularly reflected in private-sector farming. Therefore, in spite of the South's different economic system, it was unable to avoid the effects of migration on the agricultural sector.

Migration created a disincentive for agricultural production since state wages were controlled and pricing policies were enforced in terms of cooperative production. Even in light of policies and investments to promote agriculture, productivity remained low, due to the migration alternative and the inflow of remittances that allowed rural males to circumvent the system. In terms of the private sector, there was a move towards less labour-intensive yet high-return crops (such as *qat*), similar to that seen in the North.

The industrial sector

As with the agricultural sector, labour has been one of the most important factors influencing the development, or underdevelopment, of the industrial sector. As a result of large labour migration, domestic wages began to increase sharply in both North and South Yemen. Inevitably, the increase in wage rates caused many structural changes in the modern/urban sector by creating distortions in relation to Yemen's comparative advantage, and as a result this traditionally labour-intensive country began to act more like a country with a comparative advantage in capital-intensive production.

Capital-intensive industries

As entrepreneurs attempted to escape from an overpriced, poorly skilled labour market, many moved towards the introduction of either capital-intensive technology or production of goods that required few workers. Capital-intensive industries, however, were not the answer; indeed Yemen has yet to develop an infrastructure that can maintain such industries. This situation not only caused problems in terms of efficiency but also created high maintenance costs. The electricity industry is an example of a production cost where industries, especially the more capital-intensive ones, experienced increased costs. According to the Sana'a general price index, electricity prices rose from 34 in 1973/4 to 130 in 1979/80 to 643 in 1988 in North Yemen. These increases raised the cost of production and often made the goods uncompetitive against foreign imports, thus driving the local producer out of the market. Local business people were further plagued by the inconsistent and often precarious supply of electricity to a city where demand increased rapidly as foreign electronic items flooded the Yemeni market.

Although an industrialist might have been tempted in such circumstances to embark on capital-intensive industries because of high labour costs, there were other problems as well. The increased cost associated with utilising capital goods was, and is, coupled with their continuous need for maintenance. Since a skilled or semi-skilled workforce was needed to repair much of the equipment used in capital-intensive industries, there was the added cost of employing skilled or semi-skilled labour in a country where the wages of such labour reflected its scarcity. Entrepreneurs who wished to diminish labour costs invested in capital-intensive industries, especially in the subsectors of food processing and chemicals. Therefore, the share of manufacturing in the labour force in the North increased relatively rapidly, from 3 per cent in 1975 to 11.9 per cent in 1986 (for 1986 census information see CPO, 1988: 54–5; and for 1975 census information see CPO, 1977: 55).

The service sector

Since the early 1980s Yemen's service sector has had the highest percentage share of GDP. Not only have services risen as a percentage share of GDP as agriculture has fallen, but they have continued to increase while industry has remained relatively level; i.e. it appears that industry in Yemen has stagnated in spite of the fact that agriculture is decreasing, therefore allowing services to form an ever-growing share of GDP.

This growth in the service sector can be explained by a number of factors that are also related to migration. These are (1) the lack of an industrial sector, given the level of urbanisation; (2) the fact that since the early 1970s, Yemen has become a 'trading economy'; and (3) the ever-increasing role played by the public sector in providing basic services.

Although most of Yemen's population remains rural, an emerging trend of internal migration, via external migration, was evident as early as 1975.[2] In the 1994 census, 23.5 per cent of the population was defined as urban. This number is for the total Republic with a population recorded of 14,587,807 (CSO, 1996: 22). Much of this urban growth is due to the fact that many individuals who migrated to the Gulf came back to Yemen seeking urban employment. In a survey conducted by the author in the al-Hujjariyya region, 20.4 per cent of migrants interviewed defined themselves as farmers prior to migration while only 10 per cent did so upon return (Colton, 1992: 183).

Urbanisation without industrialisation is not new to the developing world. What makes the Yemeni case unique is that many of those who returned prior to the Gulf crisis often did so with enough capital to start businesses, most of which were in the service/informal sector.[3]

Yemen also saw an increase in trade since remittances were used to buy what was not being produced. This was particularly acute for North Yemen where imports increased very rapidly throughout the 1970s and 1980s. Needless to say, many service subsectors benefited greatly from this 'trading economy' which not only required the means to distribute goods from abroad, but also needed financial and bureaucratic services.

The 1970s and 1980s also witnessed a tremendous growth in public-sector activities. Not surprisingly public services in South Yemen grew from 17.5 per cent of GDP in 1970 to 25 per cent in 1985 (CSO, 1987: 176); however, the North Yemeni regime also felt pressure to provide more public works for its citizenry. As aid and remittances were often channelled through official agencies, they provided the impetus for the government to appease the masses, and at the same time to expand its role in developing the state.

It is evident that the 1970s and 1980s represented a period of tremendous economic change, regardless of whether an individual lived in the North or South of the country. Furthermore, many of the changes that took place were intimately linked to the external migration of that period.

Yemen in the 1990s: The Gulf Crisis

Before Yemen could begin to take advantage of reunification, the country was overwhelmed with tens of thousands of migrants returning from the Gulf. The magnitude and number of returnees were a shock to the country, particularly in the light of structural changes that had taken place over the previous two decades. With the onset of war, the expatriate labour in Kuwait and Iraq flooded back into Yemen. This return was further accentuated by Yemen's overt support[4] for Iraq during the crisis. Saudi Arabia reacted by requiring all Yemenis in the Kingdom to have work permits and demanding that Yemeni businesses had Saudi partners.

It is estimated that in the space of a few months Yemen received 880,000 returnees (UNESCWA, 1992: 14). Most of the returnees were from the North as they had had the most privileged status in Saudi Arabia (whereas South Yemenis had always been obliged to have work permits). If these numbers are examined in relation to the population and overall labour force, it can be seen that Yemen, with a population of 13 million after reunification, experienced an increase of 7 per cent in its population and 30 per cent in its labour force. However, the effect for Yemen of this return has been much more acute and significant than the figures suggest because of the nature and characteristics of the returning labour force. The emigrant Yemenis made up a large unskilled wage-labour class that came mainly from agriculture, but were dispersed throughout the country. Yemen found itself coping with these returned labour migrants as the mass unemployed. Many felt they had been forced home to a country offering only limited opportunities and little hope for sustainable development. Prior to their return, the economies of both the North and South had in fact relied considerably on their staying abroad in order to support the economy through remittance transfers.

Many of the Gulf crisis returnees, unlike those who had trickled home in the late 1980s, had spent a lifetime abroad and had consequently lost contact with extended families. Others who had relatives found that they were not welcomed into households that were barely subsisting even without the addition of the family members of the returnees. In desperation many of the returnees set up informal camps outside Hodeidah, and many of them even attempted unsuccessfully to return to Saudi Arabia. In 1993 the lines outside the Saudi Arabian Consulate were a testimony to the desperation many Yemenis felt upon returning home, and by 1995 a rumour that Saudi Arabia and Yemen were settling their disputes not only affected passport applications and Embassy lines, but also shook the informal banking system with currency speculation.

By the beginning of 1997 unemployment was running at a high 30 per cent.[5] This figure was due in part to the fact that those Yemeni returnees with very few skills and/or education and little diversification in background entered a labour market with a stagnant labour demand because of its move towards capital-intensive production over recent decades. Consequently, a decrease in the wage level due to increased supply and inflation has been insufficient to absorb the increase in unskilled labour. Enterprises lack the investments and capital needed for adapting production techniques to utilise this labour. Even in an era of globalisation, where speculative investment in foreign markets is on the rise, Yemen finds itself at the bottom of the disbursement ladder.

As stated earlier, a majority of the Northerners had been employed as unskilled labourers and construction workers while abroad. The Southerners were also unskilled, but a majority had also worked as vendors and office workers. However, little hope was held out for jobs, and on their return 86.37 per cent of North Yemenis and 92.67 per cent from the South reported that they were unemployed (CSO, 1991). Of those who are employed, the majority – whether from the North or South – work as farmers or drivers, indicating that even the educated or more skilled Southerners did not fare well on their return. Out of the 11.31 per cent of South Yemenis who had previously worked as office workers, less than one half of one per cent worked as office clerks on their return. Of the 44.6 per cent of North Yemenis who had been farmers before migration, only 4 per cent now claimed to be farming (CSO, 1991).

In many ways, these migrants have been Yemen's most valuable resource. However, because the Yemeni economy has never been properly established, they now find themselves living in a country that cannot easily afford or absorb them. Yemen's location on the Red Sea has always created pressure from abroad and this has caused it to remain a trading economy, subsisting on imports purchased through the export of labour. The new returnees did not infuse Yemen's formal sector with cash or otherwise raise production, and in fact, many of them became a tremendous economic and social burden for Yemen. Consequently, it is not possible to discuss a labour market that should or could absorb these people by responding to supply and demand forces. Instead it is necessary to talk about a labour market that must for the first time develop to complement Yemen's most precious resource – its people.

Yemen's returnee camps

To understand the magnitude and complexity of the situation in Yemen, in-depth interviews were conducted in 1995 in returnee camps in the Tihama. Although it is difficult to separate the issues of return migration, the 1994 civil war, and the general decline in the Yemeni economy, a number of returnees were not integrated into Yemeni society and economy.

In 1995 the UNDP reckoned that 77,000 Yemenis were still displaced because of the mass return of labourers from the Gulf.[6] Although this number may seem small compared with the 880,000 that were estimated to have entered Yemen in the post-Gulf crisis period, the fact that these individuals could not be absorbed by society was alarming. As already stated, it was difficult to think of these workers returning to a particular sector of the Yemeni economy because of the precarious nature of the Yemeni market. In addition, the size of the return meant that every sector as well as every village and town in Yemen was affected by the re-entry of such a large number of individuals.

The returnees in the camps were often migrants who had been abroad for so long that it was irrelevant to say that they had worked in agriculture fifty years ago. Others were the children of Yemenis who, prior to their mass return, had never even been taken to Yemen for a visit. However, these factors appear to be only part of the reason why they remained unemployed. They were also uneducated and unskilled, having often been employed as sanitation workers or in similar jobs in Saudi Arabia considered undesirable even for the expatriate class. Like so many Yemenis, they had no land to subsist on, and as wage labourers they had little to offer except their experience abroad. Although the returnees in camps were only a small part of the large number of unemployed who returned from abroad, they reflected a larger problem that was masked in some areas by family absorption of returnees, often at a great socio-economic cost to the family unit. Many returnees took the attitude that they had to survive until either the situation with Saudi Arabia improved or another place of prosperity enabled them to re-migrate.

The majority of these individuals lived in camps around Hodeidah, and their situation was desperate. At the time of writing (1998) these former labourers, many of whom were illiterate and unskilled, had received no aid since 1993, and the tents that were originally issued to them had fallen apart. The camps consisted of groups of shacks often made of brushwood, cardboard and plastic sheeting, and did not have electricity, running water or adequate sanitation. Most of the returnees had no possessions, having sold their personal effects over the previous five years in order to survive. Work was precarious and usually consisted of casual/day labour, either for other Yemenis living in Hodeidah or else at the port. The majority of the migrants interviewed had given up hope of any further assistance from the government or aid organisations, and had begun to adapt to their environment, having concluded that they would spend the rest of their lives in these makeshift settlements.

Thirty interviews were conducted in the Harit al-Kiatif, Um, and al-Muhaim camps. Camp Harit al-Kiatif was structured as a group of shacks in the sand next to a garbage dump, although it was not far from Hodeidah and therefore allowed easy access to the city. There were also shops of various kinds on Saddam Street, as well as a second-hand *suq* or flea market. There were approximately 250 families in the settlement. Some of the residents had not only built themselves shacks, but had also fenced in a yard area, using scrap metal and brushwood, and a few returnees were also making brick structures for themselves. However, most lived in shacks constructed out of materials found on deserted lots. The land was publicly owned. Some of the children attended the local school, which was located outside the camp, as were any health facilities.

Um al-Ma'arik (Mother of Battles) camp was located off of Sana'a Street in Hodeidah. It contained an estimated 3,000 families, was divided into four sections, and was highly organised with clearly defined alleyways and lots. Most of the structures had some type of fencing separating a family's piece of land from that of their neighbours. Although the residents did not own their lot, it was registered in their name. Many of the shacks were constructed from plywood which they had purchased. There were some cars parked around the camp, as well as a health clinic and two schools located inside the camp. Unlike the smaller camps, its organisation suggested something planned and with an element of permanence.

Al-Muhaim, the Red Crescent camp, was about 10 kilometres north of Hodeidah on the road to Harad. It was not established immediately after the Gulf crisis, but appeared some months later. Initially the Red Crescent provided tents and food subsidies; however, this aid stopped around 1993. A makeshift school functioned during the academic year for the children of the camp, with four or five teachers from Hodeidah. There were 150 families residing in this camp, and the shacks occupied by the inhabitants were fashioned from debris, brushwood and the remains of the tents that were issued to them by the Red Cross. The land on which the shacks were situated was not registered in any one name. Although the inhabitants were a long way from any health clinics, a van was sent to the camp every week by the Red Crescent to monitor the women and children and to care for the sick.

Although located at different sites, the camps had many similarities. Most importantly, they were all within a reasonable distance of the city, enabling labourers to search for work in Hodeidah, one of Yemen's most important urban and port areas. Proximity to Hodeidah was the main reason why these landless people, who depended on wage labour to survive, remained in the camps. The labourers in these camps fell into three skills categories: (1) young men who were born in Saudi Arabia and had some education but few skills; (2) young to middle-aged men who were not necessarily long-term residents in Saudi Arabia, and who had little or no education but did have a few skills; and (3) older men who, with their families, had lived almost their entire working years in Saudi Arabia and who had little or no education and skills and no connections with their village of origin.

Profiles of camp dwellers

The following three profiles help to characterise the plight of these three categories.

The first was well represented by 22-year-old Ahmed, who was born in Saudi Arabia of Yemeni parents. He lived with his mother and two young siblings at Harit al-Kiatif camp – his father had died shortly after their return. Ahmed's own house amounted to a one-room dirt-floor shack made out of material that he and his family had found. As one entered the room, it was apparent that there were no personal belongings. Ahmed had lived there since 1990 when he returned to Yemen following the Gulf crisis. Initially, this had been intended only to be temporary housing, since at the time of their return life was very uncertain and the family had wanted to wait to see what happened in the Gulf. As a result, they had not looked for work in the first year, but had lived off their savings and sold their furniture for money.

Like many of the children born in Saudi Arabia, Ahmed had attended primary school and could read and write. Although he was only 17 years old on his return to Yemen, he had already been working in Saudi Arabia, as a driver for an oil company. He had averaged six hours a day for six days a week, and had earned approximately 2,500 Saudi Riyals a month. Moreover, he had been able to save from his earnings and stated that on his return to Yemen he had SR17,000 which he brought back with him.

He had work as a driver for a transportation company which paid him 400 Yemeni Riyals per trip (US$4.00 per trip at the exchange rate prevailing during the summer of 1995), and averaged three days a week. He was fortunate to have this work, for many in this camp did not fare so well. He had a hard time adjusting socially as well as economically to Yemen, and stated that although he hoped to feel a part of Yemen, no one had given him a chance. He had tried to find work in other parts of Yemen, but had neither the means to sustain his employment search, nor the family network to assist him. What he found most difficult about his present situation was not having proper work or a home, but he liked living among the returnees and felt that they were his community.

The second group was represented by Ali Naser, who was 27 years old. He had attended four years of school and could read and write. At the age of 16, he had travelled by himself to Saudi Arabia, where he had worked for six years as a self-employed vegetable seller in Riyadh, buying the vegetables from farmers or suppliers and selling them in the street. He estimated that he made SR5,000 a month. In addition to sending money to his family throughout his ten years in Saudi Arabia, he had been able to save enough to purchase a mini-van upon his return, and also had brought back some gold and furniture that he sold to build his shelter.

He now drove a *dabbab* (a group taxi) in Hodeidah, with average earnings of YR500 per day. He did not save from his earnings and complained that the cost of living was the most difficult issue facing him. He longed to return to Saudi Arabia. Originally he came from Zabid, but he had a better life in the camp because of its proximity to Hodeidah and his job. He had married before going to Saudi Arabia, but had left his wife in Zabid with his family rather than take her with him. He had now brought his wife and their three children to live with him in the camp.

Finally there was Ahmed Yahya who represented the third group and who was too old to remember or to care how old he was. He also lived in Harit al-Kiatif camp. He went as a young man to Saudi Arabia long before the oil boom, and was illiterate. Because of his lack of skills and education, he had worked as a porter, carrying supplies on his back to transport them for short distances, much like a beast of burden. This had been his occupation for the many years that he lived in Saudi Arabia. He had never expected to return to Yemen. He had attempted to get a *kafil* (guarantor), a Saudi employer who would guarantee his employment in the Kingdom (this was required of all Yemenis following Yemen's stand on the Gulf War), but had been unsuccessful. He claimed to have worked up to 12 hours a day in Saudi Arabia for SR100 a day – such work was often paid daily rather than monthly for he had not been retained by a company but had moved from job to job as needed. He had saved nothing from his work as all his money had been needed to support his growing family in Saudi Arabia.

Since his return to Yemen in 1990, he had not worked. He had tried to find work, but had given up, and indeed he saw the lack of employment opportunities as Yemen's greatest problem. When asked why he did not return to his village, he stated that although he visited Bayt al-Faqih, where he was from, all his family and friends were either gone or dead, and he no longer knew anyone there. He claimed to have searched unsuccessfully for work all over Yemen; at least he had a place to live in the camp so it was better for him to remain there.

These profiles suggested that after the Gulf crisis many workers did not return to the countryside but instead preferred to remain in the urban areas to search for work. This might have had much to do with the fact that after decades abroad, many of these workers now either had no land or felt less keen to cultivate it. Commerce is only sustainable with remittances, so although many new shops and restaurants opened with the returnees, many more went under. Consequently, returnees were still a visible sign in an economy that had yet to embark seriously on the road to development. Furthermore, if the opportunity had arisen for most of these Yemenis to go abroad, the push factor was there to send them tumbling out of the door.

Yemen has seen much structural change to its economy over the past few decades as subsistence agriculturists were persuaded to leave the land for international urban centres. As shown here, this movement of labour caused wage levels to increase, not only in farming but also in Yemen's urban centres as they tried to compete with foreign labour markets. The net effect has been a stagnant industrial sector, an agricultural sector that has seen significant changes away from labour-intensive crops to less labour-intensive cash crops like *qat*, and a service/informal sector that is made up of small retailers dealing in imported goods.

Prospects for a different future

Since the mass return of 1990, there has been little change in the structure of the economy. The early 1990s were plagued by high unemployment as well as by inflation, apparently the product of the breakdown of the 'labour for goods' exchange that had taken place during the previous two decades. With the decline in agricultural production, Yemen has become increasingly dependent on imported foodstuffs, and this reliance on imported foodstuffs renders the country vulnerable to fluctuations in world prices. Furthermore, the lack of industrial development means that most of what is consumed in Yemen, regardless of whether it is durable or non-durable goods, comes from abroad. Even in light of Yemen's loss of remittances, imports continued to grow from YR18,867 billion in 1990 to YR64,569 billion by 1995 (CSO, 1996: 324). This inelastic supply in the early 1990s was inflationary.

A slow-down in remittances, coupled with a reduction in foreign aid receipts, has created a foreign exchange constraint. This situation was reflected in a serious balance of payments problem in the early 1990s. In 1993 the balance of payments deficit peaked at US$1,206.8 million (CSO, 1996: 311). Needless to say, this put tremendous pressure on the Yemeni government to devalue the currency, which in turn fuelled inflation. The government had also come to play a larger role as an employer, as well as the provider of social and physical infrastructure, a situation that was further exacerbated by reunification since South Yemen had always had a much larger public sector. The insufficiency of revenue led the government to deficit financing, also fuelling inflation.

By the mid-1990s, GDP had decreased by 19 per cent, inflation was reaching triple figures, unemployment was running at 30 per cent, and the number of people living in absolute poverty increased to 4.9 million (CSO, various yearbooks). The government had little choice but to turn to the International Monetary Fund for assistance in reducing its debt burden via loans and monetarist reforms to its economy. The reform programme has focused on imbalances in monetary and fiscal policies (government deficit spending, expansionist credit policies and expansionary exchange operations of the central bank). Although the programme does not deny the existence of constraints in the economy, the IMF sees them as a result of price and exchange rate distortions that were generated by the government's own behaviour and inflation.

Yemen has been working its way through the IMF's three-phase reform programme. In the first phase of stabilisation policies it has been able to reduce the rate of inflation, but this has not been without heavy social and economic costs to a society that is ill-equipped to sustain such stagnation even for a short period of time. Furthermore, it can be argued that the reforms have hindered the processes of structural change that are necessary for long-term sustainable development in Yemen.

Although it goes without saying that Yemen's economy needed reforms, there are those who have questioned its approach, particularly in the light of massive unemployment. If Yemen is ever to set a course for sustainable development in its economy, it must not be content with monetary controls in return for IMF and World Bank loans. Eventually these loans will have to be paid back. Many Yemenis hope that oil and gas will offer a way out of the country's economic ills, but Yemen's Gulf neighbours have already proved that these industries do not offer a long-term solution to their own difficulties. Yemen needs to address its structural problems even if it does mean some inflation, because without long-term change, the country may find that it has done little more than to accumulate additional debt. Not only does the Yemeni economy need to generate more capital (which it is currently attempting to do through privatisation and liberalisation), but it needs also to focus on developing its labour force through quality education. The private sector cannot make these changes alone. Yemen needs an active government that will guide it through its restructuring by providing incentives, an infrastructure, and a skilled/educated workforce.

It is crucial to understand the linkage between migration and the economic underdevelopment of the Yemeni economy. If scholars and policy makers focus on the issues that this chapter has identified as being the cause of many of Yemen's economic ills, they can begin to understand and address the consequences of migration in a way that will not leave the society vulnerable to the whims of the world labour markets. It is the very structure of the Yemeni economy that must be altered if this pattern of out-migration is to be brought to an end.

NOTES

1 Since North and South Yemen were separate countries until unification in 1990, they each had their own currency. The Yemeni Riyal was used in North Yemen while the Dinar was used in the South. See CSO, various *Statistical Yearbooks* (Aden, Government Printing).

2 In the 1975 census of North Yemen, 11 per cent of the total population was defined as living in urban centres, with over half living in Sana'a, Tai'iz and Hodeidah (CPO, 1983).

3 The informal sector has often been defined as the economic activities that take place outside government regulation and taxation. Hernando de Soto in his work on the informal sector in Peru defined the informal sector as the economic activities that fail to fulfil one or another legal requirement, even if the objectives of their endeavours are perfectly lawful. The International Labour Organization has gone further in attempting to define the informal sector with a number of characteristics. An ILO mission found the following as typifying informal activity: ease of entry, reliance on indigenous resources, family ownership of enterprises, small scale of operations, labour-intensive methods of production and adapted technology, skills acquired outside the formal school system, and unregulated/competitive markets. Another similar definition states that the composition of the informal sector is one that is more labour than capital intensive; and/or more likely to employ traditional methods of production; and/or more likely to occupy temporary or mobile facilities; and/or smaller in size (of employees, physical facilities, and total production); and/or less likely to enjoy credit, either from formal lending institutions or informal sources (De Soto, 1988: 15–74; Jenkins, 1988: 6; and ILO, 1972).

4 Via its participation on the UN Security Council.

5 This figure is an estimate as there are a number of conflicting sources for this period in terms of what unemployment was. This figure was arrived at by averaging official sources, numbers published in newspapers and communication with various Yemeni economists during the summer of 1997.

6 Interview with Abo Seif, UNDP Officer in charge of returnees, Sana'a, August 1995.

4

The Republic of Yemen: The Economic Situation and the Manufacturing Sector

Yahya Y. Almutawakel

In 1996 the Republic of Yemen (RoY) had a population of some 16 million and a land area of 555,000 km^2. In addition, an estimated 1.0–1.5 million nationals were living abroad, mostly on a temporary basis. The country's topography is rugged and its population is extremely scattered. Resources such as agricultural land and water are scarce and, with the exception of oil and gas fields, few mineral deposits have so far been found.

This contribution is intended as an introduction to the Yemeni economy, and outlines the main issues affecting it. A discussion of earlier conditions is followed by a discussion of the state of the economy at the turn of the century.

Economic conditions

Yemen is a very late starter in development. The major factor influencing the economy in the mid-1970s and the 1980s was the large labour demand in neighbouring states that could not be met locally. Yemen was able to export part of its labour force, and therefore benefited indirectly from the oil windfalls. Annual repatriated earnings during the period were estimated at around US$1 billion.

The immediate economic impact of this out-migration was an unprecedented increase in personal incomes, caused mainly by the remittances from Yemeni workers in the Gulf states, primarily in Saudi Arabia. Almost half the country's gross national product (GNP) in the late 1970s was made up of private transfers emanating from these emigrant workers, and as a result, real per capita gross national product increased considerably.

Thus, remittances were by far the most important force behind the strong performance of the economy in earlier years. However, since the national economy was unable to meet the increasing demand for consumer goods through domestic production, the growing gap was covered by a steady growth in imports, especially of foodstuffs and luxury items. Table 4.1 traces the continuous increase in nominal GNP, GDP, consumption, imports and exports in selected years between 1976 and 1996.

TABLE 4.1
Real resources and uses for selected years (US$ million)

	1976	1982	1988	1990	1994	1996
GNP	1,884	6,853	7,815	8,823	4,813	4,491
GDP	1,792	5,250	6,966	8,891	4,904	5,110
Private consumption	1,636*	4,086*	4,272*	6,654	3,830	3,575
Government consumption	189*	1,050*	693*	1,589	1,042	742
Imports of goods & services	1,026	2,970	2,033	1,824	1,858	2,568
Exports of goods & services	106	248	553	1,297	788	2,064

Note: *Data relating only to the former Yemen Arab Republic.
Sources: CSO, *Statistical Yearbook*, 1996b; IMF, *International Financial Statistics Yearbook*, 1990.

Remittances were not only a large source of private spending, but were also a major source of foreign exchange. During the period 1975–96, remittances constituted over half of Yemen's foreign exchange earnings, and became the principal source of financing for a rapidly rising import bill (Table 4.2).

TABLE 4.2
Trend in remittances (in US$ million)

Item	1975	1980	1985	1990	1994	1996
Remittances (US$ mn)	329	1,417	1,189	1,133	1,059	1,135
as % of GDP	24	40	24	17	39	22
as % of foreign exchange earnings	76	85	68	48	66	35

Sources: IMF, *International Financial Statistics Yearbook*, 1990; Central Bank of Yemen, *Annual Report*, various issues.

Although remittances grew significantly from the mid-1970s, they started to decline in the 1980s as a result of the slow-down in the growth of the construction sectors of the Gulf economies. Given the country's dependence on remittances for providing foreign exchange, their decline had – and will continue to have – far-reaching implications for the economy. In addition, many of the remittances were transferred through unofficial channels or money exchangers because of the differences between the official and the parallel market exchange rates (World Bank, 1995: 10). As a consequence, these dwindling funds could not be easily mobilised to finance productive activities in Yemen.

During the first half of the 1990s, the Yemeni economy underwent an unexpected transition. The main influencing factors were the unification process between the two parts of the homeland, and the second Gulf War, which led to the expulsion and return of some 800,000 migrants from the Gulf States and the suspension of foreign aid. The general impact of the forced return of migrants on Yemen's economy was negative. The population increased virtually overnight by around 7 per cent, and led to the following consequences:

- Macroeconomic dislocation brought about by a drastic reduction in remittances.
- Major pressures placed upon the employment situation caused by some 400,000 Yemenis seeking jobs (CSO, 1996a).
- The need to reintegrate this population and meet the additional demand for basic goods and services.

As a result, the performance of the economy was disappointing. Real non-oil GDP contracted, resulting in a decline in real per capita income from US$686 in 1990 to US$281 in 1996. While incomes declined, unemployment, inflation and demand for basic goods and services increased, exerting great pressure on the economy. Large budget deficits were recorded, reaching 16.3 per cent of GDP in 1994. These were financed primarily by the domestic banking system, mainly in the form of money creation which led to rapid monetary growth.

Large balance of payments deficits were also recorded, despite sizeable increases in oil exports in 1993–4. As indicated in Table 4.3, this situation exemplified a narrow export base, a heavy dependence on imports, particularly of food, and the continuing decline of remittances from Yemenis working abroad.[1]

TABLE 4.3
Main economic indicators

Item	1990	1994	1996
GDP per capita (US$)	686	324	281
Balance of payments deficit (US$ million)	5	688	482
as % of GNP	0	14	11
Budget deficit as % of GDP	8	16.3	3.9
Inflation*	–	104	26
Unemployment**	–	10	10

Notes: *Reflected by the Consumer Price Index. **While official documents quote unemployment at 25 per cent in 1994, use of the 1994 population census would only yield an estimate of 10 per cent.
Source: CSO, *Statistical Yearbook,* 1996b.

The origins of this situation lie in the fact that at the time the country was pursuing an expansionary expenditure policy despite its deteriorating revenue position. The country's credit rating declined because of its inability to service its loans, which had started in the heyday of petro-dollar flows. Given its debt overhang, the government had, therefore, to rely increasingly on domestic borrowing and on money issue because of its inability to borrow from foreign banks.

The external debt stock as a proportion of GDP was much higher than domestic debt stock (about 176 per cent versus 31 per cent in 1996). Hence, external debt servicing was greater than domestic debt servicing. In spite of the concessional loan conditions, the external debt service ratio soared to 73 per cent of export earnings in 1991 before falling to 38 per cent in 1996 (IMF, 1997: 40). The reason behind this improvement was the increase in oil exports and the September 1996 agreement with the Paris Club entailed a 67 per cent debt reduction at the prevailing net present value conditions. Moreover, in November 1997 Yemen reached an agreement with Russia (Yemen's major creditor) that wrote off 80 per cent of the Russian debt while subjecting the remaining 20 per cent to Naples terms (CBY, 1997).

In March 1995, the government launched the first set of reform measures to stabilise the economy and remove structural economic imbalances. These measures were intended mainly to mobilise public revenue and tighten expenditures through important price adjustments. Thus, the budget deficit was reduced to 7 per cent of GDP in 1995, down from 17 per cent in 1994. It was also a government priority to control inflation (which fell to 45 per cent in 1995), and later to address unemployment which was widely known to be much higher than the official 10 per cent figure. While unemployment is an important economic indicator, what exacerbated poverty over the decade from 1986 was the dramatic erosion of the purchasing power of the middle classes. Those living at or below the poverty line became further impoverished due to high inflation and limited access to adequate social services (World Bank, 1996a: 2). Public budget tightening resulted in financial stabilisation but was accompanied by price increases and higher unemployment.

In spite of notable and positive developments towards reform in 1995, the recovery of imports and the weak oil prices kept the country's external accounts under pressure. The current account deficit remained at a huge US$900 million. The government was aware that further policy reforms were required to achieve greater financial and exchange-rate stabilisation. A comprehensive programme of structural adjustment was agreed on, which included further reductions in budget deficit through the containment of the wage bill and the gradual reduction of subsidies to basic goods and services. It also attempted to address other issues such as trade liberalisation, privatisation and civil service reform. The government understood that implementing these reforms would cause serious social difficulties for the people.

Structure of the economy

The above events brought about changes in Yemen's economic structure, as can be seen from Table 4.4 which illustrates the contribution of various sectors to GDP for selected years. The share of the agricultural sector dropped from almost 28 per cent in 1990 to only 16.6 per cent in 1996, while manufacturing and extractive industries both raised their shares, due to the increased role of oil production and refining. Manufacturing activities, including oil refining, increased their share from 8.1 per cent to about 10.7 per cent during the same period.

An important feature of the economy was the dominant contribution of the service sector to GDP, at around 45 per cent in 1990 and 37 per cent in 1996. From the late 1980s a relatively sophisticated financial and business services sector emerged, capable of meeting the mainly financial needs of private-sector projects. Transport and communication were provided as a result of infrastructural development programmes undertaken by the previous governments over the past two decades. The growing share of the oil sector reflected a clear structural transformation of the economy, which was turning into one with increasingly dominant service and oil sectors. Manufacturing was still small and growing slowly, while agriculture – from which around half the population made a living, usually at subsistence level – was stagnant.

TABLE 4.4
Contribution of sectors to GDP (%)

Sector	1990	1996
Agriculture, forestry and fishing	27.9	16.6
Mining and quarrying	0.3	1.1
Oil and gas	13.7	29.2
Manufacturing (including oil refining)	8.1	10.7
Electricity, water and gas	3.4	1.3
Construction	2.7	3.6
Wholesale and retail trade	12.0	10.3
Restaurants and hotels	0.6	0.8
Transportation and communication	6.9	6.4
Financing and insurance	5.6	3.2
Real estate and business services	2.6	2.5
Personal and social services	1.7	2.4
Government services	15.8	11.4
Other services	3.3	3.5
Less imputed bank service charges	-2.1	-3.1
GDP at market price*	100	100
Non-oil GDP	86.3	70.8

Note: *Figures may not add up due to rounding.
Source: CSO, *Statistical Yearbook*, various issues.

There was an absolute increase in the size of the total labour force, which reached 3.3 million workers in 1994. Table 4.5 below identifies the effects of the structural change on employment, since these effects are unlikely to be limited to a fall in the output of the traditional sectors, but will also extend to the employment structure.

Although agriculture still employed most of the labour force, its relative share in 1994 had declined to 53 per cent. An opposite trend, however, could be seen in the service sectors which took up almost 33 per cent of the total labour force. The share of the manufacturing sector in the labour force was small in comparison to its contribution to GDP. The main reason for this lay in the capital-intensive techniques adopted by the modern manufacturing sector.

TABLE 4.5
Economically active population (1994)

Economic activity	Percentage
Agriculture, forestry and fishing	53.0
Mining and quarrying	<1.0
Manufacturing	4.0
Electricity, water and gas	<1.0
Construction	6.0
Wholesale, retail and catering	10.0
Transportation and communication	4.0
Financing, insurance, real estate and business services	1.0
Community, social and personal services	1.0
Government services	17.0
Other services	4.0
Total	100.0

Source: CSO (1996), *Final Results of the 1994 Population, Housing and Establishments Census: General Report*, pp. 190, 191.

It can be argued that a peculiar feature of the Yemeni experience is that the economy escaped the growing unemployment that was typical of other developing countries during the late 1970s and the 1980s. Furthermore, most developing countries in the same period enjoyed low wage costs in the early stages of industrialisation, due to labour surpluses that to some extent made up for low productivity. In Yemen, though, a significant outcome of labour emigration and the shortage of unskilled labour was the upward pressure on wages and production costs.[2]

Yemen's labour costs were very high in relation to its per capita GNP. In 1988, the ratio of the annual per worker wage to per capita GNP was in the order of 6.7, compared to 4.8, 2.1 and 1.5 for Kenya, Korea and Sri Lanka respectively.[3] However, while Yemen's labour costs were very high compared to those of other developing countries during the 1980s, its labour costs declined considerably in the 1990s in real terms, coming closer to the levels experienced elsewhere in the developing world.

Overview of the manufacturing sector

This section introduces the broad characteristics of the manufacturing sector and also discusses its limitations. As with many aspects of the economy, quantitative information on the manufacturing sector is limited. Three partial surveys of manufacturing enterprises were carried out before reunification, while the first comprehensive survey was undertaken in 1996.

Manufacturing industry formed a small part of Yemen's overall economy, accounting for 10.7 per cent of GDP in 1996 and 4 per cent of total employment in 1994. The majority of establishments were tiny, employing only one or two workers. In 1994 the sector employed 127,918 persons in total, in addition to 8,520 individuals in mining and quarrying.

During the second half of the 1970s and the early 1980s, investment in manufacturing increased rapidly in the YAR, and to a lesser extent in PDRY, thereby spurring manufacturing activity. This impressive growth was achieved mainly through a sharp increase in investment by both the public and the private sectors. Private-sector investment was fuelled by workers' remittances.

Structure of manufacturing

The production of consumer goods was predominant in the structure of manufacturing value-added (MVA). The combination of protection and assured supply of raw materials made investment highly profitable, biasing it towards consumer products, because an established market already existed. Thus, the greater part of the consumer goods industry was destined for meeting basic needs, namely food and clothing.

In 1995, as illustrated in Table 4.6, the share of the food subsector in total MVA increased substantially to 29.8 per cent. This subsector experienced the second-highest growth rate despite its large initial base, and there were still ample opportunities for growth in these branches, the main industry within the food-processing group being that of tobacco and cigarettes.

Despite its wide potential, the textiles and apparel sector contributed only 6.6 per cent to MVA. This small share reflected the difficulties facing the operations of the country's several textile factories during the preceding few years. The chemicals subsector, which covers a wide range of products such as plastic footwear, paints, plastic utensils, PVC pipes and oil refining, increased massively, raising its combined share to 20.6 per cent. Due to improved refining activity and to the fact that chemical industries started from a very low base, it was the fastest growing subsector.

TABLE 4.6
Structure of manufacturing value-added (MVA), 1995

Branch	% of MVA
Food	29.8
Textiles and clothing	6.6
Leather and leather products	1.0
Chemicals and plastics	6.6
Oil refining	14.0
Non-metal	21.1
Metal and light engineering	8.2
Wood and wood products	4.7
Paper and publishing	8.0
Total	100.0

Source: MOI and CSO, *Final Report and Results of the 1996 Industrial Survey*, p. 42.

The share of construction materials in MVA was maintained at a high 21.1 per cent, second to the food subsector. This performance might appear surprising, given the strong performance of the construction sector over recent years. However, stone – the most important construction material – is included in the mining sector, whose value-added declined between 1990 and 1996. A glance at Table 4.6 also reveals that wood products did not make a high contribution to MVA in 1995. One might conclude that the wood-product industries had lost their relative importance. This reflects the effect of the construction sector on demand for wood and wood products.

Employment, size distribution and ownership
According to the 1996 industrial survey, the food subsector, the largest manufacturing sector, accounted for almost 55 per cent of total industrial establishments and employed 42 per cent of the industrial labour force (see Table 4.7). The construction materials subsector accounted for 9.4 per cent of the industrial establishments and for 12.8 per cent of the labour force, reflecting labour-intensive methods of production. Similarly, the textiles and metal subsectors, although consisting of thousands of

establishments, employed a relatively low percentage of the workforce, suggesting the dominance of small workshops in those sectors. The chemicals subsector, on the other hand, consisted of only 45 establishments, mostly large-scale, and employed 4,924 workers, thereby averaging 109 workers per establishment.

TABLE 4.7
Establishments and employment in manufacturing

Branch	Number of establishments	Number of employees
Food	16,375	33,698
Textiles and clothing	3,425	8,501
Leather and leather products	232	1,067
Chemicals and plastics	45	4,924
Oil refining	3	2,682
Non-metal	2,814	10,278
Metal and light engineering	3,461	9,809
Wood and wood products	2,092	4,580
Paper and publishing	87	1,603
Others and not specified	1,269	3,016
Total	29,803	80,158

Source: MOI and CSO, *Final Report and Results of the 1996 Industrial Survey*, pp. 42, 45.

The 1996 Industrial Survey identified only 234 out of 28,539 manufacturing establishments employing 10 or more workers. These were considered to be large firms. Medium-sized firms were defined as those employing between 5 and 9 workers, while small firms included all those employing fewer than 5 workers.[4] Table 4.8 shows the distribution by size of manufacturing firms, and suggests that most manufacturing activity, such as the vegetable oils industry, cement blocks, clothing, many metal workshops, and most wood products, was carried out in very small establishments. Rather than involving any industrial processes, most of these operated as one- or two-man artisan or handicraft workshops. Medium- and small-scale firms were usually involved in activities that rarely had links with the foreign sector.

Most manufacturing enterprises continued to consist of small establishments that represented 95.7 per cent of all manufacturing firms even though their contribution to output did not exceed 10 per cent of the total. By the same token, although large-scale industries represented less than one per cent of the total number of firms, they continued to increase their share in output and employment.

TABLE 4.8
Size distribution of manufacturing firms

Branch	Number of firms		
	Small	Medium	Large
Food	15,992	315	69
Textiles and clothing	3,327	81	19
Leather and leather products	213	10	8
Chemicals and plastics	3	8	34
Oil refining	0	0	3
Non-metal	2,519	265	32
Metal and light engineering	3,217	201	42
Wood and wood products	2,003	87	5
Paper and publishing	29	35	22
Total	27,303	1,002	234
As % of total	95.7	3.5	0.8
Total labour force	53,390	7,390	49,562

Source: MOI and CSO, *Final Report and Results of the 1996 Industrial Survey,* various tables.

Until recently, economic policy aimed at encouraging both public- and private-sector manufacturing enterprises. The public sector employed 53 per cent of those working in large-scale industries Table 4.9), mainly in textiles, cement, and refining activities. The employment share of the public sector in small- and medium-size enterprises was much less. Public enterprises were dominant in non-traditional activities, but most of them did not generate profits, relying instead on government assistance to cover their deficits. The relatively poor performance of public enterprises has been due to lack of clear objectives, poor managerial skills, and inadequate organisation and control. If these enterprises are to succeed, priority needs to be given to improving management, organisation and the skills of the workforce.

Regarding the private sector, Yemen's first five-year plan (1996–2000) envisaged investments worth approximately YR8.0 billion in the various sectors of the economy. The private sector would provide 12 per cent of those investments, mainly in manufacturing, while foreign investments in oil and gas would amount to 48 per cent of total investments. The increased participation of private investment, which had previously been a small fraction of public investment, suggests therefore that growth will mostly occur within the modernised local and foreign private sectors.

TABLE 4.9
Manufacturing firms by size and ownership (%)

Sector	Small	Medium	Large	Total
Private	96.2	93.9	62.5	95.8
Public	0.9	3.7	28.3	1.2
Mixed	0.1	0.3	5.2	0.1
Cooperative	2.8	2.2	4.0	2.7

Source: MOI and CSO, *Final Report and Results of the 1996 Industrial Survey*, p. 29.

Government policy

During the period 1973–89, industrial investment in Yemen took a direction similar to that followed by many other developing countries: it concentrated on replacing imports of consumer goods with domestic production that was oriented towards the internal market. Potential investors could count on protected markets for their own products as well as on access to imports of capital equipment and materials required for production. Towards the end of this period, and as in many developing countries, balance of payments crises forced Yemen to undertake more import substitution (Al-Zaeem, 1994).

In order to keep its international obligations within the limits imposed by the availability of foreign exchange, both governments adopted a variety of measures to restrain imports and capital outflows, with greater emphasis being placed on import restriction. Therefore the external sector is, and has always been, an important dimension of the economic policies adopted by Yemen.

The YAR government's economic policy followed two main lines of action, both aimed at maintaining the existing pattern of the industrialisation process: (1) foreign trade policy, especially import and exchange controls which were applied through a number of different instruments (e.g. quantitative controls and multiple exchange rates); and (2) investment policy, which started to ease the main bottlenecks in the infrastructure (World Bank, 1986). However, the trade policy that was adopted mainly after 1983 had three major aspects:

(1) It maintained an overvalued currency relative to other currencies, since the government persistently refused to implement any sufficient and timely devaluation of the domestic currency. The main reason for resisting a large devaluation was probably fear of kindling a wage–price spiral.

(2) It imposed quantitative controls on imports to regulate the level and the composition of imported goods.

(3) It established a differentiated and escalating tariff structure (Almutawakel, 1992).

On the other hand, export promotion, a stated government objective since the mid-1980s, did not materialise into policy measures, and projects with export potential were not dealt with favourably under investment law. Exports were penalised through an incentive system that lacked any scheme to refund the duties and taxes on the materials used by importers in export production, nor were exporters exempted from excise or production taxes levied on a firm's total output whenever such taxes were applicable. The first measure to stimulate exports was not introduced until 1984, at which time the government abolished export taxes and initiated a draw-back scheme that enabled exporters to obtain refunds of the duty paid on the imported components of manufactured goods.

During the 1990s, however, it became evident that while stabilisation was necessary for the economic recovery of Yemen, fostering sustainable economic growth would require additional reforms, primarily to create an enabling environment for private-sector investment and employment. The first phase of the government's Economic Reform Programme (1996–2000) therefore included reforms relating to trade liberalisation and privatisation, public-enterprise reform, and improvement of the regulatory framework (World Bank, 1995). These were intended to improve the overall framework for incentives and economic efficiency and to facilitate private-sector development.

As a first step towards implementing the trade liberalisation programme, the government eliminated quantitative restrictions, reduced the level of import tariffs, and reformed and simplified the tariff structure. The system of product-based import licensing was also abolished. Recent changes in the rules governing the work of the General Investment Authority (GIA) have further simplified internal GIA procedures and have delegated more powers to its president and to its section managers. GIA licensing is, in effect, working as a registration process through which investors are able to claim incentives and are helped to obtain other clearances and licences.

Obstacles and difficulties in implementing government policy

During the 1980s, and as a result of the restrictive measures, there was some degree of success in reducing the external and internal deficits, but the shortage of foreign exchange and the resulting import-licensing restrictions also produced a somewhat crippling impact on overall manufacturing. The corrective measures managed to restrain internal demand, while the continued growth in manufacturing during that period could well have been the outcome of earlier investments made before the imposition of import restrictions (Almutawakel, 1992).

The manufacturing sector suffered from several problems, many of which persist today. Weak institutional support led to poorly prepared projects and lack of follow-up plans. Most of the import substitution projects established in the manufacturing sector were highly dependent on imported capital goods and raw materials, and although the 1996 Industrial Survey did not specify the percentage of imported inputs used by large-scale manufacturing enterprises, the percentage remained, by analogy, relatively high. This conclusion can be checked by looking at the ratio of customs duty paid to the value of material inputs.

Also, without a pool of technically skilled workers to draw upon, and given the very limited availability of training programmes, new industries usually recruit their Yemeni labour as unskilled, then provide them with the necessary on-the-job training. But the acquired skills soon tempt another employer to offer a higher wage, and workers usually quit their jobs or even seek work abroad.

Firms are often forced by water and power shortages to rely on their own high-cost and uneconomic facilities, and high capital costs, combined with high labour costs, have made some industries uncompetitive with regard to imports. Industrial facilities in Yemen also tend to operate at efficiency levels far below full capacity, often at less than 50 per cent. The main factors behind the under-utilisation of capacity are continuous interruptions in power supplies and strong competition from cheap imports.

One of the problems faced by most entrepreneurs in RoY is that in order to start an industrial project it is necessary to begin from scratch. Many entrepreneurs lack the knowledge and technical expertise to improve the efficiency of their operations, and since the plants are often family-owned, there is also a reluctance to recruit professional managers.

Due to the structure of interest rates, bank lending in RoY is concentrated in short-term loans for import financing. One obstacle to more energetic participation by the commercial banks in domestic resource mobilisation is the belief among bank officials that the regulatory environment is not conducive to the bank's well-being.

Another major obstacle to the longer-term lending to industrial concerns by the commercial banks is inadequate legal protection. It is believed that small firms which have access to the resources of the organised financial sector belong, in practice, to a small minority of owners of good standing. As a result there have been widespread appeals for interest rate policies that would reflect the costs and risks of lending to a variety of borrowers, since interest rate controls had simply led to a concentration of lending to low-risk large borrowers. Banks will not grant any loans beyond the shortest maturity. Nor have the specialised banks, which depend heavily on state financing, found the commercial banks to be a source of funds. Furthermore, the private sector has, as a result of the unstable currency, been shifting its savings abroad.

Industrial strategy
What issues need to be addressed by policy makers today? The prospects for the economic growth of the RoY (and for manufacturing in particular) depend in the main on what happens to agriculture. We have not argued this point in depth, but this conclusion is not controversial. A substantial supply response from this sector can be obtained in the short term through the implementation of suitable policy- and institutional-reform packages.

Another fruitful course of action at this stage of economic development would be to consider ways of strengthening the linkages between industry and the rest of the national economy. Industrial strategy in the RoY must be closely tied to the mainspring of rural development and agricultural growth. These, of course, are among the principal means at the disposal of the state for raising output and the demand for labour.

Yemen could thus follow a combination of import-substitution (IS) industries and other domestic resource undertakings, including agriculture. It has also been suggested that Yemen's comparative advantage lies in the processing of natural resource-based commodities, thereby adding value to the production of local raw materials. The economy can also pursue further processing of its limited exports as a means of increasing the amount of foreign exchange earned.

A more specific analysis of microeconomic policy must, however, identify exactly where comparative advantage lies, and whether and how it is likely to change over time. Broadly speaking, both trade theory and empirical work suggest that a country's comparative advantage is determined by its relative endowments of physical and human capital. By investing in physical and human capital, a country can eventually change its comparative advantage to some degree.

Agriculture, however, has been and still is undergoing major changes. Farmers are confronting new markets and changing tastes, factors that will definitely change the role of agriculture in the development process. Water as well as land suitable for arable agriculture is limited in Yemen, which implies that the prospect for increasing agricultural output will depend on a better utilisation of land and water resources. Even under such constraints and limited physical factors, though, considerable potential exists for increasing crop yields, and this can be achieved with increased use of fertilisers and insecticides, through mechanisation, and by switching to improved higher-yield seeds.

Most raw materials and semi-finished inputs to the industrial process are imported into the RoY, since only limited agricultural products, such as cotton, hides and tobacco, have significant processing potential (ESCWA, 1990). The inadequacy of local agricultural raw material necessitates a long-term strategy that will focus on agricultural research into crops for which the country's ecological conditions are suited. However, in order that the food requirement of the growing population can be met domestically and to provide input supplies for sustained industrial growth, strong producer incentives to agriculture are necessary.

Having recognised the problem of unemployment, the government should seek to diversify away from large-scale operations and to encourage the expansion of the more successful medium- and small-sized enterprises. More generally, production of appropriate goods can be linked to the promotion of small-scale units producing for local consumption, that are likely to be competitive, given the reduction in transport costs.

Such a strategy would require the identification of industries that are potentially viable outside major urban centres, taking into account transportation costs and appropriate locations for their establishment. One option might be to develop processing facilities for agricultural products in the rural areas. Other possible projects include the establishment of regional centres for the production of low-value heavy and perishable consumer goods, and industries based on local building materials.

Furthermore, it has become evident in recent years that dualism in the structure of manufacturing can be a strong and healthy trend in the industrialisation process, provided that there is a vigorous and creative interaction between the large-scale modern manufacturing sector and the more traditional small-scale sector. The informal and rural industrial sectors can be used to absorb labour, even as more capital-intensive and large-scale manufacturing develops. East Asia, where the subcontracting of small firms by large firms has long been practised between the formal and informal sectors, can be taken as an exemplar.

It is tempting to argue that unless the general structure of economic policies is more appropriate to small-scale industries, there is little that can be achieved in the way of direct interventions to solve particular problems (e.g. intervention to improve the supply of infrastructural services and finance to small industry). However, excessive concentration on small-scale enterprises could be as damaging to their growth as neglecting them. And, if overdone, the dispersion of manufacturing to help rural areas and to avoid urbanisation could adversely affect the internal and external economies of scale that are important sources of dynamic efficiency.

NOTES

1 Oil exports made up 96 per cent of all exports in 1996.
2 Particularly in the northern part of the country.
3 In 1988, for example, the average annual wage in the Yemen Arab Republic (YAR) was twice that of Kenya, and more than five times that of Sri Lanka (ILO, *Yearbook of Labour Statistics*).
4 This classification has many limitations since, in practice, every firm above micro-enterprise level is considered to be large. However, we are obliged to consider this classification in order to make use of the available data.

Part II

The Legal System

5

The Judicial System:
Framework, Institutions and Traditions

Nageeb A. R. Shamiry

The judiciary reform plans

After the 1997 general elections, the Council of Ministers approved a reform plan for the judiciary, as did the Supreme Judicial Council. The programme emphasised public security, the protection and independence of the judiciary and the stability of the judicial system, in order 'to protect people and their dignity as well as their properties, human rights and legitimate liberties'. The programme also affirmed its stand in support of justice, which it considered the basis of statehood, and asserted that the judiciary is the highest authority. It specifically reiterated government backing for the judicial system and stated, among other things, that it would make available all its resources to help the judicial authorities work efficiently. It would also support judicial inspection in eradicating corruption, bribery and favouritism and to ensure the fairness of the system. It would also develop the Supreme Judicial Institute in order to provide the system with cadres qualified in Islamic law and legal issues. By providing the necessary facilities and training, it would contribute to the development and performance of the office of the Attorney-General, and it would assist further by making legal-awareness programmes available to the population, and by setting up courts in all administrative units. Effective coordination would be established between the judiciary and the security forces, and the legal profession would be brought under the rule of law, to help ensure the practice of justice.

This chapter considers three aspects of the subject. First it gives a brief historical, but essential, account of the judicial system in the two former Yemeni states. It will be argued that, apart from slight variations, their courts systems were similar. Secondly, history shows that the Islamic *shari'a* has always been, and still is, of great significance and influence as regards the judiciary in all parts of Yemen, notwithstanding adherence to different schools of Islamic jurisprudence. Thirdly, following unification on 22 May 1990, the courts systems and Islamic *shari'a* made it possible to merge the two former judiciaries, a process that was constitutionally regulated by the 1990 and the 1994 constitutions respectively.

The judiciary before 1962/7

The Imamate period in North Yemen

Between 1872 and 1918 North Yemen was occupied by the Ottoman Turks. Despite the fact that the Ottoman States Law (*Qanun al-wilayat al-'uthmaniyya*) was enacted in 1876, its application was not uniform throughout the Ottoman Empire. It was scarcely applied in Yemen, which thus deprived the country of an opportunity to organise its judicial system. In 1904 Imam Yahya was declared head (*imam*) of the Zaydi tribes. According to Zaydi tradition an *imam* must possess the following attributes: he must be male, free-born, a taxpayer, sound in mind, in possession of all his senses, and sound of limb. He must also be just, pious, brave and generous, possess administrative ability, be *mujtahid*, and be a descendant of 'Ali (son-in-law of the Prophet), as well as of the family of Fatima (the daughter of the Prophet who was married to 'Ali).

Negotiations between the Turks and the Imam culminated in the Treaty of Da'an, which was signed on 9 October 1911. Under its terms and conditions, the Imam was to appoint governors for the Zaydi sect, and these appointments were to be endorsed by Istanbul. A Court of Appeals was to be set up to examine complaints referred to it by the Imam; based in Sana'a, its president and members were to be chosen by the Imam. The 'government' – i. e. the Turks – could appoint non-Yemenis to adjudicate in Shafi'i and Hanafi areas, while mixed Shafi'i and Zaydi courts were to be set up to look into cases of conflict of laws. The government was to appoint circuit judges (*mubashirun*) for mobile courts who would visit the villages to settle *shari'a* disputes, and it had also to appoint governors for the Shafi'is and Hanafis.

The Imam established the first Appeals Courts in 1911, but he regarded himself as 'Head of the Judiciary' and acted as a Court of Cassation. He employed a version of Islamic law that was based on the principles of the Zaydi school of Islamic jurisprudence. Where he deviated on certain matters from Zaydi principles, his opinions were called *ikhtiyarat* (sing. *ikhtiyar*). The principles of the Zaydi school of

Islamic *shari'a* and the Imam's opinions were binding on all the governors and judges, and the version of Islamic *shari'a* employed by the Imam replaced Turkish law, except in the Turkish-administered areas and the coastal plain, including Hodeidah. However, from 1918 onwards, when the Turks left Yemen, the Zaydi *shari'a* principles prevailed throughout North Yemen.

Under the judicial system that prevailed under the Imams Yahya and Ahmad, judges were appointed in the provinces and districts, and appeals went directly to the Court of Appeals. There were judges for the army, for immigrants, for state property, the municipalities, religious endowments (*awqaf*), and so on. Appeals from these judges were sent to the Court of Appeals in Sana'a, and there could be a further appeal to the Imam himself. The judges and governors appointed by the Imam were entitled to mediate and arbitrate between parties or litigants; at the same time there was a system of tribal/customary justice (*'urf*).

Imam Yahya was assassinated in 1948, and was succeeded by his son Ahmad. The courts system remained unchanged, and judges were appointed on the same basis as previously. Imam Ahmad followed his father's example by making it binding upon governors and judges to adhere to the Zaydi principles of Islamic *shari'a,* and to his father's and to his own opinions (*ikhtiyarat*). He also attempted to codify the whole Islamic *shari'a*, setting up a commission of three judges for the purpose; the commission codified 1,479 articles. In substantive law, Imam Ahmad did not introduce anything new apart from some *ikhtiyarat*, and this state of affairs continued until 26 September 1962 when the Imamate (formally a monarchy since 1926), which had lasted for about eleven centuries, was overthrown and a republic was proclaimed.

South Yemen before 1967

The territory that was known as South Yemen consisted of the Colony of Aden, the Protectorate (Federation) of South Arabia, and a number of islands. In all there were 24 administrative units, with various names including sheikhdoms, sultanates and emirates. Aden had been acquired by the British in 1839. With effect from 1 April 1937 it became a Crown Colony, governed in accordance with Orders-in-Council (1936–65) and under direct British rule. It had its own laws and courts, and jury trials in serious crimes continued up to the beginning of 1977 even though British administration had ended.

The Federation came into existence in 1959. By 1967 most of the territory that later became known as South Yemen, including Aden itself, had become part of the Federation. All the other areas outside Aden had their relations with Britain regulated by a large number of treaties, which were either for protection and/or advice but which were otherwise administered according to the principles of indirect rule. Britain had reserved the right to make laws 'for the peace, good order, and government of the Protectorate', and as a consequence of its relations with the various Protectorate states, the British Government issued various Orders-in-Council. Despite this fact, each of the states had its own form of government, developed more or less according to circumstances, and the Orders-in-Council did not form part of their domestic law.[1] In some parts of the Protectorate there was a certain amount of local legislation in Arabic, as for example in Hadhramawt, but there was very little throughout most of the western area. Apart from such legislation, the law applied in the individual states was Islamic *shari'a* and customary law (*'urf*). Federal laws were enacted in Arabic, but with regard to matters from the Courts of Aden, the right of appeal to the Judicial Committee of the Privy Council in London continued to be decided by the Federal High Court.

In pre-1967 South Yemen, the judicial system varied from area to area: Aden had a separate legal and judicial system with a comprehensive set of laws and regulations; it had magistrates' courts, a supreme court, and rights of appeal to the Court of Appeals for Eastern Africa as well as another appeal to the Judicial Committee of the Privy Council in London. There was an ad hoc judicial system in the Federation, with *shari'a* courts in the capital and courts in each of the states of the Federation, with the *shari'a* Appeals Court in the capital, in addition to a Federal High Court. The Hadhramawt had a complete legal and judicial system, and the rest of the Protectorates had *shari'a* courts and customary (*'urf*) courts. This state of affairs continued until independence from British rule or protection was achieved on 30 November 1967.

The Judicial System after 1962/1967

The YAR

On 26 September 1962 the new republic in North Yemen announced the 'Six Aims of the Revolution', one of which concerned 'the setting up of a democratic Islamic society'. The 'temporary constitution' of 13 April 1963 spoke about Islamic *shari'a*, about non-discrimination due to race, origin, language, religion or sect (*madhhab*), and about social justice. It also provided that Islam would be 'the official religion of the state', and that legislation would be 'in accordance with Islamic *shari'a* and not contrary to, or inconsistent with it'.

The constitution proclaimed on 27 April 1964 stated in Article 3 that Islam was the religion of the state, while Article 4 provided that Islamic *shari'a* would be the source of all laws. However, the 1970 Permanent Constitution, which came into force on 28 December 1970, repealed Articles 3 and 4 of the 1964 constitution, and with regard to *shari'a* went further by providing in Article 46 that no person would be appointed as a judge unless he was thoroughly conversant in *shari'a* principles. Article 162 spoke about the codification of the principles of Islamic *shari'a* on condition that such principles did not contradict the Qur'an, Hadith or *ijma'* (consensus). The article also provided that the law would set up a commission for the task of accomplishing *shari'a* codification (*al-hay'a al-'ilmiyya li taqnin ahkam al-shari'a al-islamiyya*). Article 153 stated that the courts would apply the constitution and other laws, but if there were no provisions with regard to a matter in dispute, the courts would then adjudicate in accordance with the general principles of *shari'a*. It is worth mentioning, however, that from 1962 and the declaration of the 'Six Aims of the Revolution' right up until the coming into force of the Permanent Constitution in 1970, reference to Islamic *shari'a* avoided any mention of the Zaydi, Shafi'i or Ismai'li sects. At the same time, throughout the period since 1962 no declared enactment has made any reference whatsoever to any of these sects. All enactments, without exception, refer to Islamic *shari'a* in general terms.

Law No. 7/1975 established means for practical implementation of Article 152 of the 1970 constitution. The law set up a *shari'a* Codification Commission with responsibility for codifying Islamic *shari'a* principles. This commission has successfully classified a number of codes and laws, including those of the judicature, succession, commerce, inheritance, gifts, religious endowments (*awqaf*), evidence, arbitration, family, civil, civil procedure, enforcement of civil judgment, criminal procedure, prosecution, advocates, establishment and organisation of commercial courts, and establishment of the Higher Judicial Institute.

Furthermore, since 1976, which marks the beginning of what many jurists call a legislative/judicial revolution, many laws and decrees have been enacted and issued concerning the judicial system. Briefly these are the Courts' Law, the Prosecution Law, the Advocates Law, the Ministry of Justice Law; and the laws drafted by the *shari'a* Codification Commission and promulgated by the government (noted above).

The Courts system was organised round the Supreme Court of Cassation, the Courts of Appeal in the provinces, and primary courts in the districts. There were also state security and military courts, as well as a system of disciplinary courts.

The PDRY

The laws, regulations, resolutions and bye-laws that had been in force on Independence Day on 30 November 1967 remained in force in the same manner, according to Republican Decree No. 5/1967 of 2 December 1967.

The first constitution came into effect on 30 November 1970, which was the third anniversary of independence. Stating that Islam was the official religion of the state and that Arabic was the official language, the constitution also provided for the establishment of a Supreme Court, and for the promulgation of several basic laws. It also called for the reorganisation of the judiciary, the courts, prosecution and the legal profession generally. The following laws were gradually proclaimed during the 1970s and 1980s: those relating to the Courts, Public Prosecution, the Legal Profession, and the Civil Code (including Commercial Law), as well as the Penal Code, Criminal and Civil Procedure laws, laws relating to Court Fees, Family Law, Labour Law, and Social Security Law.

The amended constitution of 1978 stated that it was not permissible to establish extraordinary courts, and called for 'the rule of law' and for all state organs, officials and citizens to adhere to the state's constitution, laws and regulations. The state gradually reorganised the judicial system and enacted the laws, which brought together the whole of the former South Yemen for the first time since the British occupation in 1839 and produced the following judicial system: (1) the Supreme Court of the Republic; (2) the provincial courts in the governorates, and (3) magistrates' courts in the districts. The state also established people's courts, as well as state security and military courts.

The judicial system since unification in 1990

The judicial system according to the amended constitution of 1994

The constitution of 1990/1 declared that Islamic *shari'a* 'shall be the principal source of legislation' (Article 3). The amended 1994 constitution provides in its Article 3 that Islamic *shari'a* 'shall be the source of all the laws'. The other main articles in the constitution of 1994 relating to the judicial system include the following:

- Article 147 states that the judicial authority is autonomous in its judicial, financial and administrative aspects, and that the office of the public prosecutor is one of its organs. The courts will settle all disputes and crimes, and the judges are independent.
- Article 148 states that the judiciary is an integrated system, and that extraordinary courts may not be established under any circumstances.
- Article 149 states that members of the judiciary and public prosecutors will not be dismissed except under the conditions stipulated by the law. The law regulates disciplinary trials of the judiciary and also organises the legal profession.
- Article 150 states that the judiciary will set up a Supreme Judicial Council that will execute guarantees for the judiciary in the fields of appointment, promotion, retirement and dismissal, according to the law. It will also study and approve the judicial budget in preparation for inserting it as an item within the overall state budget.
- Article 151 states that the Supreme Court of the Republic is the highest judicial authority. The law will specify how it should be formed, and will define its functions and the procedures that are to be followed before it. The Court will undertake to decide cases with regard to the constitutionality of laws, regulations, bye-laws and resolutions; it will settle disputes concerned with conflict of jurisdictions; and it will investigate and give opinions concerning appeals referred by the House of Representatives relating to the validity of its membership. In addition it will look into appeals against final judgments in civil, commercial, criminal, personal status and disciplinary cases as well as administrative disputes, according to law; and will attempt to determine charges against the president of the republic, the vice-president, the speaker of the parliament, the prime minister and his deputies, and the ministers and their deputies, again according to law.

- Article 152 states that court sittings are open to the public unless a court decides, for reasons of security or public morals, to hold trials *in camera*. In all events, verdicts will be pronounced in open court.

During the three years that followed unification, the principal laws concerning the unified working of the judiciary throughout the republic were promulgated or issued. These laws relate to Judicature, Civil Affairs, Commerce, Family, Traffic, Prisons, Court Fees, Evidence, *awqaf* (religious endowments), Arbitration, Authentication of Documents, State Cases, Civil Procedure and Enforcement of Judgments, Juveniles, Civil Aviation, Penal, Criminal Procedure, Maritime, Military Penal and Criminal Procedure, Labour, and Procedure Regarding Indictment and Trial of the State's Senior Executive Officials.

The courts system: Judicature Law No. 1/1991
The Judicature Law No. 1/1991, called by some jurists the Judicial Authority Law, was promulgated on 10 January 1991. The court system set up by the law, which was valid at the time of writing this account, includes:

- A uniform District Court system. In the main centres of almost all the districts there are Primary Courts (*al-mahkama al-ibtida'iyya*), dealing with, or having original jurisdiction in, all types of cases: civil, criminal (including public property, traffic and juveniles), commercial (including customs and taxation), family, and administrative.
- A Provincial Court of Appeal (*al-mahkama al-isti'nafiyya*) is found in every province (or governorate) as well as in the capital city, Sana'a. It deals with appeals against judgments and decisions of the Primary Courts (within the respective governorate) in all cases that involve legal points and determination of facts: in other words, the courts of appeal have appellate jurisdiction as regards the judgments of the lower courts.
- The Supreme Court of the Republic (*al-mahkama al-'ulya*), which is located in the capital, Sana'a, is the highest court in the land. The Supreme Court considers errors in legal procedures or in judicial interpretation of the law. Its case-load thus consists primarily of appeals involving questions of constitutional law and legal questions

of major significance. Naturally, both types of question involve *shari'a* matters, since Article 3 of the 1994 constitution determined that Islamic *shari'a* is the source of all legislation. The Supreme Court, however, also deals with appeals from convictions and/ or sentences regarding retaliation for murder (*qisas*) and corporal punishment (*hudud*).

- The Court is composed of the President (or the Chief Justice), two deputies and around 50 members (or judges). It represents the unity of the judicial system, as well as uniformity with regard to judicial supervision. The Court sits in bodies called divisions. There are eight divisions: constitutional, civil, commercial, family, criminal, administrative, military, and appeals scrutiny. A bench of five judges is responsible for each division except for the Constitutional Division which has a bench of seven judges, under the President of the Court.

Alternative dispute resolution methods

Court litigation is not the best method for solving all disputes. The length of time and the cost involved in this method of resolving disputes has been a problem for a very long time since it diminished confidence in the judicial system. The consequence of this unsatisfactory state of affairs is, first, that many people have had to resort to customary (*'urf*) justice (which is faster and less expensive); and secondly, that the state has had, as a matter of priority, to look at alternative methods of resolving disputes. The latter can be done through resorting to:

- Mediation (*sulh*).
- Arbitration (*tahkim*), although arbitration is not possible in situations that involve dissolution of marriages, cases against judges, disputes with regard to procedures of compulsory enforcement of judgments, matters related to public order, and all matters that are not compoundable.
- Government arbitration (*takhim hukumi*), in which any dispute between two or more state bodies should be settled in one of two ways: either by passing a legal opinion (*fatwa*) that is binding upon all the state bodies that are parties to the dispute, or through the machinery of government arbitration. The Ministry of Legal and Parliamentary Affairs is responsible for government arbitration, which is mandatory.

- A department of the Ministry of Legal and Parliamentary Affairs (Department of State Cases) which is responsible for representing the government in disputes for or against any ministry or public body, whether within the Republic or abroad.
- Customary tribal arbitration (*tahkim qabali/'urfi*). In practice, many people resort to arbitration, since the Arbitration Law takes note of tribal structure and, as a consequence, carefully accommodates *'urf.*

The merging of the two former judicial systems

Two factors in particular have eased the process of merging the judicial systems prevailing before May 1990 in the former North and South Yemen: first is the fact that the principles of Islamic *shari'a* were codified by the Islamic *Shari'a* Codification Commission that started in former North Yemen in the 1970s.[2] The Sana'a Declaration concerning Islamic *shari'a* was approved by the Ministers of Justice of the member states of the Arab League in February 1982. It states that the sources of codification and application of Islamic *shari'a* principles will be the Qur'an, the Sunna, *ijma'* (consensus), *qiyas* (analogy), preference (*ihtihsan, al-masalih al-mursala*), and principles of justice, provided that they do not violate Islamic *shari'a*. The second factor was the establishment of the Supreme Court of the Republic, and all the jurisdictions that are exercised by its specialised judicial bodies, the divisions.

The importance of Yemen's Supreme Court

According to the constitution of 1994 and to Judicature Law, the Supreme Court determines the constitutionality, or otherwise, of laws and regulations; it settles disputes between judicial bodies over conflict of jurisdiction; it investigates petitions, referred to it by the House of Representatives (parliament) with regard to the validity or otherwise of the membership of any of its members, and reports on its findings to the parliament; and it looks into appeals, on points of law, against decisions of the Court of Appeals in civil, criminal, commercial, personal status, and disciplinary cases, as well as in administrative disputes. In addition the Supreme Court tries and determines cases brought against the president of the Republic, the vice-president, the prime minister and his deputies, and the ministers and their deputies; looks into appeals against judgments with regard to military offences; and exercises 'judicial supervision' regarding all inferior courts in the Republic.

The role of the Supreme Court within the judiciary

In addition to being the highest court of law in the land, the importance of the Supreme Court is demonstrated by the fact that the two main bodies in the judiciary – the Supreme Judicial Council and the Judicial Inspection Commission – are elements of that Court. Its importance as an institution is also obvious in the Republic of Yemen's efforts to implement the government's Programme for Economic, Financial and Administrative Reform (1994), together with the Legal Reform Plan (1995) and the Judicial Reform Plan (approved by the Council of Ministers on 12 October 1997). The Judicial Reform Plan underlined this importance when it stated that the Yemeni constitution had confirmed the adoption and existence of a unified judiciary for the Republic of Yemen. All cases and jurisdictions were unified under a single Supreme Court, whose jurisdiction would justify the prohibition of extraordinary (or special or exceptional) courts, and ensure that errors made by subordinate courts were supervised and corrected.

The Constitutional Division is the most important division of the Supreme Court, with responsibility for constitutional jurisdiction and judicial review. Its sphere of duty concerns the constitutionality or otherwise of laws, regulations, resolutions and so on. Such jurisdiction is conferred upon the Supreme Courts (or in the case of Egypt the Supreme Constitutional Court) of only a few Arab states; Yemen is the only case in the Arabian Peninsula.

The Constitutional Division also deals with petitions against the results of elections in the constituencies that are based on irregularities, and at the request of the House of Representatives investigates complaints regarding Members and the validity or otherwise of their membership. Furthermore, it hears and determines charges against senior officials of the state.

Following the decline of totalitarian regimes, the independence of the judiciary becomes a pressing issue. This means that the judiciary becomes one of the state's three main branches, and in this respect it is important to look in some detail at the Republic's Supreme Judicial Council as well as at the Judicial Inspection Commission. It should be noted that the Supreme Judicial Council (*majlis al-qadha' al-a'la*) is not a judicial organ, in the sense that appeals may be lodged there. The Judicial Inspection Commission (*hay'at al-taftish al-qadha'i*), too, is not a judicial body, in the sense that complaints referred to it are not – and cannot be – regarded as petitions against certain judgments and decisions passed by the competent courts. Such petitions, or for that matter appeals, should be lodged at the court, or courts, superior to the court or courts that passed the judgments and decisions against which complaints have been filed.

The Supreme Judicial Council

The Supreme Judicial Council is composed of the president of the Republic, as Chairman of the Council. The President of the Supreme Court is a member (and deputises as Chairman when the president of the Republic does not attend, doing so in accordance with a resolution issued by the President of the Republic). The other members are the Minister of Justice, the Attorney-General, the two deputies to the President of the Supreme Court, the Chairman of the Judicial Inspection Commission, the Vice-Minister of Justice, and three senior judges of the Supreme Court.

According to the constitution and to judicature law, the functions of the Council are related to the implementation of the guarantees granted to the judges with regard to appointment, promotion, dismissal, discipline, transfer and retirement. Judges are appointed for life, subject to compulsory retirement at age 65; and to their good behaviour while in office.

In addition, the Council studies and approves the draft budget of the Judiciary, with a view to that budget being entered as a single item in the general budget of the state. The Council is also responsible for defining and formulating policies with regard to the development of the judiciary, as well as considering bills related to the working of the judiciary.

The Council issues resolutions that concern the divisions of the Supreme Court and the establishment of specialised courts (such as commercial courts). It also confirms proposals for the number of judges in the Supreme Court and the number of courts of appeal and approves the regulations of the Judicial Inspection Commission.

The Judicial Inspection Commission

The Judicial Inspection Commission is an autonomous authority, established in accordance with judicature law. It has a chairman, a deputy chairman, and an appropriate complement of members, approved by the Supreme Judicial Council and selected from among judges who have wide experience in the judiciary. The chairman must be a senior judge of the Supreme Court, and is seconded for a period of two to three years. He is also a member of the Supreme Judicial Council.

According to judicature law and its executive regulations, the Commission's main responsibilities are centred in the field of assessment of the judicial work and conduct of the magistrates and judges. Assessment reports on the conduct of every judge and magistrate are submitted to the Supreme Judicial Council.

The Supreme Court in action

The Supreme Court, as the highest judicial body in the land, is responsible for implementing and interpreting the principles of *shari'a*. In this connection, two points should be borne in mind. First, the codification of *shari'a* principles has at one and the same time Islamicised and systematised the laws that are deduced straight from the Qur'an and the Sunna; and secondly the main *shari'a* principles have been strictly applied as they ought to be, and not as people have become accustomed to through previous interpretations. Some examples of case law and Supreme Court decisions follow, and are meant to illustrate the above points, and in particular the importance of the role of the Supreme Court.

The constitutional principle with regard to Shari'a

The Supreme Court has interpreted the constitutional principle ('Islamic *Shari'a* is the source of all legislation') in the interest of the accused. This holds especially true with regard to cases brought before the enactment of the unified Penal Code in late 1994. The Supreme Court has, as a result, quashed many capital punishment sentences from the courts of the former South Yemen, and has ordered retrials in accordance with the constitution. There are three ways in which the accused have benefited:[3]

• the deceased's relatives have waived the right to *qisas* (retribution), whether or not the *diya* (blood money) was returned, since the act is regarded as being more civil/tort-like than criminal;

- retrials have resulted in convictions, not on the basis of murder but rather on the basis of a lesser crime (e.g. manslaughter);
- retrials might still have ended with convictions and *qisas* sentences, but the accused/convicted would have lived longer.

Composition of the Court of Appeal

The Law of Criminal Procedure provides that when trying and determining criminal appeals, the composition of the Court of Appeal should be a bench of three judges. Since its promulgation in 1979 this law has been the subject of heated debate between the modernists and their opponents. It is now accepted as not being against *shari'a* principles. The Supreme Court recently quashed a number of judgments on the grounds that a bench of only two judges, instead of three, sat in the Court of Appeal.[4]

Murder and waiver of retribution

Concerning murder, the Qur'an regards it as being more civil/tort-like than criminal. *Shari'a* principles, based on verses from the Qur'an and the Sayings of the Prophet, encourage the waiving of the right to retribution (*qisas*) by the relatives of the deceased in a murder trial. The following are examples in which the Supreme Court has commuted *qisas*, due to the deceased's relatives waiving the right to retribution:

- Appeal No. 84/1991 (murder in Aden), and Appeal Nos. 46/1992, 276/1992 and 213/1993 (murders in Sana'a): the Supreme Court held that 'waiver = *diya* + imprisonment', instead of *qiyas*.
- Appeal No. 141/1992: the Supreme Court stated that the evidence produced upheld the waiver of the father of the deceased, although other relatives had not agreed. The Court held that (1) waiver by one of the deceased's heirs is enough; (2) *qisas* lapses once there is waiver; and (3) waiver is final and irrevocable.
- Appeal No. 292/1992: the accused was the brother of the deceased's widow, and there was waiver by the widow. The Supreme Court held that *qisas* should be dropped due to proof of waiver.
- Appeal No. 103/1991: the wife murdered her husband by putting poison in a cup of milk. The parents of the husband agreed to waive the right to retribution and received their shares of the amount of *diya*. The Supreme Court affirmed the decision of the lower courts that *qisas* was not justified.

- Appeal No. 311/1992: the Supreme Court stated that the deceased's father shouted in court that he had waived the right, verbally and in writing, to retribution on the assassin of his son, in return for a lump sum. The Court held that, due to waiver, no capital punishment was to be inflicted, but that for his own safety, the accused should be released from prison only after serving five years as punishment regarding 'public right' (*al-haqq al-'amm*), and paying the amount of *diya*.
- Appeal Nos. 262/1991 and 213/1993: in these instances the accused was convicted and sentenced to be executed and the Supreme Court confirmed the judgment. However, written waivers and acceptance of *diya* were submitted later, and as a result *qisas* was commuted.

Adultery (zina)

Cases of adultery deserve special treatment. In *shari'a*, illicit intercourse is termed *zina*. The penalty (*hadd*) specified for *zina* in the Qur'an is a hundred stripes, while the Sunna laid down the punishment of stoning (lapidation) for *zina* committed by a married person (*muhsan*). The proof of *zina* is extremely difficult; the testimony of four competent male witnesses to the act itself is required, beyond a shadow of doubt.

The Supreme Court received several appeals involving the penalty of stoning/lapidation (*hadd al-zina*) but held that the evidential requirements could not be satisfied to justify application of the *hadd*. Examples include:

- Appeal No. 79/1994: the facts were that the woman was 25 years old and married, but her husband had deserted her for the last four years. He had recently agreed with her father regarding divorce, and the father had in fact already returned half the dowry. The man, who denied the indictment, was not married and had promised to marry the woman after she had obtained the divorce from her husband. The woman had become pregnant. The trial judge and the Court of Appeal passed a sentence of lapidation on the accused woman, because she was *muhsana*. In 24 July 1994 the Supreme Court unanimously reduced the sentence to one year's imprisonment, (1) because of *shubha* (doubt), for the man accused had promised to marry her, and (2) because the trial judge should have made sure of the evidential requirements for the application of lapidation (*al-musqitat*).

- Appeal No. 235/1993: here both the man and the woman accused were unmarried, and both pleaded guilty. The woman was a virgin when the act was committed, for the man had promised to marry her. She became pregnant. The trial judge and the Court of Appeal passed sentence of one hundred lashes for each. The Supreme Court affirmed the penalty but added that it should be deferred until after delivery of the infant, plus two years for feeding it.
- Appeal No. 59/1993: both the man and the woman accused pleaded guilty. The man was unmarried but the woman was married. The trial judge and the Court of Appeal held that the woman should be stoned to death and that the man should receive one hundred lashes. The Supreme Court held that the lower courts should have explained the nature of the offence and the serious consequences of any confession/plea of guilt, which had not been done. The sentence was reduced to three years' imprisonment for the woman.

Apostasy

There are two apostasy cases that for two main reasons are of vital significance. The first reason is that the accused denied allegations of blasphemous writings and asserted his attachment to, and pride in, Islam; the second is that a hard-line attitude was deemed to be against the provisions of the Law on Criminal Procedure – these correspond to the system of *hisba*, or the filing of an indictment or criminal case by an individual against another individual. The two cases concerned are:

- Appeal No. 98/1984: the accused, who was a university lecturer, wrote certain books that praised the work of Yemeni people in planting the terraces; an extremely difficult task. The books were published by the government for the Ministry of Information. The lecturer however, was, accused of blasphemous allegations (*ridda*). Having decided on his innocence, the Supreme Court acquitted him.
- Appeal No. 945/1415AH–AD1995: an advocate was accused of apostasy by another advocate regarding certain paragraphs in the pleadings. The Court of Appeal held that *hisba* is within the jurisdiction of the Attorney-General. In a Judicial Directive, the Supreme Court took the same view.

Theft and robbery

As far as theft and robbery are concerned, the Supreme Court has passed many decisions which indicate a true application of the constitution. Some examples are:

- Appeal No. 55/1992: during a two-year period, the nine persons accused had formed an armed gang to steal cars from the state and from individuals. During their criminal acts, they used armed resistance against the police. There were 22 cars involved in the case. All the nine accused were convicted of conspiracy, robbery and theft by the trial judge, who sentenced the first accused to have his right hand amputated from the wrist and all nine accused to be imprisoned for terms ranging between one and fifteen years. The Court of Appeal in Sana'a confirmed the conviction of the sentence of amputation, and reduced the terms of imprisonment. In 1992 the Supreme Court held that the requirements for robbery and theft, which justify amputation in this respect, had not been fulfilled; more importantly, *shari'a* does not provide for two penalties for the same crime. In this case, as the first accused had already spent 13 years in prison, which was a long sentence, he was to be released and ordered to return the stolen cars to their owners.
- Appeal Nos. 188/1992, 218/1992, 272/1992: in these cases, where the facts were almost identical, the accused persons had broken into certain houses and stolen property, mainly money and jewellery. They pleaded guilty. Having received back their stolen property, the owners forgave the accused persons and renounced the *hadd* of amputation of the right hand from the wrist. The Supreme Court held that the waiver constituted a circumstance that made it imperative for the courts to drop the *hadd*, as did the return of the stolen goods to the original owners. The judgments of the lower courts were quashed.

Judicial review of laws and electoral petitions

The Constitutional Division of the Supreme Court looked into two main types of appeals, in addition to many petitions, against the results of the first (April 1993) and second (April 1997) parliamentary elections held in the Republic of Yemen on the basis of a multiparty system.

- Constitutional Appeal No. 1/1992: this was submitted against the Educational Bill and then debated on the basis that some provisions were against *shari'a* and hence against the constitution. The Court rejected the case and held that its jurisdiction arose 'once the Bill is Law and before it is Law'.

- Constitutional Appeal No. 1/1993: this was filed by the prime minister and other ministers, against a decision of the Supreme Elections Commission that the prime minister and others should resign before contesting the general elections of 1993. The Court held in favour of the prime minister and others, stating that they alone, from among all public figures, could contest the elections without having to resign.

- Electoral petitions: many petitions were filed in the Supreme Court against some of the results of the 1993 and 1997 parliamentary elections, on the grounds of irregularities.

Conclusion

The experiment of the Supreme Court of the Republic of Yemen, an institution with jurisdiction in all disputes as well as an institution representing the unified judicial system under a constitution providing for the separation of powers, is worthy of study. The Supreme Court is the highest court of law in the land, protecting human rights and democracy as well as applying *shari'a* principles. The codification of the latter was an ambitious and wide-ranging programme, and indeed was the first of its kind for some 14 centuries, both in the sense of being comprehensive and in the fact that codification was accomplished without adherence to any particular school of Islamic jurisprudence. The process took nearly 20 years of hard work, and it is this which makes the Republic of Yemen unique among other Arab and Islamic countries.

NOTES

1   In Aden and the Protectorate, the judges and the courts, in addition to the laws and customs (*'urf*), resorted to such textbooks as the following: Sheikh 'Abdul Kadir bin Muhammad al-Makkawi, *The Muhammadan Law of Inheritance, Marriage and the Rights of Women* (1886); D.F. Mulla, *Principles of Mahomedan Law* (1961); N.B.E. Baillie, *Digest of Moohummudan Law* (1865/9); R.K. Wilson, *Anglo-Muhammadan Law* (1921), Ameer 'Ali, *Mahommedan Law* (1929), Al-Umm, *Al-Shafi'i* (1973), 'Abdul-Rahman 'Abdallah Bukair, *Introduction to Selected Matters of the Courts in Hadhramawt* (1966).

2   The interpretation of *shari'a* principles is, of course, based on the sources of *shari'a*, which are the Qur'an, the Sunna (or Hadith), *ijma'* (or juristic consensus), and *qiyas* (or reasoning by analogy with the previous three sources) – these constitute the primary sources. The secondary sources are *istihsan* (or *al-masalih al-mursala*); *sadd al-dhara'i*; *istishab* (or *istishab al-hal*); *'urf* and *'adat* (custom), and <u>*shar'man al-qulana*</u> (the *shari'a*s of previous messengers).

3   Examples include at least five appeals from Lahj province (Nos. 5/1992; 29/1993; 30/1993; 31/1993; and 5/1993), as well as one each from Shabwa and Hadhramawt provinces (Nos. 25/1993 and 35/1993 respectively).

4   All the examples given here, for which retrials were ordered, took place in Ta'izz, and included 55/1992 (causing bodily harm); 68/1992 (causing death); 31/1993 and 34/1993 (murder); and 20/1994 (slander).

6

Commercial Litigation and Arbitration

———

Hussein al-Hubaishi

Introduction

The following paragraphs are intended to give some brief background information on the legal systems that operated in Yemen before 1962 and 1967, and on developments that occurred in the system after independence and before reunification.

Before 1962 a dual legal system was in operation in the North. The *shari'a* was universally applied. Advanced studies revolved around mastery of *shari'a*, which was regarded as an instrument of statecraft, and as a result, *shari'a* courts had exclusive jurisdiction over all disputes. The era was characterised by highly centralised rule and by the forceful personality of the Imam, who would review around three hundred cases and issues daily. In judicial matters, civil law (or perhaps more accurately, parts of public law) would be administered by the district commissioner (*al-'amil*) and the *shari'a* was administered by a district judge (*al-hakim*) and then by the Court of Appeal. If the parties involved so chose, both these channels would lead to the Imam and his advisory board (*al-hay'a al-shar'iyya*).

It may well be, as Messick suggested (1993: 3), that uncodified *shari'a* is characterised by '[the] flexibility and interpretative ability of its constructs and open structure of its texts', but in this case the price for not codifying *shari'a* principles was high. There were different legal opinions on the same issue, parties to a dispute were uncertain of their legal position, and recourse to appeal could continue indefinitely. With regard to procedures, jurisdiction of the courts was unknown and a party to a case could take the matter under dispute to any court anywhere in Yemen. Furthermore, virtually no systems of recording or archives were kept or maintained in an orderly manner.

At the same time, tribes applied their own customary rules (*ahkam al-aslaf*) when it suited them, rather than abiding by the state's legal rules of law and order. Certain norms of tribal custom were therefore outlawed by the *shari'a*, the Imams having realised that it would mean minimal possibilities for exercising governmental control if the tribes had their own law. In some cases, sovereignty was also at stake (Al-Hubaishi, 1988: 16).

Until 1967, during the period of British rule in the South, a triple judiciary system existed. In the colony of Aden the judiciary consisted of civil and criminal courts which dealt with commercial, criminal and British Admiralty matters. Personal status matters were dealt with by *shari'a* courts, but other religious norms applied to non-Muslims.

Within tribal communities local disputes were arbitrated by tribal or religious personalities who heard cases according to the prevailing rules of custom or occasionally of *shari'a*.

The colonial courts included a Supreme Court and a number of subordinate magistrates' courts. The high court of judicature at Bombay (and later on in East Africa) acted as an appeal court for Aden's Supreme Court, and from the latter to the judicial committee of the Privy Council in London. Those courts applied various laws of British India, common law and equity. *Shari'a* courts were headed by a single *shari'a* judge (*qadhi*) in the district, and the tribal tribunals were presided over by the local sultan, sheikh or a *qadhi*.

After 1962, there were attempts in the North to modernise the judiciary. The upheaval of the social order led to urbanisation, the growth of new socioeconomic classes, and a degree of social mobility, and these factors played a significant part in the transformation of the North's legal and judicial system. Instead of individual interpretations of lengthy legal commentaries, law was recorded in a more orderly fashion as administrative acts and laws, and these were later incorporated within the national legal system of laws, decrees and regulations.

The compromise between responding to the impact of modernisation and avoiding the alienation of the traditionalists was exemplified by the codification of principles of the *shari'a* (Peterson, 1982: 69). Apart from Ottoman attempts in the late nineteenth century, the beginning of this legal movement towards codification can be traced to the few non-Zaidi principles (*al-ikhtiyarat*) incorporated into the legal system of Yemen at the times of the Imams Yahya and Ahmad (1904–62). The other attempt was made after 1971 by the Ministry of Justice and the Court of Cassation when they started to apply the idea of one set of *shari'a* principles. By 1976, it had been realised that complete codification of the *shari'a* was fundamental to the creation of a modern state and from that date the interpretative dynamics of the *shari'a* were used to legislate on personal status, commercial and judicial matters.

After the issuing of the 1970 constitution, rights of litigation and recourse to the courts were guaranteed. Regular courts of appeal followed a three-tier system consisting of courts of first instance (primary courts), courts of appeal, and the Court of Cassation (the High Court). However, as will be seen below, all was not well.

In the South, two legal systems had to be combined following independence in 1967. According to the constitution, the functioning of the judiciary was to be exercised through the courts, which had to make every endeavour to promote respect for the constitution and for the laws. Justice was to be administered by the Supreme Court, provincial high courts and divisional courts. Sources of law were the constitution, followed by legislations at different levels and issued by different bodies. In practice, Islamic law remained a source of law, although there was an attempt to accommodate a revolutionary version of Islamic beliefs. The constitution stipulated that Islam was guaranteed protection in so far as it was consonant with constitutional principles (Sections 34 and 36).

The other face of the coin showed signs of another legal system, and was evident from certain provisions in the constitution. It is easy to deduce that there was no separation of powers (legislative, judiciary and executive), since the function of the judiciary 'will promote respect . . . and loyalty to the Revolution and Homeland'. There was only one state power which was vested in the 'Sovereignty of the working people, and the Judiciary is an organ of the state power'. Lastly the Presidium had, according to the constitution, the privilege 'of interpreting the laws' (Section 97 (4)) (Amin, 1987; Al-Hubaishi, 1988: 181–98).

From 1990 there was a concerted effort to unify the two legal systems, and to submit the legal system at large to a process of reform. Both the draft constitution for a unified Yemen, completed in 1982, and the same draft constitution as provisionally amended in 1990, stipulated the unification of all Northern and Southern laws during the so-called 'transition period'. Although many unified laws were enacted, there was no detailed plan for the unifying of legislation in general. Thus, in one month, 48 laws were passed as presidential decrees before they were submitted to the Council of Representatives. This pragmatism, accompanied by a spirit of compromise aimed at pleasing parties from both the political left and the political right, resulted in certain laws either conflicting with each other or becoming inconsistent with governmental pursuit of the course of reform.

In the sphere of the judiciary, the outcome was less than ideal. The duality of the former legal systems in the North and the South surfaced, and the temporary division of power according to the constitution allowed considerable room for political manoeuvring as well as for the emergence of al-Islah (the Islam-oriented party). The combining of these elements had a distorting effect on efforts to unify and reform the judiciary, itself an unsuccessful exercise to which other factors also contributed. These included mainly the worsening financial and political situation, and above all, a general reluctance to pursue judicial reforms and their consequent deferment, a point which will be discussed further below.

Judicial courts without judicial instruments

Every Judge's shari'a

Until 1978, every judge in the North had his own interpretation of the *shari'a*, a situation that still exists in certain fields of legislation where the rules of law are blurred or not yet fully enacted. There are, of course, many jurists and commentators of different schools in traditional Islamic jurisprudence whose opinions are markedly dissimilar. Certainly this writer knows of similar cases or the same case being judged in a different manner according to where the court was located (for instance in Ta'izz, Sana'a or Sa'da). In addition, there are 'freelance' jurists who, with considerable adroitness are prepared to annul or reverse any judgment based on the *shari'a* from the times of the Caliphs or the era of the Umayyads.

Over time, *shari'a* became a human embodiment that depended on the jurist's beliefs and thoughts, and was sometimes used as a literary process leading to authority. Hence codification of the *shari'a* was to be worked on as a compromise solution, since it was fundamental to the creation of a relatively modern state. Generally, the term 'codification' is used to refer to the reduction of certain rules or principles of *shari'a* to a written and more or less clearly organised form that becomes a comprehensive piece of legislation.

In the YAR, following the issuing of Law No. 4 for 1975, codification continued unabated apart from certain intervals of political turmoil. Civil, commercial and penal laws were thus composed and enacted in a manner that would be sufficiently clear not only to judges but also to lawyers, administrative officials and perhaps even to citizens. The guiding principle for codification, as stipulated in Law No. 7 for 1975, states as follows: 'The members (of the committee) shall make use of *al-ijtihad*[1] of all schools, follow the soundest opinion, depend on abstract and universal Islamic jurisprudence and the general principles which deal with new legal situations.'

In this respect, one cannot at present claim that everybody is pleased with the process of codification. Some judges, while not necessarily feeling compelled to pronounce on matters of codified laws, are not unwilling to inform themselves of their provisions and to apply them when necessary. Other radical judges and lawyers are still pressing for understandable, clear, progressive and simply-drafted legal rules. There are, however, other reasons for dissatisfaction, including the need to systematise more, as yet uncodified, rules and principles of *shari'a*, and to simplify certain principles which have been imprecisely codified, thereby obliging any student of law to refer to the antiquated manuscripts of the Islamic jurists and commentators. An even greater irritant to young judges and lawyers is the constant reference in laws enacted by parliament to *shari'a* in general, by adding to many legal provisions the phrase 'according to the principles of *shari'a*'.

Laws with no procedure

The subject of procedure or adjective law in Yemen has become particularly important because of the difficulty of fixing the line of demarcation between substance and procedure. Until 1976 there were few statutory laws in the North or even regulations to cover procedure, but since that date many laws and regulations have been promulgated, revoked or amended. The situation in the South was different and procedural legislation was already being regularly enacted by the time of British rule in Aden and subsequently.

Our concern is the present, particularly because we find, since the establishment of Yemen unity, many instances where there is no strict application of the rules of procedure, either in pre-trial proceedings or during pleadings terms. We also notice that judges are greatly influenced by the inquisitorial nature of litigation, whereby certain lawyers make use of adversarial tactics and interlocutory injunctions to frustrate the due process of law. Even more than this, state restrictions or competence and jurisdiction are ambiguous, especially with regard to matters of commerce.

Though protracted judgments are on the decrease, most judgments and verdicts are issued without scrutiny of the facts and the law. Worse are the hearings and petitions that take place in the chambers of certain judges without any chance of rejoinders or counter-arguments being submitted. There are other instances where the court of execution may look into the facts of a case and review the entire proceedings from the start.

At the same time, those judges who abide by the rules of procedure are foiled by lack of procedural instruments imperative for courts. There are no proper archives, filing and reference systems, libraries, or qualified clerks for authentication or notarisation. Judges are not even regularly provided with the law gazette. These deficiencies can, as a result, lead to delay in hearing cases; and perhaps to an obstruction of justice.

Judges with no institutions and other frustrating factors

In addition to suffering the shortcomings afflicting judges in the towns and cities of Yemen, judges in the countryside are further deprived since they lack the means of either public or private communication and are often without decent houses or lodgings. They have no qualified clerks and are even short of items of stationery. The court buildings are far from adequate.

If we look at the judicial or semi-judicial institutions at the top of the legal hierarchy they do not fare any better. According to the chairman of the Judicial Inspection Board, this body 'is not given the necessary resources to do its job. It is not even given full authority to inspect the activities of the supreme court. The inspectors have no means of travelling, and lack documentation and information on cases' (interview with Mr Justice Shamiri, *Yemen Times*, 17 November 1997). Even so, one of the Inspection Board's bad practices in the old days was its inclination to act as an organ of rebuttal and an appeal body.

The Supreme Court (Court of Cassation) is supposed to be the highest judicial body of the land, but actually the body is run by its presiding judge who interferes in the proceedings of the lower courts, transfers cases from one bench to another and accepts judicial review of cases more or less unconditionally.

At certain times the Minister of Justice or his Ministry get involved in a process of intrusion and subversion of the judiciary, by way of indicating or directing execution of judgments. Even worse is the case of the Supreme Judicial Council, a part-time body whose function is to guarantee the rights and privileges of judges and administer and oversee their discipline and removal. Yet most of the time the Council or its chairman acts as a full-time administrative, executive and judicial body, giving directives and instructions to judges and courts alike.

The consequential corruption of most of the judicial system is a logical conclusion to the above-mentioned misbehaviours or shortcomings. Administrative corruption is indicated by the absence of judges from the Bench, prolongation of hearings and sometimes inducement of the parties concerned to attend hearings that are held in the judge chambers.

Financial corruption is initiated by means of bribing lower-graded clerks of the court and, through them, directly buying off underpaid or greedy judges with incentives, financial inducements and backhanders. The upshot of all this is an outcry against the judiciary and lack of respect or contempt for judges.

The writer personally disagrees with reformers who blame the judges for such a situation and who think the judiciary should be restructured from the top; rather, reform should begin with re-education, instruction and postgraduate training for most of the judges, preceded by the guaranteeing of their rights and privileges. Reform would thus start from the bottom, with the majority of the judges found in rural and urban areas.

Reluctant judicial reforms
The reforms intended for the judiciary in Yemen can be classified into three categories. After 1974, certain reformers in North Yemen tried the dogmatic approach – 'old is bad, new is good'. To their way of thinking, traditional judges needed to be discharged and replaced by recently qualified university graduates. At around the same time in the South, the Left took over the reins of government and attempted to apply the same dogma.

From the 1980s until the present, reformers who believe in what might be called 'the theoretical approach' have tried their hand. They have continued to believe that long-term planning should proceed at a measured pace for the entire judiciary and that reforms should take place hierarchically. This approach exposed their intentions to those with vested interests and they were quickly shaken off by the old guard before they had made any progress, but having possibly learnt their lesson, they continue to promote their theories.

The third category, which might be called 'the realistic approach', was actually formulated in the mid-1970s and still has some supporters among those who participated in the trials at that time. Reformers who followed this approach to a certain extent combined elements of both the first and the second approaches. On the one hand they believed in introducing a number of university graduates into the judiciary without, however, removing or dismissing all the traditionally minded or elderly judges. On the other, these reformers believed in planning for judicial reform but were careful to reveal their long-term plans gradually, thereby avoiding conflict with the opponents of reform.

One of their methods was the establishing of dedicated courts for commerce, administration, financial and constitutional matters, staffed by law graduates specialising in these fields, but without, on the whole, impinging on the theoretical unity of the judiciary that they are envisaging. They concluded that when the regular courts had been influenced by the examples of the new specialised courts, then, and only then, the principle of judicial unity would be upheld. In fact there are still a few courts and benches that are composed partly of university graduates, but they are not immune from either the impression of overall corruption or from visible abuse of the system. The first real break from this unsatisfying situation was the establishment of the commercial courts in 1976.

Commercial courts: from success to downfall

In search of model courts in the YAR

In 1976, for all the reasons noted above, along with the most important cause identified – that of inertia (indeed outright resistance) to reform, and no accountability – the reformers seized their chance and convinced the authorities to promulgate a number of laws regulating commercial matters. Due to administrative incompetence of the Supreme Court and the Ministry of Justice, the State Legal Office reluctantly agreed that for a time it would control the commercial courts. These were intended to be the focal point of judicial reform and a model to be copied by the usual courts.

In addition new and related laws were issued, such as Law No. 116 on court fees, as well as laws on civil and commercial procedure. The main legislation on commercial courts (Law No. 40 for 1976) provided for the courts to be constituted at central locations within the provinces according to economic and judicial needs. The law's stipulation on the cases to be decided by the courts was related to matters of public order, thereby putting matters beyond the influence of the parties concerned. On matters of appeal, a commercial appeal circuit was established in Sana'a, the capital, and acted as an intermediate court.

There were other reasons besides judicial ones for setting up the commercial courts, including in particular the pace of economic change. This was determined by the transformation from subsistence agriculture to a cash economy and the consequent partial integration of the country into the international economy. Yemen began to seek foreign participation in economic investment, and efficient and speedy litigation was one of the main incentives for prospective investors. (This is why commercial courts are known in some countries as the 'investment judiciary'.)

Commercial courts: a success and a model for others

As noted above, the main aims in establishing commercial courts as a partly separate judicial institution were to set an example that would be followed by the regular courts, to discourage any delaying tactics in the due processes of the law, and thereby to enhance the performance of the judiciary as a whole. The concept of the commercial courts was not meant to diminish anything of good quality in the old system, whether in the *shari'a* itself or in relation to the judges who administered *shari'a*. The bill introducing commercial law was discussed and consented to by some of the best-qualified judges in *shari'a*, and the first judge appointed to a commercial court was chosen from among the senior judges versed in *shari'a*. Even so, resistance to reform and intrigue against any kind of judicial reform continued, although the evident success of the commercial courts kept the opponents quiescent for a time.

This early success was due to many factors. First, judges were well paid and received other work-related benefits, such as accommodation, transportation and incidental expenses. Secondly, the court buildings were well chosen for judicial functioning. Thirdly, judges were well protected from interference from litigants and from the judicial and/or political hierarchy; at the same time they were held accountable by means of inspection and reports. Indeed, they were immune from corruption to the extent that very few instances of attempted bribery were actually reported to me. For the first time in Yemen, litigation rates and dutiable charges were collected by law, and covered all the running costs of the courts. Commercial court judges were pleased and proud when foreign courts started quoting their rulings. There were even calls in Egypt for courts to be established on the Yemen model.[2]

The new guard takes over: segregation or affiliation?

In many developing countries, including Yemen, important matters often depend on personalities rather than on institutions. Thus, when a new incumbent takes over responsibility for a governmental body he generally has a certain freedom to apply his theories since there are very few binding regulations and institutions to check and balance his deeds and actions.

This happened in Yemen when a new government was formed at the end of the 1970s. The new guard ended the semi-independence of the commercial courts from the decaying judiciary, first by creating a first degree of appeal, thus killing off the notion of speedy litigation in commercial matters, and secondly by decreeing that the Supreme Court was to have the final say. With all due respect, this was the last court equipped to deal with worldly concepts of commerce and investment. Thirdly, the State Office for Legal Affairs, which had temporarily administered the commercial courts, suggested, in good faith, the transfer of their administration to the Ministry of Justice, provided that all the work structures and related facilities were maintained. In the event none of these provisos was met. Instead the commercial courts were amalgamated with the regular courts and all the good work that had been done was swallowed up by the decaying system.

This raised the theoretical question as to whether courts needed to be segregated or affiliated – i.e. whether the good courts should be detached from those that required reform, given the length of time that this would take. Such separation would be temporary until reform had succeeded and all courts could be united under one judicial administration. Alternatively the regular courts and the newly created

[128]

commercial, administrative and constitutional courts could affiliate under one administration and one High Court, whether or not it was qualified to deal with new concepts of law and its institutions.

In countries where the judiciary functions well and according to law, the idea of a unified judiciary is simple, and indeed preferable, but in a country like Yemen, amalgamating modern and efficient courts with traditional and inefficient ones tends to lead to the former becoming 'infected' with all the ills of the latter. However, although separate or segregated courts may not represent the ideal, as a means of gradual reform it is worth trying, given that overall reform is likely to take a very long time to achieve.

The slow death of the commercial courts

The beginning of the end of the commercial courts was marked by ignorant and unsympathetic acts deliberately performed and designed to undermine their specific functions. The final blow came when the Supreme Council appointed judges, the majority of whom had no knowledge whatsoever of commercial, financial or investment matters. In addition the Court of Appeal in Sana'a declared that all commercial suits would be dealt with by its civil law circuit. From these moves, observers deduced that there was a fight behind the scenes to take over the commercial courts and to enlarge the payoffs of certain circles. It was pointed out to those jurists who opposed the functioning of the commercial courts that the Egyptian government, which had embarked on a drive to encourage investment, had started to set up special commercial litigation units. But in Yemen, where the government, while claiming support for economic reforms, lacked enthusiasm for the institutions needed to support them, those in the judiciary with vested interests had the first say and the upper hand.

It is unfortunate that the commercial courts that had previously excelled in their performance went into decline during the 1980s. But there is usually light after darkness, and at the end of 1996 the World Bank suddenly started to press the government to see that there were regular or special courts to deal equitably and speedily with legal suits concerning investment and credits. The government's initial plan was to create new courts for settling financial disputes but at the last moment it was persuaded to revive the remnants of the commercial courts since these were matters that concerned investment and commerce as a whole.

New decrees were therefore passed to give the commercial courts a degree of administrative and financial independence.

However the old guard saw to it that judges from among their ranks were nominated to the restored courts. Other more competent judges did not fall into the trap and thus refused appointment. Thus the last attempt to save the commercial courts was doomed to failure and the reformers had to start thinking of another way out, turning this time to the idea of arbitration.

Arbitration as a partial remedy for judicial ills

Seeing that the task of reforming the judiciary system with separate or affiliated courts had become almost impossible, the financiers started to think about referring their disputes to pre- or post-arranged arbitration. Next, jurists within and outside governmental bodies embarked on a campaign for legislating for and setting in motion the process of arbitration, as well as for setting up centres for that purpose.

There are certain advantages for the parties to a dispute to refer it to arbitration rather than to take action through the courts. These include the following:

- the process can be advantageous;
- details of the subject matter can be kept relatively unpublicised;
- when the dispute concerns a technical matter, those chosen to arbitrate generally possess the appropriate professional qualifications;
- the parties choose, or agree to, the applicable laws and rules of procedure;
- there can be cost savings;
- the parties are able to consider the time and place of arbitration to suit themselves.

In Yemen the statutory definition of arbitration is: 'the voluntary choice of two parties, another person or other persons, other than the competent court, to arbitrate their differences and disputes'. This kind of generalised definition helps those involved to think of arbitration as if it was conciliation or a sort of tribal arbitration by custom. Conciliation or mediation in Yemen does not need a written agreement, and on the whole the conciliators are individuals who do not necessarily have to be versed in law or even specialised in one or another field of knowledge. No specific procedure, written or otherwise, is followed, and unless the conciliator or conciliators are men of power and authority, the decision of the conciliator is often ignored.

On the other hand, tribally affiliated Yemenis think of arbitration, whether commercial or otherwise, as belonging to the domain of customary norms (*al-'araf*). It is known among tribes that there are commonly enunciated and accepted norms – both of behaviour and for the settling of disputes. An approximate definition of the term 'custom' as observed by the tribes views customary law (*'urf*) as the body of accepted unformulated rules and principles established by human conduct over time and in accordance with accepted criteria, and forming part of the inherent sources of law (cf. Twining and Miers, 1982). There were therefore attempts in Yemen to introduce some of these rules into the laws and regulations governing arbitration.

Misconceived and thwarted attempts

When Law No. 33 on Arbitration was promulgated in 1981 in Sana'a it included a few rules on conciliation and a great many rules on tribal customs. As with conciliation, the law did not mention the applicable legislation or stipulate procedural rules to be followed in arbitration. Article 22 of the law envisaged a binding decision 'by the conciliator' but generally spoke of the 'arbitrator' rather than a 'conciliator'. Concerning tribunals, Article A made it a condition that if an arbitrator was not familiar with the *shari'a* he should be familiar with tribal customary rules. Article 6 went further in envisaging a situation where the entire tribe would be the arbitrators, Article 16 tackled cases of manslaughter and sedition, and Article 24 left the handing of the verdict to the guarantors of enforcement.

The relevant statutory law governing arbitration was thus a blending of traditional rules of conciliation, tribal customs, *shari'a* and modern provisions, and as such was born dead. However, although arbitration (under different names) has always been practised in Yemen as an alternative to ordinary litigation, no official arbitration tribunals were set up, apart from some quasi-judicial committees on tax and customs tariffs. And although the law allowed the Chamber of Commerce to establish a tribunal for settling commercial disputes, the Chamber of Commerce never took advantage of this privilege.

It is interesting to note that in Aden, under British rule, an arbitration ordinance was promulgated as early as 19 March 1941. It concerned voluntary arbitration that allowed any court to halt proceedings whenever there was a valid submission. Once filed in court an award was enforceable as if it was a decree of the court (Article 13); however, the court could set the award aside if it had been improperly procured (Article 13).

Calls for economic reform

Yemen, like any other underdeveloped country, progressed to some extent through most of the requisite economic conditions for a comparatively modern state – development of a non-agricultural society, an influx of Arab and Western capital and entrepreneurs, and development of light industry. It was, however, hindered by various political and economic factors that threatened its antiquated financial policy and also its political stability.

Since the mid-1990s the government has battled with the planned economic and administrative reforms, and has succeeded in regaining some control of the financial situation, though not of the overall economic situation, where reforms were achieved at the expense of the poor and the middle class in the short term. However, for political and other reasons the government has been reluctant to press ahead with administrative and judicial reforms.

To attract both Arab and non-Arab foreign capital, in particular for investment purposes, the government established a semi-independent Public Authority for Investment in the early 1990s which adopted a law that was reasonably welcoming to investors, Yemenis and foreigners alike. However, one of Yemen's economic problems has been that local entrepreneurs preferred to establish limited family companies, and the banks were not brave enough to back long-term enterprises. In addition there was a lot of unused capital funding in the country because of the lack of joint-stock public companies. The great need to attract foreign capital will, however, have to wait for concrete guarantees and facilities. As the World Bank's initial demands indicated, the first requirement was, if possible, to establish an independent and efficient regular judiciary, if not a specialised system of courts to deal with commercial and financial disputes. Failing this it was desirable to achieve any kind of legal system that could settle disputes swiftly and impartially.

Law No. 22 (1992): a leap forward

Attempts by the government authorities to respond to the first requirement were inconclusive; their response to the second was favourable but only partly successful. They did, however, decide to take a short cut to the settling of disputes by replacing the old Yemen Arab Republic legislation and promulgating a new statute on arbitration; this was done by issuing Law No. 22 in 1992. Overall this was a diligent piece of legal work, though it did have certain pitfalls, as indicated in the following sections (cf. also Al-Hubaishi, 1997a).

The Arbitration Agreement

Unlike arbitration laws elsewhere in the region, Article 2 of Yemen's Law No. 22 (1992) defined arbitration according to the 'place' and not to the 'party'. In addition the law did not expressly declare the need for mentioning the subject-matter under dispute in the agreement. This unintentional omission was subsequently amended by Article 15 of Law No. 33 (1997).

Arbitration and tribunal

Ignoring an obvious and well-used term found in similar legislations, the legislator replaced 'tribunal' with the word 'committee'. Furthermore, paragraph 1 of Article 22 allowed the competent court to select the sole arbitrator without giving the parties any choice, and the law also allowed the parties to elect two arbitrators without an intermediary, contrary to arbitration usage. Worse than that, Article 6 specified certain qualifications for arbitrators, such as 'just' and 'eligible' – *shari'a* terms which were legally ambiguous and which required time and knowledge to explain.

Procedure and applicable law

Article 33 did not go into detail on the equal nature of the parties and assistants before the tribunal: 'such parties should not be excluded without good grounds or the award may be set aside'. Furthermore, in the case of a motion to remove an arbitrator, the request was to be forwarded to the tribunal, although in corresponding laws the request was to be sent to the court. Article 45 did not differentiate between the applicable laws with regard to merit and procedure.

The award

The law did not consider the case of the parties re-petitioning the tribunal on a merit that had been ignored by the arbitration, nor did Yemeni legislators grant a *res judicat* to the award in spite of an action for nullity. Furthermore the law did not expressly stipulate that the award had to comply with the submission.[3] Nor did it require that the making of the award had to be delegated to another person, stating only that 'a legal adviser may draw up the award'.[4]

Other comments and legal arguments concerning the execution of Law 22 could also be put forward, but none of these or the foregoing points should in any way denigrate the serious attempt by the policy maker to enact an up-to-date piece of legislation (Hubaishi, 1997b). The removal of certain provisions that make non-Yemenis hesitant about referring disputes to the judiciary or to arbitration in Yemen would, however, be advisable. They are reluctant to invest capital in Yemen, and when contracting a deal, will often stipulate that legal action takes place outside Yemen and that the law applied, whether to merit, interpretation or procedure, should be other than Yemeni law. In addition, if Yemen wants foreign capital and investment it is high time to begin negotiating for accession to international agreements for settlement of investment disputes and execution of foreign awards.

Arbitration tribunals in the making

Some years ago, Yemen had no official ad hoc tribunals in the relevant ministries. The State Legal Office (now the Ministry of Legal and Parliamentary Affairs), which was set up in the 1970s, established quasi-judicial committees to arbitrate customs tariffs, tax disputes and labour disputes. Since 1997, however, there has been an awareness of the importance of arbitration, and a group of jurists and other professionals, in cooperation with the Association of Banks and Chambers of Commerce, founded the Yemeni Centre for Conciliation and Arbitration (YCCA). So far this organisation has been doing well. Individual lawyers have also followed the lead of the YCCA and have established their own centres, while another organisation has been set up mainly for settling tribunal disputes.

In the long run, however, the problem of lack of efficiency in the judiciary will not be solved by the promotion of commercial courts or the formation of arbitration tribunals. What will count is a persistent effort to make the three institutions run efficiently, either as a unified institution or as parallel organisations.

Prospects for litigation in Yemen
Current struggles for legal reform
On the surface it seems that the struggle for judicial reform is between the old guard and the new, between traditionally oriented learning and the graduates of new universities, and between the sacred scriptures and secular legislation. It also falls between judgments handwritten on lengthy scrolls and electronically printed verdicts, and lastly between the concepts of a non-territorial Islamic *umma* and those circumscribed by the contemporary nation-state.

In fact around a third of those who oppose reform are concerned about losing their vested interests and possibly their jobs at the same time. A further third of the opposition consists of those who find it very difficult to deal with a new body of law, even if it is codified rules of the *shari'a*, not to mention the complicated rules of procedure and execution of judgments, and the system of separate jurisdictions of criminal, civil and sometimes commercial courts. There are also other issues of constitutional and administrative issues, or for instance, maritime concerns.

Most of those who oppose reform – i.e. a third or more of the personnel of the judiciary – do not care either way. They behave as typical civil servants, as passive observers who will join the victors when the battle has ended. In this context, however, it is not correct to classify jurists and their stand on reform according to their academic background and whether they acquired their knowledge at the local mosque or at a foreign university, or whether they wear the traditional turban or not. The writer is personally acquainted with jurists from the first category who are able to coexist with reform and some of whom have joined the ranks of the reformers. On the other hand there are certain university graduates who strongly oppose any reform for reasons of cultural background or political partisanship.

Economic, administrative or judicial reforms
Which of the above-mentioned subjects should be considered as a priority for reform? Few planners consider the problem, and the government

itself, being particularly occupied with the economic crisis identified by the World Bank, has been too busy with day-to-day challenges to answer the question. Apart from the dilemma resulting from inflation, the government has performed fairly well in dealing with economic or financial exigencies but, other than some discussion, has given little time or attention to administrative reform (perhaps to avoid disturbing the political balance). Nor has it had much time for reforming the judiciary, and, despite much rustling of government papers, nothing concrete had been achieved by the beginning of 1998. The authorities may feel that judicial reform is not a high priority or that other socioeconomic problems need to be disentangled first. The opposition is critical of the government's performance but, apart from politicising every judicial issue, has no specific reform programmes or plans of its own.

The university-trained lawyers and the *shari'a* judges who call for reform may differ among themselves as to ways and means of reform but are all of the opinion that reform of the judiciary cannot wait. The government considers that economic matters come first but how can the relevant ministries apply laws and settle disputes with regard to customs tariffs, taxes, investment, trade, tourism and all sorts of other economic and financial matters without reform of the judicial system? This argument also applies to administrative reform, which requires conforming to law and order and abiding by court rulings. All in all, reformers believe that reform of the judiciary, the administration and the economy should be dealt with concurrently.

Conclusion

No country can deal with everyday or long-terms problems and questions without a proper and impartial judiciary. If the regular courts and their administrations do not function as such, then specialised courts for urgent needs should be established. Yemen's experiment with commercial courts proved successful for a certain period. If the country has no alternative solutions for the inept and inefficient judiciary, then perhaps the constitutional and administrative courts should also be detached before the contagion of the regular courts affects them.

At the same time Yemen needs the law, system and institution of arbitration, since this is likely to become increasingly important and popular in the future, for reasons that include the country's growing need for investment. Arbitration also gives an opportunity to disputing parties to reject the law or the judges that they do not want.

Generally speaking, the judicial system in Yemen, which still lacks many substances, devices and facilities, needs laws (commercial and penal) that do not contradict each other, and judges who are kept up to date through post-qualification courses and who are not isolated from developments in legislation and litigation. It also needs acceptability and the means for due processes of law, as well as such practicalities as trained court clerks, archives and filing systems, and procedures for inspection.

The main crisis of the judiciary, however, is the fact that most of those responsible for it do not admit that there is a crisis. If asked how the system is functioning, the old guard will respond that 90 per cent of it is excellent and the new guard will reply that 90 per cent of it is bad, an interesting agreement as to the figure but not the substance. The judiciary, in which is vested the constitutional authority of the state, needs above all the will of the ruling circles and the ability to save itself from interference from the executive, from the distorting laws issued by the legislative authority, and from the private prejudices of judges.[5]

A modern or new Yemen means new responsibilities. Yemen is endeavouring to preserve its unity, to promote its newly gained democracy, and to achieve prosperity for its people. However, those aspirations and responsibilities need to be safeguarded and the most effective protection is justice, which 'drives us to action whenever an instance of injustice affronts our sight'.[6] Yemen requires justice with a judiciary adaptable to changing national needs.

NOTES

1 Independent reasoning with regard to religious issues.
2 Dr N. Omar of Alexandria University, quoted in Hubaishi, 1988: 158ff.).
3 See Gatliff v. Dunn, 1738, and Johnson v. Latham, 1850.
4 Cf. re Underwood and Bedford Ry, 1861.
5 Chief Justice E. Warren, cited in Enid Marshall (ed.), Gill, *The Law of Arbitration*, 3rd edn, London: Sweet and Maxwell, 1973 and 20th edn of Russel.
6 Public papers of Chief Justice Earl Warren, edited by Henry M. Christman, Capricorn Books, New York, 1996, p. 123.

7

Yemeni Judicial History
as Political History, 1970–97[1]

Anna Würth

Introduction

Unification of the Yemen Arab Republic (YAR) and the People's Democratic Republic of Yemen (PDRY) generated a lively debate about the development of democracy and the rule of law (*siyadat al-qanun*). The role of the judiciary was central to the debate, and was part of the international, post-1990 discourse on democracy, human rights, civil society, economic liberalisation and good governance. However, there was also a home-grown debate that arose both from the increasing juridification of social and political relationships, as reflected in a steadily rising number of court cases,[2] and from the confrontation and unification of two very different legal and judicial systems and traditions in the North and in the South. This debate continues to be a lively one, and is subject to party politics. This chapter will look particularly at the institutional development of the judiciary in Yemen and its political implications, based on developments in the former YAR and the Republic of Yemen (RoY) (for developments in the former PDRY see Shamiry, 1995: 175–94).

Separation of powers is a concept that is central to the principles of modern government. It presupposes, and also results in, de facto and de jure power-sharing between the executive, legislative and judicial branches of government, and ideally the independence of the latter effectively controls the former (on this subject see, *inter alia*, Mayer, 1991). However, power is not easily ceded, and in most states the judicature must perpetually wrest power from the other branches of government which generally try to avoid power-sharing and reject judicial control, preferring to use the judiciary for their own political ends (cf. Shapiro, 1981). Yemen is no exception to this rule.

Legal and judicial reforms in the YAR during the 1970s illustrate the powers granted to the judicature. In order to grasp the significance of the reforms and of the subsequent developments of the 1990s, one needs to understand the educational background of legal professionals. I argue that during the 1990s the judiciary – or at least part of it – has systematically attempted to exercise the constitutional function previously denied to it. This effort can be explained, among other factors, by a change in the composition and education of the judiciary. The relevant legislation, the Programmes for Judicial Reform in 1979 and in 1997, and some recent judgments in administrative law, will be used to illustrate this.

Legal and judicial development during the 1970s

Legal development in the Yemen Arab Republic before the mid-1970s was diffuse but existed nevertheless. Between 1962 and 1970 six constitutions were enacted (for an overview of constitutional development until 1991, see Tarbush, 1993: 145–212), and a large number of new state institutions were established. Legislation in basic civil, penal and family matters was issued in 68 ordinances (*qararat*) by the Ministry of Justice in 1971 (on legislation at this period see Al-'Alimi, 1989: 131–63; for Ministry of Justice ordinances see Al-'Amrani, 1984: 233–44). These ordinances were in essence the codification of Yemeni judicial practice as it had been during the Imamate, and were partly based on judgments of the Imamic Supreme Court of Cassation (*al-mahkama al-isti'nafiyya al-'ulya*), established in 1911.[3] These precedent decisions, together with legal opinions (*ikhtiyarat*) of Imam Yahya and Imam Ahmad (1904–62) (to be found in abbreviated form in Al-'Alimi, 1989: 258–9; and Haykel, 1997: 380–2), and the works of Islamic jurisprudence did not assume the shape of law codes but seem to have functioned as such for all practical purposes.[4] By the mid-1970s, however, this legal framework had proved to be incapable of coping with the structural transformations that were taking place in the Yemeni economy and society (for a comprehensive account of economic change in the 1970s and 1980s see Chaudhry, 1997; and Carapico, 1998: 33ff.).

Between 1975 and 1977 major pieces of legislation in commercial and procedural law were therefore passed. Even though this period has been dubbed a 'legislative awakening' (*al-nahda al-tashri'iyya*), thus linking it to the efforts of the prominent Egyptian jurist 'Abd al-Razzaq Al-Sanhuri (Hill, 1987),[5] the Yemeni 'legislative awakening' by-passed the legislature. Parliament was suspended in 1974, and this led to a political stalemate (cf. Burrowes, 1987: 57–94; Peterson, 1982: 113–35; Carapico, 1998: 33ff., 118ff.), as a result of which most laws were passed by presidential decree. This practice has since become a well-established tradition, familiar in other states as well.[6]

Most of the laws enacted during this early period were prepared by the Law Office (*al-maktab al-qanuni*), which was established in 1968, whereas the Codification Commission (*hai'at taqnin ahkam al-shari'a al-islamiyya*) was set up only in 1975.[7] The commission prepared legislation in the core areas of Islamic jurisprudence and, *inter alia*, codified the laws of endowment, proof, and the family, as well as the civil code.

As noted, the Law Office and the Codification Commission were different institutions, staffed with different types of jurists and dealing with different areas of legal expertise. The Law Office was attached to the Presidential Office, and became the Ministry of Legal and Parliamentary Affairs in the 1980s. Staffed mainly by technocrats and university-trained jurists, it drafted laws on institution-building and procedural laws, frequently adapting legislation from other Arab states, and thus from European (mostly French) law. The Codification Commission, on the other hand, was initially independent, institutionally speaking, though obliged to present draft laws to parliament. Its task was to prepare legislation in substantive law, and to adapt Yemeni judicial practice as well as Yemeni legal traditions, both Zaydi and Shafi'i, since according to Article 2.2 of Law 7/1975, it was bound to Islamic jurisprudence but not to any particular school of law (YAR Law Office, n.d.(a): 329). However, when a new legislature (*al-majlis al-ta'sisi*) was appointed in 1978, one of its committees assumed the role of the former Codification Commission (Al-Fadli, n.d.: 32).

The Codification Commission and the later Codification Committee in the legislature were dominated by jurists who had been trained under the Imamic system and who had been active as judges, teachers of law and in government service.[8] However, this split in legislation and in the legal profession was to last for only two decades and is destined to disappear. Thus, as will be discussed below, most legislation based on an adaptation of foreign law has now been amended to fit Yemeni circumstances, and nowadays the majority of judges in office have a university education.

One of the important laws passed during the 1970s was Law 23/1976 on Judicial Authority (YAR Ministry of Justice, n.d.: 145–76). The Imamic system in force until that time had a two-tiered system of courts, consisting of first instance courts in the provinces and the Supreme Court of Cassation in Sana'a. The first instance courts enjoyed general jurisdiction without any limitations. However, there were judges in administrative positions in such areas as endowments, the military, customs etc. (cf. Al-'Alimi 1989: 151).[9]

The new law of 1976, which was taken almost verbatim from the 1972 Egyptian law of Judicial Authority (Botiveau, 1986: 81–113) changed this judicial organisation completely by introducing functionally specialised jurisdiction. Henceforth the jurisdiction of lower courts was to be restricted to small civil claims, while the control of higher courts over lower courts was tightened by introducing the previously unknown courts of appeal. This was followed by the setting up of commercial courts, and an evaluation of commercial law decisions was published with the intention of making the commercial courts into model courts for judicial reform (YAR Law Office, 1979). It was intended that this functional differentiation of courts would serve two interrelated goals. The specialisation and increased 'hierarchisation' of courts would simultaneously strengthen inner judicial control and legal security since, by introducing the principle of appeal, cases could be retried by collegiate tribunals. In this way cases would be submitted to judicial scrutiny, not only on points of law but also on points of fact, and this would produce a more unified interpretation of the social facts and relationships at issue in court cases. Simultaneously, the growth in the unified application of law would also lead to greater legal security, which was essential for the centralising and consolidating of state power that had been striven for since the mid-1970s.

For several reasons, this Egyptian model (itself inspired by French judicial organisation) proved to be a failure in Yemen. The commercial courts did not turn into model courts, but instead remained as ordinary courts (see the contribution by Al-Hubaishi in the present volume). In the other courts, the principle of restricted jurisdiction could not be enforced, first because the law itself was not sufficiently clear, and secondly because parties and judges alike could not be convinced of the new system: nor, as the Ministry of Justice itself admitted, was much effort made to alter this (YAR Ministry of Justice, 1980a: 64).

For this reason, a new law on judicial authority that revived the pre-1976 organisation of courts was passed in 1979 (Law 28/1979); in theory this has prevailed ever since. The post-unification law on judicial authority (Law 1/1991) granted unlimited jurisdiction in civil, penal and family matters to the courts of first instance. Only the commercial courts and the courts of appeal remained outside these attempts at functional differentiation.

Two other elements of Egyptian judicial policy were applied with more success in Yemen – namely, the by-passing of parliament and legislation by decree – and resulted in the establishment of extra-judicial courts in the mid-1970s. Military courts were set up under the adminis-tration of the military, as was the state security court; this had been established in 1965 and was legally regulated in the mid-1970s.[10] The executive's obvious mistrust of the judiciary was reflected in the attempt to deprive the latter of jurisdictional authority in sensitive areas. This lack of trust in the judiciary becomes even more transparent when one examines the judicial institutions that were potentially able to impede legislative and executive powers and decisions.

The constitution of 1970 had provided for parliament to elect a Supreme Constitutional Court with broadly defined judicial and legislative powers: it also allowed for the establishment of administrative courts. Theoretically, these two institutions can be the most powerful instruments of judicial control in modern states. In practice, however, neither of these was established in Yemen. The Yemeni Court of Cassation was granted jurisdiction in constitutional matters, but had fewer powers than the originally planned Supreme Constitutional Court. Nor were its judges elected by parliament, as envisaged for the Supreme Constitutional Court. No administrative courts were established at all, and administrative cases have continued to be heard at the courts of first instance or at the Supreme Court of Cassation.

The so-called Supreme Judicial Council (*majlis al-qada' al-a'la*) was also in line with the Egyptian system. In principle, this council safeguards the professionalism and independence of the judiciary, and is responsible for the nomination and rotation of judges: it should therefore be a purely judicial institution. In practice, however, and again following the Egyptian model, the president of the Republic is the head of this

Council, and consequently has a potentially direct influence on the nomination of judges.[11]

Certain elements of Egyptian-French judicial policy were thus easily adapted in the Yemen Arab Republic. They served the government's need to concentrate and centralise power in a much more immediate fashion than the attempts at functional differentiation of the judicial system as described above.

The result of these policies was that, by the end of the 1970s, the executive had managed to pull out of certain areas of judicial control, while the judicature itself had rather limited channels through which to control the actions of the executive and the legislature.

Developments in the legal profession between the 1970s and the 1990s

Institutionally the judicial set-up did not change very much in the 1990s. Although some functionally differentiated courts, including Maritime Courts, Courts for Public Property, and Custom Courts, were established in the mid-1990s, by 1998 there were no separate administrative courts (for an overview, see Shamiri, 1995: 236–45). Despite institutional continuity, though, the composition of the legal profession has changed profoundly – it has, however, remained a male preserve. Although some women judges work in the Southern Provinces (Carapico, 1998: 197, 200), the Judicial Institute in Sana'a have not yet accepted female candidates. There is a tiny but increasing number of women lawyers, and while only a very small minority of law students at Sana'a university were women, almost half the Law Faculty students at Aden University in 1987/8 were female (PDRY, CSO, 1990: 92).

The change in the composition of the profession is first of all a question of numbers. It was estimated that in 1972 there were about 250 trained judges in the YAR (see Al-Abdin, 1975: 189). By 1989, the Judicial Institute in Sana'a had trained 200 new judges, and by 1997 there were around 100 judges in Sana'a alone (RoY, 1997b: 56; RoY, 1989: 102). Furthermore, the number of law graduates has multiplied. In the academic year 1996/7 the Faculty of Law at the University of Sana'a had more than 15,000 students, compared with only 300 students 20 years earlier (RoY, 1997a; YAR, CPO, n.d.: 229; and cf. Al-'Alimi, 1989: 176).

Members of the legal profession can be divided into the following groups, according to their educational background:

- A small minority of jurists has been trained in modern law abroad, mainly in Egypt, Iraq, Syria, the United Kingdom, the former USSR, and the US. Most are professional lawyers, either in private law firms or in governmental departments. Only a small number of judges have been professionally educated abroad, and all seem to be from the former PDRY.

- Much more numerous are the jurists who have acquired their education in Yemen. They can be subdivided into three groups, differing in both age and education.

  (1) Jurists born before the 1940s – who are now in their 60s, if not older – dominated the legal profession, the codification committees, and the judiciary during the 1970s and early 1980s. Trained in the Judicial Academy (*al-madrasa al-ʿilmiyya*, 1925–64) or at comparable institutions in the provinces, they studied Islamic jurisprudence and related sciences.[12] Many have continued to follow legal developments closely and thus also have a solid knowledge of the codified laws of the Republic of Yemen. Many also have a long family tradition in law, working in the judiciary, teaching law, and working in governmental service. Today, this group of jurists is employed in the Ministries of Justice and Endowments, the Supreme Court, and the Codification Committees in the respective legislatures. While many still held judgeships in the early 1990s, they are gradually being pensioned off.

  (2) The second group of jurists, the most numerous in the contemporary RoY, has university training at Sanaʿa or Aden through a four- or five-year programme that concentrates on a background of codified law and Islamic jurisprudence (for curricular development in the Sanaʿa Law Faculty see Al-ʿAlimi, 1989: 174–94). Between 25 and 50 years of age, they generally work as professional lawyers, either in private law firms or with governmental departments.

  (3) Members of the third group have acquired a diploma from the Judicial Institute (*al-maʿhad al-ʿaliy li'l-qadaʾ*, established in 1983) after a two- or three-year training course. The Judicial

Institute was designed to educate judges in judicial administration and special areas of law, but in practice functions as a more general training institution for aspiring judges.[13] The Institute's training programme places a strong emphasis on Islamic jurisprudence, the assumption being that students already have a background in codified law.[14] During the early 1980s some individuals were admitted without previous university studies, having acquired their initial legal education in mosques or by private tutoring, but now most graduates have also acquired a university degree before entering the Institute. By 1991, admission to the judiciary was restricted to those holding both a university degree and a degree from the Judicial Institute,[15] and as a result the majority of judges have a solid background in Islamic jurisprudence and codified Yemeni law.[16] Currently most courts of first instance are staffed by graduates of the Institute who are between 30 and 50 years of age.

The end result is that, generally speaking, lawyers are trained mainly in codified law, while two generations of jurists are represented in the judiciary. Most of the older generation was trained in Islamic jurisprudence, while the younger generation has been trained in both Islamic jurisprudence and codified law, and holds degrees from the Judicial Institute as well as a university.

In general, Yemeni jurists seem to have more training in Islamic jurisprudence than do jurists in other Arab countries. This indeed is to be expected, given that the laws in force have consistently retained a closer relationship to Islamic jurisprudence than is common in other Middle Eastern republican states. The younger generation of judges is currently employed in the courts of first instance, and many have recently been promoted to the courts of appeal. Thus it is only in the Supreme Court that the number of judges who also graduated from a university remained limited in the late 1990s. However, this is simply a question of time; for instance, in July 1998 some younger university-educated judges were nominated to the Supreme Court (*Al-Qistas*, June 1998: 7), and the trend seems likely to continue.

Judicial reform in the 1990s

Unification in 1990 raised many hopes among Yemenis, including the expectation that the judiciary would safeguard constitutional guarantees, such as press freedom, and prevent the arbitrary infringement by government of individual liberties. The judiciary was widely criticised by the public for allegedly being inefficient, corrupt and slow (*Sawt Al-'Ummal*, 17 January 1994; *Al-Thawri*, 3 February 1994; *Al-Mustaqbal*, 8 December 1991, 6 February 1994; *Al-Shura*, 23 November 1997, 30 November 1997, 7 December 1997). Such criticisms had been voiced since the late 1970s, but the tone sharpened as political tensions rose following unification in 1990.

One response to this political and popular pressure was the founding in 1991 of a professional association, the Judges' Club (*al-muntada al-qadha'i*). The aim of the Club was to organise the professional interests of judges and to function as a forum for discussions. Its goals were to raise educational and ethical standards, and by way of commentary and research to involve judges in the codification effort (Al-Muntada al-qada'i, 1991, 1992). However, the success of the association as a pressure group was limited. Two unsuccessful strikes in 1992 and early 1993 had called respectively for higher wages and increased security, and as the economic crisis escalated, attacks on judges by litigants did in fact increase (*Al-Thawra*, 15 February 1993; *Al-Sahwa*, 14 October 1993; *Al-Shura*, 24 August 1997). The pay rise was achieved only in late 1994, in which year the long-awaited promotion of judges was also carried out (cf. interview with 'Abd al-Wahhab ad-Dailami, Minister of Justice 1994–97, in *Al-Sahwa*, 29 December 1994).

Judges also discussed the consequences of the new 1994 constitution. Officially, this was promulgated as an amended constitution. However, since it completely changed the governmental system and also abandoned some of the basic rights and liberties of the 1991 constitution, there is some justification for speaking of 'the new constitution of 1994' (on the respective discussions see Al-Saqqaf, 1993: 149–62; Glosemeyer, 1995: 18–29, 164–70). This 'new constitution' increased judicial powers by defining judicial independence administratively, financially and judicially.[17] The *raison d'être* of the Ministry of Justice and the Supreme Judicial Council had therefore to be reconsidered. In April 1995 a committee was set up to amend Law 1/1991 on judicial authority in the light of constitutional developments (Shamiri 1995: 236; cf. also RoY, 1997c:

8ff., 19f., 22–5; and for a draft law on judicial authority see *Al-Qistas*, June 1998, 38–41).

The Judicial Reform Programme submitted by the Minister of Justice in December 1997 meticulously elaborated on the current system, both theoretically and practically; however, the suggested solutions are modest. Instead of changing the composition of the Supreme Judicial Council and abolishing the Ministry of Justice, which had been two of the earlier suggestions,[18] the programme merely advocated the more precise regulation of their powers (RoY, 1997c: 14, 20, 25).

Discussions on institutional guarantees of judicial independence have been accompanied by major developments in constitutional and administrative case law. The constitutional division of the Supreme Court was thus turned into an important forum for legislative and political development, especially between 1990 and 1994. In 1992, the division heard a case on the constitutionality of draft laws, and decided that its jurisdiction covered only questions concerning the constitutionality of laws passed by parliament and not of those presented as drafts to parliament. In 1993, the court decided a case in which the constitutionality of one article of the Elections Law 41/1992 and its interpretation by the Supreme Elections Committee (*al-lajna al-'ulya li'l-intikhabat*) was at issue. The Supreme Court's opinion was increasingly sought as a means of establishing guidelines for interpreting the relevant laws and the constitution (for the decisions in these cases see Mallat, 1995: 71–91).

Developments in administrative law are less obvious and attract less attention than those in constitutional case law. However, the non-establishment of administrative courts resulted in a number of interesting cases in which jurisdiction in administrative cases was disputed between the courts of first instance and the Supreme Court.

In 1996, a case was brought against the Supreme Election Committee claiming that the guidelines and programme for the elections issued by the Committee violated the provisions of the Elections Law. The defendant pleaded that the case needed to be heard at the Supreme Court, since the matter seemed to hinge on the interpretation of the Elections Law. However, this argument was not accepted by the court of first instance. Maintaining that the disputed guidelines and programme were not laws but administrative guidelines, the court of first instance claimed jurisdiction on the grounds that the jurisdiction of the Supreme Court was limited to the interpretation and constitutionality of laws.[19]

The same problem of jurisdiction was raised in another case when a member of parliament, 'Abd al-Habib Muqbil, challenged the administrative procedures followed by the Board of Parliament in connection with his resignation from office. The judicial reasoning in this case is a useful example for a clear understanding of judicial control. The court first established that the issue was one of jurisdiction, and then examined the question of whether parliament was subject to judicial control. On the basis of the constitution of 1994, which defined the *shari'a* as constituting the only source of legislation,[20] the court quoted evidence from the Qur'an and Hadith to support judicial control over governing agencies, and further claimed that separation of powers was a principle enshrined in the constitution and the laws in force. The court thereby deemed that governmental power was subject to judicial control. As the judge, quoting from an Egyptian law book, expressed it, judicial control was needed if the government's power was not to lose its legitimacy and turn the country 'into a police-state'. The court also expressed its views concerning the extent of judicial control over other governmental branches. It explained that the absence of administrative courts meant that the courts of first instance had full jurisdiction 'in all disputes over the legality of administrative acts, regardless of whether these acts emanate from the executive, legislature or the judicature, as long as they are not of a judicial or legislative nature'.[21]

Both courts declare themselves competent to deal with the administrative acts of leading state institutions, and are openly critical of the failure to establish administrative courts. The presiding judges have therefore insisted on demanding the exercise of their judicial function: their intention is to submit the executive and legislative bodies to judicial control. To achieve this, they use the legal methods they have been educated to employ, and argue on the level of the constitution, Islamic and comparative jurisprudence, and applicable Yemeni legislation.

Some will argue that only a minority of judges has the will and courage to do this, or that this is merely party politics, or that this movement is in any case long overdue. There is some truth in these reservations. It should be remembered, however, that the courage of individual judges has rarely been respected: nor will it be respected as long as the professionalism of judges remains largely ignored in the process of nominating and promoting them. Secondly, it is the educational background of the younger generation of judges which allows them systematically to attempt to control the administrative measures that emerge from governmental agencies. This is not to say that judges trained under the Imamic system were less critical – there are numerous examples of scathing judicial criticism of the abuse of executive power under the Imamate (see, for example, Al-Mu'allimi, 1954 and 1981: 65–120). But today's younger judges have different legal means at their disposal. Separation of powers and the rule of law are principles enshrined in Yemeni legislation and the constitution; and judges can resort to these principles and can in addition reason on the level of Islamic jurisprudence.

During the 1970s, critics argued that because it failed to rely on codified law and specifically disregarded the laws of procedure, the judiciary was thereby prevented from functioning as a third, independent, power. As has been shown, it was in fact quite difficult for the judiciary to operate in the way that it was meant to do. Extra-judicial bodies were established in politically sensitive areas, the nomination of judges was determined by the executive, and the setting up of important judicial institutions was neglected. By the 1990s, however, the situation had changed and it had become the business of the judiciary to remind the other governmental authorities about judicial independence, and of the right of the judicial establishment to control the legislature and the executive.

Even though the Yemeni judiciary continues to be widely criticised for being, among other things, dysfunctional, corrupt and slow, there are elements within it who attempt to exercise their constitutional function. This opens up the judiciary to all kinds of political manipulation, as illustrated in numerous administrative cases raised against the press in which the judiciary had, in fact, to decide on questions of party politics.

It remains to be seen whether the government will respect these developments. There are also a number of questions that are still to be answered. Is there a willingness to accept judicial independence and to share power with the judiciary? Will extra-judicial bodies be brought back into the judicial realm? And will the government bow to judicial control by enforcing judicial decisions, even if it is found that such decisions are contrary to its own goals?

NOTES

1 This contribution draws on the first chapter of my PhD thesis, submitted to the Free University of Berlin (1998).

2 Whereas resort to legal assistance was said to be marginal in most areas of Yemen during the 1970s and 1980s, the population nowadays seems increasingly to turn to the courts, judging by case loads in the Yemeni court system (compare YAR, 1983: 53; RoY, 1997a: 304; and *Al-Qistas*, June 1998: 6).

3 Because of its Arabic name, this court is generally regarded as having been adapted from the Court of Appeal introduced by the Ottomans during their second occupation of Yemen (Messick, 1993: 107, 190f.). However, as the procedural legislation (*al-ta'limat al-sharifa*) issued by Imam Yahya in 1354/1936 reveals (Al-'Alimi 1989: 265–70), this court did not retry cases but reviewed judgements issued by courts of first instance on points of law only. For a selection of later decisions of the courts on penal, civil and family matters see YAR, 1980b.

4 It has often been assumed that uncodified law and the existence of several legal opinions on one matter leads to a non-unified application of law (Coulson, 1969: 24, 38; Messick, 1993: 34f., 56). However, the extent of the unified application of law should be checked against applied law, e.g. court judgments, and not against legal texts (on this debate see Fadel, 1996: 193–233).

5 Al-Sanhuri, the architect of Egyptian civil law and of several other Arab codifications in civil and commercial law, attempted to combine Islamic jurisprudence with modern law. He died in 1975.

6 As with many other Arab constitutions, the Yemeni constitutions of 1970 (art. 88), 1991 (art. 95), and 1994 (art. 119), give the president the right to legislate by decree if the need should arise and if parliament is in recess (Tarbush 1993: 189–90).

7 The 'Permanent Constitution' of 1970 (art. 152) had provided for the establishment of such a body but its formation was delayed until 1975. See Law 7/1975 and Decree 74/1975 on the Establishment of the Codification Commission and Nomination of its Members in YAR, Law Office, n.d.(a): 329.

8 The 1975 Codification Commission was headed by 'Abd al-Qadir 'Abdallah, already a prominent and influential jurist under Imam Ahmad (for biographical information see Zabarah, 1979: 382f., and Al-Akwa', 1995). In general it seems that the respective codification committees were, and to some extent continue to be, dominated by jurists educated under the Imamic system (for the members of the parliamentary codification committees between 1993 and 1997 see Glosemeyer, 1995: 282). Botiveau claims that members of the *Islah* party are increasingly influential in legislative politics but offers no evidence for this assumption (Botiveau, 1996/7: 103–14).

9 The organisation of Yemeni courts under Ottoman and pre-Ottoman rule is entirely unclear and awaits further archival research.

10 For the relevant laws see YAR Law Office, n.d.(b): 213, 237ff.; and YAR Law Office, n.d.(c): 115–57. There was no appeal against judgments of the state security courts, whereas it was possible to appeal to the military division at the Supreme Court against the judgments of military courts. For similar extra-judicial jurisdictions in other Arab states, see Botiveau 1986: 104–8; Al-Taïb, 1995: 123–45, 127f., note 16; and Welchman, 1988: 868–86, 869.

11 Cf. Taïb, 1995: 125, 141f., for a similar situation in Algeria.

12 On the Judicial Academy and its curriculum, see Messick, 1993: 108–14; Al-Akwaʾ, 1986: 400–34. For an exhaustive treatment of these institutions in the provinces, cf. Al-Akwaʾ, 1995.

13 The original idea was to establish an institution for legal specialisation, for example in commercial, administrative and constitutional law (see: YAR, 1980a: 20; Al-ʿAlimi 1989: 181ff.). For many reasons this plan did not materialise. The Judicial Reform Programme of 1997 took up the issue of specialised training of judges again (see RoY, 1997c: 32). For a highly critical and polemic evaluation of the current training activities of the Judicial Institute and the educational level of judges, see Al-Tayyib, 1995: 59–65).

14 For the curriculum of the Judicial Institute and its development see Al-ʿAlimi 1989: 182–4; RoY, 1989: 24–6).

15 For the different criteria for admission to the judiciary see the following Laws on Judicial Authority: 23/1976 (art. 21h); Law 28/1979 (art. 22jim); and Law 1/1991 (art. 57jim).

16 Botiveau (1996/7) errs in assuming that lawyers and judges are educated in different types of law and institutions and that there still exists a significant split between legal education and culture. Judges and lawyers are educated in the same university departments. Because of their additional training at the Institute, judges simply have more education in Islamic jurisprudence and related sciences, including Arabic, than do most lawyers.

17 Constitution 1994, art. 147. Former constitutions had understood the independence of the judiciary to pertain to judicial matters only: see Constitution 1970, arts. 144 and 145; Constitution 1991, art. 120.

18 Author's informal discussions with judges in 1994 and 1995. These suggestions were, of course, connected to party politics and to the struggle between *Al-Islah* and the General People's Congress over control of the Ministry of Justice.

19 South-West Court, Sanaʿa, Muhammad Najiʾ Alaw et al. vs. Supreme Elections Committee, No. 85/1417; 20.2.1417/6.7.1996.

20 Art. 3 of the 1994 constitution is identical to art. 3 of the YAR's Permanent Constitution of 1970. Only in the constitution of 1991 was Islamic jurisprudence considered to be one source of legislation.

21 Western Court, Sanaʿa; ʿAbd al-Habib Muqbil vs. Board of Parliament, No. 6/1415, 3.3.1416/3.8.1995.

PART III

ENVIRONMENT, WATER AND AGRICULTURAL LAND TENURE

8

Practical Responses to Extreme
Groundwater Overdraft in Yemen

Christopher Ward[1]

Yemen's water problem[2]

The principal water problems in Yemen

The chapter looks briefly at Yemen's water resources, and then identifies
three major water management problems that the country has now
to face. Yemen's total annually renewed water resources are estimated at
2.1 billion m³ (BCM), and with a population of around 15.2 million,
available resources thus amount to about 140 m³ per person each year.
This compares with the Middle East and North Africa average of 1,250
m³, and the worldwide average of 7,500 m³. According to worldwide
norms, domestic uses alone require up to 100 m³ per person per year,
and food self-sufficiency requires 1,000 m³. Yemen is thus a dry country,
and can never again be self-sufficient in food. Notable is the prevalence
of groundwater in water resources – 60 per cent of renewed resources
(1.3 BCM) is groundwater recharge.

Since time immemorial Yemen has practised sustainable irrigation
and lived in balance with its resources. The last thirty years or so have
seen a very rapid development of water resources in Yemen, including
the harnessing of a high proportion of surface flows by modern spate
irrigation schemes, and considerable provision of tubewells. Most of
the economically exploitable surface water sources in Yemen are now
harnessed and exploited, and in most areas groundwater is already fully
exploited. The pace of this development has brought with it three main
problems which are briefly discussed in the following paragraphs.

First, groundwater is being mined at such a rate that parts of
the rural economy could disappear within a generation. It is estimated
that there are about 45,000 private wells in the country (although some
estimates are considerably higher) and about 200 drilling rigs (Ward,
1997). In some of the most stressed areas of the country, agriculture is

running out of water. For example, in Wadi Bani Khawlan near Ta'izz, uncontrolled groundwater extraction for agriculture and water sales by upstream riparians have drained the aquifer and led to drying up and the abandonment of agriculture further down the wadi. Shooting incidents over water in the wadi during 1997 confirm the tensions generated by competition for this scarce resource (Moench, 1997).

Second, major cities have grown very short of water. The present main sources of supply to Sana'a – the Eastern and Western Wellfields – which are currently delivering 600 litres per second (lps), are drying up and by 2008 will deliver only 100 lps (Kruseman, 1996). In the summer of 1995, Ta'izz, Yemen's third city, received water once every forty days, a period popularly referred to as 'The Crisis'.

Third, many people, particularly the poor in the cities and the countryside, do not have access to safe water. It is estimated that about 60 per cent of urban households nationwide are connected to mains supply – but often this supply is inadequate. In Sana'a, the public utility supplies little more than a third of households: two-thirds of the water consumed in the capital does not come from a safe public supply, and much comes from shallow wells in contaminated groundwater beneath the city. In rural areas, the most recent estimates put access to safe water at little more than 20 per cent of households. In this contribution, we concentrate on the groundwater problem.

Causes of increased groundwater use

Since the 1970s, Yemen has witnessed very rapid changes, often not matched by development of instruments of governance. The present section analyses how these changes have fuelled a rapid increase in the demand for water and in its supply.

The most obvious change is demographic. The population has doubled in the last twenty years, and Yemen currently has one of the highest rates of increase in the world (3.9 per cent average for the 1990s), which implies that the population will double again in twenty years (World Bank, 2002). Demographic changes have increased demand for water and for goods whose production requires water, particularly agricultural produce. The same changes have contributed to a large increase in the rural population.

A second and related factor on the demand side is the development of markets for cash crops. With the growth of market opportunities, agriculture has developed rapidly. Profitable cash crops have been adopted – particularly fruit, vegetables and, of course, *qat* which has exploded in the last twenty years or so as a social and agricultural phenomenon. The profitability of *qat* can justify irrigation by tankered water (at a cost of over US$1/m³). The development of profitable agricultural markets has increased the incentives to use water.

On the supply side, exploitation of groundwater has been stimulated by new technology. The advent of tractors, chemical inputs and, in particular, tubewell technology has made possible the shift away from age-old farming practice based on careful husbandry and family labour. Technological changes have made extracting groundwater easy, and this has been encouraged by economic policy. Government has actively encouraged groundwater use for years, and is still doing so by a series of direct and indirect subsidies. Diesel fuel, used to run most water pumps, is priced at half of its equivalent international level. The Cooperative and Agricultural Credit Bank (CACB) for many years lent for the purchase of water pumps at interest rates of 9 to 11 per cent, compared to market interest rates above 20 per cent. Fruit, vegetables and *qat*, which are water-intensive crops, are favoured by import bans that raise their profit margins and hence their attractiveness for farmers. It is evident that current policies constitute a powerful engine pushing in the direction of exhaustion of Yemen's aquifers.

With these powerful forces driving both demand and supply, how has water management developed? First, there has been little control from law and tradition. For centuries, traditional society managed common resources like water and pasture in a sustainable way. Social changes and powerful economic incentives have relaxed traditional controls over resource use and, in the case of groundwater, law and tradition have favoured exploitation rather than conservation.

There has been little capacity in the public sector for water resources management. Although the government did create a High Water Council in the 1980s, it never convened in a decade of existence. There has been virtually no planning for conservation, and no regulation. The creation of a new National Water Resources Authority (NWRA) in 1997 has done little to improve the situation. The effect of government policy and practice has been to promote groundwater exploitation and not to regulate it, and until very recently public expenditure patterns have been skewed towards water resource development rather than conservation.

Results of increased groundwater use

This section examines the striking costs (and some equally striking benefits) for Yemen of the pattern of increased groundwater use that has developed. It emerges that the costs are now beginning to outweigh the benefits as the resource is depleted. The section also looks at how the benefits have tended to be somewhat unequally shared, and at how the opportunity for groundwater use to contribute to rural poverty alleviation has been largely missed.

The first and most striking result of increased groundwater use has been the extent of groundwater depletion. It is clear that Yemen is grossly overdrawing its aquifers. In 1994, national water use was estimated at about 2.8 BCM. The country thus overdrew its renewed resources of 2.1 BCM by 0.7 BCM. The most stressed area is the western part of the country – the mountains, escarpments and coastal plains that contain more than 90 per cent of the population. In 1994, groundwater use was 1.8 BCM, recharge was 1.1 BCM, a 70 per cent overdraft. Usable storage in the western half is about 35 BCM, so at present rates of extraction the area will be dry within fifty years.

In the densely populated highland valleys and plains, the situation is even worse. In the Sana'a basin, where 10 per cent of the population live (1.5 million people), water use in 1994 was 224 million m³ (MCM), and recharge was 42 MCM, a 400 per cent overdraft. The water is literally running out. Groundwater is expected to be pumped dry in the northern part of the Sana'a basin early in the second decade of this century. In Qa' Al-Boun, near Amran, water levels have dropped 60 m in the last twenty years.

What have been the economic benefits and costs of this rapid groundwater exploitation? First and most remarkable among the benefits has been the resilience of the agriculture sector, which still accounts for 17 per cent of GDP according to the national accounts (1996). More importantly, the sector provides a livelihood for about 70 per cent of the population. Over the last thirty years the sector has absorbed a vast increase in the population at a higher level of income than previously and, as a result, Yemen has largely avoided the rural-urban drift that has plagued other developing countries.

This viability of the rural economy has been sustained in large measure by increased use of water. The sector uses 95 per cent of Yemen's water in an increasingly market-oriented agriculture. The leading example of this change towards water-intensive cash crop production is the explosion in the cultivation of *qat*, now far and away the most important crop in Yemen and the country's greatest consumer of water.[3]

This resilience of the agricultural economy is counterbalanced by the lack of sustainability. In areas where groundwater is being overused for agriculture – i.e. where use exceeds recharge and the resource is being mined like a mineral – the economic outlook is bleak. In the Al-Irra area north of Sana'a, a typical farmer will have deepened his well by 50 m over the last 12 years – increasing his costs – but will still have seen the amount of water he can extract drop by two-thirds. With higher costs and only one-third of the water, this farmer can no longer make a living from farming. As this pattern of resource depletion is repeated in groundwater areas, the existence of the rural economy will be threatened.

The overexploitation of groundwater in rural areas is also likely to have severe economic consequences for Yemen's towns. As all groundwater around cities is effectively harnessed and overexploited for agricultural usage, the cost of new supplies of water for cities is likely to rise sharply since water has to be brought from further and deeper. Already, shortages of water are constraining urban and industrial development. In Sana'a, the urban utility is unable to keep pace with new housing and industrial developments. New development is obliged to buy water from private sources at prices as high as YR50–200/m^3 (35–140 US cents). Most of the options now being explored for the next source of supply to the capital cost over $1/m^3, and drilling for new groundwater sources has taken place to a depth of over 2 km. The ultimate – and nightmare – option for the capital is desalination and transport up from the coast, estimated to cost up to $7.60/m^3 (Kruseman, 1996: 8ff.).

In addition to the economic costs, the search for new water for growing cities raises the spectre of conflict over water resources between town and country. The city of Ta'izz negotiated for ten years with the nearby rural area of Habir to extract new water. After some frank confrontations, the rural people in Habir reluctantly agreed in 1996 to allow the city to extract water from a previously untapped deep aquifer in exchange for investments in village water supply, schools and women's centres, and for support to community water management. The wells were drilled for the city, but in 2003 there were continuing frictions over the transfer.

The benefits of groundwater development have been spread through all agricultural areas where groundwater is to be found. Visiting a prosperous village south of Amran where nothing but *qat* is grown, the author learned that in the early 1970s the population was only a third of what it is today and the living then was from a poor sort of rainfed sorghum. The Sa'ada orange farmer will display with pride the massive fruits hanging from his '*trees of blessing*' (Lichtenthaler, 2003).

But there have been losers, too. The proliferation of tubewells has certainly increased inequity in many rural areas. This has occurred because access to groundwater requires not only ownership of the land where the well is drilled but also sufficient capital to drill and equip the well. Once a well is drilled the groundwater is appropriated and the well owner owns the water he pumps. The result has been an 'enclosure' of what had hitherto been the property of nobody (*mubah*), and the vesting of extraction rights in perpetuity in a comparatively small number of well owners. In many areas, well owners now sell water to those who are not lucky enough to have their own well.

Public policy has tended to confirm this inequitable distribution of water through its 'hands off' approach to groundwater development. The absence of any administrative or traditional controls on drilling has concentrated a valuable resource in the hands of those with land and capital, i.e. the locally powerful. In addition, public policy has given the landowners access to the cheap credit and equipment that enable them to drill. The poor who lack the means to develop their own water resource then have to pay for irrigation or rely on rainfed cultivation. In some cases, like that of Wadi Bani Khawlan mentioned above, some users in an aquifer have been able to appropriate the resource at the expense of others.

Regarding the contribution of groundwater development to poverty alleviation, there has been a first-rate opportunity to solve one of the problems that has contributed most to poverty and poor health status in rural areas – access to safe water and sanitation. Many communities have benefited, often through self-help programmes financed with the assistance of remittances of emigrant workers. However, the overall picture is surprisingly sombre. It is estimated that even after thirty years of intensive groundwater development, only a fifth of rural households have access to safe water. Government programmes for rural water supply have concentrated on the area around the capital to the neglect of the poorer, further-flung areas. Sanitation has been largely neglected, with consequent environmental and health problems. As a result, Yemen still has quite poor rural health indicators, with the region's lowest life expectancy (51 years) and the highest infant mortality (11.7 per cent of live births). A leading cause of death in infants and children remains diarrhoea, partly caused by unsafe water and poor sanitation. Children living in rural areas experience on average seven cases of diarrhoea a year. Rural under-five mortality rates deteriorate markedly in households that do not have access to safe water or sanitation. Lack of access to drinking water also has an important impact on the lives of women. In rural areas unserved by piped water, women and girls typically spend up to seven hours a day fetching water.[4]

Government policy and options

Political economy of groundwater

At the level of overall political economy, groundwater has, by and large, been a godsend for the first generation of the new Republic. Initially, when remittances from the oil countries started some thirty years ago, the arrival of cheap capital allowed development of groundwater. After the first Gulf War, many Yemenis had to return home, and a lean period for remittances began. However, the capital invested in groundwater extraction produced its returns and oil discoveries allowed government to keep diesel prices down so that the water was pumped out at very low cost. *Qat* came in, too, on a rising curve, a crop that responded well to the extra irrigation and which had a rich market. And all along a complaisant government and an enabling socioeconomic and legal environment allowed the groundwater boom simply to happen, and in doing so helped the rural economy to stay alive and to support a vast increase in the population. But now all this is threatened with disappearance, or at least with a painful attenuation.

Past and current policy

In discussing here how the government's past policy towards groundwater has encouraged its full development, we argue that policy has to change as groundwater is depleted. Over the last thirty years the government has generally adopted a *laissez-faire* approach to economic management. Within such a framework, specific policies have been drawn up that have tended to promote the rural economy and to encourage a move to higher output and value-added, partly through the increasing use of groundwater. Specific policy instruments (credit subsidies, import bans, cheap diesel etc.) have been quite successful in this regard. Groundwater is fully exploited after only three decades of development of tubewells. The country is self-sufficient in fruit and vegetables. The country is well supplied with food and some industrial inputs.

To its credit, the government has rarely indulged in the rhetoric of food self-sufficiency common in some countries, and has never created distortions in the rural economy by pursuing what would – for a dry country like Yemen – be the illusory goal of producing all its own food needs. Instead, it has quietly accepted the logic that Yemen should import 'virtual water' embedded in cereals, and use its scanty domestic water resource for whatever gives the highest return. Thus, food security has been efficiently ensured through an increasing level of cereal imports that have been made at low cost, thanks to the cereal subsidies practised in the European Union and the US that have kept world cereal prices below production cost for a number of years. This has enabled Yemen to feed itself cheaply (most recently buying cereals from the proceeds of oil exports), while allocating water resources to producing higher-value cash crops like fruit, vegetables and *qat*. The success of this approach should not be underestimated, as it has resulted in food security and high rural incomes on a relatively sparse natural resource base.[5]

On the other hand, the wide gap between the financial cost of water at the well head and its scarcity or opportunity value has led to some misallocation of water within agriculture and between agriculture and urban uses.

Even so, whatever the success of this policy over the last thirty years, the world has changed. Groundwater is running out and the cities are running on empty. Providing for sustainability of the rural economy has to be given as much importance as providing for production and income. And it would be desirable too for the voice of equity to be heard as policies change. Like most governments, the government of Yemen may only act when the writing is on the wall. But the letters of scarcity are spelled out clearly enough now.

Future policy

What are the choices that Yemen faces? One choice is to do nothing, and to continue current rates of depletion of groundwater resources. This approach is consistent with what is practised in other sectors and other economies. Mining is a policy choice for many other natural resources. It goes against the grain with water, which is seen as a basic necessity, but after all drinking water makes up only about 5 per cent of national water use in Yemen, and the rest is used for production. Yemen can make the choice whether to have that production now or in the future. It can listen to policy guidance from those who cite the example of the US, which has mined natural resources to create capital that now supports a higher level of development. This argument has been made for the mining of groundwater elsewhere in the Arabian Peninsula.

The result of continued mining would be that aquifers in many regions of Yemen would be progressively exhausted – some within a few years, the bulk within the next fifty years. Pumping costs would increase progressively, and as mining tapped into the last third or so of the remaining storage, the water quality would decline sharply until the remaining stored water became unusable. During this period, costs would increase progressively and sections of the population would leave agriculture; rural people would probably move to the towns. Lack of water would become a growing constraint in the modern sectors, and friction between town and countryside over water allocation would be exacerbated. Finally, there would be an intergenerational problem – there would be no usable water for future generations in some areas since all usable amounts would have been mined and the balance would be polluted.

The economic and social cost of these results can be calculated, but even without the arithmetic it is clear that the cost would be enormous and that it would create very strong social and political tensions.

Is groundwater mining a credible option for Yemen? In practice, there are strong arguments against it. Given the dependence of such a large proportion of the population on revenue from agriculture, it is unlikely that the urban and modern sectors would be capable over a short period of absorbing a huge increase in labour. Nor has the rural off-farm economy so far proved particularly buoyant. In any case, the model of capital accumulation and productive investment from a mining policy does not correspond to the behaviour of Yemen with its low savings and investment rates, and the predominant tendency to invest in land and construction rather than in the production of goods and services. The most likely outcome of a mining policy is that natural resource capital will be consumed as income, and that within several decades the country will emerge decapitalized and further impoverished.

However, the alternative to a mining policy is unlikely to be a complete halt to mining. Once it gets out of hand, groundwater exploitation is very hard to check. Apart from the United States and Israel there is no instance of any state having been able effectively to reassert central control over groundwater once it has been lost. In Yemen, the momentum is so great that many aquifers will in any case be exhausted, regardless of what is done to arrest the pace. It was predicted for the Sana'a basin that, with all conceivable supply and demand management measures successfully applied, the horizon by which water would run out would simply be extended beyond the current predicted date of 2008 (Chaudhry *et al.*, 1992: 53). Any solution would be imperfect – no more than a buying of time. In fact, the objective of a recent project being financed by the World Bank is precisely to push back the date at which water will have to be transferred into the Sana'a basin from elsewhere.

The alternative to a mining policy can thus only be a 'mitigation plan', a package of management measures that would at least slow the rate of depletion and give time for the economy and society to adjust. This alternative would attempt substantially to increase the efficiency of water use and to reduce rates of overdraft through supply and demand management. The plan would at the same time promote the shift toward non-agricultural activities as the basis of both the rural and the urban economy.

The questions to be answered concern the instruments available for a 'mining mitigation plan' and whether there is any evidence that such instruments might work. Can the government in Yemen effectively influence outcomes in groundwater depletion?

Elements for a mitigation plan

Possibilities for central control and regulation

The model for water resources management that is generally advocated supposes an integrated government management function responsible for policy, water allocation, regulation and environmental aspects. In Yemen, there are several reasons why it is difficult for government to execute this integrated function.

Modern public institutions and systems are developing slowly in Yemen. The creation in 1997 of the National Water Resources Authority

(NWRA), the passage of a new Water Law (in 2003), and the creation of a single water ministry (also in 2003) are useful steps. But these institutions are new and in the governance conditions of Yemen, groundwater regulation by government is unlikely to be successful.

The physical configuration of Yemen makes central control of water resources difficult. The fragmented geography and hydrology, and the predominance of dispersed rural water uses make central control and master planning difficult. Indeed, central control of groundwater is, for several reasons, inherently difficult throughout the world. Groundwater is a 'fugitive uncharted resource'. It cannot be seen, its assessment is an approximate art, and it is hard to delimit it into discrete management areas.

In addition, the system of laws and rights with which government is attempting to work is confused. The civil code is at variance with the constitution over groundwater rights.[6] The 2003 water law sets up a system of licensing and regulation that requires good governance. To date, neither modern nor traditional systems have proved effective in controlling groundwater development. If anything, they have been overwhelmed by the sudden irruption of tubewell technology, which has the power to produce water and to mine resources quite unforeseen in modern law or in the *shari'a*.

On a larger scale, the role of central government in economic management is limited by the strong influence of decentralised, traditional structures. This makes it difficult to impose a vision of development from the centre.

Thus, it is clear that a planning approach involving regulation and centrally imposed management cannot be the solution, or at least not the total solution. Government will certainly have a role but other partners will have to be incorporated too. A collaborative approach is required and because of the nature of both groundwater and of Yemeni society, this will require action at the local level.

Local interests and institutions

In looking for a solution to the groundwater problem involving partnerships at the local level, it is necessary to consider what interests are at stake, and what institutions articulate those interests. In Yemen three basic interests in groundwater can generally be distinguished: *domestic users*, *productive users* and *owners*. *Domestic users* represent the basic needs of urban and rural people for water for drinking as well as washing, cooking and other domestic purposes. This need is a priority in any scheme, but as we have seen in Yemen, it is often not well served. The second interest, *productive users*, concerns those who use water for production that enables them to earn their living. As already noted, agriculture is far and away the dominant user of water in Yemen, but urban use – for industry, commerce and tourism – is also significant and generally contributes much higher value-added. The third interest, *owners*, is represented by those who have rights over the resource; they all, of course, are also domestic users, and most of them will also be productive users. This interest is particularly important in Yemen because, as discussed above, title to Yemen's groundwater has effectively been vested in the owners of the 45,000 tubewells, and each owner is a sovereign decision maker over his resource.

The institutional structures through which these interests may be articulated can also be described under three broad headings – *government*, *traditional structures*, and *'modern' groups*. In Yemen, the institution of *government* – that is to say, the superstructure of a modern political state – is a relatively new phenomenon. Central government departments concerned with water have been formed, but the state and its institutions remain comparatively weak. *Traditional structures of local governance*, by contrast, remain strong, particularly in rural areas: historically, these controlled Yemeni life and were generally place-centred – dominated by shaikh, tribe and locality. *Modern groups* are not a homogeneous class like the first two. They are characterised by their non-governmental and non-traditional status rather than by any specific positive attribute. They are generally organised around economic activities – examples are the local development councils, remnants of the local development associations, groups formed to manage village water supply systems, and the occasional irrigation or agricultural cooperative. They usually have a more democratic (or 'participatory' or 'inclusive') character than traditional structures.

The way in which the three 'institutional structures' articulate the three 'interests' can be illustrated by examples. A first example is where the shaikhs and the traditional leaders own the wells in an area, a not uncommon situation. Here the *traditional structure*, headed by these same shaikhs, represents the interest of the *owners*, and this traditional structure validates and enforces the owners' rights. But there may well be other 'interests' as well, for example, domestic or productive users who access water from the owner's well. The latter are not represented in the traditional structure, but have an interest, and this interest may be represented by a different institutional structure, such as a modern group (e.g. a water users' association) or – in a remoter sense – by some arm of government.

Or, in another example, a community may have clubbed together to bring drinking water to the village, and in the process set up a modern group such as a water users' association for financing and running the scheme. Here there is a close overlap between the members of the modern group and the same members as domestic users. But there are other interests, too. For example, the traditional élite in the area may, as users, wish to drill wells for farming or water sales, and these wells may tap into the same aquifer and interfere with the yield of the drinking wells.

The lesson is that water management of the shared aquifer has somehow to proceed by reconciliation between the different interests that are articulated through different institutions. In the first example, any proposal to alter or improve groundwater management in such an area will have to deal with traditional structures as 'owners'. But the proposal also has to take into account the interests of users other than the owners. Change could be initiated by any of the three institutions – by a wise government, by the traditional structures or by the modern group. But in all cases, change would have to incorporate incentives for both owners and users. Incentives could take many forms, and could as well be moral or spiritual as economic – public spirit, *noblesse oblige*, piety – all of which can, if well seated, be powerful forces in traditional structures.

In the second example, the democratic basis of the modern group may initially be in opposition to the traditional structure, with its hierarchical and capitalistic character. Good management of the aquifer that is shared by both parties will depend on cooperation, and change will require incentives for each party.

Three ways in which improvements in groundwater management can be possible are examined in the following sections. The argument builds upon the typology of the interests and institutions outlined above, and provides examples from case studies. Local partnership solutions, market-based solutions, and the complementary role of government are considered.

Local partnerships to achieve water management[7]
In the absence of regulation, cooperation is of key importance. Groundwater extraction depends on decisions by individuals about pumping, but management of the groundwater aquifer requires cooperation among all those who draw from or benefit from the common aquifer.

Because the possibility of better aquifer management seems to require local actions by different institutions representing different interests, recent fieldwork has concentrated on understanding the attitudes, incentives and constraints of the different interests drawing from the aquifer (domestic and productive users and owners), and on understanding institutions for collective action (the traditional structures, modern groups, and the role of government, together with their various laws, rules, ethical codes, etc.). The fieldwork included a number of case studies, two of which will illustrate the challenge and the potential.

Example one
The first example concerns al Haima, a *nahia* (a rural parish) near the major city of Ta'izz. The *nahia* is reached by a rough track from the main road. There are no telephones, none of the villages in the *nahia* is connected either to electricity or piped drinking water, and there are no permanent health facilities in the area. The only significant economic activity is agriculture. This was based on rainfall and on pumping from the alluvial aquifer until the 1980s, but because the wells have dried up in most of the area, there has been a reversion to rainfed agriculture and no land remains under permanent cropping. How did this come about?

In the late 1980s the area was dominated by a *shaikh* who was regarded as being close to the government. In 1989 the city, which was experiencing chronic water shortages, negotiated with the *shaikh* to tap into the deeper aquifer underlying the *nahia*. Seven wells were drilled in the area and some compensation was paid, including the drilling of an agricultural well. The *shaikh* apparently succeeded in gaining full control of the compensation for his personal use.

Local users assert that this 'agreement' was not respected. They claim to have been told that pumping from lower aquifers would not affect existing resources in the alluvial aquifer, but in fact most of the wells in the upper aquifer have long since become dry. They say also that thirty wells were actually drilled, not seven, and that even though initially the city wells were to be drilled to 120 m, the city later decided to drill to 500 m. Nor was compensation paid to them for the land used for city wells, for damaged and lost crops, or for the large number of agricultural wells that dried up.

At one stage, the locals stopped the drilling and the army was sent in. This led to a long history of confrontation, which ended in capitulation by the local people. Visitors described them after the imposed settlement as demoralised and broken.

During 1997, with some encouragement and training from a non-governmental organisation and a new government project, the local people decided to form a community association. Initially, the aim was to manage two centres for women and some potable water schemes that government was constructing in the area. However, the leaders of the association have also seen this as the beginning of a movement that will help them improve groundwater management, on which they would like to cooperate along with the new government project. The *shaikh* was not invited to join the association and opposed its creation. He was told by the local governor: 'If you object, form your own association!'

This example provides an illustration of a traditional structure initially cooperating with government in a deal that helped the interests of some of the owners and of the urban users, but which rode roughshod over the interests of other rural users. Under extreme groundwater stress, other users and owners then created a modern group that has started to obtain some support for other rural interests (drinking water), and which intends to cooperate with (a now wiser?) government – and probably ultimately with the traditional structure – in improved groundwater management.

In order to follow best practices, the newly formed association for this *nahia* has formed links with another modern group in the region (which provides our second example) that has a much longer track record.

Example two

Our second example is a local community association that represents a high level of community solidarity. It is located in al Sina, an *'uzla* (village) to the south of the same city, and is reached via an unsealed road leading up into the mountain range whose northern face overlooks the city. The only local activity in the area is agriculture. Rainfall here is very low, since the clouds gather and rain falls further north. It is a traditional area of emigration.

In 1975, emigrants from the village met in their various countries of migration and created clubs to support their home village. Their first activity was to collect funds for a domestic water-supply project, a scheme that was strongly supported by the community back home. The women sold their gold and other possessions to contribute towards the project, which benefited them greatly since they had to walk for up to 7 km and climb 700 m uphill to bring water to their homes.

The initial network brought water 700 m up from the *wadi* below the village to water tanks installed outside the community school, and women then collected water in the traditional way, in jerrycans carried on their heads. In 1980 the network was extended from distribution tanks at the school site to the centre of each hamlet where a tank was installed. By 1983 all the hamlets had been connected and the association started to install standpipes for every house, with a meter at the tap, though water had to be carried to the house. Connections were only made into the houses themselves if the householder agreed to pay a fee and to dig a cesspit according to specifications prepared by the association.

In 1985 the water in the original wells dried up. Other sources of water were sought and found south-east of the old wells in a neighbouring *'uzla*. The inhabitants of the neighbouring *'uzla* objected to water being taken out of their *'uzla* even though it was only for drinking, arguing that they needed drinking water as well. The association then had to find water elsewhere and eventually did so. However, although it was on land belonging to members of the community, it was also in another *'uzla*. Fortunately, the traditional leaders of this *'uzla* agreed that since the water was for drinking and not for irrigation, the wells could be drilled. Eventually some of their households were also supplied by the scheme.

However, after the new wells had begun to operate, agricultural wells started to proliferate in the same valley, creating the real risk that the drinking-water supply would dry up. In order to protect this last source of water, the association began surreptitiously to buy up plots of land in the area, then to drill wells and cap them. This was because custom in the region broadly recognises spacing restrictions of 500 m to 1,000 m between wells. The capped wells counted, and no one else could drill near them.

From the start, the association has been managed democratically. The community holds annual meetings attended by all adult males who choose to be present. These meetings are held during the Eid when most of the emigrants are at home.

According to the association leaders, there are several reasons for success. One is the democratic basis of the association. The second was the association's ability to survive the initial opposition of traditional leaders in the community. Once the water-supply scheme became operational, the importance of the activities meant that no one in the community could oppose the concept, since it brought such benefits to the entire population. At this point, traditional leaders lent it their support. A third reason was the association's independence from government support. Occasional benefits have been accepted from various government projects (but only where they fit within the association's own plans) and they are taken on the community's own terms. Finally, sustainability is ensured by the association's ability to protect its water source and to maintain the operation of the scheme by full cost recovery. This well-established association now provides advice to other associations in water management.

This example provides an illustration of a modern group that has managed water resources and services successfully and sustainably, which has coopted the traditional institution's leaders by the strength of a good idea, capably executed, and has made local rules concerned with well-spacing work to its advantage. It has also cooperated with government – but only on an equal basis and in the service of its own interests.

The findings from this recent fieldwork suggest that modern groups have the greatest potential to contribute to better groundwater management. Because of their broader representation, they can represent drinkers or users or owners, or all three. In effect, they are 'inclusive' institutions, in a way that traditional structures can never be. In the second case, a modern group was actually able to absorb or eclipse the interests of traditional structures.

In addition, modern groups can serve as the nucleus from which different management techniques – regulation, dissemination of technologies, conflict resolution, education, development of alternative sources of income, etc. – can be developed and adapted to local conditions.

Constraints on the local partnership approach

We should not underestimate the multiple tensions involved in this kind of change. Between government and other participants a deep gulf already exists – that between the planner and the reality. Government's perspective is that of planning, setting objectives, and formulating policy. Inevitably this perspective focuses on water scarcity as a constraint to Yemen's growing economy; on water resource sustainability in terms of quantity and quality; and on equitable access for users. But up till now the 'beneficiaries' – the domestic users, the productive users, and the owners – have rarely been consulted on the problems, their constraints, or their solutions.

This tension between planner and beneficiary is paralleled by the tensions between central and local power bases, between town and country, and between all the different interests and their representative institutions. In the first of our two examples, we saw this combination between a government concerned largely for the interests of urban users and a traditional institution (the *shaikh*) driven by self-interest. The situation may now correct itself in the form of a new partnership between a (wiser) government and a modern group, but tensions will persist and others will arise.

And of course Yemen is a vastly heterogeneous country. In some more traditional areas in the north, the notion of a 'modern group' may be a weak one to set alongside the powerful tribal structure, and in fact the traditional structure may prove more representative. In other areas, the traditional structure may be weak, and the modern structure may play a greater role from the beginning.

In some cases, a partnership approach may simply happen; in other cases, it may be that social engineers (government, non-governmental organisations, donors) will find ways to make it happen.[8] But there is another management instrument that has sprung up all over Yemen entirely without the intervention of any planners and that brings about water transfers to the satisfaction of both supplier and recipient. This is the phenomenon of the water market.

Market-based solutions: achieving allocative efficiency

Water markets are widespread in Yemen. They were documented in a recent case study (Moench 1997:11ff.) undertaken in the Ta'izz region where two separate categories of market were found to exist. First, there are local sales of irrigation water to farmers around the well. These sales are made by the well owner directly to the farmer, and are usually on the basis of share-cropping or hourly water-sale arrangements. Secondly, there are tanker water sales, where water is conveyed to domestic, industrial and non-local agricultural users, generally by way of at least one middleman (a truck owner and/or a water purification shop). In this instance, water sales are made on a volumetric basis. The market structure is open, with a large number of individual truck owners purchasing water from well owners and selling water on the open market.

The development of these water markets represents a natural evolutionary response to growing water scarcity as well as to the need for mechanisms to allocate available supplies to those who require them and who can afford to pay for them. It seems that in Yemen, water is now accepted as an economic commodity in daily life, bypassing the anguished debates of policy makers in other countries.

Water markets can achieve many of the goals of good water policy, by transferring water to the highest value uses (allocative efficiency), providing incentives for efficiency within uses (end use efficiency), and compensating those who transfer water out of lower value uses (equity).

Markets do, in fact, have many advantages over administrative methods of allocation. They bring flexibility, so that those requiring water can purchase it from the most convenient and affordable source while those having excess water can sell it for productive use in other areas. Markets also build up conservation incentives – since new users pay hard cash for water, they have a strong incentive to use it as efficiently as possible, while owners are also encouraged to be efficient since they can sell water that is surplus to their needs. Furthermore, markets contain an inherent mechanism for compensating owners who transfer water from existing uses: and this compensation mechanism is not dependent on government resources. Finally, in the case of Yemen, markets have the merit of existing. It is not necessary to devise or even legislate for them. They have already evolved to meet a need and they are already working in many areas of the country.

Markets seem a good way of matching the interests of rural owners with users and drinkers who require water. This is certainly the case if we compare the difficult and antagonistic transfer of water from the *nahia* to the city with the apparently mutually advantageous possibilities of a market-based transfer, as discussed above. This was a finding of the

Ta'izz study, where respondents stated that transferring water to urban uses would face far less opposition if the urban area was to purchase the water, and if returns from those purchases flowed both to the community and to any individual well owner whose own water supply was affected.

However, there are also very substantial drawbacks to water markets. The first and most obvious is that markets do not in themselves solve the problem of groundwater overdraft. If anything, they may increase the incentives for individual well owners to overdraw, as they will receive higher prices. Secondly, the contract is between the owner and the buyer and since there is no provision for compensating other users, there may be a wide variety of uncompensated third-party impacts that could affect the entire rural community. A third problem is that since there is no workable definition of groundwater rights in Yemen, there is thus no legal way of formulating the right to sell and buy. Up till now, this does not seem to have hindered the development of markets, but recognising these rights could prove to be a stumbling-block for the government.

Of course, solutions could be found to these problems. Were the government to recognise and promote purchases of water from representative community-level management organisations (modern groups) controlling groundwater over some hydrologically meaningful area where aquifer management was possible, then it is conceivable that sustainable extraction levels could be respected and a fair distribution of benefits and compensation could take place. However, to date no such organisation exists. Unless the government is prepared to promote such an arrangement, perhaps in the context of a new water-supply project, it is likely that water markets will continue to spread, although without resolution of the drawbacks noted above.

A role for a wise government

It was argued above that the capacity of the central government to plan and regulate groundwater is extremely limited. However, it will be clear from the following discussion of the partnership approach and of the water market phenomenon that government, even in a weak state, can never be absent and that there are, in fact, areas where government can play an important role.

First, government can exert considerable influence on water resource management through correction of the distorted incentive framework. Government could change the economics of crop choice and irrigation in ways that would strongly encourage water conservation, in effect changing relative prices to discourage groundwater use. The possibilities include introducing a higher price for diesel, levying higher tariffs and taxes on pumping equipment, eliminating credit subsidies for pumps, and removing incentives (such as import controls) to the production of water-intensive agricultural products.

In the long term, it might be hoped that these policy adjustments would encourage water conservation activities that would at the same time yield good incomes. Changes in cropping patterns and in irrigation technology could yield higher returns to water, so that as costs went up, gross margins would go up as well. In the short term, however, there is a risk that the change in relative prices might simply erode the basis for much rural prosperity and undermine much of the positive impact of rural development over the last thirty years.

In fact, the government, encouraged by the International Monetary Fund, has begun to implement elements of an adjustment programme. Diesel prices have been increased: domestic prices in 2004 are about one-half of border prices, and are expected to continue to rise towards border parity. It is clear that these changes are driven by the need for macroeconomic stabilisation and by structural adjustment policy rather than by a water resources conservation strategy or rural development strategy. Nonetheless, government has shown concern for the impact on farmers. Part of the proceeds of the successive diesel price increases since the mid-1990s has been allocated to the Agriculture and Fisheries Production Promotion Fund, whose mandate is to make productive investments in the sector and so compensate in part for the impact of the increases. This approach would work best if the investments of the fund were specifically made in water-use efficiency and in other productive investments that relieved groundwater stress and helped sustain incomes in affected areas.

At the institutional level, government is trying to improve its management capacity through the creation of NWRA. Plainly this institution should have a role at the centre, in information, policy, public awareness, etc. But if government is to play a positive role in the kind of collaborative approaches to groundwater management that were discussed above, it also needs to build a decentralised capability.

The argument that Yemen is by nature and circumstance decentralised has been made above. In effect, this 'natural decentralisation' has the advantage of making it easier to deal with a more manageable hydrological, social and economic unit. Decentralisation also increases the likelihood that government and traditional and modern institutions can work together at the local level. Certainly the different interests can be better articulated at the local level and each participant can better understand the attitudes, incentives and constraints of others, and develop communications channels. Where needed, the government can design incentives and support programmes at local level that can favour changes in behaviour.

NWRA has actually begun with a decentralised approach, and is giving priority to particularly vulnerable areas, for which it is developing regional water management plans. These plans include working with a manageable local area – the Ta'izz region, the Sana'a basin – and bringing together all the water resources and the economic and social information needed to enable rational choices to be made about water allocation and management.

The next key step will be to forge the partnerships at the local level – government, and traditional and modern structures – that will be needed to bring about change. Recent studies and pilot projects have shown the particular promise of the modern structures (the water-user associations, etc.). Government should therefore develop an active policy and programme to promote modern water-user groups that are 'inclusive' of all local interests in water and that can cooperate across significant parts of the aquifer. The non-governmental sector would be natural partners in promoting this development.

At the technical level, the government's potential contribution should not be ignored. Specifically, government can draw up a programme for water conservation in agriculture. The imperative to preserve as much as possible of the rural economy while reducing water use highlights the need for efficiency improvements that will maximise returns to water.

The aim is to increase the return per m^3 of water. Government is already encouraging and financing some technical improvements. There have been a number of pilot programmes to promote improved irrigation technology (drip irrigation, plasticulture, greenhouses), and there is currently a national programme to promote the conveyance and distribution of irrigation water by pipe rather than open channel. More can be done. An expanded programme should include revived research and extension, incentives for conservation activities, review of the potential for small dams, spate rehabilitation and management, and testing of other sources like treated wastewater and saline water. At the same time, government should increase support to rural water supplies and sanitation, as this is a way of ensuring that the benefits of groundwater are widely spread and have an impact on poverty alleviation in rural areas. There should also be promotion of alternative rural enterprises, since diversification out of agriculture will be necessary in the long run.

Government has also to mediate equitably between the interest of the city and the use of water for rural incomes. Here the possibility of incorporating a market-based solution should not be neglected. Despite the problems of markets discussed above, the government could support market development that would respect both sustainability and equity if it were able to contract for urban water supply with a representative modern association of the kind mentioned above.

Finally, the role of good law should not be neglected, even in a country of minimal governance. The key question is water rights; it is essential that the formulation of these reflect both traditional approaches and the new partnership approach. The example given above of the association that was able to defend its water rights by appealing to a traditional rule in the locality about spacing between wells shows the power of rules, even where the rule maker lacks the capability to enforce. Government should work out simple rules for conservation that build on local tradition and that can be broadly applied and regulated by rural people themselves. Government could, for example, set a national regulation for a 500-metre spacing between wells.

Long-term prospects
This chapter has discussed the possibilities of mitigating groundwater mining by promoting a partnership between all interests at the local level. The essence of the partnership approach is for agents of change (government, non-governmental organisations, donors) to work with local interests and institutions to develop practical programmes for local groundwater management, working from existing rights systems and management practices. Recent studies, as noted above, have suggested that there is a basis for these local partnership solutions. Initial attempts to implement partnership solutions have had mixed results. Many lessons have been learned, but government and its external partners have shown

insufficient stamina in pursuing pilot experiences to a conclusion. Many lessons have, however, been learned and they are being incorporated in new programmes.

At the same time, markets, although imperfect, are an alternative 'solution' that has emerged organically, and can achieve some goals.

Finally, there is scope for a more proactive government role, even in a weak state, in promoting the partnership approach, developing instruments of supply and demand management, and ensuring equity.

If Yemen achieves some measure of success in these approaches, what is likely to happen in the rural economy? The course followed by other water-scarce countries can provide an instructive lesson. For example, Jordan has very little more water than Yemen – about 200 m³ per head annually against Yemen's 140 m³ – but has managed to transform its agriculture to a high income, high value-added activity, dominated by market-garden crops grown in plastic houses under drip irrigation. This has been made possible by rising demand based on rising incomes, by good market organisation, and by the availability of technology, education, capital and inputs. At the same time, the Jordanian agriculture sector has progressively shed labour into other sectors, and this has been made possible by high levels of investment in human resources and in enterprise development.

The Jordanian experience represents a model that Yemen might hope to move towards over the next generation. Yemen cannot and probably will not follow precisely in Jordan's footsteps, but the example is potent. Orderly management of dwindling water resources and a transition from low value agriculture to an efficient, high-value, market-oriented agriculture sector matched with a growing modern urban sector, is possible if it can be phased over a reasonable period and if it is accompanied by the kind of supporting policies and programmes discussed above.

NOTES

1   This chapter draws on work that the author has done in partnership with many others, including work on the Yemen Local Water Management Study with Marcus Moench, Helen Lackner, Ghazi Al-Saqqaf, Tony Zagni, Chris Handley and others; work on the Yemen Water Strategy Report with John Hayward, Alex McPhail, Roger Norton, Mohammed Al-Eryani, Ton Negenman, Janusz Kindler and others; and work on the Ta'izz Water Supply Pilot Project with Andrew Macoun, Helen Lackner, Tony Milroy, Abdul Rahman Al-Eryani, Ghazi Al-Saqqaf, Mario Zelaya, Shaheena Khan and others. The chapter also draws on discussions with many more people in recent years, including Mohammed al-Eryani, Anwer Sahooly, Mohammad al-Hamdi, Jamal Mohammed Abdo, Ja'ffer Hamed, Abdul Karim Al Fusayl, Ali Jabr Alawi, Thabet Al Hoot, Hamoud Al Rubaidi, Abdallah Saif, Aslam Chaudhry, Jeremy Berkoff, Elizabeth Monosowski, Stephen Mink, Tony Allen, Gerhard Lichtenthaler and Shelagh Weir. Comments on a draft of this chapter were provided by Alex McPhail and Chris Handley.

2   The section describing Yemen's water problems is partly based on the paper recently written by the author for the World Bank (cf. Ward, 1997). In this section, and throughout the chapter, quantities and process are for 1999 unless otherwise stated.

3   *Qat* is a much-debated crop. From the standpoint of the viability of the rural economy, it has many favourable characteristics. It has the highest return to water of any crop, so is ideal for an agriculture where water is the scarce factor; it produces a regular flow of cash from town to country; the benefits are quite widely spread in rural areas among the predominantly smallholder producers, labour and the marketing chain; and the flow of cash paid to *qat* producers has increased demand for other rural produce. Some have seen *qat* as the mainstay of the rural economy: 'In *qat* producing areas, the crop has performed a holding operation – it has kept alive the agricultural potential and kept the people on the land, tied socially and economically to their small rural communities' (Weir, 1985). Moves to restrict *qat* – from the 1970s to date – have produced little discernible change in behaviour.

4   For a full discussion of the relation between rural water and sanitation and the incidence of poverty in rural areas see Cosgrove *et al.*, 1996: *passim* and World Bank, 1996: *passim*.

5   The author thanks Professor J. A. Allan of SOAS for the useful 'virtual water' concept. See, for example, his paper 'Virtual Water' presented at the 1997 British Association Festival of Science.

6   Civil Code Article 1163: ' "Landownership is inclusive of what is above and beneath it to any useful depth", whereas the Constitution Article 8 says: "All types of natural resource ... underground ... are property of the state" ' (quoted by Dr Salah Haddash, *Yemen Times*, 23 February 1998 and 2 March 1998).

7   This section and the section on markets draw heavily on work done for the Local Water Management Study directed by Dr Marcus Moench (Natural Heritage Institute) with Helen Lackner and others (see Moench, 1997, and Ward and Moench, 1999. The section also benefits greatly from the work done on the

World Bank-financed Ta'izz Water Supply Pilot Project with Helen Lackner, Tony Milroy, Abdul Rahman Al-Eryani and Dr Ghazi Al-Saqqaf.

8 The World Bank-financed Ta'izz Water Supply Pilot Project tested this partnership approach in two wadis near to Ta'izz. The results are documented in the Implementation Completion report, and will be developed in detail in a broader study by the present author of water management in Yemen.

9

Land Tenure and Resource Management in the Yemeni Highlands

M. Mosleh Al-Sanabani

Introduction

This contribution describes property rights and land tenure arrangements in the highlands of Yemen and their effects on land management, and examines in particular the impact of land tenure on terrace maintenance. Indigenous land tenure arrangements have been forced to accommodate the consequences of social and economic change. In addition, fragmentation of land holdings and a growing scarcity of land (due to high population growth) continue to generate disputes about land. Nevertheless, the preparation by trusted individuals of the title deeds of land ownership at subdistrict level and the recording of all land transactions are regarded as an adequate tough temporary solution to the absence of officially certified land registrations.

The Republic of Yemen has limited arable land, estimated in 1996 at 1.66 million hectares (ha). Of this total area, 64 per cent of the total area was cultivated and 36 per cent was uncultivated (MAWR, 1997). A large portion of the arable land on the highlands is in the form of manmade terraces. Over centuries Yemeni farmers developed indigenous techniques of water spreading and water harvesting through terracing of mountain slopes and superb landscape engineering. These and other community-based practices were responsible for the long-term sustainability of agriculture in Yemen. However, socioeconomic changes, including rapid population growth and urbanisation, migration, improved infrastructure and the growing role of markets, have brought with them new trends in land use. At the same time, soil erosion due to land abandonment and lack of regular maintenance has caused degradation of the highland terraces.

This chapter focuses on the mountain terrace area that covers most of the western escarpments on the country's highlands, not only because the terraced area represents a national heritage or a monument to environmental sustainability, but also because it has the highest population density in rural Yemen. In some districts, the population density can at times exceed 720 persons/km^2 (compared with 28 persons/km^2 on the national level). Agriculture, which occupies some 80 per cent of the local population, is the principal economic activity in the area. Even so, agriculture is unable to support the swelling population, and as a result out-migration has occurred in the region.

The intention is (1) to describe land property rights and tenancy arrangements; (2) to examine their effects on land management; and (3) to analyse the changes in indigenous land tenure arrangements and their effect on terrace management. It is based on data collected in 1996 and 1997 in the Kuhlan-Affar and Shariss districts in Hajjah province, located in the northern part of the western escarpments. The data were presented in an earlier case study (Alsanabani, Land Tenure and Water Rights, 1997), but information about the rest of the terraced area was limited. Details were therefore sought from certain farmers and other key figures in the subdistricts (*uzla*), as noted in the text.

Land property rights

Types of land ownership

There are four types of agricultural land ownership in Yemen; namely, private land (*mulk khas*), state land (*aradi al-dawla*), religious endowment land (*aradi waqf*), and run-off hill areas which are sometimes terraced (*maraheq al-mal*).

Private land (mulk khas)

Privately owned land predominates, and is estimated at 85 per cent of total landholding in Yemen (World Bank, 1993). In the highlands it is estimated at 81 per cent in the northern provinces (No'man, 1989). However, these are not reliable estimates due to the lack of land registration records and cadastral maps. Private land can be sold or used without restrictions.

State land (aradi al-dawla)

State land includes land that was confiscated by the Imam before the 1962 revolution from certain large landholders, land taken from tribes in settlement of disputes, and the land that was confiscated from the Imam's family after the revolution. As a rough estimate, state land makes up 2–3 per cent of arable land in the northern provinces (Table 9.1). According to Decree No. 21 for 1995, the Authority for State Land, under the Ministry of Housing and Urban Planning, is responsible for state land, but since the authority has no reliable records, state land continues to be lost by illegal seizure (land grabbing).

TABLE 9.1
Types of land ownership in Yemen

Type of land ownership	Per cent area (approximate)
Private ownership	85
Endowment (*Waqf*)	10–15
State	2–3

Source: Noaman, 1989.

*Religious endowment land (*waqf *land)*

The religious endowment land, known as *waqf* land, is the land donated by individuals for the enhancement of religious institutions such as mosques and schools. This land cannot be transferred by sale, gift or inheritance. Total *waqf* land is estimated at 10 to 15 per cent of the agricultural land in Yemen (Table 9.1). The Ministry of *Waqf* and Spiritual Guidance holds the *waqf* land, but has no countrywide records of such land, although its provincial offices have some records of the lands (*ayan*) under their jurisdiction. The *waqf* land is cultivated by tenant farmers through sharecropping arrangements.

Like *aradi al-dawla* land, *waqf* land is not registered in the Survey and Land Registration Authority (SLRA) in Sana'a. As a result *waqf* land is also grabbed by big landholders. In response to the increasing losses of *waqf* land, the Council of Ministers formed a committee in August 1997 to investigate the matter and to collect the land records from every province in the country. This in fact was not the government's first attempt to collect the records, but previous attempts had had limited success.

The maraheq al-mal *areas*

Maraheq al-mal (sing. *marhaq*) are the run-off areas adjacent to farmland, and are located mostly upstream of cultivated fields (Alsanabani, 1997). In more arid districts where rainfall is limited, farmland should have some access into run-off water to support plant growth. Traditionally, such matters are arranged by regarding any run-off area that allows rainwater to run directly on to a plot as a *maraheq* (run-on area) for such a plot. Priority for the utilisation of *maraheq al-mal* is given to the farmer who first reclaimed the land. In size, a *marhaq al-mal* area can cover a whole slope or hillside or extend all the way to the top of a hill.

Traditionally, property rights in *maraheq al-mal* belong to the farmland owner whose land receives run-off from such a *marhaq*. Although land owners in the area may consider *marhaq*s as their property, they have no idea of their size. *Marhaq* areas may reach several fold of the cultivated areas, and ratios of cultivated to run-off areas range from 1:1–1:3 and in the terraced areas to 1:15 (Eger, 1987). Decree No. 21 issued in 1995 considers *maraheq al-mal* to be extensions to areas of farmland, with the exception of *maraheq al-mal* that are located on land surfaces with a slope that exceeds 20 degrees.

Land registration

There is no agricultural land registration in Yemen. The Survey and Land Registration Authority (SLRA), based in Sana'a, deals only with urban land registration; there are no cadastral maps for agricultural land. Traditionally, local elders, who had knowledge of the land and of property boundaries, resolved ownership disputes through customary rules. However, increasing scarcity of land and changing attitudes have begun to render the traditional methods ineffective, and as a result most of the disputes currently end up in the courts.

Inevitably, the lack of land registration and of cadastral maps makes the implementation of court decisions difficult. At the local level, there is the *basirah* (title deed; pl. *basayir*), which is the only document that proves an individual land ownership. Most of the *basayir* that were prepared before the 1962 revolution were written by the *faqih* (the only individual in the community who could read and write and who had some understanding of the technicalities of *shari'a*). The *basirah* recorded the cadastral information, which included farm boundaries, when land delineation was carried out within the community. This document is accepted in court litigation processes. As a result of increasing land scarcity, false title deeds are increasingly being produced, which leads to more conflicts over land ownership and farm boundaries. This makes the *basirah* a less reliable proof of land ownership.

Holding size and fragmentation
In the highlands, holding sizes are relatively small in the governorates of Ibb and Mahwit which contain most of the cultivated lands in the terraced area (Table 9.2). They are about three times higher in Sana'a governorate where most of the cultivated land is found on the plains. However, for the purposes of this discussion it is more meaningful to analyse the distribution of holding sizes at the district level. For instance Table 9.2 shows a clear concentration of holdings in the Kuhlan-Affar district. Out of the sample of farmers interviewed, about 51 per cent with holding sizes of less than one hectare occupied only 15 per cent of the area. At the same time a mere 2 per cent of the farmers had around 14 per cent of the area. Other studies have documented the concentration of the more productive land in Yemen, and this varies in different areas. In some areas a small number of landlords own large tracts of the agricultural land.

TABLE 9.2
Land holding size and distribution of the sample farmers in Kuhlan, 1997

Holding size	Per cent area	Per cent farmers
Less than 1 ha	15	51
1–2 ha	31	27
2–4 ha	20	16
4–8 ha	19	5
More than 8 ha	14	2

Source: M. Moslih Alsanabani, 1997.

Land fragmentation is also a phenomenon that is present in predominantly agrarian economies where a major section of the population is involved in agriculture. Land fragmentation affects the scale of agricultural production and reduces farmers' ability to invest in land improvement. Small landholders have relatively fewer resources to invest and lower capacity to absorb the risk involved. Small farmers, who often do not have access to credit due to institutional or bureaucratic obstacles, are simply too poor to invest for the long term.

In Kuhlan-Affar, 11 farmers were asked specifically about the number of plots of land and the time spent in walking to those plots. The average holdings of 1.8 ha owned by these farmers consisted of 45 terraces (abr), which were fragmented into 4 plots of about 11 terraces each with an approximate area of less than half a hectare. Each of these plots was located in a different micro-agroecological zone, locally known as *wattan*, and on average farmers spent 65 minutes in walking to reach them. Land fragmentation is generally a result of the inheritance law. Some farmers in the study area had tried to consolidate their land by exchanging plots with other farmers (*monaqala*), but due to the variations in land quality, this was not a common practice. Furthermore, the distribution of land into plots located in different micro-agroecological zones would reduce the risks due to weather fluctuations and might thereby discourage land consolidation. However, the fragmentation of holdings in irrigated areas is more severe than in the rainfed areas.

Land tenure arrangements

Tenancy arrangements

There are two main types of tenancy arrangements common in Yemen, namely fixed rent and sharecropping arrangements. The fixed rent form is more common in the irrigated systems, while sharecropping is found in both the irrigated and rainfed areas. Although the predominant type of landholding in Yemen is that of the owner-cultivator (67 to 95 per cent of holdings in Yemen), a sizeable area of land is cultivated by sharecropping. The proportion of land under sharecropping is greater in the regions with a higher number of large landholders, such as Tihama, Ibb and Mahwit (No'man, 1989).

In the highland provinces the land cultivated by sharecropping ranges from 9 per cent in Sana'a Governorate to 33 per cent in Mahwit (Table 9.3). The sharecropped area in Hajja province is 5 per cent. However, the area cultivated by sharecropping is higher in the terraced areas than in the whole province (19 per cent), the reason being that large holdings are more frequent in the terraced lands than in the flat lands (No'man, 1989).

TABLE 9.3
Total cultivated area and sharecropping

| | | | | Sharecropped land | |
	Total area	Proportion in Yemen	Average holding size	All province	Terraced area
	Ha	Per cent	Ha	Per cent	Per cent
Hajja	124,594	7.5	1.5	5	19
Mahwit	29,169	1.8	0.8	33	32
Sanaʻa	380,726	22.9	2.6	9	26
Thamar	138,220	8.3	1.5	31	37
Ibb	101,521	6.0	0.7	26	26
Taʻizz	123,432	7.4	0.9	14	17
Average				18	35

Source: Agricultural Statistics Year Book 1985 and 1996, Ministry of Agriculture and Irrigation, Sanaʻa.

Formalising land tenure arrangements

It was common for land tenure arrangements to be binding simply by oral agreement. To become effective, agreements needed to be witnessed by one or two adults. Furthermore, if both tenant and landowner abided by the norms of the community, this provided security for the tenant and satisfaction for the owner. It is not uncommon for such tenancies to have lasted for life and indeed for generations. For instance, an oral agreement that was made in Raymah in the nineteenth century had reached the third generation and still remained effective (Table 9.5). By contrast, in an area such as Kuhlan-Affar (in the Hajja governorate) a written contract was, according to local people, required even in the nineteenth century (personal communication, 1997), particularly in *waqf* land.

The indigenous tenure system has been facing pressure to adapt to socioeconomic changes for nearly four decades. Such changes include the growing scarcity of land. Per capita arable land had decreased from 0.2 ha in 1970 to 0.06 ha in 1995, and as a result of the high population growth rate (3.5 per cent), people's attitudes towards land have been affected. In addition, a reduction in the number of illiterates (from 99 per cent in the early 1960s to 55 per cent in 1994) has prompted more farmers to make use of written contracts in tenancy agreements.

The government's response to such changes was to move towards formalising the tenure system in 1990 by approving the election by the community of a trusted individual to be the *ma'moon*. However, to have the government's approval, the elected individual must be able to show some knowledge of *shari'a*. The *ma'moon's* responsibilities include: (1) preparing the *waraqat ijarah* for the tenancy arrangement; (2) writing the title deed (*basirah*) of land ownership for the purposes of inheritance and for the new owners; and (3) preparing marriage contracts. The *ma'moon* is also responsible for keeping records of all land transactions that take place in the subdistrict. The government encourages the use of written contracts on land tenure agreements to reduce disputes, and the local administration authorities at subdistrict levels (*'uzla*) are therefore required to endorse and keep records of tenancy contracts and other land transactions.

Typical waraqat ijarah

A typical *waraqat ijarah* that binds a tenancy arrangement (prepared by the *ma'moon*) indicates that the tenure agreement is based on the customary rules. It states the names of the landowner and the tenant, location of the farm and boundaries with other farms, and occasionally records the shares of the two parties. It also states that it is the tenant's responsibility to keep the land in a cultivable condition (*iqama al-mal*): the document does not, however, include the crops to be cultivated on the land.

The sharecropping system

Share of harvested crop

Sharecropping is an old system in Yemen and one that has adapted to many different situations. It varies according to region, type of land, availability of irrigation water, and the crops that are grown. The most common sharecropping arrangements in the area that was studied are half-and-half, two-thirds to one-third, and three-quarters to one-quarter of harvested crop for the tenant and the landowner respectively. These shares are based on the prevailing customary rules in each community. Hence, all farmers in a community or in a subdistrict apply only one ratio of shares.

Sharing the cost of production

Traditionally, the landowner should contribute to farm inputs, share in cost of production, participate in crop harvesting, and/or share the cost of terrace maintenance so that he can claim his share of the harvested crop according to customary rules. However, the importance of the landowner's contribution at any point varies according to region. For example, in Al-Hayma Dakhilia, if the landowner shares the cost of the harvest with the tenant farmer he is entitled to 50 per cent of the harvested crop; otherwise he receives only one-third. Crop shares also depend on sharing the cost of terrace maintenance. Table 9.4 shows the tenant's share in production and in terrace maintenance costs in the various highland governorates. It is worth noting that while the landowners claim that decisions about sharing the crops are based on customary rules, at the same time they are not necessarily making their contribution according to community norms (see section on Terrace Maintenance and Land Tenure below).

TABLE 9.4
Tenant's share of production and costs of major terrace maintenance

District/Province	Production shares	Major terrace maintenance cost shares
	Per cent	Per cent
Kuhlan/Hajja	50	50
Bni Awam/Hajja	67	100
Mahwit	67	50
Jahala/Sana'a	50	50
Raymah/Sana'a	67	100
Humir/Thammar	50	67
Otoma/Thammar	75	100
Habali/Ibb	50	50
Suhool/Ibb	67	100
Saber/Ta'izz	67	50

Source: M. Moslih Alsanabani, 1997.

Common sharecropping agreements

With regard to sharecropping arrangements, two types of agreement were identified in the study area, namely an open agreement and a long-term agreement. In both types, the tenant and the landowner normally sign a written contract (*waraqut ijarah*). In the open agreement, which is the type most commonly used in this area, the period of tenancy is not mentioned in the contract, although the arrangement is intended to last for years. However, the period of the tenancy is mentioned in any contract that is concerned with a long-term tenure arrangement.

Tenancy agreements lasting 20, 30 or 50 years are to be found in the study area, and these can be transferred across generations through inheritance. The short-term pattern of tenancy arrangement is the least common form: it can be found in Habali (Ibb Governorate) and lasts for only one season or for one year. No written contract is required with this type of tenure arrangement, which is usually limited to the rainfed area.

Security of tenure and long-term investment

Customary land tenure systems in Yemen acknowledge the importance of a secure tenancy for any long-term investment in land improvement, and offers assurance to tenants that they will receive a return on their investment. In the study area, for example, if uncultivated land is reclaimed and transformed to farmland the tenant may keep the whole harvest for a period of four to six years (varying according to region) so as to cover the cost of land reclamation. Only after such a period had elapsed would the landowner's share be collected.

Special tenancy arrangements may also apply, for instance if a rangeland is reclaimed and transformed to farming land. In Sahool (Ibb), a tenant may claim ownership of one quarter of the reclaimed land if the landowner decides to terminate the tenancy arrangement. In Hayma al-Dakhel, another district in northern Sana'a Governorate, tenants are allowed to keep half of the land, while any tenant in Hayma who plants coffee or qat bushes is entitled to half the trees if the landowner decides to terminate the tenancy. A tenant who plants coffee in Raymah may take 75 per cent of the production; otherwise the 50:50 rule applies.

Terrace maintenance and land tenure

Customary rules of terrace maintenance

The shared responsibility between tenants and landowners for terrace maintenance is based on customary rules. The tenant bears the full cost of any 'minor' damage that is considered an unavoidable part of farm husbandry, and shares the cost of 'major' damage caused by heavy storms or by floods with the landlord on a 50 per cent basis. However, this rule is not included in written tenure contracts. Instead, what is stated is that the tenant should keep the land in a cultivable condition (*iqamat al mal*).

Furthermore, the definition of minor and major damage may be contested. Farmers have developed the term *mathber* to describe what happens when a portion of the terrace wall falls and the soil behind the wall is washed away (Alsanabani, 1997). This term is common in Hajja and Mahwit governorates, and in the western districts of Sana'a Governorate. A partial collapse of terrace walls without soil erosion is not considered a *mathber*. Farmers indicated that damage to terrace walls which requires two to three working days to reconstruct is within the range of 'minor' damage, and that the tenant should bear the full cost of repairs.

Deviation from the common rules

Although the prevailing view is that responsibility for terrace maintenance is determined according to customary rules, there is a lack of clarity about such responsibility and the customary rules are weakening. It was a customary rule that farmers repaired damaged terraces and that the landlord's portion of the cost was deducted from the production share. This was done by mutual agreement and was a way to avoid delays in terrace repairs. However, this understanding has been affected by uncertainty about payment of the landlord's share of the cost and this has resulted in terrace repairs being held up.

The 50:50 cost-sharing rule is not always respected because of the vague nature of the responsibility for terrace maintenance in the customary rules. The fact that tenants have to repair all 'minor' damages and keep the land in a cultivable condition puts landlords in a strong position, and enforcement of the customary rules is weak. Although a tenant could, in principle, withhold the landowner's share if the latter's share of tenancy maintenance was not paid, he might find himself in a weaker position by doing so. Farmers stated that proper enforcement of the 50:50 rule would significantly increase investment in land improvement, such as terrace maintenance.

Among the tenant farmers who were interviewed, only the 46 per cent who cultivated *waqf* land mentioned that they were allowed to subtract the share of major terrace maintenance costs from the harvest share. At the same time, a similar percentage indicated that they had to bear the whole cost of both minor and major damage. Around 7 per cent of tenants indicated that the *waqf* authorities refused to share the costs, but 4 per cent of the tenants did not try to ask the *waqf*, nor were they asked to repair damage that had occurred more than five years previously. Farmers reported that landlords avoided and sometimes refused outright any sharing of the costs of major damage with tenants. Without any assurance that they would receive a return on their investment, the tenants in turn saw no reason to carry out the repairs. Thus, terraces continue to degrade due to lack of proper maintenance.

Some tenant farmers (47 per cent) on the *waqf* land said, however, that they carried the whole cost in order to avoid the loss of productive land. Similarly, 62 per cent of the tenant farmers sharecropping on private land stated that they had, for the same reason, to bear the full cost of terrace repair for both minor and major damage. Only 38 per cent indicated that the landowner shared the cost. Furthermore, the unreliability of production estimates led some landlords to delay or to refuse their share of terrace maintenance on sharecropped land.

Effect of land tenure on terrace maintenance
Table 9.5 shows the average number of broken terrace walls on farms with different land tenure systems for a sample of farmers in the study area. The data shows that owner-cultivated land has the largest number of damaged terraces per farm. However, sharecropped *waqf* and private land had significantly higher numbers of broken terraces (21 *mathaber*) per hectare than the owner-cultivated land (13 *mathaber*). The higher number of terraces on the sharecropped land is to be expected since the rules and responsibilities on terrace maintenance are increasingly contested and landlords tend to avoid paying their share of the costs.

TABLE 9.5
Average number of broken terrace walls on farms
of different land tenure systems

Type of land tenure	Average farm size	Broken walls (*Mathaber*)	Broken walls (*Mathaber*)
	Ha	Per farm	Per ha
Private-cultivated land	1.35	16	12
Sharecropped private land	0.43	8	19
Sharecropped *Waqf* land	0.3	8	25

Source: M. Moslih Alsanabani, 1997.

During the interviews farmers ranked state land as the most degraded, followed by *waqf* land, though private land was considered to be in a relatively better condition. The level of degradation was attributed to landlords' unwillingness to contribute to terrace maintenance.

The cumulative average numbers of broken terrace walls per hectare for different land tenure systems until 1997 are shown in Figure 9.1. The relatively higher number of broken terrace walls that were dealt with in 1997 does not correspond strictly to the number which collapsed that year, since terrace repairs are usually postponed until after the harvest, at which time tenants will receive the landowner's share of the cost of repairing terraces as a portion of the harvested crops. The remaining number of broken walls that occurred in and before 1996 indicates the slowness of the response to terrace maintenance. There is a clear trend towards an increasing number of *mathaber* that are not repaired. Tenant farmers regard many of the terrace collapses that occurred in the past as constituting major damage – which is the responsibility of the landlord. Such damage on private land is considered expensive and lack of financial resources is seen as the limiting factor.

FIGURE 9.1
Cumulative degraded terraces

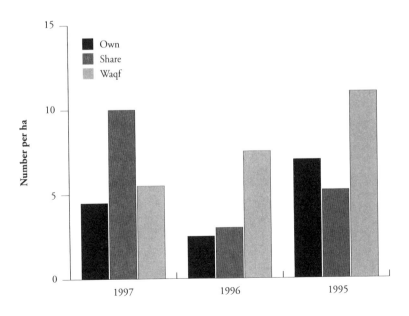

However, the author's study (Alsanabani, 1997) indicates that the recurrence of *mathaber* is second only to high costs as one of the main constraints. Farmers in Kuhlan-Affar and the Wadi Sharis area reported frequent recurrence of terrace-wall damage, which may imply that the essential indigenous knowledge of terrace construction and repair is eroding. Some farmers indicated that the constant occurrence of *mathaber* was sufficiently frustrating to make them consider abandoning their terraces.

Collective actions and terrace management

Over many centuries, collective action has played an important rule in constructing and maintaining mountain terraces in Yemen. For instance, *jaysh* and *'awn* are terms that describe collective actions in different highland regions. *Jaysh* occurs when a farmer or a household requires assistance for major terrace repairs or for other urgent situations such as flood diversion or repair of damaged houses, and is unable to carry these out alone. The farmer concerned would inform each household in the community of his need for collective action (*jaysh*) to repair damaged terraces, and provide food for those who would participate in the *jaysh*. An announcement accompanied by drum beats was made early in the morning and people – normally an adult male from each household – were summoned to join this community action. Although participation in *jaysh* was regarded as voluntary, it was also seen as shameful not to join in.

Unlike *jaysh*, which happens only in cases of urgent need, the collective action of *'awn* can also take place in less urgent cases. In *'awn* the number of participants in the collective action may vary according to the size and nature of the task. Whereas most of the farmers in the community would participate in *'awn* if it was a case of flood diversion, only a few might become involved if it was an instance of help with harvesting. Nor is *'awn* limited to men: women may also participate in collective actions. In Raymah, for example, women may help in crop harvesting or in carrying manure to the fields. Participation in *'awn* is also common in the mountain terrace region for collecting fodder from *mahajer*, and is a form of assistance that is offered by one farmer to another for less urgent activities such as harvesting, or repairing minor damage to terraces. However, *'awn* may be considered as a debt.

These practices have largely disappeared due to migration, urbanisation and changing attitudes among the population. As a result, many terraces have become severely degraded and are no longer cultivable.

In spite of the modern-day decline of systems of collective action, village rotation systems were still found in the area under study. In these systems, the entire community adopts the same cropping pattern on fields in the same area, *wattan*, and this is rotated seasonally. Farmers are convinced that this practice will maintain soil productivity.

Tenancy arrangements in rangelands

Mahjer (pl. *mahajer*) is a designation of *marhaq al-mal* (Alsanabani *et al.*, 1997) as a reserve area in which grazing is prohibited at certain times, such as the wet season. However, the traditional practice of *mahajer* is limited to private ownership such as *maraheq al-mal*. The *qabal* arrangement in the *mahajer* is not the same, being a rental arrangement that is not fixed, as with farmland, and that is restricted to the *mahajer* rangeland areas (*mahajer* being privately owned areas of rangeland). The purpose of such an arrangement is to utilise the fodder that grows in such areas during the wet season. The basis for estimating the fees that a tenant should pay the *mahjer* owner is neither the unit area nor the average yield of fodder in the *mahjer*. Rather it is based on the number of workers that are required per day to collect fodder from a whole *mahjer*. Normally the fees for workers increase annually, and as a result so do the fees for *mahajer*. In other words, the fee is not fixed for the rate of workers' fees on the date of signing the *qabal* agreement. The *qabal* in *mahajer* is found in areas with a relatively high production of fodder such as Raymah, Othmah and Hymah districts (Sana'a Province).

The most common feature of the sharecropping arrangements is that the use of the natural vegetative cover of *maraheq al-mal* adjacent to farmland may implicitly be included. In fact there are no separate arrangements made with regard to such use. In practice, both landowner and tenant farmer follow common rules in the area, whereby the latter is allowed to benefit on a limited basis from the natural vegetation on the *maraheq*. He is permitted to collect fodder from *maraheq al-mal* and to graze livestock. He may also collect fodder (leaves) from certain trees but is not permitted to cut trees as fuel-wood.

On *waqf* land a farmer is similarly allowed to collect fodder and graze livestock on *maraheq al-mal*. He is also allowed to utilise trees growing on the rangelands for fodder collection (leaves). Furthermore, a tenant may also cut trees on an annual basis for fuel-wood though may not fell the whole tree.

Conclusion

Abandonment of terraced agricultural land in the highlands of Yemen had resulted in degradation of productive land, which was historically constructed and sustained with indigenous knowledge and by cooperation within local communities.

There are private, estate and endowment cultivated land ownerships, and *marhaq* land. However, there is no agricultural land registration and the figures of different land properties are only estimates. At the local (sub-district or *'uzla*) level, a trusted person, locally known as *amin*, keeps records of land transactions such as sales and tenancy arrangements and this is encouraged by the Ministry of Local Administration. Private land is mainly cultivated by owners (70 per cent), but it is also rented out to tenants under sharecropping arrangements which depend on the crop, agro-ecological zone, availability of irrigation water, the cost sharing arrangements and the terrace maintenance cost-sharing arrangements. State and *waqf* land are cultivated by tenants under sharecropping.

The study found that the number of degraded terraces in land under sharecropping arrangements is higher than in examples of land which is owner-cultivated. Lack of clearly defined responsibility between tenants and landowners for the maintenance and cost-sharing was one of the main reasons for that. Although these responsibilities are defined in the customary rules of land use, there are no effective enforcement mechanisms.

Future studies, therefore, should address this aspect, and identify options and measures to enhance terrace maintenance, particularly under food crops.

10

Land Tenure, Social Structure and the State in the Southern Governorates in the Mid-1990s

Helen Lackner

Introduction[1]

Land tenure, whether for cultivation, pasture or any other use, is a core issue in all societies. The state's management of tenure conflicts is indicative of the nature of the relationship existing between the state, individuals and locally based authorities and power groups; in particular, tenure issues also reflect the tensions inherent in these relations and changes in the balance of power over time. In Yemen's Southern Governorates, the opportunities and problems brought about by unification and the changed political environment have both found their main focus in matters relating to land tenure during the 1990s. The area's history over the past two or more centuries has become a source of contemporary reference for a variety of ownership claims. It is clearly a case where historical knowledge and study are of immediate socioeconomic relevance and are not merely of remote academic interest.

An early measure taken by the unified Yemeni state was the denationalisation of agricultural land that the socialist regime in the PDRY had distributed to those farming it in the 1970s. This decision resulted in the return of land to those who had owned it under the British Protectorate and the dispossession of the farmers who had been cultivating it for the past generation. According to the Council of Ministers Decree No. 65,[2] which provided the legal framework for this measure, the farmers who had benefited from the Land Reform were to be given state lands in compensation. The allocation of state lands has raised many issues, locally and nationally, and these are central to the new relationships developing between locally based power and the state.

This chapter is based on work carried out in Shabwa, Wadi Hadhramawt and Abyan in 1996 and 1997; although Lahej Governorate was not covered in detail, a few observations will also be made concerning the Tuban Delta area. Through an analysis of some of the issues which emerged in the course of discussions with the communities concerned,[3] the chapter sets out to illustrate the ability of the various social groups involved to influence changes in their present socioeconomic and political status. It outlines the basic social and historical background to the present situation, and then looks at the issues more broadly in order to identify what these specific examples and cases indicate with respect to changes in the power and status of the different social groups concerned and their interrelationships, both within the area concerned and with respect to the broader state authorities.

Background

Relevant aspects of Yemeni social structure

Yemeni social stratification is complex (for pre-independence social structure in the Hadhramawt see Bujra, 1971; for PDRY social structure see Lackner, 1985; on Yemen in general see Chelhod, 1985, esp. Vol. 3). In addition to groupings based on status at birth, the many changes which have taken place in the past three decades or so have created new possibilities for social mobility. As will be seen below, the criteria for ascribed status also vary in different areas of the country, both in their definitions and in the strictness with which they are enforced. Before I discuss the situation found during fieldwork, an extremely rough sketch is given of the broad features of social stratification in the country.

The highest social stratum is that of the *sada* (sing. *sayyid*), also known in some areas as *ashraf* (sing. *sharif*), who claim descent from the Prophet. Occupationally they are the stratum which has responsibility for knowledge; initially this was religious and was later extended to other forms of knowledge. They hold positions connected with religious and legal affairs, are often landowners but do not cultivate the land themselves, and are generally seen as the 'intellectual' stratum. The *mashaykh* (sing. and plural) have slightly lower social status but are also associated with mediation and legal affairs.

The largest social group is that of the tribesmen (*qaba'il*, sing. *qabili*) who are warriors and farmers, usually owning their land but also sometimes working other people's land. They are also very conscious of their ancestries and their relations with other tribes and groups.

A medium status group is that of traders and artisans (*qarar*), who are not very numerous. In recent decades, they have gradually merged into either the higher or lower social strata depending on the changes in their financial situation. The fact that many migrants of different social strata have returned to Yemen and set themselves up in commerce is an important factor in assimilating this group with others.

The lower social strata are the *du'afa* (sing. *da'if*) and *masakin* (sing. *miskin*), i.e. the weak and poor. They include the *harthan* and other farming groups who cultivate land owned by others: in Hadhramawt they are known as *fellahin*.[4] Below them are the 'servant' groups, the *'abid* (sing. *'abd*), the *sibyan* and the *akhdam*, who are the lowest strata and sometimes not even considered to be Yemenis by tribesmen and *sada*.

The above description is extremely sketchy and there is considerable debate about the borders between the different groups and their definitions. Moreover the situation varies in different areas. The considerable transformations which have affected Yemeni society in recent decades have not only allowed some people to change their status situation gradually but have also reduced the strength of the rules governing relations between the strata.

Land tenure prior to independence

As a general rule, pre-colonial land ownership was only slightly modified during British rule, since Britain was only indirectly involved in the management of socioeconomic affairs in the Protectorates. Control over land was of three main types:

- tribal *mathawi* (sing. *mithwa*) lands, which were areas within whose borders a tribe was responsible for the protection of travellers and of social groups under its guardianship; they were also used as grazing land for its livestock. They could briefly and crudely be summarised as the equivalent of political borders;
- private ownership by individuals or families over agricultural, building and other small plots of land. These could belong to tribespeople or other social groups, particularly the *sada*, and even traders; some social groups in some areas were not 'allowed' to own land;
- state ownership by the various states/amirates of lands which were used for cultivation, public or other purposes and controlled by the state authorities, individual rulers or their officials.

During the colonial period, the main transformation was the interruption of the process of fluidity and change, resulting from the strengthening of the control exercised by certain families and individuals whose position was stabilised by the support they got from the British authorities. Hence a process of continuous transformation and modification of borders through various power struggles was in effect 'petrified' at the moment when Protection Treaties were signed with Britain, thus empowering certain individuals and families at the expense of others for a variety of more or less rational reasons. In this way the Protectorates were composed of a few substantive states, such as the Qu'ayti and 'Abdali, and many minor or microscopic ones (e.g. Wahedi, Yafi', etc.) who might have disappeared or developed different balances of power and areas of control had the former ebb and flow of local power struggles been allowed to continue. Britain also encouraged some of the states, particularly in Hadhramawt, to introduce various aspects of modern administration, including recording changes in land ownership on a more systematic and centralised basis (see Lackner, 1985, among others).

On the whole, regardless of what socialist ideology asserted in the 1970s, land tenure in the Aden Protectorates had not been monopolised by a few large 'feudal' landowners. While there were a number of such owners, in particular the leading and ruling families in Lahej ('Abdali, al-Jifri, Aidrus), 'Abyan (Fadli, Awaliq), and Hadhramawt (al-Kaf, Qu'ayti, etc.), in other areas, particularly Shabwa, there were no very large landowners. On the whole most agricultural landholdings were small and belonged to people who either cultivated themselves, or had the land cultivated on their behalf according to different types of arrangements. The size of holdings could range up to 100 *feddans* (40 ha) which is not particularly large for a rainfed or spate-irrigated holding. Permanent irrigated agriculture was developed only in the twentieth century when mechanically operated pumps and engines were introduced. This also took place mostly on smallholdings, where the well owner took a major share of the income, thus reducing the income of the landowner when land and water were owned by different individuals. The country cannot be described as one of large feudal landowners, and most holdings were barely sufficient to support a nuclear, let alone an extended, family.

Land tenure in the People's Democratic Republic of Yemen

Independence brought an entirely different situation. The Constitution of the PDRY asserted state ownership over all land, and a process of nationalisation was implemented from 1969 onwards. This will be discussed in some detail here, as it has direct and immediate relevance to the contemporary situation. The Land Reform Law (No. 27 for 1970) restricted individual land ownership to 20 *feddans* of irrigated and up to 40 *feddans* of rainfed land, while families were allowed to own twice this amount. In the revolutionary fervour of the early 1970s, the authorities encouraged peasants to get involved in uprisings known as *intifadhat* to evict landowners and take over the lands, but this presented certain practical problems. It was intended as a move to overthrow the feudal landowners and to empower the oppressed peasantry but it did not always work out that way, particularly as most landowners in Yemen were not feudal or pseudo-feudal landowners. Most of the few who were had fled at independence, since they had either been supporters of the British or of FLOSY, the defeated Liberation movement (as was the case of the 'Abdali in Lahej or the Qu'ayti and Kathiri ruling families in Hadhramawt, or large owners such as the Al-Kaf *sada* and others). Much of this land was turned into state farms and rather than creating a group of dispossessed farmers, its repossession instead produced a group of unemployed salaried and casual workers.

In most areas, agricultural land had been held in small plots by farmers of tribal and other origins. However, the revolutionary zeal of the NLF[5] militants, who lacked political sophistication and training, meant that they insisted on implementing the Land Reform through *intifadhat*, even in areas where there was no social basis to do so. As a result, farmers in many areas exchanged plots of land, handing their own plots to their colleagues and taking others of similar size and condition in exchange. This process usually took place without bitterness and by mutual agreement, thus ensuring formal implementation of the Land Reform while making little difference to local socioeconomic conditions. In these areas there was almost no violence; if there was any it was unrelated to land redistribution.

In other areas, the situation was different and the *intifadhat* were an opportunity for settling scores, both through land redistribution and through the infliction of violence on former landowners and other 'oppressors' of the farming classes; this was the case in some parts of

Wadi Hadhramawt (particularly near Shibam and Seiyun), in Abyan Delta and Wadi Tuban. The bitterness left by the implementation of the Land Reform is still very much in evidence, since although these events took place in the early 1970s, the people involved are still in many cases alive and present in the area. Many of those who left the country during this period are now returning with thoughts of revenge.

Once the lands were taken over, the farmers were encouraged to group into cooperatives. Initially it was intended that these would gradually progress towards common ownership and cultivation of the land, but this never materialised. In practice they were similar to cooperatives in other countries, functioning as institutions providing agricultural services (inputs, extension) and organising access to machinery through the Machinery Rental Stations. They were also representatives of the state since they collected taxes from the farmers and organised marketing through the centralised agencies for the various 'strategic' crops (wheat, cotton, etc.). They were also responsible for devising the cropping pattern within their area so as to fit into national production plans, but found this difficult to implement effectively since farmers on the whole continued to cultivate the crops they favoured.

By the 1980s, there was no longer talk of collectivisation. As agriculture in the PDRY became increasingly privatised, the cooperatives lost their controlling aspects, particularly with respect to cropping patterns, and turned into mere service providers. The state began to distribute long-term usufruct titles that gave farmers full rights of inheritance etc. over their plots, and the role of the cooperatives was restricted to providing extension, inputs and collection of taxes. Newly reclaimed lands were all distributed with individual usufruct titles. By the time of unification, the situation in practice was one of smallholders with access to cooperative services.

Land tenure after unification
Unification in 1990 brought about another sudden and massive change in rural social structure and in particular in the living and working conditions of the smallholder farmers. The Council of Ministers' Decree No. 65, issued in May 1991, stated that all lands were to be returned to their pre-independence owners and that dispossessed farmers would be compensated with five *feddans* of irrigated land ready for cultivation; farmers were also to be compensated for any investment they had made

on the owners' lands during their tenure. If owners were unable to pay this compensation, they might decide to give up this land to the farmers and themselves accept new compensation land. In practice this decree was implemented unevenly, with the repossession component being widely implemented while the compensation aspect was practically ignored. Most cooperative farmers on land owned by formerly exiled landowners were evicted by force, particularly in Abyan Governorate. Many who resisted eviction were either threatened or imprisoned. As a result only a few former tenants continue to cultivate the land they had under the PDRY regime, either on the basis of agreement with the repossessing landowner or, more exceptionally, because they have successfully resisted eviction.

Out of those who were dispossessed, those who had 'exchanged' lands have returned to their own original lands. Many others have accepted unfavourable agreements from repossessing landlords who have revived pre-independence tenancy terms, and many remain landless sharecroppers on insecure short-term agreements. Since unification, the situation which has been re-created is broadly one of smallholding agriculture in precarious conditions, but with one notable change: in the course of the previous generation, the population has more than doubled throughout the country, thus increasing the pressure on very limited and fragile resources.

The situation in the Southern Governorates since unification and particularly after the 1994 Civil War has been characterised by uncertainty. It is a phase of transition from a situation where land tenure as well as other aspects of life were clearly managed according to known rules (whether liked or not) to a new form of administration which is still unclear. This uncertainty creates opportunities for a variety of claims and counterclaims in all aspects of social life, and in particular with respect to a sensitive issue such as land tenure.

Aspects of social structure directly relevant to land tenure issues
Wadi Hadhramawt
The land tenure situation in Hadhramawt differs from that prevailing in other governorates for one main reason: in this area a clear distinction exists between the social groups which own land and are traditionally allowed to do so, and members of the social group who cultivate the land and who are traditionally not allowed to own it. The former include tribespeople, *sada*, *mashaykh*, and trades people (*qarar*), while

the latter are all from the *du'afa* (i.e. weak people) social group, known locally as *fellahin*, who cultivate the land or can work in construction but for whom landownership in pre-colonial days was impossible. While these ascribed status characteristics weakened during the half-century that encompassed British and socialist rule, the former higher status groups have recently been trying to revive them and these attempts are being resisted by the people concerned. Therefore those making claims on the land do not include any *fellahin* and, because the claims involve status as well as land, the claimants are particularly virulent and unwilling to compromise.

Many former leaders of Hadhrami society, whether tribesmen, *sada* or others, spent much of the socialist period in Saudi Arabia where they gained a different experience of rule, and where they also observed some of the characteristics of the position of Yemeni tribes who live in the border areas with Saudi Arabia. Their interpretation and understanding of relations between tribes and central government, based on observation of the relations of some of the border tribes, was generalised to cover all tribe–government relations in the YAR and has also become a model for their approach to their relationship with the state in unified Yemen. This interpretation of contemporary political dynamics is the basis for many of the existing broad undocumented claims.

Under both British rule and that of the YSP during the period of the PDRY, tribesmen found that central government power reached everywhere, particularly when there were conflicts and when the authority of the state was challenged. After the Yemeni revolution in Sana'a in 1962, and particularly up to the late 1970s, there was a widespread belief in the PDRY that the YAR was a lawless area where the state was unable to enforce its authority and where tribal rule and tribal conflicts could take place at will and be won by the strongest, who would then force the state to accept the result. While this may have been the case for brief periods and in certain areas, it ceased to be true soon after the current president, 'Ali 'Abdullah Saleh, came to power in 1978. However, this conviction is one that has encouraged would-be tribal leaders from Hadhramawt and other border areas to believe that they could act in defiance of state laws and that such behaviour would be endorsed by the president and the rulers in Sana'a. But this is only the case when the activities undertaken fit in with the political strategy of the authorities, and within the context of Saudi–Yemeni relations.

In Saudi Arabia, by contrast, exiles lived within the framework of a very authoritarian environment in which their room for manoeuvre was greater than that of Saudi nationals with respect to some activities. They were supported and given the opportunity to bear arms along the borders and were allowed, and at certain times encouraged, to cause problems across the borders. However their activities were firmly delimited by Saudi Arabian foreign policy objectives. This was clearly seen in May 2000 when the border agreement was made between Saudi Arabia and Yemen: the Yemeni opposition, based in Saudi Arabia and with offices in various locations around the world, ceased to operate overnight.

Shabwa Governorate

The land tenure situation in Shabwa Governorate is somewhat different from that prevailing in Hadhramawt. In this governorate in particular most land was grazing land and was *mithwa*, i.e. common land within the borders of a particular tribe. Small patches which were irrigated were privately owned, and most agriculture took place on spate-irrigated land. As stated above, it was only in the course of the twentieth century that permanent irrigation was introduced, and even then it is very limited in scope and area.

It is important to note that farming is marginal in this governorate. Socioeconomic inequality did not emerge from taxation on agriculture, but rather from trade and other activities: agriculture on its own was insufficient to sustain the population of the area, and had to be supplemented by livestock keeping. Indeed, most tribesmen were primarily semi-nomadic livestock herders, who had taken up agriculture in recent decades, rather than the opposite. While landholdings were on the whole larger than elsewhere, this is because yields were very low; the infrequency of spate flows and their unpredictability has meant that Shabwa has for a long time been an area that lives from emigration as much as from agriculture. A spate-irrigated holding of 50 *feddans*[6] in Shabwa is probably enough in most years to keep a family.

Social structure is less strictly defined than in Hadhramawt, and while similar social groups are found, their relationships are more relaxed. Traditional landowners are primarily tribesmen along with some *sada* and *fuqaha'* (sing. *faqih* – who are comparable to the *mashaykh* in Hadhramawt). These three groups own most of the land that they formerly cultivated themselves with their families. The small amount of land that was irrigated by wells was partly cultivated by the *harthan* (equivalent to *fellahin* in Hadhramawt), particularly when it belonged to the *fuqaha'* and *ashraf* rather than to tribesmen, since the former were the main rulers of the area, particularly in Bayhan.

At the time of the *intifadhat* of the Land Reform, most land was exchanged between members of the landowning group, thus formally implementing the Reform without making significant changes in social and political relationships. This was reasonable given that there was little social differentiation between the various tribespeople, most of whom were equally poor; their income was based on a combination of livestock herding, agriculture and external income, particularly participation in the armed forces and later emigration to the Gulf states. In addition, land that was later reclaimed by the state through projects was mostly distributed to former semi-nomads and to members of the farming group, the *harthan*.

Abyan and Lahej

Pre-independence land tenure in the Abyan Delta is similar to that prevailing in the Tuban Delta, with a few large landowners, mostly from the ruling families and their allies. From the 1940s onwards, the British encouraged the rulers in both areas to introduce cultivation of cotton to diversify British sources of supply. Spate-irrigation structures were modernised and groundwater irrigation was introduced. Tenure, with a number of larger landowners, was closer to the 'feudal' model that the socialists wanted to eradicate. Smallholdings also existed.

In Ahwar, located 100 km to the east of Zinjibar, along the coast, the situation was slightly different. Much of the land belonged to the state – i.e. the Lower Awlaqi state – through its treasury, and is known as *beit al-mal* land. Although much of it was leased in the mid-1960s to individuals for farming, with the long-term objective of irrigating the land for cotton and other cultivation, no significant development was carried out on this land prior to independence. At the time of the Land Reform, these lands were distributed to farmers, most of whom were tribesmen, and in the early 1970s a series of spate-diversion structures were constructed with Soviet assistance. Thereafter these lands were cultivated, mostly under cash crops, i.e. largely cotton, fruit and vegetables. Other lands were owned in small plots by tribesmen and *harthan*. As was done elsewhere in the country, these lands were mostly exchanged during the period of the *intifadhat* to comply formally with the Land Reform, but without making any substantial social transformation among groups of equally deprived people.

Broadly speaking, the socialist Land Reform in the Abyan and Tuban deltas did dispossess 'feudal' landowners and the lands were distributed to small farmers from the tribes as well as from the lower social-status groups. This distribution was implemented with varying degrees of violence, though on the whole most large landowners, having been associated with the previous rulers, had left the country by the time of the Land Reform. Much of this land, which had previously been cultivated in large estates, was turned into state farms, while the cooperatives divided the land into smaller plots.

Additionally, both these deltas are areas where the repossession process in the 1990s took place largely by force and the threat of force. Most former beneficiaries of the Land Reform are working now as casual labourers or sharecroppers on very short contracts, rarely on the same lands as those they had received in the Land Reform.

Socially, as in other ways, the situation in Abyan Governorate is again different, though the trend of change between Hadhramawt and Shabwa continues towards Abyan. The differentiation between social strata is less strict, with greater possibilities for social mixing and a further reduction in the rigidity of barriers between ascribed social groups. With respect to the strictness of enforcement of traditional rights to land tenure, there is a clear gradation, with Hadhramawt being the area where ascribed status was most strongly enforced, and the Western Governorates the region where it was weakest and where it was easier for low-status people to own land.

The debate surrounding state-owned lands

The situation should be straightforward: the state has denationalised the formerly privately owned lands which had been nationalised by the socialist regime, thus restoring private property as it was during the period of the British Protectorates. Other land should return to its former status and, broadly speaking, should become state owned as it was under the Protectorates. However, the situation is complicated by misconceptions about the way the country is currently ruled, and is also subject to attempts at political manipulation by individuals with a variety of interests. Changes in the balance of power between social groups as well as tribal allegiances are currently very important. This was particularly the case in the period preceding the 1997 elections. In the current uncertain situation, the state does not, on the whole, systematically enforce its right to control state lands. It does so when it needs the lands for its own purposes (road construction, construction of government establishments, military use), or when it is politically expedient. Therefore local groups can often engage in power struggles over land, particularly when these struggles do not challenge the state's authority and indeed may even serve its interests.

In practice this means that, at the local level, anyone with a grudge against the former regime who hopes to gain personal or political benefit or who is trying to assert his[7] political clout, is liable to make a variety of claims on the land. These claims are based on any number of what are often mutually contradictory types of arguments: e.g. interpretation of colonial or pre-colonial 'customary law' or history, customary rights, *shari'a*, documented and undocumented agreements of centuries past and present, and so on. In particular most of the broad claims deny the existence of state-owned lands by the states which existed prior to the Protectorates period, despite the fact that such ownership is clearly documented and well known in all the earlier states and statelets. State-owned lands were in many cases defined and confirmed during the Protectorate period; in some cases these documents were formally endorsed by the British officials responsible for the areas.

The claimants feel encouraged by their widespread misunderstanding of the land situation in the former YAR and believe that force remains the main criterion in deciding disputes in the Northern Governorates. They completely ignore the role of customary law and local legal authorities in the settling of disputes in the former YAR, let alone the right of the state, which it enforced whenever it was considered appropriate.

Types of claims
There are two main types of claims on the land. The first are tribal claims over vast undefined areas; they are based on traditional tribal borders and have no legal basis as private property, despite the assertions made by the claimants. The claims are 'justified' by an instant trans-formation of tribal, i.e. political, borders into private property claims. No court (customary, *shari'a* or secular) would take them seriously; moreover neither does the state, when it gives any attention to the matter, since

the recognition of such claims would deny its rights to drill for oil, to construct roads and buildings, and so on.

The second are individual or family claims; they come from tribes-men, *sada* and any other individuals from any social group that owned land prior to the socialist period. These are more serious and substantive claims and are based on customary documentation identifying both the site and its owners. These claims are over cultivated land, or land that was once cultivated and that covers known and identifiable areas. Customary documentation is sometimes available and is of some degree of precision.

Within this broad description there are local differences in the areas covered by the present study. These are based on a number of factors, including changes in social status, balance of power between social groups, rigidity of ascribed status, relationships with the power structure, and others. The claiming groups in Wadi Hadhramawt are all from the traditional landowning social strata and they object to land being given to *fellahin* for social and political reasons as much as for straightforward economic motives. Distributing land as freehold would fundamentally transform the social status of the *fellahin* from that of an inferior group to one that would be on a level comparable with that of the *sada* or tribespeople. The latter already resent the advantages obtained during the socialist period by the *fellahin* who not only had privileged access to land, but were also given opportunities to improve their social status and encouraged to take up important political positions. The *sada* regard unification and in particular the post-civil-war period as an opportunity to regain their own superior status at the expense of the *fellahin* and object strongly to any move which assists the *fellahin* to retain, or even occasionally to strengthen, some of the gains they had made during the socialist period.

A further cause for claims is the widespread belief that in the last years of the socialist period and during the first three years after unification, many middle-ranking and senior officials of the ruling party and other influential people obtained land with private property titles. This was usually in prime sites where it could be expected that high profits would be obtained in future through building. This is viewed critically both by the poor who compare the behaviour of officials and their stated ideology, and by those whose private property had been nationalised earlier.

Hence, to some extent, what are presented in Wadi Hadhramawt as problems of tenure are in fact problems of social relations and resistance to a change in social status. This has three main aspects:

1. the former higher-status social groups are trying to reassert the status they had lost during the colonial and socialist periods;
2. these groups are resisting any action which would confirm the status of equality which the lower social groups have acquired in the past half-century; and
3. the lower-social-status people concerned are torn between hope that they might retain the sociopolitical gains made during recent decades as well as re-establish their household economic viability, and the fear that nothing will happen and that their current situation of social and economic deprivation will continue.

In Shabwa Governorate, after unification and Decree 65, most people re-exchanged land and re-established the situation that had prevailed prior to independence. The only situations where claims have emerged involve (1) the newly reclaimed lands, which tribesmen and others were tempted to claim because they had been transformed into cultivable land from being mere grazing land; and (2) the lands which had been improved and developed by cooperative holders and which they had no interest in relinquishing in favour of far inferior and less developed land, regardless of whether it 'belonged' to them or not. This means, in effect, that social tension is focused on disagreements between *harthan* and tribesmen who hold lands developed during the socialist period, and the 'owners' of these lands who want to benefit from the investment made in the 1970s and 1980s without contributing any payment or compensation for it.

In the Abyan Delta no lands have been made available for the compensation process; hence there are no claims. In Ahwar claims are limited in most areas. In Lahej Governorate very large areas were proposed for compensation but have been found technically unsuitable, although some plots have been distributed. Since the author did not conduct any fieldwork there, no information concerning claims in this governorate is given in this chapter.

With a few notable exceptions, it also seems to be a general rule that claims are strongest where past relations between the tribesmen and *sada* on the one hand and the *fellahin/harthan* on the other have been tense and the *intifadhat* more violent. Where these relations are good, claims are weak or non-existent.

Major issues raised by the contemporary situation

The distribution process and the social issues raised

The proposed distribution of state land to the former beneficiaries of the Agrarian Reform is an opportunity for bringing into the open many of the social tensions that underlie Yemeni society in the Southern Governorates after unification. Although there were many changes in the balance of power in rural areas during the PDRY period, the fundamental facts of policy remained out of the realm of discussion: former landowners and particularly former rulers had no opportunity to air their complaints, let alone repossess their properties. Those changes that took place over the two decades concerned focused on the status of holdings maintained by the beneficiaries of the Land Reform and the extent to which land was to be cultivated collectively or individually. By the time of unification it was clear that smallholder private agriculture was the dominant form, accepted by the overwhelming majority of farmers. Even the state farms were in the process of being privatised. Unification and Decree 65 brought back the former landowners who had been exiled or marginalised and gave them the opportunity to criticise openly what had happened in the past and also to 'take revenge' on those whom they blamed for their earlier losses. However, most of their victims have been the farmers who had received the land rather than the politicians who had taken the decision to implement the Land Reform. Not content with recovering their land, many of these landowners want to prevent the former beneficiaries of the Land Reform from obtaining any compensation. The main tools in this struggle are claims on the land.

Who controls the land?

The land which has been allocated by the state for distribution is mostly barren land that has either never been cultivated or has been left fallow for decades and even centuries. Hence, according to customary and *shari'a* law as well as to the constitution, these lands belong to the state. However in view of the government's recent unwillingness to enforce this right firmly, local individuals and groups have challenged state ownership of these lands. This has been done primarily by people who want both to increase or restore their authority in their home areas and to demonstrate to the former beneficiaries of the Land Reform that they are now those in power and in control. It is a form of 'settling of accounts' between, on the one hand, the social groups who dominated in the pre-Independence period, were suppressed under the socialist regime, and who are now determined to reassert their supremacy, and on the other, the lower-status groups whose position was the opposite in these periods. In Yemen, the state does not usually intervene in local power struggles unless its overall authority is threatened. Because most of these disputes do not present any such threat and are, on the contrary, opportunities for the regime to gain support from local forces, there is only limited intervention.

In brief, there is little doubt that the state ultimately controls land distribution and ownership, but that it chooses to enforce its authority only when this assists it in demonstrating its control at the wider national level, or if it serves the interests of powerful individuals or groups at the central state level.

Changes in social status of the cultivating social groups

Overall, one of the major achievements of the British Protectorates and the socialist regime in the PDRY was to empower individuals from the lower-social-status groups. This was done in a number of different ways:

- by giving them access to education at all levels: in Hadhramawt in particular, during the Protectorates many individuals from lower social strata entered the modern education system. As a result, they were later in a position to take up senior positions in the civil service and in government as they were the most highly educated and competent people;
- through land: the socialist regime gave land to people from these lower social strata, thus bringing them to equal status with tribesmen and *sada*, and officially eliminating the status differentials which have been a long-standing feature of Yemeni society.

Although, following unification and Decree 65, the former beneficiaries were to lose the land they had been given, there was no suggestion that they should return to their former lower social status. Indeed the

1994 Constitution of the RoY, like those of the YAR and PDRY previously, affirms the equality of all citizens and rejects distinctions based on ascribed status. The lower-status people who have lost their lands are therefore resisting attempts by tribesmen and *sada* to deprive them of their other achievements and reduce them, once again, to the status of 'servant farmers'.

Changes in circumstances of the other social groups

Other social groups lost status during the socialist period, and in the case of the richer groups, lost property as well. Their current attempts to re-establish their supremacy are based primarily on their former ascribed social status. However, their success is largely determined by factors other than the social group into which they were born: their wealth is a primary determinant of their current potential power, closely followed by possession of a currently powerful network of political allies and supporters, locally and nationally. With respect to wealth, those who are wealthiest are generally people who were successful migrants to Saudi Arabia, where they either obtained wealth through trade and enterprise, or received an income from the Saudi state as a mark of support for them as former rulers opposed to the socialist regime.

Among people with political aspirations who emigrated and returned after unification, a distinction must be made between two groups. First are the poor, mostly farmers, who were expelled from Saudi Arabia and Kuwait. While some of these returned with some wealth, politically speaking, few have developed any influence beyond their villages. The other migrant group, mostly larger traders and people who left for political reasons in the 1960s and 1970s, are mainly tribal shaikhs, *sada*, and other formerly powerful people who are determined to re-establish their political influence. Some of these operate at the local level and take up positions as 'traditional' shaikhs, something that cannot be achieved without support from the central government authorities. Others are trying to use their local areas as bases for increasing their wealth through land and property ownership as well as to insert themselves into the wider political framework, and are therefore more active in national 'party' politics.

Potential and constraints of the new rural land tenure situation
The restoration of private property in farming and a completely free market in agricultural products have brought about changes in rural society and economy. The effect of rescinding the Land Reform means that there are now two main types of social relations emerging in agriculture. On the one hand smallholders are now operating much as they were in the late 1980s, though in some cases with different people managing individual farms. The main difference for the smallholders is the effective disappearance of the cooperatives with respect to the supply of inputs and support in marketing, activities that have now been taken over by the private sector. Farming on smallholdings varies in its productivity according to soils and irrigation potential, but there is little doubt that most such farmers are, at best, not far above the poverty line. In areas which are more remote from markets or where soils and irrigation are poor, they are likely to be below the poverty line. This type of agriculture does not create much in the way of labour opportunities, and indeed most farming families would have surplus labour available for other activities for most, if not all, of the year. Most family members are likely to be busy only during sowing and harvesting time. Although partly mechanised, such farming is probably uneconomic when full mechanisation costs are taken into consideration.[8]

On the other hand, the restoration of land to the few large landowners has deprived many smallholders of their farms and has thus created a large pool of labourers, who are available either for sharecropping (even on relatively bad terms) or as casual labourers on daily or seasonal contracts. While there was a time when Yemen had a shortage of labour, the situation has now changed, and the transformation of rural relations in the Southern Governorates has contributed to this situation. In the absence of employment opportunities in their villages, whether agricultural or other, many former farmers who have lost their lands migrate temporarily or seasonally to towns in search of unskilled work in construction or any other activity.

Causes and significance of the differences between the areas
The restoration of private landownership and the return of former landlords is having a different social impact in each area. The difference is based on the specific history of social relations between the different status groups. In Hadhramawt, where the distinction within the social

strata between those who are traditionally allowed to own land and those who are not is at its greatest and most inflexible, the process of distributing land to the former beneficiaries of the Land Reform meets with strong resistance from the landowning classes. This is because it would, if implemented as intended (i.e. through giving freehold titles to the farmers), formalise an official change in the social hierarchy that is as fiercely resisted by the landowning classes as it is desired by the non-landowning classes. Here the process is seen as a challenge to traditional social relations that goes against what the returning landlords believe is the philosophy of the new Yemeni state. They regard unification as a defeat of the 'modern' progressive forces that were embodied in the socialist regime and, failing to recognise the state's 'modernisation' tendencies, are surprised to find that the state might be willing to help the 'lower' social strata to change their status by giving them access to landownership.

In other governorates, the significance of the allocation of state lands to the former beneficiaries of the Land Reform is seen merely as a form of support for the poorer farmers, many of whom are tribesmen, and is not regarded as a fundamental challenge to any existing or desired social order. Challenges are based primarily on alternative claims to the land, whether justified or not, that are caused by hopes of gaining material benefits. Because land ownership by the low-status cultivating classes already exists and is not viewed as a fundamental challenge to the 'traditional' social order, giving land to these classes is not seen as a major political issue but merely as one of economics and local influence.

Conclusions

Is the state being weakened or strengthened through this process?
The state in Yemen is often described as weak. However, in the past decades it has strengthened its grip on the country and is now able to enforce its authority throughout the country when the authorities choose to do so. The process of transformation of land tenure in the Southern Governorates takes place within this context: in itself it neither weakens nor strengthens the state. Indeed it is an opportunity for central authorities to allow a local balance of power to develop, and it is only when the state has other concerns or has a vested interest that it will intervene to enforce its authority.

Except where the state has specific proposed uses for land, it is likely that the problem of claims on land will remain unsolved in the foreseeable future, at least for the next few years and probably longer. There will be a solution only when the state asserts its rights to control land which is not clearly privately owned; the nature of the solution will depend on *how* the state decides to do so, i.e. in whose interests. This may well not be in the interests of the poor. However, this is an opportunity for the authorities to demonstrate their support for the constitutionally defined equal rights for all people regardless of origin. It could also be used to strengthen state authority by taking a firmly 'modernising' stand, upholding the constitution and its laws, and demonstrating the strength of its modern institutions, such as ministries and projects, rather than allowing manipulation of change by 'tribal'-type politics.

Implications for the development of a new social structure of the areas

Regardless of anyone's wishes, a new social structure is emerging through-out Yemen which, yet again, will differ from the ones that prevailed in the 1970s and 1980s. Even leaving aside unification, the underlying socioeconomic circumstances of the country changed dramatically during the 1990s, due among other things to the sharp reduction in labour out-migration, the fall in remittances by migrant workers, the reduced ability of the state to employ citizens, the rapid increase in population, and the unsustainable exploitation of groundwater. Agriculture remains the main form of employment in rural areas, where 70 per cent of the population still lives. The reappearance of large landlords in Lahej, Abyan and Hadhramawt contributes towards the re-establishment of a significant divide between the few wealthy rural people and the majority of poor farmers. More generally, wealth acquisition by small numbers of people from all social origins is contributing towards the strengthening of social differentiation on the basis of wealth rather than of origin and descent.

Implications for national unity

The unification of Yemen is an unarguable fact. Whatever difficulties may exist and despite the considerable stresses suffered by people in the Southern Governorates, the populations of these areas have no desire to challenge the unity of the country. The vast majority of Yemenis have supported unification and believed in the existence of a 'Yemeni nation' for many decades. This is why the slogan of 'Yemeni Unity' was popular throughout Yemen in the 1970s and 1980s, regardless of the political differences then existing between the two regimes. Population movements in Yemen over the centuries and in particular in the last half century mean that almost all Yemenis have relatives elsewhere within the country, frequently in more than one distant governorate. Although this creates some tensions it also strengthens the cultural bonds and the identity of the people as Yemenis.

Within this context the current debates and challenges to state authority in the land redistribution process are no more than elements in the overall process of the country's political development. Those who challenge the state's right to land do so on the basis that they claim it as individuals or tribes, but these debates take place within the accepted premise that the country is one. These are struggles for local power and private control of resources; they are not in any way challenges to the state as a united entity. If anything they are a challenge to state ownership to the benefit of private property.

This fieldwork was carried out over six years following the short civil conflict of 1994 during which the Yemeni Socialist Party was defeated and effectively exiled. Its members remaining in the country, who opposed the 'secession', were not rewarded by the regime, which continued to repress the party's activities. Perception in the areas where this work was carried out was that those who were supposed to receive state lands (the dispossessed) were supporters of the YSP, while those who claimed the land and/or denied the existence of state lands were opponents of the YSP and supporters either of the GPC or the Islah, which at that time were in alliance. There is no doubt that all the groups involved in the land issues discussed in this chapter considered that the outcome would be determined according to political rather than any other criteria, whether legal or historical. Insofar as the poor and landless found – and to some extent still find – their political voice in the YSP and given that this party is effectively powerless, it is not surprising that by 2004, when the World Bank-financed project to allocate lands to the dispossessed farmers was reaching its end, the total area distributed was 850 feddans to 190 families, by comparison with the originally designed 9,300 feddans to 1,950 families.

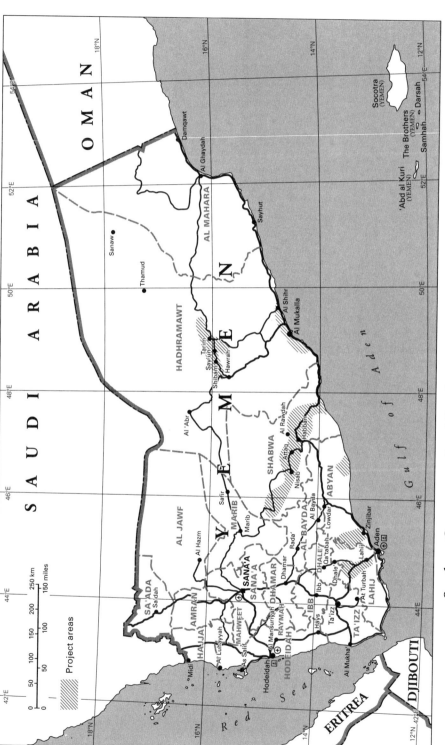

Southern Governorates Rural Development Project, Republic of Yemen

NOTES

1 This chapter is based on work I carried out for the World Bank and the Government of Yemen in 1996–7 as Chair of the Committee for the Selection of Beneficiaries of Project Land Development, within the framework of the design phase of the Southern Governorates Rural Development Project. The responsibility of the Committee was, in association with the local communities concerned, to select poor dispossessed farmers and other poor rural people who would benefit from the allocation of state lands for agricultural purposes. I am grateful to the World Bank for permission to use for this contribution some of the experiences I gained during that work. The views expressed here are my own and do not reflect either those of the World Bank, the Ministry of Agriculture and Water Resources (MAWR) or those of other Committee members. However, I acknowledge with gratitude the contribution made to my understanding of the problems by my colleagues on the Committee and in particular Muhammed Aidrus Ali, Lutf Lutf al-Ansi and Abdul Aziz Bin Aqil.

2 No further details are available for this and other decrees.

3 Fieldwork associated with the selection of beneficiaries for the allocation of land to people dispossessed by the denationalisation of land was carried out in 1996 and January 1997.

4 *Fellah* (pl. *fellahin*) is the normal Arabic word for farmer, but is little used in Yemen where the term *muzari'* is preferred. In the context of Wadi Hadhramawt, the word *fellahin* is used exclusively to describe the cultivating social group, i.e. the *du'afa*.

5 The National Liberation Front (NLF) or *Al-Jabha al-Qawmiyya* took over from Britain at independence, after having defeated the Nasserite FLOSY (Front for the Liberation of Occupied South Yemen) a few weeks earlier. The NLF became the National Liberation Front Political Organisation in 1973, the Unified Political Organisation (the National Front) in 1975 after allying with other small left-wing parties, and the Yemeni Socialist Party in 1978.

6 In Yemen 1 hectare = 2.4 feddans.

7 Women own land only exceptionally, and very few were beneficiaries of the Land Reform. The current debate is exclusively the domain of men: even when women own land they do not actively participate in these types of sociopolitical issues.

8 Taking full mechanisation costs into consideration, such farming is probably uneconomic because farm machines were originally either bought through subsidies (via the Cooperative and Agriculture Credit Bank) or were financed by remittances as investments. Since the rental price for farm equipment is below operating costs plus depreciation, this means that once items of farm equipment break down, the income from them will be insufficient to replace them.

11

Research Agenda for Sustainable Agricultural Growth and Natural Resource Management in Yemen

Richard N. Tutwiler[1]

Introduction

Agricultural research in the Republic of Yemen has reached an historic turning point. Following an extensive review and assessment of past efforts to raise productivity in agriculture, the Agricultural Research and Extension Authority (AREA) produced the country's first Agricultural Research Strategy (AREA, 1997). With the official approval of the government, the Strategy has been adopted as the guiding framework for future national research efforts in the agricultural sector.

The Strategy builds upon over twenty years of successive development plans, projects and policies, and addresses the enduring goals of achieving self-sufficiency in food production, increasing the incomes of agricultural households, and reducing the widening trade deficit in agricultural commodities. Although there have been some notable achievements in a few areas, the Strategy recognises that national goals in agriculture remain largely unfulfilled. It continues to subscribe to these goals, but past experience and present realities indicate strongly that in order to achieve them, research and development efforts need considerable changes in emphasis and direction.

The major changes incorporated in the Strategy include: recognition of the overwhelming importance of rainfed agriculture for Yemen's future prosperity; the need adequately to address the present environmental crisis resulting from degradation of the nation's limited and fragile soil, water and vegetative resources; and, not least, the imperative for research and development to address the needs of the majority of rural producers who live in conditions of poverty. The fundamental vision embodied in the Strategy is that, given the mandate to improve productivity, research, extension and associated institutions must assume an expanded mission that seeks to alleviate the poverty of the agricultural population while fostering the conservation and protection of the natural resources upon which the present and future generations of rural producers must depend for their livelihoods.

Agricultural research in Yemen faces a challenging agenda. Nevertheless, the agenda must be addressed if agricultural research is to make a meaningful contribution to national development goals. This chapter reviews the major issues involved, including food security, income enhancement for poor farmers, past strategies to improve productivity, and the sustainability of natural resources in agriculture. The concluding section summarises the major features of the AREA's Research Strategy and considers research approaches relevant to achieving its principal objectives.

Development goals and agricultural research

The goals for the agricultural sector under the 1996–2000 Development Plan are consistent with those expressed by previous national and regional development plans (Al-Agbari and Al-Hebshi, 1993; AREA, 1997). In summary, national development goals in agriculture include the following main points:

- achieving an agricultural sector growth target of 5 per cent per annum;
- raising self-sufficiency levels in key commodities in order to decrease import bills and improve food security;
- improving employment opportunities in agriculture to reduce rural-urban migration;
- enabling the poor majority of farmers to become genuine partners in national development, through self-sustained improvements in their incomes and resource endowments.

Specific policy measures being pursued include market liberalisation and encouragement of private-sector investment in production enterprises and services related to agriculture. With regard to the provision of agricultural inputs, the government is to seek a system for providing inputs to farmers with suitable timing, amounts and prices. The private sector is to be encouraged to provide input supplies through both private and joint companies. The structural adjustment programme initiated in 1994–5 stipulated a reduction in subsidies and other measures to encourage domestic production of major agricultural commodities. The export of products such as vegetables and fruits, where Yemen has adequate supplies, are to be encouraged.

In order to provide farmers with a greater range of technological options for increasing economic returns and improving household incomes while sustaining the natural resource base upon which future production depends, the government will strengthen national agricultural research and extension institutions. They are to be given an explicit mandate to generate appropriate technologies and to facilitate their transfer to the poor majority of Yemen's farmers and livestock producers.

AREA has emerged as the principal agricultural research institution in Yemen, following the unification of the country and the merger of the previous Department of Research and Extension of the southern region and the Agricultural Research Authority of the northern region. In addition to AREA, there are two agricultural faculties, one at Aden University (est. 1975) and one at Sana'a University (est. 1984), which carry out scientific research as part of their academic programmes. Other agricultural colleges were established in 1996 at Ibb, Hodeidah, and Dhamar universities. Modest research activities are also conducted by the Fisheries and Marine Research Centre, the National Veterinary Services Development Programme, and the General Directorate of Plant Protection in the Ministry of Agriculture and Irrigation.

From modest beginnings at El-Kod Research Station (established in the 1950s by the British as a research adjunct to the Abyan Scheme), agricultural research activities have been attached to development projects. Of the seven regional research stations now attached to AREA, virtually all have been inherited from previous development projects. The past research agenda was largely determined by the needs, objectives and funding of these projects, and there was little or no attention given to establishing a coherent and integrated national agricultural research strategy. Research was mostly directed to the improvement of the various crops and production systems that were the concern of the different projects. The purpose of developing a national agricultural research strategy is to translate the development goals of the whole country into a relevant and practical research agenda that will be implemented by AREA and other associated agricultural research institutions.

Agriculture and food security

Yemen's social and economic development depends on maintaining a strong and vibrant agricultural sector. Unfortunately, the cumulative result of past research and development efforts to increase the contribution of agriculture to the national economy is discouraging. There has been a marked decline in agriculture's share of the Gross Domestic Product (GDP) over the past several decades, although sectoral performance varies considerably from year to year, due largely to fluctuations in the areas planted and harvested. Total value of agricultural production has increased only marginally, at around 1 to 2 per cent per year, far below annual population growth rate and the rate of increased national food consumption. In the first half of the 1990s, the agricultural sector contributed about 17 per cent of GDP (MAWR, 1997), declining to 15.7 per cent in 2001 (ESCWA, 2003). By far the greatest share of production value continues to come from staple foods, particularly crops and livestock products. Industrial crops and non-food products represent only a small proportion of total agricultural output.

The sluggish performance of the agricultural sector should be interpreted in the light of national demographic trends. According to the latest population census, Yemen's population was 14.6 million in 1994. It is believed that the average annual increase in population during the period 1959–75 was 1.9 per cent. From the mid-1970s onwards annual increases are estimated at 3.3 per cent, and this appears to have risen to 3.7 per cent in the latter part of the 1990s. Yemen now has one of the highest natural population growth rates in the world, and its 2003 population was estimated to have been 20.7 million (ESCWA, 2003).

Food production has not kept pace with demand, and per capita food production over the period 1961–92 did in fact decline at an annual rate of 1.2 per cent. Yemen's food staple self-sufficiency ratio for the base year 1961 has been estimated at 90 per cent: this ratio had fallen to 38 per cent by 1992. Nevertheless, there was an increase in the national per capita food supply over the three decades, from 1,730 to 2,203 calories per capita per day (FAOSTAT-PC, 1996).

The increase in food availability was achieved through large-scale imports of basic foodstuffs, and by 1992 the net value food import bill was estimated at almost US$56 per person per year (FAOSTAT-PC, 1996). This figure, and the national economic burden it represents, should be compared to the estimates of GDP per capita of only US$277 in 1995 and to an average of just over US$300 during the 1997–2001 period, measured at constant 1995 prices (ESCWA, 2003). The implications of these figures for household food security, particularly among low-income families, are as ominous as they are obvious.

Government import and subsidy programmes in the 1970s and 1980s ensured adequate supplies and access to basic foodstuffs. There have been no major occurrences of famine or widespread hunger. There have, however, been noticeable changes in the composition of the national diet. Although the caloric consumption has risen by some 27 per cent since the 1960s, protein consumption has increased by only a third this much, and most of this is accounted for by increases in quantity of cereals consumed, plus a small but significant increase in poultry consumption. In terms of total calories, almost all the increase can be explained by increases in three foods: cereals, sugar, and edible oils (FAOSTAT-PC, 1996), commodities that have been the major components of Yemen's food import and subsidy programmes.

While food supplies have been adequately maintained without significant growth in domestic production, the quality of the food available may be a cause for concern, particularly among the younger members of the population. Malnutrition and the frequency of its occurrence is difficult to assess, but it is estimated that almost a third of Yemeni children under the age of five are under- or malnourished (UNDP, 1994). There are, of course, many factors that contribute to malnourishment, ranging from economic to social and environmental causes, but the adequacy and the nutritional quality of diet, particularly among the poorer households, is a cause for concern.

The conclusion to be drawn from these figures is that adequate national food supplies have not been obtained through the agricultural sector. Rather, there is a national dependency on imported food. This situation has created numerous problems, among which is a loss of national financial resources that otherwise could be invested in development activities. In addition, food security through imports does not ensure nutritional security, particularly for the younger and poorer segments of the population. Agricultural research, if applied to improving the production of food crops, could certainly contribute to both food and nutritional security. However, it is not enough to target food crops in the research strategy. It is, perhaps, equally important to consider carefully who will produce them and under what conditions.

Agriculture and poverty

On the basis of national statistics, Yemen is among the poorest countries in the world, and the situation appears to be getting worse. Due to the continuing economic vicissitudes that started in the 1980s, including serious inflation problems, and the falling off of remittance transfers, per capita income figures show a sharp decline over the past decade or so until the mid-1990s before stabilising close to the World Bank's absolute poverty line for Yemen of US$230 per annum (World Bank, 1996b).

Although uncritical use of aggregate statistics can be dangerously misleading, there is no doubt that a large proportion of the Yemeni population is living in poverty. The poor are unevenly distributed geographically and occupationally. Although there is little systematic data, it is generally perceived that urban dwellers, on average, have higher disposable income levels than rural people, and that they have much better access to employment opportunities and to crucial social, educational and health services. Indeed, the higher living standards and quality of life in the towns and cities is the most often cited reason for a high urban population annual growth rate. To complement the lure of the urban areas, there are the rural push factors of low economic opportunities and lack of essential infrastructure and services.

Even with the high urban growth rate, there continues to be considerable rural population growth, estimated at about 2.6 per cent annually. At present, about 70 per cent of the total population are rural. The International Fund for Rural Development (IFAD) in its landmark study of rural poverty throughout the developing world (1992) estimated that 30 per cent of Yemen's rural population were living in conditions of absolute poverty in 1988. This figure was revised slightly upwards for the early 1990s by UNDP (1997). In any event, the conclusion must be that, no matter what the proportion, the absolute number of people living in poverty is increasing. Most of the rural poor depend on agriculture, in one way or another, for their livelihoods. In its profile of the rural poor, IFAD identified three groups in Yemen most vulnerable to poverty: smallholder farmers, the landless, and nomadic pastoralists. Together, these groups constitute close to three-quarters of the rural population.

The fundamental contributor to poverty in rural Yemen is limited resource endowment. The total land area of the country is estimated at 55.5 million hectares. Amounts of rainfall and other water resources impose severe limits on the amount of land suitable for cultivation. The total estimated potentially arable area is only 2.9 million hectares (5.2 per cent of the land area). Of this potential, only about 1.4 million hectares are regularly cultivated. Of this total, between 26 and 30 per cent is irrigated, and the rest depends on rainfall (AREA, 1997).

Rainfall is the basic resource governing agricultural production, but its supply varies greatly in amount and distribution from year to year. Long-term averages vary from less than 350 mm, which can be considered the minimal amount needed for rainfed agriculture, to almost 1500 mm. The former figure characterises most of the rainfed areas; the latter applies only to a few fortunate areas in the southern uplands. Soil conditions often limit agricultural potential. In general, the soils of Yemen are low in nitrogen, phosphorus and organic matter. In the highland areas, they are often shallow and stony, and have little moisture-retention capacity. Salinity can be a problem, particularly in coastal areas.

Even though traditional water-harvesting techniques improve rainfall utilisation considerably, rainfed farming is often precarious, simply because of the capricious environment. Without the controlled application of irrigation water, the yields of the most commonly grown crops tend to be low and variable. There are frequent droughts. Moisture stress is compounded by low soil fertility, and this is exacerbated by the needs of farmers to utilise all crop by-products and residues as animal feed and domestic fuel. The benefits of manuring are understood, but animal dung is often utilised as domestic fuel. Very little organic material is returned to the soil. Landrace crop varieties predominate and, although they are well adapted to survive and produce a minimum yield in difficult conditions, their genetic potential to produce high yields under more favourable circumstances may be limited. Pests and diseases are endemic and pervasive, and periodic outbreaks of disease frequently devastate crops.

Throughout the country, most agricultural holdings, whether owned by the farmer or not, are small. There are roughly 700,000 agricultural households in the country, annually cultivating approximately 1.4 million hectares (MAWR, 1996). This translates into an average farm size of only two hectares. In reality, farm sizes vary considerably. Farms tend to be larger in the coastal regions, the eastern plateau, and the central highland plains. In the higher rainfall mountain areas, average sizes are smaller, and the population densities are greater than in the other areas. In the six highland provinces covering the area from Hajja in the north to Ta'izz in the south, only Sana'a province has an average farm size greater that 1.5 hectares (Alsanabani *et al.*, 1997).

Since the late 1970s, there have been numerous farm-level studies describing the economic returns to crop and livestock production in different parts of Yemen. Most of these have focused on crop enterprise budgets, including labour requirements. A number of the earlier studies have been summarised by Tutwiler (1990), and reveal the great variability in production practices under different farming systems in different agro-ecological circumstances. The capacity of traditional production methods, and particularly terrace agriculture, to absorb and respond to high labour inputs is a feature of most of these studies. Nevertheless, the economic returns to labour inputs are generally low. For most cereal and food legume crops, high labour inputs are economic only if unpaid family labour is used, or if the opportunity costs of farm labour are low. Under conditions of rising opportunity costs for farm labour, improved farm incomes must depend on either raising the value or price per unit of output, increasing the capital inputs relative to labour, or raising the technical efficiency of production by adopting improved technologies.

The Agricultural Research and Extension Authority undertook an extensive study of production among different farm types in several rainfall zones of the central highlands in order to estimate the economic returns from traditional farming practices in comparison with available new technologies (Khalid and Johaish, 1997). The results of the whole farm models and budgets generated by the study are striking in their implications. Using a farm size of two hectares producing cereals, legumes and livestock with traditional techniques where rainfall is above 800 mm, it is estimated on the basis of enterprise budgets that a typical family of seven persons would receive a per capita income of only US$187 per year. Where rainfall is lower and farms are smaller, farm income is so low that it is difficult to satisfy minimal food requirements. In cases where subsistence cannot be obtained from the holding, additional income must be sought through off-farm employment, either with other farming households, within the rural community, or in urban areas or abroad.

Using the results of station experiments and on-farm trials, the AREA study argues that it is possible to make considerable improvements in farm income through the application of new technologies adapted to rainfed conditions. In particular, the evaluation of chemical fertilisers, improved varieties, and better animal husbandry indicates that their adoption by farmers could raise net income by as much as 76 per cent even for the farms with the smallest resource endowments.

In contrast to the situation in rainfed farming, irrigated farms show a much better economic performance. Based on survey data, a one-hectare farm (representing 70 per cent of the farms in the central plains) with well irrigation and producing potatoes will gain a per capita farm family income that is around 24 per cent above the absolute poverty line. In other models with mixed rainfed and irrigated production and larger farm sizes with moderate rainfall, the return is almost four times above the poverty line.

These irrigated-farm models use prevailing cropping patterns with low cropping intensities and low-to-moderate value crops. If irrigation is combined with higher cropping intensity and high value crops, particularly *qat*² and fruit trees, even small farms can obtain relatively high incomes. For example, an irrigated *qat* farm of just one hectare can net twelve or more times the poverty level.

A note of caution towards the optimism aroused by the benefits from improving technology and intensifying production is sounded by an IFAD report (1985) from the mountain foothills of southern Yemen. In this location, farmers have to maintain traditional terraced systems, but have augmented rainfall with tubewells and pumps. Irrigation water has allowed them to double cropping intensities and to introduce new cash crops, but the improvements realised seem to have reached their endpoint. Underground water supply and quality are in decline and soil fertility is much reduced from overcropping. Investments in land and water are experiencing diminishing returns. The report concludes that the farmers' incomes are in danger of being undermined by their own previous successes.

Nevertheless, this brief examination of the character of poverty among the agricultural population indicates several important considerations in directing agricultural research towards poverty alleviation. First, poverty is concentrated in the rainfed areas and among smallholders where productivity is variable and highly risky. These factors coincide with the environmental realities of the great majority of the farming population. Second, poor farmers have very limited resource endowments. If they are to be effective and relevant, research products and new technologies designed to raise productivity cannot require either favourable agro-ecological conditions or considerable increases in the amount of external inputs applied.

Past efforts to improve productivity

From the 1970s, Yemeni governments sought major improvements in agricultural production through ambitious development projects and incentive-based policy instruments. Although agricultural research was not a major player in these initiatives, the lessons learned from them are important for developing a national research agenda. Three broad categories of interventions are briefly considered: large-scale irrigation systems, extension and technology transfer, and policy incentives for private investment.

Large-scale irrigation systems

In the southern region in particular, but also in the north, there have been considerable efforts to increase supplies and capacity to manage irrigation water, usually in development schemes based in the flood plains of the major *wadi* systems. Subsequent construction of large irrigation works, including diversion weirs, delivery canals, and protection structures, changed traditional spate-irrigation systems significantly. Coupled with the installation of tubewells to augment seasonal floods with perennial underground water resources, increased cropping intensities, introduction of new crops, extension of cultivated areas, and stabilisation of crop yield levels were made possible by these projects, simply through the provision of larger and more dependable amounts of water. Before these development projects, small-scale spate-irrigation systems that used simple construction techniques and structures had been built and maintained by local communities. Because the modern systems introduced by development projects needed large capital investments, had to be operated on a large scale to be economically justified, and required the provision of outside expertise and services to operate, local management arrangements were inevitably supplanted by government-created institutions.

While there is no question that large-scale irrigation projects have increased the potential for production, there have been shortcomings in realising project objectives and serious constraints to sustainable increases in production (FAO, 1989). All the schemes have experienced major problems with destructive floods and high sedimentation levels within the water delivery systems, often to the point where the system becomes inoperable. There has been a lack of adequate operation and maintenance procedures after completion of the construction works, and maintenance of the financing system has been a considerable problem. Finally, the inclusion of tubewells in most schemes, whether planned or unplanned, has led to a rapid exhaustion of groundwater resources due to over-exploitation of aquifers and inattention to recharge requirements. Depletion is compounded by salinisation in many areas.

Following an extensive review of irrigation projects in Yemen, FAO, UNDP and relevant government officials concluded that future projects should be based on: a clearer understanding and incorporation of traditional spate systems into project design; utilisation of development concepts appropriate to the needs of the intended users; attention to the development and adaptation of more appropriate crop production technology; and the institutionalisation of monitoring and maintenance arrangements following completion of physical improvements, especially for the exploitation of groundwater resources (FAO, 1989).

It should be noted in this regard that irrigation projects of more modest scope and ambition may prove to be more successful in achieving sustainable improvements, both in productivity and income generation. One example of this is the development of tubewell-based farming covering several hundred hectares of small-sized holdings in central Wadi Hadhramawt, an area where the traditional spate-irrigation systems have all but disappeared due to lack of continued labour and financial investment by the local population (Tutwiler and Aw-Hassan, 1996). The two keys to the success of these new 'model' farms are (1) close attention to the balance between exploiting and replenishing the groundwater resource, and (2) utilisation of the most appropriate technology in crop production. Agricultural researchers, extensionists and farmers have worked together to introduce new and very profitable crops into a production system closely attuned to the imperative of maintaining the integrity of the water resource. Through careful research and extension work, it has been possible significantly to reduce the amount of irrigation water applied without reducing crop yields.

Agricultural extension and technology transfer

In highland areas where the development of large-scale irrigation works is not feasible, the agricultural development strategy for the past 25 years has consisted of regional projects that are concerned mainly with establishing the necessary physical and institutional infrastructure for agricultural extension and technology transfer. This includes constructing extension centres, training extension agents, instituting farmer credit and loan mechanisms, and providing modern inputs.

The first large extension and technology transfer project of this type was the Southern Upland Rural Development Project (SURDP), which began in the Ta'izz and Ibb areas in the early 1970s. The SURDP model was later extended to cover, to a greater or lesser extent, virtually all the highland areas in the northern region of the country. The impression given by field observations (GTZ, 1993, Khalid, 1996) is that the sustainability of project efforts in the absence of external support is questionable. Nevertheless, despite a noticeable decline in the provision of services due to financial constraints, projects of this nature have had noticeable success in introducing farmers to modern production technologies, particularly chemical fertilisers, pesticides and improved crop varieties.

However, in recent years the utilisation of fertilisers and pesticides has been in decline. Several explanations are given. First, many farmers had previously adopted chemical inputs through contact with regional development project personnel when these inputs were provided by the project on very reasonable terms. Subsequently, conditions for obtaining credit to purchase inputs were tightened. Many farmers now find that they cannot meet loan conditions, and those that can feel that the transaction costs in obtaining a loan may be too high to justify the step. Additionally, inputs previously available through project channels are now less accessible and more costly. Most fertilisers and pesticides now move through market and private-sector channels, and they have become more expensive, to the point that farmers feel their cost does not justify their use, even if they have the cash to buy them (Dameem, 1993). It appears that fertilisers are now mainly applied to irrigated, high-value crops, especially vegetables, fruit trees and *qat*. Import controls on pesticides, introduced to bar the use of dangerous substances, have further restricted supplies available to farmers. As a costly external input to production, it can be assumed that pesticides are now restricted to high-value crops, and especially to *qat*. Unfortunately, due to the way in which *qat* is consumed, pesticide application can be particularly dangerous to the health of consumers.

Cereals are the most important crop in Yemen. Over the millennia of settled agriculture, a wide genetic variation has developed in sorghum, millet, wheat and barley. The vast majority of farmers grow local landraces adapted through natural and traditional human selection to specific agro-ecological niches, but their genetic yield potential is low. In the attempt to increase the productivity of cereal cultivation, research and development activities have given greatest attention to varietal introduction, while agronomic practices, local genetic resources, and resource management have been relatively neglected. Several new sorghum, wheat and maize varieties based on introduced genetic material have been tested and released for cultivation in Yemen. Seeds of certified quality are being produced through public-sector seed multiplication enterprises for distribution and sale through project and market channels.

The new sorghum varieties have not been well received by farmers because their grain quality is not up to the standard of the farmers' own landraces. In contrast, there has been substantial adoption of new wheat varieties, and certified seed production of these varieties is increasing. There has also been noticeable adoption of imported maize varieties. In general, the new varieties are grown either under full or supplemental irrigation conditions, often with chemical fertiliser application. Substantial yield gains can be achieved, often as much as several times the yield of the landrace variety.

However, as is the case with modern cereal varieties elsewhere, there are certain attendant conditions. Improved varieties are more water- and nutrient-demanding than landraces, and their genetic homogeneity can make them more vulnerable to devastation by disease epidemics and pests. Quality and marketing can also be an issue. For example, Yemeni farmers report that the modern wheat varieties have lower grain quality and taste than landraces; consequently, they fetch lower prices in the market. Nevertheless, their higher productivity is enough to overcome the quality and price limitations to their profitability.

Private investment and policy incentives
Perhaps the greatest success story to emerge from agriculture in the 1980s was the growth of the poultry industry and the reaching of near

self-sufficiency. This is often cited as an example of the potential benefits to be gained from a complementary relationship between government policy measures and private-sector investment. Traditionally, poultry production was a household, and particularly woman's, activity. No more than a score or so birds were kept in the house and yard, existing as scavengers. Very little care was given them apart from protection from larger animals, and what eggs and birds they produced were either eaten by the family as a dietary supplement or sold by the women to neighbours or the local market. People still prefer these 'free range' birds and eggs for their taste, but by the 1990s the great majority of both chickens and eggs consumed in Yemen were commercially produced.

The commercial poultry industry started modestly in 1975 with government encouragement and assistance in obtaining necessary equipment, expertise and imported materials. To protect local producers and encourage greater investment, government approvals to import frozen chickens were first reduced and then stopped completely, although importing of chickens was subsequently allowed to a limited extent (Albar, 1993). These measures had the desired effect. The output of broilers was 1,400 tons in 1976 and reached over 70,000 tons in the late 1980s. Egg production achieved a similar quantum leap. According to a government survey, there were 1,240 broiler farms and 36 layer farms, mainly in the central highlands area serving the major cities and towns, by the end of the decade (MAWR, 1990). The poultry industry employs thousands of people directly, and provides employment opportunities to many more through the rapidly growing networks that market products and provision the industry with the required supplies of feed, chicks and veterinary services.

Despite the nature of its products, the poultry industry is not well integrated into the rest of the agricultural sector. Most of the enterprises are operated by large- and medium-scale producers, most of the small operators who proliferated in the 1980s having gone out of business because of inadequate financing, low profitability, and lack of access to supplies and markets. The majority of the inputs, including feed, are imported, although there have been attempts to encourage domestic production of feed, principally maize. Apart from private sources, usually merchant capital, much of the financing for the industry comes from the Bank for Agriculture Credit and Cooperatives and the Yemen Bank for Reconstruction and Development (Albar, 1993).

Significant production gains have been made in other commodities, particularly vegetables and fruits. This is largely attributed to protectionist import bans and restrictions which maintained high producer prices and resulted in expanded cultivation. Incidentally, encouraging the cultivation of these particular crops also encouraged higher rates of groundwater extraction. For other agricultural products, especially traditional staples such as cereals, legumes and small ruminants, there has been little growth and even some alarming declines in production.

An examination of these successes brings into question their sustainability and actual contribution to poverty alleviation. Capital-intensive enterprises, such as modern poultry and dairy operations, are not well integrated in the agricultural sector and are often dependent on imported materials and favourable trading arrangements. As Yemen makes the necessary policy and regulatory adjustments in line with the emerging global trading agreements, these enterprises will need to look to domestic sources of supply to ensure their future profitability.

Agriculture and natural resources

The greatest threat to sustainable increases in crop and animal production in Yemen is the rapid deterioration of the water, soil and vegetative resources upon which production depends. The most important causes of resource degradation can be found within two seemingly divergent trends in contemporary farming systems development. The first of these is intensification – increasing productivity per unit area through increasing inputs in the production process, particularly the application of irrigation water. Groundwater extraction has now reached a point at which the future sustainability of irrigated production is seriously threatened.

The second cause of resource degradation is the de-intensification – i.e. a reduction in the amount of agricultural labour applied per unit area – of traditional rainfed farming, particularly on terraced slopes in the highlands (Tutwiler and Bailey, 1997). Failure to devote sufficient labour to maintain terraces has allowed vast areas to become subject to ever-increasing soil erosion, the collapse of extensive water-harvesting structures, and loss of productive capacity.

The groundwater dilemma

Yemen is not unique among the dry areas of the Middle East and North Africa in its exploitation of limited groundwater resources to intensify agricultural production (Tutwiler and Bailey, 1997). Unfortunately, the relative lack of alternative routes to intensification, due largely to climatic and topographical constraints, has made groundwater extraction virtually the only means by which farmers can increase their productivity. Furthermore, groundwater use, expansion of irrigated areas and increased extraction rates have been encouraged and supported by government policies, through a number of direct and indirect subsidies for tubewells, pumps, pipes and fuel. Restricting imports of water-intensive crops such as fruits, vegetables and *qat* has made these more economically attractive to farmers. It is estimated that by the mid-1990s there were over 45,000 private tubewells and perhaps as many as 200 mobile drilling rigs operating in the country (Al-Fatesh and de Nooy, 1993, and Ward, Chapter 8 in this volume). The area served by these wells exceeds all other irrigated schemes combined (AREA, 1997). Given crop yield response to the controlled application of water and the higher-value crops possible under reliable irrigation, groundwater irrigation is arguably the most important contributor to increased farm incomes in Yemen.

Many smallholders have benefited from the proliferation of tube-wells, which has enabled the climatic constraint of limited and variable rainfall to be overcome and encouraged the use of modern inputs and diversified cropping systems. But overpumping, high water losses, and low water-use efficiency have resulted in alarming drops in water tables throughout the country, as well as a possibly irreversible depletion of water resources in many areas. Many shallow aquifers are drying up, and the draw-down rate for many deep aquifers is a minimum of one metre per year. In many key basins in the highlands, the annual cumulative fall in the water table is over four metres (Al-Fatesh and de Nooy, 1993).

The total groundwater extracted per year is estimated at about 2.8 billion m³, and of this amount, only some 1.3 billion m³ is considered to be renewable (AREA, 1997). Although there are no estimates of the total supply within the various aquifers, it is clear that at present extraction rates the supply cannot be considered endless. Moreover, the energy costs of extraction will steadily increase. The phenomenon of redrilling tubewells to deeper depths in order to secure water from falling water tables is already widespread, particularly in the highlands and the drier regions of the country.

As these estimates indicate, continued agricultural growth based upon the present system of water management and use is probably not sustainable in the long term. The dilemma faced by national policy makers is how to preserve the productivity gains achieved through groundwater exploitation while simultaneously making major reductions in the rate of extraction. Various suggestions have been made for controlling the extraction rate through direct and indirect means of demand management, all of which are aimed at increasing the social and economic costs of extraction to well owners.

Few, if any, of these measures to control groundwater exploitation are within the purview of agricultural research. However, research can make a contribution in the area of increasing the efficiency of groundwater resource productivity. In effect, the objective is to preserve productivity gains, or even to increase production, while using less water. Yemeni researchers estimate that only 35 per cent of the water applied through surface irrigation systems using basins, furrows and unlined canals reaches the plants (Al-Fatesh and de Nooy, 1993). The rest is lost through evaporation and seepage. Moreover, it is also thought that the amount of water reaching the plant is often considerably greater than the crop water requirement. In essence, present irrigation systems waste vast quantities of water, and improved techniques can be used that would actually increase productivity per unit of water applied without decreasing production levels.

While research to improve the productivity of water can contribute to reduced water demand in agriculture, it cannot by itself solve the problem of groundwater depletion. Ultimately, this must be solved by means beyond the agricultural sector. However, in the longer term, agricultural research can help to alleviate the pressure on limited groundwater resources by enhancing and making more productive the estimated 40 per cent of renewable water resources that are not in aquifers. Essentially, this can only be done through a revitalisation of traditional rainfed farming systems.

Revitalisation of traditional rainfed production

The approximately 70 per cent of Yemen's cropped area that is dependent upon rainfall is primarily devoted to cereal-based mixed farming using traditional techniques. Unlike the case of irrigated farming, farmers dependent on rainfall are still largely subsistence-oriented. Available technologies, as well as those under development, hold the potential significantly to raise the productivity of rainfed agriculture. Efforts to adapt these improvements to real farm conditions and to make technologies available to farmers must therefore continue. However, the real challenge in rainfed agriculture is simply to maintain the productive capacity of the natural resource base.

In order to make agriculture viable in the steeply sloped areas of the highlands where most Yemenis live, farmers have over centuries developed a technologically simple, yet sophisticated, system of water harvesting and soil retention. This is based on contour terracing, most commonly using stone walls to retain soil and create cultivation surfaces and to supplement direct rainfall with diverted run-off flows from adjacent, uncultivated slopes. The percentage of Yemen's total cultivated land (including both slopes and plains) equipped with terraces could reach as high as 44 per cent (Alsanabani *et al.*, 1997). The terracing system is an effective way of enabling farmers to increase the supply of moisture delivered to crops, to control soil structure, and to manipulate soil fertility. It is also quite labour intensive and requires continuous and considerable maintenance to preserve the terraces against the erosive effects of rainstorms. Moreover, the continued existence and functioning of each terrace in the chain of terraces along a slope depends on the maintenance of the adjacent and neighbouring terraces that serve as breaks in the down-slope flow of water and soil following a rainstorm.

Production in rainfed systems has been in steady decline for decades, not as a result of a long-term fall in precipitation levels, but from fundamental social and economic changes within Yemeni society. Such changes include the development of a market-oriented rural economy, improved communication and mobility, and above all, the opening of alternative employment opportunities outside agriculture. The opportunity costs of agricultural labour have increased greatly, and there has been a reduction in the amount of labour devoted to maintaining the water-harvesting, water-spreading and soil-retention structures that enable continued cultivation on the mountain slopes, in the valleys and on the flood plains. Large expanses of terraced land, particularly in less productive environments, have been abandoned or neglected, with devastating results in terms of increased erosion, loss of surface water, and destructive downstream effects. Once lost, terraced land will probably never be replaced.

It is ironic that the social and economic conditions that produced a sustainable rainfed agricultural system in the past are now seen as extreme poverty and underdevelopment. Although poor, and not infrequently suffering hunger and even famine, the majority of the people relied on rainfed terraces and other traditional technologies to meet their basic subsistence needs. They had few alternative livelihoods. When alternative sources of food (largely through imports) and alternative employment (largely through male labour migration) became available in the 1960s and 1970s, a high proportion of people left the land, and the conditions under which terraces and associated water-harvesting systems were constructed and maintained altered. There was a marked decline in community cooperative arrangements for land and terrace maintenance (Alsanabani *et al.*, 1997). Without subsistence dependency on the land, the disincentives to invest the labour and capital that are inherent in traditional tenure arrangements became more pronounced. Overall, there was a marked decline in the amount of labour that was applied to producing rainfed cereals and maintaining soil resources. The situation is reminiscent of other highland areas in the Middle East (cf. Tutwiler, 1995) in which smallholder farmers lack resource endowments and sufficient incomes to break the cycle of poverty. They continue with a minimum level of production at close to zero value of their labour's marginal product while depleting their fixed capital assets, in this case the soil retained by terraces.

With a few notable exceptions, money earned in off-farm activities is rarely invested in land or crop improvements. Apart from those fortunate few with land endowed with the requisite soil and moisture conditions to produce high-value market crops, such as *qat* or fruits, the income from sorghum and other subsistence crops hardly justifies unpaid family or hired labour investments in maintaining terraces.[3] If a household has land in an area with access to groundwater, then it is difficult not to justify investing in a tubewell.

Apart from these options there are, under present economic circumstances, few economic incentives to investment in traditional rainfed production. Lacking the financial or ecological resources to produce lucrative crops, poor farming households find themselves constantly engaged in an uphill struggle for survival. In the past three decades, they have most often sought off-farm employment. They have shown a willingness to implement and maintain conservation practices on rainfed farmland only when such activities produce substantial and quick returns at relatively low cost. Even when they manage by any means to achieve a total income above the poverty threshold, their possession and access to key productivity assets may be insufficient to make critical investments in the natural resource base attractive (Reardon and Vosti, 1995).

The problem of devising strategies to revitalise terrace agriculture is compounded by the fact that benefits from soil conservation activities are long term, usually shared among neighbouring farms, and often intangible. For the majority of poor farmers dependent on rainfall, the issue at stake is not which soil conservation or water-harvesting measures to implement. Rather, it is the more fundamental issue of ensuring that rainfed agriculture can support the household. The appropriate incentives needed to persuade farmers to participate in sustained soil and water conservation activities are enhanced food security and improved incomes.

Therefore, the appropriate strategy for research addressing rainfed agriculture does not lie in improved soil conservation or water-harvesting techniques, *per se*, but rather in improving the economic returns to labour within an integrated farming system. The productivity of crops and livestock is the starting point, and efforts should be made to provide farmers with an improved range of options in varieties and crops to grow under their ecological conditions. Ensuring that new technologies are well adapted to specific circumstances is a crucial aspect of this strategy. Poor farmers have little to invest in increasing productivity apart from their labour, so the emphasis should be on low external input systems, and enterprises that raise labour productivity. Integrated crop-livestock systems, adapted to local climate and soil conditions, may have a particular advantage in this regard (Tutwiler *et al.*, 1997). Once farmers begin to reap the benefits from improved production, they will inevitably devote more time and effort towards maintaining the natural resource base.

A research agenda for sustainable agricultural growth

The strategy of Yemen's Agricultural Research and Extension Authority is appropriately based on recognising that the country's limited and fragile endowment of natural resources of water, soil and vegetation is the factor which most constrains national agricultural growth. Production improvements will have to be made in productivity increases per unit of area, rather than in expansion of cropped area. Moreover, productivity per area will be the result of increased technical efficiency of production in individual crops. The increasing of annual cropping intensity is held back by limited water resources and the fragility of soils and soil fertility.

In identifying ways in which research can make a meaningful contribution to sustainable agricultural growth, AREA recognises that development must be built on what already exists. Improvements must be made in such a way that further growth is generated from within the farming systems themselves, without creating dependencies on external factors or agencies. Productivity increases must not be at the expense of further depletion and degradation of natural resources. It is the responsibility of research to develop means to increase productivity while conserving resources and fostering their enhancement and sustainability. Above all, research products must be utilisable by the poor majority of farming households and enable them to improve their incomes and food security. For this to be possible, the development and adaptation of new technologies should take place as much as possible within the needs, abilities and conditions of the farming population.

The emerging research agenda of AREA falls conveniently into four areas: high input (irrigated) systems, rainfed agriculture, decentralisation of research, and re-definition of beneficiaries.

High input, irrigated systems

The scientists and research managers in AREA recognise the magnitude and significance of Yemen's natural resource crisis, particularly the critical situation of groundwater depletion and degradation. The government is taking steps to formulate a national water management policy, including institutions and agencies to promote practices and to implement regulations to foster more sustainable use of groundwater and other water resources. Whatever solution is eventually found, it must involve all stakeholders in the conservation and use of water resources: domestic and municipal users, industry and manufacturing, services, and agricultural producers. Whether water is allocated through regulation, demand management or market forces, there will inevitably be less water available for agriculture. Moreover, its cost to users will be higher than at present.

For agricultural research and development in the medium term, there will be a shift away from the previous focus on increasing irrigation water used towards the sustainable use of limited water resources, including attention to water-use efficiency at the farm level, irrigation efficiency within delivery systems, and water management at the scales of aquifers and watersheds.

To take account of cost-effectiveness, sustainability and ease of management, research emphasis will shift from complex, large-scale irrigation systems to small-scale irrigation and water-harvesting methods. Small-scale irrigation schemes have been found to be conducive (1) to improving smallholder production by increasing the carrying capacity of the land, and (2) to sustainability through management by the users themselves. Smaller-scale management arrangements allow greater responsiveness to the incentives offered by technologies that improve irrigation and water-use efficiencies. To a great extent, research in small-scale irrigation systems will build upon the experience and management infrastructure of local, private systems that have spontaneously arisen throughout Yemen in the past few decades. The objective of research will be to develop ways and means to enable these producers to obtain higher production per unit of water used.

Rainfed agriculture

Although research in irrigated agriculture will continue, albeit with a different emphasis and focus, the major strategic shift in research is away from irrigated production towards rainfed agriculture. The emphasis in rainfed agriculture is on integrated crop-livestock systems. These can achieve higher and more stable yield levels through use of improved cultivars and management practices that increase water- and nutrient-use efficiencies while maintaining the essential integrity and productive capacity of the natural resource base. Research priorities are food and forage crops, as opposed to industrial and other non-food crops.

Resource conservation and management in terraced, rainfed agriculture must be approached indirectly. The range of technological innovations specific to soil and water conservation is extremely limited. Most conservation measures currently available have their origins in traditional practices, and all involve continuous and considerable labour inputs from farming households and communities. In order to encourage these inputs, research to increase the value of production on terraces is the highest priority. Similarly, improvements in livestock production of smallholder, rainfed farming will enhance the value of forage material grown on terraces, while at the same time providing higher returns to farm labour through increases in milk and other animal products.

Income generation for farming households will be sought through net factor productivity increases (higher net return per inputs used, including labour), diversification of cropping patterns (to reduce crop-loss risks and take better advantage of market opportunities), and improvements in soil fertility and water-use efficiency (to reduce input costs). Optimal crop selection and crop rotations with sound resource management practices are essential components of a sustainable, income-enhancing farming system. With regard to further income enhancement and improved food security, research is needed on ways to reduce post-harvest losses, improve product quality, and add value to farm production through the processing of primary products within households and local communities.

In conjunction with increasing the returns to labour in rainfed agriculture, research will be initiated on the rehabilitation and sustainable management of the degraded, non-arable grazing areas adjacent to farming communities. Natural vegetation is an important complement to forage production on arable land, but most of the rangeland has been seriously overgrazed and denuded in recent decades. This has contributed to a further decline in forage material available to livestock, as well as to accelerated soil erosion, increased rainfall moisture loss and destructive run-off, and a general loss in natural resources available to poor farmers.

Decentralisation of research

In the past, formal research conducted by national agricultural research institutions has been virtually confined to research stations. Work 'outside the fence' on farmers' fields has been limited to some verification trials and extension demonstrations. Research on individual crops was assigned to different stations, resulting in an inappropriate distribution between adaptive research activities and target agro-ecological environments. The AREA strategy is to decentralise technology development and adaptive research to specific target environments throughout the country. In addition, multidisciplinary teams are to be formed to address productivity and resource management problems for each agro-ecology and associated farming system. Although these teams will be based in the respective regional research centres (i.e. research stations), their mission is to work with extension agents and farmers directly in actual farm conditions.

Decentralising research to target environments and conducting research activities on-farm are deliberate measures to ensure that research products are adapted and relevant to the reality of conditions faced by farmers. All too often in the past, technologies selected for transfer to farmers have proved to be ill-adapted to farmer conditions, and their performance in farmers' hands has been disappointing. By conducting applied and adaptive research with farmers in their farm environments, the problem of 'recommended technologies' that do not perform well in actual field conditions should be avoided at an early stage in the research and development process.

Monitoring progress towards achieving desired objectives is an essential part of the research process. Monitoring will be done at various levels of research management, including research teams, regional centres and AREA headquarters. It is equally important in the monitoring process to consider how research results are evaluated. Research results will be measured in terms of their contribution to production increases, but the evaluation of results in terms of their contribution to the sustainability of production and the natural resource base is of equal importance.

Redefinition of beneficiaries

As is common in agricultural research systems throughout the world, the intended beneficiary of previous research efforts in Yemen has been the (mostly hypothetical) individual *farmer*, usually assumed to be a male who has more or less independent control over resources and production decisions. The objective has been to provide this 'typical farmer' with the technological means to combine his labour, land and other resources in more productive and economically rewarding ways. AREA has, however, begun to redefine the intended beneficiaries of its research outputs; first, because of its concern with enabling farming *households* to improve their food security and incomes, and secondly because of its concern with natural resource management. Households represent a complex decision-making unit, composed of different people with distinct, if complementary, roles, capacities and responsibilities. It is likely that any given technological option to improve productivity or resource sustainability will be received and acted upon in different ways by the people of the household. In terms of developing technologies appropriate for households, research must therefore consider the variety and complexity of needs, objectives and decision-making *within* the household. Differences *among* households must also be taken into account if the relevance of research outputs is to be assessed adequately.

Moreover, resource management and sustainability concerns often require researchers to move beyond the limits of households as beneficiaries of research. This is simply because many of the natural resources are managed by local *communities* of households. Water resources in Yemen, for instance, are often managed at village, territorial group, or user-group level. Similarly, non-agricultural land used for grazing or woodlots is often subject to decision-making and control by social groups larger than the household. In the case of terraced agriculture, neighbours are often affected by each other's maintenance or lack of maintenance of terrace walls and water-harvesting structures.

The redefinition of target beneficiaries in terms of households and communities of households implies the adoption of innovative research approaches. Several of these are being considered by AREA. The first is participatory research in which farmers, households and communities are involved from the outset in identifying production and resource management problems with researchers, participating in research activities and testing or validating research results. The second is a resource domain approach, an example of which is research conducted on the scale of small watersheds that encompass numerous farm households, all of whom have a common concern with the sustainable management of the resource. Research will seek the improvement of watershed management with respect to water balance, land conservation and crop productivity. Integrated watershed management will include the development of cost-effective water-harvesting techniques that can be implemented and managed by communities of small farmers. AREA is proposing to undertake participatory research in a selected number of pilot areas into the integrated management of small watersheds, incorporating annual and perennial crop production, livestock husbandry and range rehabilitation.

NOTES

1 At the time of writing, the author was Programme Leader, Natural Resource Management Program, International Center for Agricultural Research in the Dry Areas (ICARDA), Aleppo, Syria. The views and opinions expressed are those of the author and not necessarily those of ICARDA.

2 *Qat* (*Catha edulis* Forsk.) is a perennial shrub whose young, tender leaves are chewed to produce a mildly euphoric effect. Economically, *qat* is arguably the most important crop in Yemen. *Qat* cultivation reduces land and water available for food production, and its consumption is a serious drain on disposable incomes. However, producers enjoy high incomes, and its cultivation, transportation and marketing employs tens of thousands of people.

3 One of the concomitants to men leaving rainfed agriculture for off-farm employment is an increasing feminisation of household self-provisioning through cereal and livestock production (Tutwiler, 1990). In fact, it can be argued that women continue growing sorghum on terraces not so much for grain but for forage to feed the animals that are their primary responsibility, and often their property, in the traditional gender division of labour. It follows that if agricultural research is to focus on crop-livestock integration and productivity of this system, then much more work needs to be done with the women farmers who constitute the majority of the labour force, decision makers, and beneficiaries of this farming system.

PART IV

SOCIAL AND REGIONAL ISSUES

12

Poverty Reduction in Yemen:
A Social Exclusion Perspective

Mouna H. Hashem

Introduction

Since the 1970s, development efforts in Yemen have aimed at improving people's livelihoods by increasing access to basic services such as literacy, health care, agricultural development and employment opportunities.[1] Nonetheless, poverty today is more evident in the country than ever before. The per capita GNP dropped from US$540 in 1991 to US$350 in 1999 (World Bank, 2001): it was also estimated that inflation was over 50 per cent in 1992 and had risen to over 100 per cent by 1994 (ibid.). The Human Development Report (UNDP, 2000) ranked Yemen 148 among 178 countries in the Human Development Index. A Poverty Survey (CSO, 1999) reported that 30 per cent of Yemeni households live below the poverty line; this includes food and access to social services. Two sets of indicators were used to measure poverty: (1) consumption, expenditure and monetary income metric indicators, and (2) social indicators such as health, nutrition, education and reproduction. In addition, findings show that the majority of the poor reside in rural areas.

The government has identified poverty reduction as a major objective in its Five Year Plan (2001–5), and foreign donors have also emphasised poverty reduction as a major priority in their technical aid packages. However, ongoing poverty-oriented projects have not resulted in any significant improvement in reducing poverty.

A central argument of this study is that while poverty is a complex and multidimensional issue, explaining it within the narrow realm of the macroeconomic framework suffices only in relation to economic growth and provision of basic services. Determinants affecting poverty are not constant, but change with political, economic and social trends. Factors that led to the impoverishment of citizens during the Imamate regime in the 1950s, for example, are not the same as those that have affected society under the republican regime of the 1990s. Thus, explaining poverty and establishing strategies to combat it has to be performed within the current economic, political and social context, which the prevailing approach fails to do. For example, its targeting methodology fails to identify critically poor groups who are entrapped in impoverishment and marginalisation from society, a process also known as social exclusion. A critical criterion in analysing poverty is to examine the process of poverty in relation to access and participation in civil society – economic, social and political. In other words, individuals or groups encountering impediments to access and participation in any civil society realm are those deprived from attaining a productive livelihood and thus entrapped in a process of poverty and social exclusion.

Identifying processes of poverty and social exclusion and, on this basis, promoting the integration of excluded individuals and groups will be essential for the country's success in reducing poverty and attaining social and economic development. Until this is done, Yemen will continue to be pulled apart by two opposing dynamic forces: the efforts to transform the country into a modern market society, and the acute problems of poverty and poor mobilisation of human and natural resources.

Issues of poverty reduction and social exclusion

The World Summit for Social Development held in Copenhagen March 1995 was an important opportunity for the international community to revisit the development experiences of the past couple of decades. The dominant issue at the conference was the rise in poverty. Estimates in 1990 suggested that 1.1 billion people in developing countries were living in poverty, some 8 per cent more than in 1985 (World Bank, 1993). For example, in the Middle East, North Africa, Latin America and the Caribbean the proportion of the population living on less than US$1.00 a day had increased. In the Middle East and North Africa the increase in the number of poor people was estimated to have exceeded population growth (ibid: 4). The conference underlined a new agenda for social development and defined three major objectives: 'the eradication of poverty, the expansion of productive employment and reduction of unemployment, and the promotion of social integration' (UN, 1995).

These objectives define the notion of social exclusion that indicates a new dimension in poverty.

Poverty-reduction strategies aim to promote economic growth in order to expand employment opportunities and provision of basic services. The Yemeni strategy is based on the assumption that economic growth will allow governments to invest in human development, such that subsequently it can contribute more to economic growth. For example, the World Bank's country-assistance poverty-reduction strategy is designed to complement a country's capacity to reduce poverty. In countries where poverty is narrowly concentrated and the government's implementation ability is good, targeted programmes are considered an effective poverty-reduction strategy. In countries where poverty is widespread and the government's implementation capacity is weak, broad-based growth and support for basic social services may be the most effective strategy for poverty reduction (World Bank, 1993: 13).

The strength of this poverty-reduction strategy is the importance placed on human resources development, including sectoral policy reforms. This is an essential criterion for improving the country's capacity in the distribution of basic services. Conversely, the weakness of this strategy is its analysis of poverty. In examining the new rise in poverty rates, no account is taken of a country's social and political dimensions, important components that provide an overall profile of the country's development and that identify factors affecting economic growth and distribution of basic services. This is especially the case in developing countries with dual societies where the distribution of development benefits and social services is influenced by traditional social networks that persist within the newly established modern systems. Furthermore, factors such as a weak institutional capacity, and the impact of external shocks from the global economy are disregarded. Hence, traditional poverty analysis provides insufficient information to explain the barriers to basic services or income-earning opportunities. It does not question how certain groups are able to improve their living standards while others continue to suffer deprivation. Processes that make individuals or groups vulnerable to impoverishment are overlooked. Moreover, identification of the poor is not based on reliable data.

Poverty-reduction strategies for Yemen

There are various challenging issues involved in dealing with poverty in Yemen. These include widespread deprivation from access to basic services (such as piped water, health care services, schools, roads), along with problems of identifying the poor due to insufficient data. Moreover, the government's outreach capacity, both technical and financial, is inadequate, the institutional infrastructure to provide assistance programmes is limited, as is the sociopolitical configuration that affects the distribution of social provisioning. To achieve their effectiveness these concerns need, therefore, to be incorporated into the design and implementation of poverty-reduction strategies.

The World Bank notes that the Yemen government's poverty-reduction strategy consists of: (1) cash and in-kind assistance to the unemployable poor; (2) training and grants to help the employable poor obtain jobs or establish micro-enterprises; (3) provision of basic services to a larger share of the population; and (4) universal wheat and flour consumer subsidies (World Bank, 1997). The government defines its target population primarily as those in rural villages. It recognises the difficulty in targeting the poor due to insufficient household data and therefore employs geographical or self-selection targeting mechanisms. This strategy is implemented through public-sector entities.

In 1997 the World Bank assisted the government to establish the Social Fund for Development (SFD) as a social safety net institution for the poor. The need for such an institution was in response to the increase in the poverty rate that was one of the side-effects of the government's Economic Reform Program (SFD, 1999). The SFD's objectives consist of assistance programmes for the poor aimed at improving their living conditions by providing access to social services and generating income opportunities. The SFD's poverty-reduction strategy differs, however, from that of the government in that its approach is primarily decentralised and demand-driven. In other words, the SFD aims to reach the poor by meeting local demand for social services, and it depends on the use of community associations, NGOs, the private sector and local government in providing such services. It defines its target population as the poor and disadvantaged communities that lack access to essential services or that suffer from high unemployment or underemployment. Components of the SFD include community development, micro-credit enterprise and institutional capacity building.

A common denominator between the government and the SFD is that their poverty-reduction strategies are based on the traditional definition of poverty based on static economic and social measurements. Their efforts therefore are aimed at altering this status quo. The causes that lead individuals and groups into a process of deprivations and marginalisation and from there into impoverishment go unexplained. As a consequence, evolving factors contributing to current problems of poverty are also overlooked and new impoverished groups are not recognised. The government's strategy suggests short-term prescriptions that would meet the immediate needs of the poor: their limited financial resources, however, will hinder the implementation of these efforts. The SFD's strategy, on the other hand, is broadly based, and will require long-term efforts to build up the institutional capacity of the poor communities and orient them towards the demand-driven approach. Nor is their strategy innovative since it resembles previous development strategies. Furthermore, it is based on the assumption that poor communities know how to organise themselves and have access to social representatives even though this is not usually the case with the critically poor.

In both strategies, an underlying problem that results from the limited definition of poverty is the lack of an efficient methodology for identifying the target group. Poor groups are no longer concentrated in rural areas and although the unemployed are poor that is only a single determinant of their poverty. The failure to target different groups entrapped in poverty reflects how poor groups become vulnerable to social exclusion. Furthermore, failure to identify the processes that expose individuals and groups to destitution disqualifies poverty-reduction strategies from reversing these processes. Thus, although such strategies are important, they are inadequate in combating the processes of impoverishment and in promoting equitable access to economic and social participation and development.

The concept of social exclusion
Social exclusion is a broader notion of poverty that includes non-material deprivation and the marginalisation of groups from the benefits of social and economic development. What distinguishes the poor from the excluded is that the poor may still be within the mainstream of society. The excluded, on the other hand, are groups that have been marginalised. As well as being deprived of basic goods and services they also lack the

social networks and effective political representation that will assist them in reintegration. Thus, unlike the limited definition of poverty that describes only a standard of living, social indicators and purchasing power, social exclusion includes the multidimensional causes of deprivation and disadvantage – social, economic and political – that push individuals and groups to the periphery of society. These dynamic forces are related to attributes of the individual and society, and as this relationship advances, it reveals a causal relationship of deprivation and social disaffiliation. Thus, as development proceeds, those who are left behind are trapped in a cycle of poverty and exclusion.

The term 'social exclusion' is not new. What is new in this evolving concept is the notion of exclusion as it relates to modern and economic changes and social ties. During the 1980s the French began to use it to refer to the 'new poor', who were the long-term unemployed, the poor, unskilled workers, and immigrants. The term was taken over by the European Commission in the late 1980s, when unemployment and poverty had risen and the disadvantages among these groups came to be regarded as an issue that questioned the 'social rights' and 'equity' of a country's welfare systems. Social rights, as conveyed in the term 'citizenship', address questions about the rights of the citizen in relation to employment, housing, health care, justice, etc., and the effectiveness of national polices in securing these rights.

In the early 1990s, the International Institute for Labour Studies (IILS) undertook a major study of the notion of social exclusion as it relates to developing countries and transitional societies.[2] Empirical evidence gathered from country case studies showed that the interpretation of social exclusion in developing countries differs somewhat from that in industrialised societies. In the latter, exclusion is based on the rupture of the legal relationship between the citizen and the state. This relationship is founded on the 'social contract'. Employment is the most important of these social rights, and is considered fundamental for maintaining the social relationships between citizens. In developing societies, by contrast, social exclusion is based on the relationship defined by membership of and status within various kinds of groups and networks. Unlike in industrialised societies, social exclusion in developing societies is not the breakdown of social ties but rather the lack of social membership. Social rights are not yet fully nationalised but are based in part on customary laws (Hashem, 1996). Thus exclusion can result from involuntary individual attributes or formal or informal institutions. It is therefore vital for poverty-reduction strategists to focus on the dynamics of cumulative causation by describing the effects that reinforce disadvantage, marginalisation and social disaffiliation (IILS, 1996: 12).

Thus the concept of social exclusion builds on the traditional definition of poverty to include a multidimensional analysis of the issue that incorporates aspects of social participation and rights into its conceptualisation. Non-material dimensions of impoverishment are important issues in developing societies. The issues of citizenship and social rights are, in this scenario, in a state of flux as a result of the changing position of the individual in society from a social system based on kinship and a traditional productive livelihood to one based on individualism and merit. The concept focuses, therefore, on the process of poverty rather than on the outcome of poverty. Consequently, it allows a causal analysis to explain the ways people become poor and excluded from access to development benefits.

In conclusion, the concept of social exclusion complements a poverty-reduction strategy. It reveals different attributes of impoverishment in society that go beyond those of income levels and purchasing power and deals with the ways in which mechanisms of impoverishment and exclusion can be reversed to social integration and income acquisition.

Poverty and social exclusion in Yemen

An overview of Yemen's history during the 1990s highlights certain events in the society's political economy and the transition to a market economy that have contributed to problems of poverty and social exclusion. Processes of poverty and social exclusion are influenced by factors such as the political economy, national development policies and structural norms.

The political economy

Since access to resources and entitlements in low-income countries is centred on the distributive powers of the political system, Yemen's political economy is crucial for understanding poverty and social exclusion. In developing countries such as Yemen, the *realpolitik* shows that political stability (or instability) is an important determinant of trends of economic growth, social provisioning, and poverty.

Faltering economic growth in Yemen became evident in the mid-1980s as a consequence of the Iran–Iraq war and the international oil glut.[3] It was, however, the Gulf War in 1990 that led to a domino effect in paralysing the country's economy and social development. The government of the newly unified Yemen was punished for its neutral stand at the United Nations in not joining the international alliance to bomb Iraq. Almost one million emigrant Yemeni labourers and their families were expelled from the Gulf States with a consequent reduction in remittances, a major source of external hard currency to the country. Foreign grants, specifically from Arab oil states, were halted, and foreign technical development assistance was drastically curtailed. Within a few months, the country underwent a population increase of 8 per cent.

The government was overwhelmed by this sudden crisis of national refugees and by its responsibility for providing emergency assistance. Short-term labour migrants reintegrated into their villages while camps had to be built around the major cities to accommodate emigrants who could no longer trace their family roots. Social services such as schools, health services, housing, and food subsidies were stretched to the limits, and the labour market in a stagnant economy was glutted with unskilled and semi-skilled workers.

By 1994, the unification honeymoon between the previous South Yemen Socialist Party (YSP) of Ali Salem Al-Beedh and the Congress Party of President Ali Saleh was deteriorating. Conflict was brewing, thereby impeding economic recovery. Government offices were slow in implementing social projects, and some technical assistance was put on hold. On 5 May 1994, war finally broke out when the YSP attempted to dissolve the unification process.

Although there was more infrastructure damage in the South, the economic collapse was nationwide. Private investment was halted and the depleted government budget led to the dysfunction of social services. The middle class shrank, those already in the lower-income strata were pushed further into an insecure livelihood, and extreme cases of poverty, unemployment and marginalised groups in society started to become visible throughout the country. Schools witnessed a decline in student enrolments and a rise in student dropouts, since education was perceived among lower-income groups as a commodity rather than a necessity. Medical care became unreachable for many, especially because of the high costs of medicine. The market economy was strained by a depreciated national currency; inflation was at an all-time high; and employment opportunities became rare. As a result, the competition over limited resources made social networks a dominant factor in social and economic participation.[4]

In such circumstances, individuals resort to their traditional groups in search of support. Those who lack social membership in subgroups are pushed out to the margins of society (Hashem, 1996: 97–102). Their exclusion is thus twofold: they are excluded from government institutions that would provide them with social welfare, as well as from traditional subgroups that would provide them with support and solidarity.

National development policies
During the transition from a society based on subsistence agriculture to a market economy, society undergoes restructuring as a result of economic and technological changes. In order to integrate into a market economy, the transformation process is contingent on social and economic development. For example, education and training in professional skills appropriate to the demands of the new labour market are essential.

However, the Yemen government's capacity for distributing social services (especially those relating to human resource development) has been limited. Consequently, some groups in society that have access to development benefits advance socially and economically, while others are left behind. Those who lack access to development benefits, especially human resource development, are hindered from participating in the market economy. This emphasises their vulnerability to impoverishment and accentuates their gradual marginalisation from civil society.

Cultural and modern processes of social exclusion
Cultural structural norms in Yemeni society did not diminish during the country's transformation process from a primordial state to a modern market economy state; rather, they persisted and competed with the evolving norms of the market economy. As a result, the country is characterised as having a dual society, i.e. one that includes norms of both a primordial and a civil society. Consequently, dual processes of social exclusion exist, i.e. those related to structural norms and those embedded in national development policies of the market economy. Different groups are excluded as a result of one or both of these factors. These dual processes are not mutually exclusive. Individuals and groups

that lack access to membership in one or other of these systems represent those who are most vulnerable to poverty and exclusion.

This section briefly summarises the primordial dimension of social exclusion – structural norms – and three important new dimensions of social exclusion embedded in the modern economy-state – exclusion from basic needs, the labour market, and social and political representation.

Structural norms

Traditionally, genealogy and access to land are important structural norms that have determined social stratification, and political and economic power in Yemen (Shaher, 1991: 218; Al-Sharjaby, 1986: 55). These norms also reflect the structural processes of inclusion and exclusion in social membership. The economic status of the individual is secondary to genealogy. In the major cities these norms are slowly changing with the emergence of a market-economy society, but they continue to be dominant among the rural population.

Although new socioeconomic groups such as the military and the entrepreneurs are emerging, Yemen's traditional social stratification continues to define the overall social order.[5] Individuals or groups most vulnerable to exclusion are those that are outside the social order or the traditional legal code. Their exclusion from social membership is passive and discriminatory. Although the rights of the excluded may be protected nationally, their exclusion is enforced by social behaviour. As is the case in most traditional practices, this social behaviour is resistant to change.

Exclusion from basic needs

Basic needs include goods and services (e.g. health care services, schools, piped water, roads, electricity) essential for improving the quality of life. A large portion of society continues to be deprived of these basics. For example, health services are accessible to only 42 per cent of the total population, of whom 75 per cent are located in urban areas and 25 per cent in rural areas (UN, 2001: 5). Only 58 per cent of the total population in the age group 6–15 years are enrolled in formal education (CSO, 1998: 15).[6] There is also wide enrolment disparity between urban and rural populations and gender. The enrolment rate in urban primary schools is 81 per cent as opposed to 52 per cent in rural areas; while gross enrolment rates in primary schools are 76 per cent boys and 40 per cent girls (UN, 2001: 14).

Basic-needs deprivation takes on different guises. First, exclusion of some groups from basic needs can be explained by a simple supply-and-demand equation. Though the government acknowledges its responsibilities, its ability to provide basic social services has been constrained by various interdependent factors, mainly the state's financial limitations. This problem has been compounded by the geographic dispersion of the population, the rapid population growth rate, and the overall stagnant economy. The effectiveness of the state's efforts in social provisioning are also restricted by technical limitations that include shortages of physicians, nurses, teachers and other professionals who tend to be concentrated in the major cities, and a poorly developed infrastructure (lack of paved roads, school buildings, hospitals, electricity, etc.).

Secondly, even in situations where basic services are available, people are deprived of access to these services by their inability to pay for them, especially where opportunity costs are concerned. This is particularly evident in education and health. For example, although free education is guaranteed by the state, the income sacrifices demanded of the poor to pay for related expenses (textbooks, registration fees, clothing, etc.) are such that their children are more likely to be excluded from schooling. Similarly in health, the inability to pay for medicine excludes the poor from adequate heath care.

In the past, deprivation from basic needs may have gone un-recognised by some. More recently, exposure of the population to the mass media and other sources of information has alerted them to the importance of education, health care, safe drinking water and proper nutrition. Their deprivation from these services has become more acutely felt since they now realise the importance of these services and feel that they and their children are being denied a chance to improve their livelihood.

Exclusion from the labour market
Changes in patterns of employment inevitably result as the country pursues the transformation to a market economy. Concentrations of poor, illiterate and professionally unskilled individuals in rural areas are in the frontline of exclusion from the labour market. They have been squeezed out of their traditional livelihoods, and lack the opportunity to insert themselves into the modern economy.

Exclusion from the labour market worsens during the following: (1) a slow economy and a high proportion of unskilled labour; (2) lack of investment in industrial and modern-sector activities; (3) conventional development planning (such as industries, services and utilities concentrated in the major cities and their outskirts); (4) use of capital-intensive techniques that have led to an increase in productivity with no additional employment opportunities; and (5) lack of training programmes to provide untrained and illiterate labourers with skills that fulfil the needs of the economy.

The large influx of Yemeni workers returning from neighbouring Gulf countries during the Gulf War in 1990 resulted in high levels of unemployment. It was estimated that 23.3 per cent of the labour force was employed in 1990: by 1994 the figure had risen to 40 per cent (EIU, 1995). A major characteristic of this labour force was the high level of semi-skilled and unskilled workers for whom there was little demand. Between 1995 and 2000, the labour force in Yemen has grown at a rate of 4.3 per cent per annum (UN, 2001).

Open unemployment demonstrates exclusion from the labour market. However, exclusion can also occur within the labour market. This is the position with labourers who can find only casual work or employment in menial jobs. In this case, labourers are confined to poorly paid and low-skilled occupations. The underlying issue in this case is a dual process (Rodgers, 1994: 10). On the one hand, there are 'bad jobs' with easier access but where upward mobility is prohibited and poverty is concentrated; and on the other hand, there are 'good jobs' that provide a degree of financial security, promotion and acceptable working conditions but have restricted access. There are, therefore, different levels of exclusion from the labour market whereby it is possible to be included but at the same time excluded from the 'good jobs'.

Exclusion from social and political representation
Exclusion from social and political representation is closely associated with the issue of access to social membership at the local and national level. Political and social institutions that are accessible to citizens are essential for the promotion of integration in society, since it is through these institutions that the notion of citizenship is promoted.

Shortly after unification, in an effort to promote public participation and representation, the government of the Republic of Yemen allowed the organisation of political parties, of which there were almost 45 by the year 1992. However, many of these political parties remain strongly influenced by the traditional social order and networks of power, and political affiliation is based more on patronage and personal relationships than on ideology (HRW, 1992: 13).[7] Nor have the parties improved the participation and representation of poor citizens, basically because the notion of participation in political parties, democracy and political pluralism are concepts familiar only to the educated minority. The poor and disadvantaged, for example, lack awareness of how to organise or utilise the parties to represent their needs and demands, and the combination of their poverty and illiteracy is a major barrier to information, organisation and participation in the political process. Thus, poor groups do not regard the emergence of political parties as a means of solving their problems of being deprived of basic needs or employment.[8]

For various reasons, the ability of citizens, particularly the poor, individually or collectively, to voice their demands and needs to government is often limited. Unofficial channels and networks have become the norm for citizens to process government-related activities or gain access to government officials. In addition, a significant number of government employees do not seem to function according to their roles as 'civil servants' with responsibilities for a 'public service'. Some of these civil servants work in the public sector basically because it was the biggest employment agency in the 1970s and 1980s, while other civil servants are merely interested in enhancing their own political image (Hashem, 1996). As a result, poor and disadvantaged citizens who lack social networks are overwhelmed by what is involved in interacting with their government, and often give up what is within their social rights. Although these rights may be protected by the state, such people are confronted by too many obstacles as a consequence of their lack of access to mediating institutions and agencies. This problem is not peculiar to Yemen but prevails in many developing countries.

Thus exclusion from representation compounds the other dimensions of exclusion (i.e. access to basic services and to the labour market). This fosters feelings of insecurity and vulnerability among poor groups and pushes them to the margin of society.

Excluded groups

The case study on Yemen, undertaken for the IILS research project on social exclusion in developing countries, identified four groups most vulnerable to the dimensions of exclusion discussed above: (1) an ethnic minority group, the *akhdam*; (2) day labourers; (3) inhabitants in remote villages; and (4) emigrant returnees of the Gulf War.[9] This does not imply that these are the only excluded groups in Yemen; merely that, in the first study to be conducted on social exclusion, these four groups were significantly represented.

Ethnic minority group: the akhdam

As is particularly evident in the Northern Governorates, the *akhdam* provide a perfect example of a group caught in a vicious cycle of poverty and social exclusion. The term *akhdam* (plural for *khadem* – servant) is discriminatory; its use in this study is dictated by the lack of any alternative means of identification for this group.

The experience of the *akhdam* in the Southern Governorates (the former South Yemen) has been different as a result of the policies of the socialist regime that outlawed the use of social status terminology. The *akhdam* in the South were encouraged to seek education and training. More importantly, they were given equal employment opportunities (Hashem, 1996: 70). Several studies have described the *akhdam* in the Northern Governorates as the poorest and most marginal group in Yemen (Othman, 1978; Globovaskaya, 1981; Al-Sharjaby, 1986; Shaher, 1991).

Generally, their physical features are African, while their language and religious practices are the same as the rest of Yemeni society. Numerous studies have attempted to establish a link between the *akhdam* and Africa, though none have been able to confirm this hypothesis. Another hypothesis states that the *akhdam* are descendants of the Ethiopian invaders left behind in Yemen after the Ethiopians were overthrown by the Yemenis in the sixth century. In retaliation, the Yemenis made the Ethiopians who were left behind their servants (Shaher, 1991: 236). A further hypothesis suggests that the *akhdam* were originally people of Yemeni descent who migrated to Ethiopia before the spread of Islam and resided there and assimilated with the local population (Othman, 1978). They later returned to Yemen during the Ethiopian invasion in 525 AD. Similar to all hypotheses on the *akhdam*, there has been no evidence to confirm this, although some believe it is the more likely explanation. Yet what this hypothesis also implies is that the *akhdam* are an indigenous minority group rather than an out-group ethnic minority.

Consequently, in a society where genealogy is fundamental for social membership and status, the social status of the *akhdam* has been based on their occupation, mainly in jobs such as street cleaners, waste collectors and butchers, that are considered degrading in Yemeni society. Consequently, their poverty and social exclusion can be traced to persisting cultural structural norms in society embedded in social behaviour.

For several reasons they are politically weak and subservient. They consist of small and scattered groups, and as a result of the lack of occupational stability, they always segment and disperse before they reach an optimum size in any particular location. In times of drought or other hardships they are the first to become redundant, and their economic dependence has always put them in a status of clientship. Furthermore, instead of a single leader they may have fifty, each heading his own small group (Bujra, 1971: 43).

The *akhdam* tend to keep to themselves, knowing that if they try to mix with others in society they will not be welcomed. They live in closed ghettos of tin huts that have no piped water, sanitation facilities or sewage systems. Their children are seldom educated, since they cannot afford the expense of sending them to school; in addition, children may be required to participate in work that will add to the family's income. In some cases those that do attend school drop out as a result of discriminatory practices by their peers. The racial and emotional uneasiness and uncertainty in dealing with the *akhdam* is best character-ised as 'aversive racism'. Hagendoorn (1993: 26–51) explains this as a more hidden form of racism which is expressed in simple avoidance. Social distance is maintained, separating this minority group from the rest of society in relation to work, neighbourhood, friendships and marriage.

Day labourers

Day labourers in Yemen are referred to as *al-mouhamasheen*, or the marginalised. In general, the term *mouhamasheen* (sing. *mouhamash*) could refer to any peripheral underclass group (or individual) in Yemeni society. Recently, it has become widely used to describe poor casual labourers who seek work on a daily basis and who gather in several locations in the major cities, especially Sana'a and Aden. They are primarily landless workers and marginal landowners who migrate to the cities with expectations of improving their economic status. Instead, they arrive in urban centres that are poorly prepared to absorb them.

There are several factors that may have contributed to the increasing numbers of day labourers, including:

- conventional development planning, which has resulted in a maldistribution of employment opportunities (i.e. industries, services and utilities were concentrated in the major cities and their outskirts, leading to stagnation in the productive capability of the rural population and in turn to an increase in rural-urban migration). The large numbers coming from rural areas to urban centres were unable to find sufficient job opportunities, which resulted in high levels of unemployment and underemployment;
- a high population growth, especially in the 15–65 age group (44 per cent), and a high illiteracy rate among this group;
- the sudden return of emigrant workers from the Arab oil states as a result of the Gulf War crisis, which created a surplus of unskilled and semi-skilled workers.
- the high costs of agricultural production and its low output, leading many farmers to abandon their land and migrate to the cities in search of work;
- the increased use of modern technology on the more affluent farms may have resulted in job loss that forced peasants to migrate to the city.

Day labourers who have been squeezed out of the traditional market thus do not have the skills to integrate into the new market economy. Hence, the transformation process that includes changes in the economy and the characteristics of the labour force is an important underlying mechanism contributing to the marginal economic participation of day labourers.

Inhabitants of remote villages

The exclusion of the inhabitants of remote villages is associated with territorial exclusion. Remote villages may be only a few miles away from the country's main road network but lack paved roads and are difficult to reach without a guide and a proper vehicle. Major characteristics of these villages include problems of high emigration, no productive investment, no communication and transportation network facilities and no essential services (such as piped water, electricity, health centres or schools). The villagers live in impoverished conditions and believe that the government is not interested in including them in overall national social and economic development. Although the state has always considered the social integration of these villages a major priority, providing basic services to geographically distant and scattered settlements in which traditional social structures still predominate is, however, a complex and costly endeavour.

The livelihood of inhabitants in remote villages is also restricted. Agriculture is the predominant employment sector (58 per cent). Share-cropping is a major characteristic in this sector. In recent years, there has been a reduction in the amount of land that is cultivated annually, due to meagre water supply, deterioration of soil, migration to urban areas or abroad, limited availability of production inputs, and rising production costs (UN, 2001: 10). This has had a serious impact on the livelihood of the majority of the rural population.

The returnee emigrants of the Gulf War

A few months after Yemen's unification (May 1990), the Iraqi invasion of Kuwait launched events leading to the Gulf War. As a result of the neutral political stance on the war adopted by the government of the Yemen Republic, close to a million Yemeni emigrants in Kuwait, Bahrain, Saudi Arabia, the United Arab Emirates and Iraq were forced to return home. This represented a population increase of about 8 per cent (CSO, 1991).

A survey by the Central Statistical Organisation (CSO, 1990: 17–35) provides some information on the characteristics of these returnees. The majority (65 per cent) had been out of the country for over 10 years; 61 per cent were born in Saudi Arabia; 75 per cent did not own land and/or housing in Yemen, and 74 per cent of the returnees were aged between 15 and 45 years. Almost half were illiterate, while only 18 per cent had received some formal education. Fifty-one per cent had previously been employed as skilled labourers. Most of these returnees did not go back to their villages but settled in the cities. At the time the survey was conducted only 13 per cent had found employment. These statistics illustrate the difficulties of incorporating returnees with few skills into an already congested labour market.

The largest group of returnees (92 per cent) had returned from Saudi Arabia, and were forced to sell their property and possessions at absurdly low prices. Some returnees faced more obstacles to re-integration than others; those who lacked strong family ties in their villages experienced the greatest difficulties. The state provided temporary housing in schools and hospitals. The hardest-hit areas were in Hodeidah and Aden, where vacant lands were transformed into tent cities. The majority of the returnees who had limited resources were confronted with exorbitant rents and had no place to live other than the state-sponsored camps. In 1994, about 75,000 families of returnee emigrants were still living in wretched conditions in camps on the outskirts of major cities. The difficulties of camp life – which include uncertain water delivery, lack of electricity, lack of privacy, and unpredictable food supplies – continue to define the livelihood of these refugees. Malaria and other diseases are widespread in these camps. A decade later, the situation of the returnee emigrants in these camps remains the same (UN, 2000).

Conclusion

Processes of poverty and social exclusion: macro-micro linkages

There is a strong relationship between poverty and social exclusion. The concept of social exclusion in Yemen must be understood as it relates to the notion of social integration. It is a process that denies social membership within the context of a dualistic transitional society. In relation to the traditional society it denies membership in the social order, while in a modern market-economy it denies citizens the right to equal social participation. The former reflects the dominant social order that continues to determine access and entitlements, while the latter reflects national development policies that fail to deliver equal access to development benefits. These processes are not mutually exclusive.

The exclusionary process is transposed to community level by certain factors that make some groups more vulnerable than others. In the case of the four excluded groups in the study – the *akhdam*, the day labourers, the inhabitants of remote villages, and the returnees – these factors include emigration, geographic location and structural norms. The four excluded groups reflect the diversity of the processes of exclusion.

The process of exclusion of the *akhdam* is embedded in cultural practices that define membership in the social order. This process of exclusion is transposed by structural norms, which continue to be practised by society. The untraceable social identity of the *akhdam* impedes their economic and social participation at the community level. The processes of exclusion of the day labourers are associated with development policies that fail to integrate this group in the market economy. Emigration has further promoted the exclusion process of day labourers. In other words, the migration from rural to urban centres of day labourers with insufficient skills and lack of social networks makes this group vulnerable. As a result, they experience peripheral participation in the labour force and marginal social participation in the cities.

The interaction of processes of social exclusion in the dualistic Yemeni society is illustrated in the exclusion process of inhabitants of remote villages and the returnees. The exclusion of inhabitants of remote villages can be explained by national development policies that have not included them in the development process. However, what makes inhabitants of remote villages vulnerable to exclusion is their geographic location. Thus, the more remote the village, the more likely its exclusion from development benefits. Cultural norms also play a covert role in the process of exclusion of this group, particularly in the northern regions where the social order is more obvious. If the village is connected to a prestigious tribal clan, its chances of inclusion in development benefits increase, since tribal *shaikhs* in government positions can influence the provision of social welfare to their clan. For returnees, on the other hand, the process of exclusion is associated with development policies that have not been sufficiently extended to include their citizenship rights. It was assumed that their vulnerability to exclusion was related to migration, since these returnees had been permanent emigrants who had established their livelihoods elsewhere. Their exclusion reflected a rupture from major community and social networks of origin. This group no longer had any social ties to a clan or village in Yemen to help them re-integrate.

Prevalent dimensions of exclusion – basic needs, labour market and social and political representation – are not mutually exclusive; rather, their interaction leads to a dynamic cycle of poverty and downward mobility. This reflects the multidimensionality of processes of exclusion at the micro-level. Each excluded group encounters a certain dimension of exclusion, which sets in motion the compound process of exclusion. For example, the day labourers are primarily excluded from the formal labour market. This dimension of exclusion is associated with their exclusion from social and political representation. Their lack of protection in the labour market and insecure livelihood accentuates their poverty, and consequently excludes them from access to basic services as a result of their low purchasing power.

The inhabitants in remote villages are primarily excluded from basic needs. As a result of this exclusion, their lack of education and training leads, for example, to their exclusion from the labour market. Moreover, their exclusion from effective political representation to oversee their access to development benefits sustains their exclusion from the development process that is taking place in the rest of the country. The *akhdam*, on the other hand, are primarily excluded from social and political representation that would help abolish the social stigma from which they suffer, and would confirm their social integration into mainstream society. However, exclusion from representation has also led to their exclusion from access to remunerative jobs in the labour market, and exclusion from basic needs. As for the returnees, when they first arrived they were excluded from basic goods and services while surviving in the camps. Their poverty was made more severe by their exclusion from the labour market due to the degenerating economy as well as to their depleting personal funds. Lack of political representation to demand their citizens' rights to assist them in reintegrating into their homeland accentuated their peripheral social existence.

These dimensions of exclusion not only represent outcomes of exclusion, but also come to reflect mechanisms that sustain the exclusionary process. This is observed in the effects of deprivation, which are spilling over to the younger generations. For example, many children are not currently enrolled in school for the same reasons that kept their parents out of schools: lack of financial resources and unavailability of schools. Thus, processes of exclusion can form a vicious cycle from which it is difficult to escape. This problem should be taken seriously, especially in relation to the high population growth rate among these groups.

Poverty and social exclusion of each group also provide a time profile of the dynamic process that reflects economic, social and political change. For example, the exclusion of the *akhdam* is an historical prejudice maintained by structural norms. Their exclusion appears to be permanent, unless affirmative action is taken by the government to ensure their integration into society. The returnees, on the other hand, are victims of an international political conflict. In 2000, their plight was similar to that of refugees. It is a temporary situation, but one that is fragile under the degenerating economy. The returnees are thus a vulnerable group whose exclusion may be transformed into one that is more permanent. The exclusion of day labourers is cyclical. In other words, their exclusion depends on the state of the economy. However, their exclusion is different from that of the other three groups, since they are vulnerable to exclusion only while they are in the cities. Day labourers who maintain links with their villages belong to a community, and have a social base upon their return to their village. The exclusion process of day labourers reflects the serious social calamities in transitional societies that result from economic transformation and its volatility.

The exclusion of inhabitants of remote villages is more complex in nature, since it has been going on for many decades. Historically, in the North, this was a result of the weakness of these villages as social groups, due to weak tribal affiliation or leadership. In the South, however, it was a result of the subversive policies of the colonial power. Although structural norms continue to have some underlying influence, more recently their process of exclusion is associated with the economic constraints of the state and the overall problems in the development of the country.

This study has also shown a strong relationship between poverty and social exclusion. Poverty and exclusion seem to reinforce each other, regardless of which occurs first. In the case of the returnees, for example, their inability to reintegrate their villages led to their exclusion. Their long-term unemployment then depleted their savings and made them poor and vulnerable. The day labourers, on the other hand, are poor rural men, whose migration to a new city and inability to participate in the labour market contributed to their exclusion. Among the inhabitants of remote villages and the *akhdam*, poverty and exclusion have always coexisted. At some stage, poverty and exclusion may become indistinguishable. This is perhaps the basis of the common assumption that the poor are also the excluded in low-income societies.

An important finding of the study is the fact that poverty and unemployment did not affect an individual's social ties with his/her family and the immediate community. Family ties were strong and people depended on each other during times of hardship. People perceived the problem of exclusion and poverty as a problem that involved the family and the community as a whole and not as a problem limited to the individual. This reflects a positive aspect of traditional societies. Unlike Western industrialised societies that have become individualised, and where employment is a major determinant for establishing social ties and for social integration, the social values of traditional societies, based on family and religion, maintain a fundamental social bond. This bond represents a significant social safety net that has helped sustain these excluded groups.

Policy implications

The concept of social exclusion in relation to developing countries has developed at a particularly important time, when poverty is at an all-time high and resources are at an all-time low. Its usage helps confirm that the most impoverished of the vulnerable groups in society are those who are not receiving development benefits and whose entitlements are not protected. Examining poverty in relation to social change and social policies is a useful analytical tool, especially in a transitional developing country. The integration of the concept of social exclusion in poverty-reduction strategies is therefore essential, since it provides a multidimensional approach to examining poverty and marginalisation in relation to economic, political and social change. The four excluded groups discussed in this study are exemplars.

The exclusion of the returnees, for example, represents social change as a consequence of political change. The returnees are victims of a political crisis who need immediate attention, and assistance, in the form of poverty-reduction strategies and programmes that would especially help them to integrate, includes housing and employment opportunities. There are no clear policies or projects that focus on the provision of low-income housing, yet housing policies are essential for social integration since housing gives people a feeling of belonging and security.

The day labourers reflect social change to which economic change has contributed. The social problem of day labourers also reflects the absence of policies to secure them employment rights and social insurance. These workers, who are unskilled and semi-skilled, represent a large majority of Yemen's active labour force. They are part of the country's human resources, in which the government should make a serious investment. Their marginal participation in the labour market emphasises the need for on-the-job training and the importance of protection in the labour market. Employment entitlements in the public sector, such as a minimum wage and social insurance, are not applied to such workers. However, according to the Social Security Corporation (under Law No. 26 for 1991, cited in MPD, 1992), establishments in the private sector that employ five or more workers should provide their employees with social insurance. This law needs close monitoring for more effective implementation. Workers in the private and informal sectors do not have any protective regulations regarding their work environment, wages or social insurance; nor is there any welfare system to sustain the poor when the principal provider suddenly loses his/her job. Labour unions are governmental agencies and have been ineffective in safeguarding the rights of poor casual labourers. There is an urgent need for the establishment of a labour organisation or union that would specifically represent this group by assisting them to find employment; obtain training and advancement in their occupations (e.g. from temporary to permanent employment), while overseeing their employment conditions.

The process of exclusion of the *akhdam* reflects social behaviour that continues to be influenced by structural norms. The obvious social exclusion of the *akhdam*, particularly in the Northern Governorates, illustrates discriminatory behaviour towards this group. The social change currently taking place in Yemen has not been sufficiently dynamic to eliminate structural norms that promote processes of exclusion.

The status of social change and the dynamics of social relationships are important information for policy makers. Affirmative social policies that specifically aim to eradicate the social stigma of the *akhdam* may help their inclusion into mainstream society and upward economic mobility. The success of such social policies was demonstrated by the experience of the *akhdam* in Aden, where the state developed specific policies to prevent social discrimination against them. The use of the term *khadem/akhdam* was forbidden. The catalyst for the *akhdam*'s integration was the availability of education and training and equal employment opportunities. As a result, although short-lived, the policies of the 1980s proved successful in freeing the *akhdam* from the social stigma attached to them in allowing their upward mobility and most importantly, in promoting their social integration. Such policies can also be applied to include the integration of other groups, vulnerable to structural norms that embody processes of exclusion.

The exclusion of inhabitants of remote villages indicates social change that reflects a widening gap between rural and urban centres, and even between different rural areas. Rural inhabitants are the backbone of Yemeni society and its economy. The continuing marginalisation of this population in the development process, and thus in their human resource development, is a serious problem that will delay the development of the country. The concept of social exclusion, in this case, highlights the importance of evaluating, monitoring and reviewing development policies. It confirms the view that the most vulnerable groups are not at the receiving end of development benefits.

Current development policies, such as rural development designed to increase agriculture productivity, would benefit from a review of their embedded processes of exclusion (MPD, 1992: 9). In a list of strategies for the implementation of this policy, the only one that relates to improving the livelihood of small farm-holders is increased production. There do not appear to be any specific plans for human resource development by means of education and training, provision of health care services or safe drinking water. Instead, the emphasis is primarily on the industrialisation of agriculture. These strategies do not take into consideration the economic participation of landless people in rural areas. This group can, for example, be included in training programmes for the use of modern agricultural technology and other skills. Alternatively, the landless may be employed in construction projects to develop the infrastructure of the villages, such as the building of roads, the installation of water systems, and the building of schools and health centres. This would enable them to sustain their livelihoods in their own villages.

Poverty-reduction strategies designed regionally rather than centrally can effectively meet different needs and utilise available local resources. Private investment in rural areas can also contribute to improving the livelihood of inhabitants in remote villages and integrating them into economic development. As a result, this would provide employment opportunities, reduce rural-urban migration and alleviate urban congestion. Expansion of the country's road network represents an ideal example with obvious multidimensional benefits. Most importantly, it would integrate the country (i.e. rural-rural, and rural-urban) and enhance its transformation into a modern market economy. This includes facilitating the transportation and communication of markets, services and ideas.

Other social actors, such as foreign-country donors, international organisations and NGOs, can also benefit from the use of the concept of social exclusion in their poverty-reduction strategies and projects. It would assist them in identifying the socially disadvantaged and in designing development projects that would meet the needs of these people for equal participation in society.

Many sceptics will claim that the concept of social exclusion is another discourse on poverty and deprivation in developing countries. As this study explains, poverty and social exclusion are strongly associated. The causal relationship is not uniform in differentiating the independent from the dependent variables. Yet what makes the concept of exclusion important to poverty issues is that it encompasses the issue of the rights of social membership. This membership represents a fundamental human right. Development is not complete when it provides only basic services that would subsequently improve an individual's economic value. Development is complete when all citizens, regardless of their identity, religion or economic status, are aware of and able to participate in society, and when the state oversees and protects these rights.

NOTES

1 This takes into consideration the political and economic history of the two Yemens.

2 The International Institute for Labour Studies (IILS) and the UNDP conducted a global research project in 1993, to develop the concept of social exclusion in low-income and transitional societies. Researchers from 11 countries (Brazil, India, Mali, Mexico, Peru, Russia, Tanzania, Thailand, Tunisia, Venezuela and Yemen) participated in the project. This chapter is based on the study conducted in Yemen by the author. See M. H. Hashem (1996), *Goals for Social Integration and Realties of Social Exclusion*, Geneva: Institute for Labour Studies.

3 This was evident in both the previous North and South Yemens.

4 This is based on observations and interviews with government officials, NGOs and poor groups while collecting data for this study.

5 Studies relating to Yemen's social hierarchy vary, especially with regard to describing the lower strata. See Shaher (1991), pp. 217–20.

6 The Ministry of Planning and Development (MPD) uses this percentage only as a general indicator; it is difficult to establish an accurate estimate of enrolment percentages due to the fact that many of those in school are above this overall age group.

7 There is a 301-seat parliament composed of 159 members of the Shura Council, 111 from the People's Assembly and 31 representatives nominated by the president (Human Rights Watch, 1992: 4).

8 These findings are from the research survey, which included a section in the questionnaire that addressed poor people's attitudes towards their social and political representation. See M. H. Hashem 1996: 98–100).

9 Ibid. The selection process of 'excluded groups' was complex because of insufficient data on social and economic indicators pertaining to poverty: thus there were no measurable criteria to use in the selection process of the target population. As a result, identification of excluded groups was based on preliminary analysis of data (primary and secondary) collected by the author during a visit to Yemen in November 1993. During this visit, several interviews were conducted with officials and representatives in different ministries, international organisations and NGOs (local and foreign). During these interviews information was solicited as to which groups they felt encountered barriers in attaining access to basic services, which groups encountered barriers in the labour market, and which groups appeared to have marginal participation and representation in society. The author also visited different neighbourhoods that obviously consisted of the poorest groups. However, since poverty is becoming more prevalent in Yemen, it was very important to be able to differentiate between those who are 'poor' and those who are 'excluded'. Furthermore, applying the concept of 'excluded' at a more individual level is a sensitive procedure, since this issue, unlike the issue of poverty, questions the individual's position in society in relation to social membership. It also involves the way in which this membership, or lack of it, affects access to goods and services, employment, safety nets and entitlements.

13

Women's Health and Politics in Yemen

Ilse Worm

Introduction

Studies on women's health in Yemen usually focus on the medical, social and demographic aspects of health behaviour and very often neglect the political dimension of health care.[1] This chapter sets women's health in the context of the political process which took place in Yemen during the 1990s, in order to investigate how women's health was defined in the policy-making process and how health strategies affecting women's health were implemented.[2]

The health status and health needs of Yemeni women and the public health care services offered to women are described, and the development of Yemeni health and population policies are examined in the context of the political liberalisation at the beginning of the 1990s, the participation of the Islah party in the government between 1993 and 1997, the international debate on population, women and development, and the national discussions on economic reform. An analysis of the main health and population policy documents issued in the 1990s indicates that it was not possible to achieve a political consensus on the definition of women's health and on the strategies needed to improve the health of Yemeni women.

The chapter then looks at how Mother and Child Health (MCH) and Family Planning (FP) services were managed in the Ministry of Public Health between 1993 and 1997, and argues that despite the ideological influence of the Islah party on the policy-making process, the management of health care under the Islah leadership was characterised by pragmatism and continuity of existing practices.

Aspects of women's health in Yemen

Seen in its social context, women's health in Yemen is determined by their position in the family and the household, by their legal status, and by their access to social services. The complex interplay between these factors cannot be developed here, but there are a number of issues that should be taken into consideration.

Current family law in Yemen still allows early marriage and hence encourages early pregnancies. Although the reform of family law endorsed in 1992 prohibited girls under 15 years of age from marrying, it did not ensure the enforcement of this regulation,[3] and in practice early marriage is still frequent, although it has been decreasing since the 1980s.[4] Although this decline is due mainly to the higher educational status of Yemeni women, the economic crisis might also have pushed the age of marriage upwards.

Education also has a high impact on the fertility of Yemeni women.[5] However, access by Yemeni girls and women to formal and informal education is still very low, especially in rural areas. More than 75 per cent of Yemeni women are illiterate, in comparison to 36 per cent of men. In rural areas approximately 15 per cent only of women can read and write, and the school enrolment ratio is still very low (27.3 per cent), while being noticeably higher in cities (74.6 per cent) (CSO, 1996).

Since the adoption of the primary health care approach in 1978, MCH services have been established at different levels of the Yemeni health systems, with a focus on infant immunisation and antenatal care. Although some experience has been gained with outreach activities regarding immunisation and health education, MCH services still continue to be overwhelmingly facility-based.

One of the main problems in the health sector lies in the severe shortage of qualified female health staff. There were only 550 qualified Yemeni midwives employed by the Ministry of Public Health in 1996, most of whom were working in urban areas (CSO, 1996).

Family planning (FP) services were introduced in South Yemen in the late 1970s and in North Yemen in the mid-1980s. They were restricted to the urban areas until the beginning of the 1990s and then started to expand to the countryside. In public health facilities, contraceptives are only provided to married women on condition that their husbands agree. They can, nevertheless, be procured from pharmacies and in private health clinics.

Despite the efforts made in the last two decades to improve primary health care, estimates of maternal mortality in Yemen range between 1,000 and 1,400 per 100,000 live births (Bahobeishi *et al.*, 1992: 99;

UNFPA, 1997: 68). This rate is one of the highest in the world, and did not decrease significantly during the 1990s. Direct obstetric causes, in particular haemorrhage and obstructed labour, appear to account for more than 60 per cent of maternal deaths (Bahobeishi *et al.*, 1992: 99).[6] Indirect causes of maternal deaths are mainly related to the high prevalence of anaemia and of endemic diseases among pregnant women, such as viral hepatitis or malaria. Malnutrition, early, recurrent and late pregnancies, as well as the high number of deliveries carried out without trained attendance, are the most important underlying factors leading to maternal morbidity and mortality. Although the number of women using modern methods of contraception has risen, contraceptive prevalence was still as low as 6 per cent in 1992 (CSO, 1992a). Pills and intrauterine devices are the most common methods. Lack of knowledge, fears of side-effects and the difficulty of access to family planning services are the main reasons why women do not use contraceptives (CSO, 1992a; Al-Sa'edi, 1996: 27).

Most of the recent surveys on women's health in Yemen focus on maternal health. This is certainly justified insofar as childbearing constitutes a recurrent event in the life of most Yemeni women. However, by restricting the focus to women's roles as mothers, other health concerns are overlooked. Information on other reproductive health concerns affecting the life of Yemeni women, such as abortion, circumcision, reproductive tract infections, sexually transmitted diseases and HIV/AIDS, is rare and very often inaccurate.

Although abortion is prohibited by penal and civil law unless pregnancy threatens the life of the mother,[7] it currently seems to be practised in private and public facilities, provided the unwanted pregnancy results from a marital relationship and both wife and husband consent to it.[8] There are, of course, no statistics on the number of women dying or suffering injuries as a result of illegal unsafe abortions.[9] Female circumcision, consisting of the removal of the clitoral hood of newly born female children, is apparently widespread in the Tihama, though seldom practised in other regions. Unlike other more severe forms of female genital mutilation, it does not seem to be a significant physical health concern.[10] Data on reproductive tract infections affecting women as a result of sexually transmitted diseases or in interaction with the use of intrauterine devices are virtually non-existent.[11] Since the establishment of the National AIDS Programme in 1988 efforts were made to collect information on the prevalence of HIV infections. According to official data HIV/AIDS cases, although still infrequent, are rising steadily, and 36 per cent of the cases known in 1997 were women.[12]

Seen from the perspective of Yemeni women, the current health system – which should encompass easy access to health services for themselves and their children, affordable medical care, and respect for their privacy – does not respond adequately to their health needs. High transport costs and the lack of female health staff and of drugs in the majority of public health facilities are key determinants of the low use of MCH/FP services. For these reasons, and because they prefer the familiarity of a home setting, most women, despite regional differences, still deliver their babies at home with the assistance of relatives. Even when trained midwives are available, they often lack the knowledge to handle emergency deliveries.[13] Furthermore, the needs of those divorced or widowed women who do not receive the social support of their enlarged family are often not taken into consideration by governmental health services, which are targeted primarily to married women.[14]

In 1995 the Government of Yemen agreed to implement a structural adjustment programme; had it been implemented fully, this would have had a negative impact on rural women's access to health services, as it was not linked to a compensating reform of the health sector. High transportation and accommodation costs meant that health care in 1995 was three times as expensive for the rural population than for urban residents (World Bank, 1995: 33). The increase in the price of transport after the proposed removal of subsidies on diesel prices was bound to result in reduced use of preventative health services for poor users, primarily women. Similarly the civil service reform involved a freeze in recruitment in government employment: this included a freeze on hiring female health staff, thus obstructing efforts to improve the quality of MCH/FP services.

Health and politics in Yemen

From 1990–3

At the beginning of the 1990s, when the Yemeni government had to face the social realities of a steadily rising population at a time of rapidly shrinking internal and external economic resources, health, and in particular women's health, increasingly became a subject of political debate. The government was being pressured to deliver social services by rapid population growth and by the return of some 800,000 Yemeni migrants in the aftermath of the Gulf War. Moreover, as Saudi Arabia and Kuwait cut off their financial support, the failure of the public health sector to meet the essential needs of Yemeni citizens became evident.

In August 1991 the government reacted to this changing reality by endorsing a National Population Strategy, which it justified on the basis both of the need to reduce the gap between population growth and economic resources and to depart from the prevailing *laisser-faire* approach to population issues.[15] Improving the social and economic status of Yemeni women was central to this strategy, assuming as it did a positive relationship between the enhanced access of women to health and education services, the integration of women in the labour market, the reform of family law, and the decrease in fertility (CSO, 1992c). Following the First National Population Policy Conference, held in Sana'a in October 1991 with support from international donors, the National Population Strategy was further developed into a Population Action Plan. In July 1992 the government established an interministerial National Population Council to coordinate and supervise the implementation of this official population policy.

As a result of the political liberalisation process, initiated at the beginning of the 1990s, health became a subject of competition between political parties. Between 1990 and 1993 the Islah party, in opposition to the government, regularly blamed the state for the deterioration of medical services in the country. The Islamist weekly *Al-Sahwa* also criticised the state for proclaiming cost-free treatment, although in reality most patients could not have access to medical services without intermediaries. Public health facilities were described as suffering from financial and administrative mismanagement, lack of motivated health staff, and bad maintenance. Women were seen as the main victims of the system: they entered hospitals to deliver under poor conditions, and were treated either by foreign nurses or by men without respect for their privacy (*Al-Sahwa*, 15 February 1990; 8 August 1991; 6 February 1992, 15 April 1993). *Al-Sahwa* even urged the Ministry of Public Health 'to force all health facilities, public and private, to employ enough female staff' (ibid., 6 February 1992). On several occasions the paper attacked international agencies such as USAID and the World Bank for financing family planning programmes in Yemen and following a deliberate plan 'to tear apart the Yemeni family' and 'destroy the Islamic world' (ibid., 11 July 1991; 8 August 1991; 25 June 1992).[16]

The spring 1993 election campaign focused on the unification process, constitutional reform and political liberalisation. However, the provision of social services was an issue as well (Detalle, 1993: 9), and in their election programmes the three main parties committed themselves to developing sufficient primary health care services, especially in deprived rural areas. All three parties further advocated the development of health manpower and the promotion of private investments in the curative sector. The YSP (Yemen Socialist Party), in accordance with its call for decentralisation, emphasised the need for local councils to participate in supervising health services. The Islah party in particular stressed the close relationship between health and preservation of the moral integrity of Yemeni society, and spoke of the need to fight infectious diseases, especially AIDS, by controlling immigration and setting up quarantine clinics. Cultural and information policy in the social field was to focus on health education for mothers, and as such to be free of disruptive and immoral influences.[17]

From 1993–7

When Islah entered the government alongside the GPC (General People's Congress) and the YSP following the April 1993 elections, it was given responsibility for the Ministry of Public Health. The new Minister, Dr Najib Sa'id Ghanim, adopted a pragmatic approach in describing the core priorities of his policy. These involved administrative and financial reform and the development of health manpower, as well as the improvement of coordination mechanisms between the Ministry of Public Health, other sectoral ministries or health-related institutions, and donor organisations (*Al-Sahwa*, 5 August 1993).[18]

Initially Islah experienced great difficulties with the Ministry of Public Health in gaining support and legitimacy from those public servants who were either members of the GPC or the YSP or whose sympathies lay with those parties. Officials, particularly those at the central and higher levels of the health administration, mistrusted each other, feared political and ideological control, and competed over donor resources. The lines of conflict were related not only to political affiliation but also to diverging understandings of management: in contrast to the minister, many high-ranking health officials had had long experience in the health ministries either of North or South Yemen and also held higher degrees in public health administration. These factors, combined with the overall power struggle between the Northern and the Southern ruling élites, led to a gradual paralysis of the Ministry of Public Health.

Despite these conflicts the ministry managed to convene the First National Conference for Health Development in February 1994. Although the conference received the official support of the Islah party,[19] it was mainly prepared and organised by representatives of the Islah-critical wing in the ministry. The conference brought together officials from the central and governorate-level health administrations, as well as representatives from other ministries, and Yemeni non-governmental and donor organisations.

One of the main outcomes of the conference was a document that was published in a draft version under the title 'Forward-looking Policies and Strategies for Health Development in the Republic of Yemen'. While referring to the National Population Strategy endorsed by the government in 1991, the paper also set health, and in particular women's health, in a broad social and economic context and recognised the need to link health services with other development efforts (Ministry of Public Health, 1994a: 5–6).[20]

After the war had ended in July 1994 and with the defeat of the YSP, the Islah party asserted its position in health administration at central and governorate level. Officials critical of the party gradually left the ministry and were replaced by persons whom the minister trusted. Nevertheless, the health policy-making process continued at both international and national levels, and Islah pursued its pragmatic approach by participating in the international debate on population, health, women and development and by exerting ideological influence within the framework of existing institutions.

The Yemeni government participated in the International Conference on Population and Development held in Cairo 1994, and in the Fourth World Conference on Women in Beijing in 1995, and agreed to the respective final resolutions and action programmes.[21] However, official representatives made it clear after both conferences that Yemen would interpret international documents in the light of its own national legislation. It would therefore not implement any regulation which contradicted the *shari'a*, wherein most of these conflictual matters, especially parental power and inheritance rights, were related to personal status and family law.[22] In Cairo, the Yemeni delegation accepted the final Programme of Action with several reservations,[23] in particular with regard to abortion[24] and the provision of sexual health education to adolescents, and the Yemeni delegation in Beijing put forward what were basically the same reservations.[25]

At the national level, the discussions on health and population issues were increasingly related to the structural adjustment programme that was signed with the International Monetary Fund and the World Bank in 1995 and initially only partly implemented. At the end of 1995, and at the request of the Ministry of Planning and Development, the Ministry of Public Health worked out a Five-Year Plan for Health Development. In its policy preamble the plan showed the ideological influence of Islah insofar as health-specific strategies were no longer linked to other efforts to improve women's status (Ministry of Public Health, 1995: 14, 32–3). An even more restrictive interpretation of women's health was brought forward in the *Shari'a Guidelines for Family Planning*, issued by the Minister's Office in May 1996. In this document women's health and the use of contraceptive methods were clearly subordinated to the need to protect the moral integrity of Yemeni society as a whole (Ministry of Public Health, 1996b).

These radical positions obviously did not gain much support within the government as a whole, since it was preoccupied with the social costs of the structural adjustment programme. In a speech celebrating the anniversary of the 1962 revolution, the president, 'Ali 'Abdullah Salih, highlighted the negative effects of Yemen's population growth on the country's structural adjustment programme (*Al-Thawra*, 26 September 1996).

The Second National Population Policy Conference was held in Sana'a in October 1996. It confirmed the validity of the National Population Strategy adopted in 1991 and drafted a new Population Action Plan.[26] In addition to emphasising poverty alleviation, this plan introduced the international concept of reproductive health into the Yemeni context. Although less explicit than the previous Population Action Plan of 1991, especially in matters related to family law, it nevertheless reaffirmed the need to improve the social and economic status of Yemeni women (Republic of Yemen, 1996: 1–3).

Women's health in the policy-making process

The policy-making process which took place between 1991 and 1996 illustrates that a political consensus could not be achieved on defining the issue of women's health and on the strategies needed to improve the health status of Yemeni women.

Women's health in its social context

As noted above, the improvement of the social, economic and health status of Yemeni women was central to the National Population Strategy endorsed by the government in 1991. This aimed to expand the provision of education services, especially to girls in rural areas; to combat female adult illiteracy; to improve conditions for working women as well as social security especially for pregnant women, widows and divorced women; and to raise the minimum age of marriage for women (CSO, 1992c: 24, 26). The 1991 Population Action Plan called for the reform of the family and labour laws, explicitly mentioning the need to increase the minimum legal age of marriage for women to 18 years and to ensure its enforcement (CSO, 1992c: 54).

At the National Health Conference of 1994 and in the document issued subsequently, the limited participation of women in health, social and economic development was described as an important factor negatively influencing their health status. This limited participation was in turn related to the high rate of female illiteracy, low education and to 'the wrong perceptions regarding women's role beyond their traditional duties at home' (Ministry of Public Health, 1994a: 5). However there was no mention of raising the minimum age of marriage as one possible strategy for improving women's health.

The final draft document of the National Health Conference obviously did not wholly conform to the convictions of the leadership of the Ministry of Public Health. Most of its form and its contents were taken over in the policy preamble to the Five-Year Plan for Health Development issued in 1995. A thorough comparison of both documents reveals that the Five-Year Plan followed a more restrictive concept of women's health. Hence, illiteracy, low educational status and mistaken perceptions regarding women's role were still mentioned but the phrase 'beyond their traditional duties at home' was omitted (Ministry of Public Health, 1995: 14).

In the *Shari'a Guidelines for Family Planning Methods* the argument linking women's health to an improvement of their social status was turned upside down. The authors, allegedly medical practitioners and religious scholars, argued that the heavy social problems encountered in Yemen were also the result of the use of hormonal and mechanical contraceptives. They therefore encouraged early marriage in order to preserve the integrity (*hasana*) of the individual and the society (Ministry of Public Health, 1996b: 2).

In contrast with this position and more in accordance with the National Population Strategy, the revised Population Plan of 1996 reaffirmed the need to improve women's social, economic and political status. However, it subordinated the achievement of equality between men and women to the principles of the *shari'a* (*ahkam al-shari'a*) (ibid.: 12), and while it called for a review of the family law, it did not demand that the minimum legal age of marriage be raised (ibid.: 25).

Health-specific strategies to improve women's health

The health-specific strategies which were brought forward in the Yemeni discussions on population, health and development range from a narrow focus on facility-based maternal health services to broader concepts of reproductive health services.

The National Population Strategy endorsed in 1991 aimed both at reducing maternal mortality and morbidity and at lowering fertility rates, and it therefore focused on the provision of maternal health services and in particular on family planning services.[27] It was planned that the prevalence of contraceptive use would be raised to 35 per cent by the year 2000 (CSO, 1992c: 22). The 1991 Population Action Plan proposed to expand preventive and curative maternal health services to rural areas, and anticipated the development of emergency obstetric services and the training of traditional birth attendants in local communities (ibid.: 32). The demand for family planning in Yemeni society was to be increased by awareness-raising programmes on various levels (national, regional, community) and targeted to different social groups (men, religious leaders, decision makers, women's groups). FP services were to be improved by expanding the health infrastructure, by training health personnel, especially midwives, and by involving the private sector (ibid.: 35).

The authors of the Ministry of Public Health's *Forward-looking Policies* identified maternal health as a priority issue. They advocated the expansion and improvement of MCH/FP services, including the development of emergency delivery and outreach services (Ministry of Public Health, 1994a: 20). They envisaged the establishment of nursing schools in the governorate hospitals for the training of female nurses and midwives (ibid.: 28), while malnutrition was to be addressed by establishing a national nutrition programme, specifically targeting mothers and children (ibid.: 19). The authors reaffirmed the importance of family planning by referring to the National Population Strategy and called for the discouraging of pregnancies among teenagers and mothers above 35 years of age. In accordance with Arabic and Islamic values, awareness-raising programmes regarding reproductive norms were to be linked to concerted efforts to improve women's status (ibid.: 20–1). Finally, sexually transmitted diseases and AIDS were regarded for the first time as an issue for health policy, and development of a prevention programme that would include health education and control of blood transfusions, was recommended (ibid.: 18).

In the policy preamble to the Five-Year Health Plan there was no mention of family planning as a major component of the strategy to improve women's health. The authors called for discouraging early (though not teenage) pregnancies, but omitted late pregnancies over the age of 35. They did not recommend raising awareness with regard to reproductive norms in general, but only in relation to pregnancy and delivery; nor did they link these strategies to efforts to improve women's status. Finally, a paragraph which had not been included in the *Forward-looking Policies* was added to the Plan. It recommended reducing the risks related to serial pregnancies by providing FP services which did not contradict the Ministry of Public Health's policies (Ministry of Public Health, 1995: 32–3).

In the Five-Year Health Plan itself, the improvement of women's health was mainly restricted to the expansion of facility-based maternal health services: reducing total fertility rates or increasing the prevalence rate of contraceptives were therefore not part of its objectives.[28] The overall strategy adopted to improve maternal health was to expand and strengthen MCH/FP services in public health facilities by focusing on nutrition, antenatal and delivery care. The main target groups were pregnant women and children. The main implementation mechanisms referred to were the training of health personnel, and health education (ibid.: 117–21; 125–32; 198–201).

Several factors contributing to the spread of sexually transmitted diseases and AIDS were mentioned, including lack of awareness about the disease and prevention methods; the geographical location of Yemen next to the Horn of Africa; Yemeni migration to Arab and other foreign countries; uncontrolled blood transfusions; and also high dowry prices which, it was assumed, led young men to unhealthy sexual practices before marriage. The measures to be taken included establishing a control system for blood transfusions, raising public awareness and targeting health education to groups at risk, training health staff and regulating the work of the National AIDS Committee through a specific law (ibid.: 149–53).

The authors of the *Shari'a Guidelines for Family Planning Methods* further restricted the provision and use of family planning services. In general, they strongly recommended that modern contraceptive methods should not be provided to women before the birth of a third child, except when a pregnancy threatened the mother's health. Families were to be made aware of the risks of pregnancies below 18 years of age, and in the case of early marriage modern contraceptives could be used. Instead of discouraging pregnancies in women over 35 years old, pregnant women below 18 and above 39 were to receive intensive health care. The authors upheld that the permission of the husband as well as the agreement of the wife was an essential condition for the provision of FP services, and that contraceptives were not to be provided under any circumstances to unmarried women. They further asserted that abortion was legally forbidden except when the mother's life was endangered by pregnancy. Finally, the use of 'morning after' pills was to be allowed in emergency situations such as rape (Ministry of Public Health, 1996b: 2–3).

In contrast to this restrictive view the expansion of primary health care, including reproductive health services, was considered as a priority by the Population Action Plan of 1996. Although the nature and range of these services were not clearly defined,[29] young people were included as a target group for health education relating to safe pregnancies and the prevention of sexually transmitted diseases. The importance of providing accessible, integrated and low-cost FP services and improving their quality was stressed. Contraceptive methods were described as a way of preventing unwanted pregnancies and abortions as well as providing protection against sexually transmitted diseases and AIDS (Population Action Plan, Republic of Yemen, 1996: 4–7).

The management of women's health in the ministry of public health

After the Islah party took over the Ministry of Public Health in 1993, the management of MCH and FP services was at the core of interministerial conflicts over donor resources. From its establishment in the Ministry in 1974 the department for MCH had been dependent on external resources (Abdulghani, 1993: 2). Until the beginning of the 1990s, however, most of the foreign assistance to the health sector was generally channelled to primary health care (World Bank, 1994: 48, 66). In the 1990s, and particularly after the Yemeni government adopted a National Population Strategy in 1991, donors attached more importance, and consequently more funds, to the direct support of MCH/FP services.[30]

The interministerial conflicts focused on the question of which department was to coordinate and ultimately to control the donor resources channelled to MCH/FP services. Early in 1994 the new Islah leadership in the Ministry of Health was unsuccessful in establishing a new 'Family Health Donor Coordination Unit', since important changes in the organisational structure of the Public Health Ministry required the approval of the Ministry of Civil Services and Administrative Reform. The health minister resorted instead to the appointment of new high-ranking officials, such as the Director General for Technical Cooperation and the Director for MCH. Since neither individual held key positions in terms of decision-making power, but remained subordinate to the under-secretaries for Health Planning and Development and Health Care and Services, the minister decreed more power for his personal office, which was mandated to supervise and coordinate all his ministry's internal and external partners (Ministry of Public Health, 1994b).

Although the MCH department did not itself decide on the allocation of funds, it nevertheless gained a better standing in the donor community by reorganising its own administrative structures. This reform, which was supported by external advisers, left the basic tasks of the department unchanged (i.e. the planning and supervision of MCH/FP programmes in the governorates, the training of female health staff and the supply of contraceptives to the governorates' health offices). Although the efficiency of the administration was improved at central level, between 1993 and 1997 the management of MCH/FP services nationwide was characterised by overall continuity rather than change. In general, MCH/FP services still focused on facility-based antenatal care and family planning. The policy to develop outreach and emergency delivery services was not put into practice, nor were the restrictive guidelines on the provision of FP services implemented.

The training of female staff was the only strategy which was vehemently pushed by the new leadership and, in part, realised. In an interview given to *Al-Sahwa* in December 1994 the minister urged young Yemeni women to become nurses and stressed that practising this 'noble' profession was fully in accordance with Islamic values. He also mentioned that the Ministry of Public Health intended to establish new nursing colleges in several governorates (*Al-Sahwa*, 1 December 1994). The minister himself attached great importance to the new national community midwifery training programme, which was developed in 1995/6 and was partly implemented during his tenure. This programme, elaborated by the MCH department with the support of other institutions such as the Health Manpower Institutes, initially planned to train 4,000 community midwives by the year 2000. A new two-year training curriculum was drafted, combining elements of previous curricula for primary health guides and midwives in former North and South Yemen. It included preventive health care (antenatal care, immunisation, family planning) and basic obstetric care, including home deliveries. The initial idea was to select girls from rural areas and train them in rural health centres. In accordance with the civil service reform programme, only 20 per cent of the graduates were to be employed in the public health sector's rural health facilities. The remaining graduates were to work privately as community midwives. However, the programme failed to specify how the private sector could be involved effectively in the provision of MCH/FP services and how community-based services could be developed during and after the initial training phase.[31]

Furthermore, after the programme started in 1997, most rural health centres were unable to absorb the required number of trainees (20 per health facility) without severe shortcomings in the quality of the training. Local communities were rarely involved in the selection of trainees, which was mostly carried out directly by the MCH department in Sana'a. Eventually, trainers were recruited from a central pool at ministerial level, thus bypassing the local training capacities of the Health Manpower Institutes at governorate level. These highly centralised management structures stood in contradiction to the decentralisation policy adopted by the Five-Year Health Plan. They were justified, according to the ministry, by the need to channel donor resources efficiently and to exert a social control over the midwifery trainees, which could not, according to the perception of higher-ranking officials in the Public Health Ministry, be left to the local communities.[32]

Between 1993 and 1997, interministerial and intersectoral co-operation, which had been advocated as a core strategy both by the 1991 National Population Strategy and the 1994 *Policies and Strategies for Health Development*, had virtually ceased to exist at the higher institutional level. In practice the National Population Council and its attached technical secretariat did not exert any noticeable influence on the Ministry of Public Health. The low performance of formal coordinating institutions is not new to Yemen, as is shown by the experience of the Council for Maternal and Child Care, which was founded as an interministerial coordinating body for MCH policies and strategies in 1990 but has never functioned in the 1990s (Abdulghani, 1993: 2; Republic of Yemen, 1994: 28). Nevertheless, health officials continued to request the establishment of a Health Board or a National Primary Health Care Council that would consist of representatives of the Ministry of Public Health and other related ministries and organisations (Ministry of Public Health, 1995: 42, 227).

The Islah leadership in the Ministry of Public Health obviously resented the dominant role claimed by the National Population Council in promoting a family planning strategy. However, the idea of creating structures parallel to the National Population Council should not be interpreted as a direct outcome of political conflict over strategies towards health in general and women's health in particular, but rather as an inherent function of institutional life in Yemen. The paralysis of formal coordinating bodies illustrates that where a political consensus on sensitive social issues cannot be established, the search for an institutional solution remains fruitless.

NOTES

1   For a critical discussion of demographic literature on Arab countries see C. Makhlouf Obermeyer (1992), who argues that 'a better understanding of demographic change must include attention to the political context of fertility and health behaviour' (p. 34).

2   This contribution is based on an analysis of official documents, the press and development reports, as well as on my own professional experience in Yemen between 1993 and 1997 within the framework of two Yemeni–German Health Projects. The views expressed here are my own and do not reflect the standpoint of any organisation. Nevertheless, I would like to thank all Yemeni and non-Yemeni men and women with whom I worked during this period and with whom I discussed many of the issues raised here. In Berlin my thanks go to Anna Würth, Iris Glosemeyer and Eva Weidnitzer for giving me valuable information and material and discussing my ideas with me.

3   Information from Anna Würth; see her PhD thesis on Family Law in Yemen.

4   In 1994, 34.1 per cent of Yemeni women aged between 15 and 19 were married, compared with 48.2 per cent in 1975. The mean age of marriage for women aged 15 to 49 was 15.8 in 1992 (CSO, 1992a).

5   In 1992 the fertility rate for illiterate women aged 15 to 49 was 8.1, for women who had attended primary school 5.7 and for women with secondary education 3.5 (CSO, 1992a). According to the National Population Census of 1994 the total fertility rate in 1994 was 7.2 (CSO 1996).

6   These, however, are hospital-based data which do not reflect maternal mortality in the community. For a critical discussion of methods measuring maternal health see Graham and Campbell, 1992.

7   Articles 239 and 240 of Penal Law 12/1994 prohibit abortion except when it is necessary to protect the life of the mother. If the abortion is carried out without the agreement of the wife, the physician or midwife can be sentenced to five to ten years in prison. If the abortion is carried out with the wife's agreement, the penal law considers only private compensation (*diya*) to the child's father (Law 12/1994 in *Official Gazette*, Vol. 19, No. 3, 15 October 1995). Law 32/92 on the practice of health professions specifies that all legal abortions have to be undertaken in a public health facility by qualified personnel and after the written agreement of both husband and wife. In non-urgent cases the decision must be taken by at least two doctors. If an illegal abortion is conducted, practitioners can be sentenced to one year's imprisonment or fined up to YR 30000 (Law 32/1992 in *Official Gazette*, Vol. 7, No. 2, 15 April 1992).

8   Personal impression following discussions with Yemeni women and practitioners.

9   Development workers in health projects are at times confronted with the difficult situation of unmarried pregnant Yemeni women (Köhler, 1996).

10 Meneley states in a recent study that the impact of *zabid* (female circumcision) on sexual well-being is apparently rarely discussed, even among women (1996: 84–6).

11 The fact that 32.3 per cent of the women using intrauterine devices (IUDs) in 1992 were concerned about the side-effects of this method (CSO,1992a) is possibly related, among other factors, to reproductive-tract infections. For a

discussion of the high prevalence of gynaecological morbidity among women using IUDs in Egypt see Younis *et al.*, 1993.

12 In 1994 there were 144 officially known cases of AIDS (Ministry of Public Health, 1995: 149), and in 1997 there were 350 such cases (Director of National AIDS Programme, quoted in *Al-Ummal*, 16 August 1997). Although AIDS was seen mainly as a problem of male Yemeni and foreign migrants at the beginning of the 1990s, the probability of the disease spreading through Yemeni society through uncontrolled blood transfusions or sexual intercourse is increasingly discussed in the media (see *Al-Ayyam*, 31 January 1996 and 26 June 1996; *26 September*, 7 July 1996; *Al-Haqq*, 30 March 1997).

13 See Kempe, 1994, on health needs as expressed by Yemeni women.

14 The number of rural and especially urban female-headed households has apparently risen in recent years (UNDP and GoY, 1997: 9).

15 See the opening speech by Dr Farag Bin Ghanem at the First National Population Policy Conference in October 1991 (CSO, 1992b: 6–9).

16 After the 1993 elections these attacks slowed down but did not cease completely: see *Al-Sahwa*, 3 February 1994.

17 See the election programmes of the GPC, the YSP and Islah in Glosemeyer, 1995: 215–41.

18 On 1 July 1993, and in line with this pragmatic reform approach, *Al-Sahwa* published an interview with the director of the national AIDS Programme, who stated openly that isolating HIV-positive patients in special clinics was, on the one hand, unfair for 'innocent' persons infected by blood transfusions, and on the other, far too expensive for the government.

19 The conference was officially opened by Shaikh Zindani, an influential Islah politician and member of the presidential council (*Al-Sahwa*, 10 February 1994).

20 The main organiser of the conference and the document's main author was Dr Abdullah Al-Sa'edi, at that time Deputy Minister for Planning and Development in the Ministry of Public Health. He left the ministry in spring 1995.

21 Although the draft programme presented at the Cairo Conference was strongly criticised in *Al-Sahwa* (1 September 1994), the Islah party did not follow the call of the Islamic World League or of the Saudi Arabian government to boycott the conference. For a brief overview of the debate across the Middle East on the Cairo Conference, see Franz, 1995.

22 For statements after the Cairo Conference see *Al-Sahwa*, 15 September 1994; for statements after Beijing see National Committee for Women, 1995a and 1995b.

23 For the official statement and reservations of the Yemeni delegation in Cairo see Bundesinstitut für Bevöelkerungsforschung, 1994: 107; 114.

24 The Yemeni delegation rejected the notion of 'unsafe abortion', which, in its view, was in contradiction to Yemeni religious beliefs and to the *shari'a*. Paragraph 8.25 of the Cairo Action Programme requests governments 'to deal with the health impact of unsafe abortion as a major public health concern and to reduce recourse to abortion through expanded and improved family planning services. [. . .] In circumstances where abortion is not against the law, such abortion should be safe' (United Nations, 1995). For the recent Arabic–Islamic debate on abortion see Bowen, 1997.

25 Yemen expressed reservations towards paragraph 97 of the Beijing Action Platform related to the sexual and reproductive rights of women, as well as towards paragraph 107, which requests governments to 'consider reviewing laws containing punitive measures against women who have undergone illegal abortions'. For the standpoint of Yemen in Beijing, see National Committee for Women, 1995a and 1995b.

26 For media coverage see *Al-Thawra*, 29 October 1996 and *14 October*, 27 October 1996.

27 The National Population Strategy aimed at reducing the maternal mortality rate by 50 per cent and at reducing the total fertility rate to 6.0 per cent by the year 2000 (CSO, 1992c: 22).

28 Its main objectives are to reduce the maternal mortality rate by 50 per cent of its 1995 level by the year 2000, to reduce the prevalence of anaemia by 30 per cent among women aged 15 to 49, to raise the coverage of MCH services by 60 per cent by the year 2000, and to increase antenatal coverage by 60 per cent (Ministry of Public Health, 1995: 49, 117).

29 According to Paragraph 7.6 of the Cairo Action Programme these services should include

> family-planning counselling, communication and services; education and services for prenatal care, safe delivery and post-natal care, especially breast-feeding, infant and women's health care; prevention and appropriate treatment of infertility; abortion as specified in paragraph 8.25, including prevention of abortion and the management of the consequences of abortion; treatment of reproductive tract infections; sexually transmitted diseases and other reproductive health conditions; and information, education and counselling, as appropriate, on human sexuality, reproductive health and responsible parenthood. [. . .] Active discouragement of female genital mutilation should also be an integral component of primary health care, including reproductive health-care programmes. (United Nations, 1995)

30 See World Bank, 1994: 35 for a positive assessment of the impact of the National Population Strategy on donor support to the health sector. In 1993 IDA/World Bank agreed to a credit of approximately US$26.6 million to the health sector as a contribution to the implementation of the National Population Strategy (ibid.: 49). Multilateral support to the health sector was also provided by UNFPA, UNICEF and WHO, while the Netherlands and Germany were major bilateral donors. See UNDP, 1996a and 1996b for an assessment of the rise in donor assistance to family planning services by comparison with support for primary health care.

31 Information on the midwifery training programme taken from Ministry of Public Health, 1996a, and from personal discussions with ministry officials.

32 Here I draw from my own experiences in the GTZ project on *Family Health/Family Planning in the Governorates of Ibb and Abyan* and from personal discussions with officials in the MCH department of the Ministry of Public Health in Sana'a.

14

Lack of Treatment Capacity, Lack of Trust: Yemenis' Medical Treatment Abroad

Beth Kangas

Introduction

When Shaikh 'Abdallah bin Hussein Al-Ahmar returned home to Yemen from successful heart surgery at the Cleveland Clinic in Ohio in March 1998, tens of thousands of citizens – drawn from the *'ulama*, *shaikhs*, politicians, academics, businessmen, youth, students, workers, military personnel and the upper crust, from all districts and governorates including Hadhramawt and Mahra, gathered to greet him. Unable to descend from the Yemenia[1] bus to his waiting cars because of the cheering crowds, Shaikh 'Abdallah rode the transit bus home through the well-wishing multitudes lining the city streets. He was back in Yemen at last from his three-month therapeutic journey through America, France, Egypt and Saudi Arabia.[2]

High-profile medical travellers like Shaikh 'Abdallah are not the primary focus of this chapter. Rather, I am interested in the tens of thousands of Yemenis who often spent sums of money far exceeding their own disposable incomes to board a plane and seek medical care outside the country, mainly in Jordan, Egypt, Iraq, India, Germany and Russia, and occasionally in the UK (London) and America. This chapter draws on over two years of anthropological research in Yemen and among Yemeni medical travellers in Bombay and Amman, and looks at options and constraints in providing reliable curative medical care for Yemeni patients inside and/or outside the country.

According to post-revolutionary rhetoric, Yemen experienced, over the past forty years, a dramatic increase in its general medical facilities, building up from the mere three hospitals of Imamate Yemen. In the second half of the 1990s, an almost dizzying number of private hospitals sprang up. Despite the ongoing expansion in medical facilities, patients and their family members continued to leave the country in ever-growing numbers. Precise figures on how many Yemenis went abroad each year for medical care were difficult to obtain, but estimates range from 40,000 to 200,000 annually. Each patient was said to spend an average of US$3,000 for treatment abroad.[3]

Reasons for medical travel

Yemenis commonly gave two reasons why people left the country for medical care: a lack of facilities and a lack of confidence in the services that did exist. While there were CT scans and cardiac catheterisation labs in Yemen to diagnose cases, the capabilities to treat cancer, heart disease and kidney failure did not exist. Patients suffering from these conditions needed to leave the country for radiotherapy or complicated surgery. Over the years, awareness of symptoms and of susceptibilities to degenerative diseases – if not their actual prevalence – increased, as did the knowledge that these conditions must be treated abroad. This awareness and knowledge, in turn, contributed to an increase in international medical travel.

In addition, patients and family members said they travelled because they doubted Yemen's medical system could provide proper care, even if services were available. Several patients I interviewed sought an accurate diagnosis abroad, having collected an assortment of different ones from each facility they had visited in Yemen. Others travelled to correct errors that had occurred in their own country. As one man described medical care in Yemen:

> If you find a suitable doctor, you won't find the suitable laboratory, you won't find the suitable x-ray, you won't find the suitable medicines. It's like an electric circuit: the switch, wire, and lamp. If the electricity goes out in any part of the circuit, the light won't go on. If the doctor is not suitable, and the medicine, laboratory and x-ray are suitable, then the patient won't get what he wants because of a missing part. And I believe that not only one part is missing [in Yemen], it's more likely two or three.

This man's sentiments were not unusual. Deteriorating medical services disgruntled people throughout the country. In the 1990s, Yemen's medical system was affected by the additional pressure on the already-strained health facilities of 800,000 returning migrants (UNICEF,

1993: 37); the discontinuation of donor support by the Gulf countries in reaction to Yemen's stance on the Gulf War; and unregulated private facilities often rumoured to cause more harm than good. Dissatisfied with their own medical system, many people, if they could afford it, travelled for what they believed to be more reliable care.

However, many Yemenis that I met in Bombay and Jordan resented having to travel for medical care. They wished the government would devote more interest and resources than they currently had to improving health services. For example, a governmental employee in telecommunications from Aden who had travelled to Bombay to treat his wife's cancer lamented: 'I'll be paying people back for five or six years. And, why? If only we had had doctors and such in the beginning, during the first two years [of her illness]!' Many medical travellers said they would prefer to use their money inside their own country rather than on high costs elsewhere. They also recognised discrepancies in the affordability of medical care abroad. For example, an inventory clerk in a governmental hospital in Shabwa, after spending $800 during a week in Bombay and learning that the operation his daughter needed to treat her epilepsy would cost an impossible $4,200, commented: 'For the financially able, they can be treated abroad. But for people like us, it's better to stay [in Yemen] and die.'

In order to be treated in Yemen, medical travellers said, the country's medical system – its equipment and cadres – would need to reach the level at which current treatment destinations were. A specialist practising in Sanaa's al-Thawra Hospital concurred: 'If you take medical services as a 12-storey building,' he explained, 'we are at the fifth or sixth floor. People would prefer to go to the top floor, anywhere they can afford it.' Yemen had attempted to develop its medical capabilities; yet the overall system, as UNICEF reported (1993: 61–2), lacked credibility among Yemenis because of shortages of funds, medicines, equipment and qualified staff.

Over the years, the budget allotted to health had increased. As a United Nations Development Programme (UNDP) report (1996: 17) stated, until 1992 the health budget represented only YR2.3 billion out of 57.0 billion. It increased to YR3 billion (out of YR69 billion) in 1993. In 1995 and 1996, the health budget rose remarkably to YR5.6 billion and YR7.6 billion, respectively. The proportion of total expenditures allotted to health moved from 4 per cent in 1992 up to 4.5 per cent in 1995, and to almost 4.9 per cent in 1996.

One area of development had been in medical personnel, particularly physicians. In 1972, according to a UNDP report (1973: 81), there were 203 doctors in former North Yemen. Almost half of them (a total of 92, or 45 per cent) were expatriates. All Yemeni physicians were trained abroad. By contrast, the *Statistical Year Book* for 1993 reported that 3,132 doctors were working in unified Yemen, of which only 817 (26 per cent) were expatriates (CSO, 1994: 131). The Statistical Year Book for 1996 listed a total of 3,812 doctors, with only 304 (8 per cent) of them being non-Yemenis (CSO, 1997: 184). In addition, two medical schools had opened in the country (in Aden in 1975 and in Sana'a in 1983) to train men and women to become physicians. During the academic year 1995–6, for example, 1,044 students (720 males and 324 females) were registered in the faculty of medicine (a six-year programme) at Sana'a University (CSO 1997: 160). Table 14.1 lists the number of graduates from the faculties of medicine in Aden and Sana'a universities from 1992 to 1996.

TABLE 14.1

Numbers of graduates from the faculties of medicine in Aden and Sana'a universities by academic year, 1992–6

	1992–3			1993–4			1994–5			1995–6			Total		
	Male	Female	Total	Male	Female	Total	Male	Female	Total	Male	Female	Total	Male	Female	Total
Aden	36	47	83	57	64	121	34	26	60	63	42	105	190	179	369
Sana'a	108	58	166	115	86	201	187	84	271	210	78	288	620	306	926
Total	144	105	249	172	150	322	221	110	331	273	120	393	810	485	1,295

Source: *Statistical Year Book 1996* (CSO, 1997: 166–7).

In addition, in 1998, in a survey I conducted with 205 doctors in four governmental hospitals in Sana'a about whether they inform terminally ill patients of their condition, all but 19 doctors (9 per cent) were from Yemen. Ten of them were from Iraq (all practising in Kuwait Hospital), five from Cuba (in the Military Hospital), and four from Egypt (in Kuwait Hospital). At that time in al-Thawra Hospital, the one Cuban neurologist was preparing to return to his country. Of the 186 Yemeni physicians and residents surveyed, 129 (69 per cent) had received their training outside Yemen. The largest group of the 129 (46 physicians) were trained in the former Soviet Union. Two Yemeni physicians had been practising medicine for over 30 years. Almost one-fourth of the total respondents (48 respondents, or 23 per cent) were trained in Yemen and had practised less than two years. These were mainly medical students and residents practising in Sana'a's two teaching hospitals (Kuwait and al-Thawra Hospitals).

That almost all specialists practising in al-Thawra Hospital (the country's most advanced governmental facility) in 1998 were Yemeni contrasted significantly with the numerous specialists coming from Iraq and other Arab countries that I noticed when I first conducted anthropological observations at al-Thawra in 1993. Several doctors and administrators explained that following the 1994 civil war and subsequent reforms, Yemen had less hard currency than before to pay expatriate specialists, although they were still employed at private hospitals. The large difference in the salaries that a Yemeni and non-Yemeni physician received did little to motivate the local cadre, nor did the obvious preference patients granted to non-Yemeni doctors. One interaction that I observed in 1993 highlighted the high regard that Yemeni patients had at the time for Iraqi physicians. One day at the end of the morning shift in the outpatient clinics, a man with a problem in his foot came into the paediatrics clinic in search of any remaining doctor. The Iraqi paediatrician referred him to the orthopaedics clinic, explaining that he was a children's doctor. 'But you're Iraqi,' the man replied, 'you can treat it.'

One doctor in 1997 referred to the English adage 'Familiarity breeds contempt' to explain people's low perception of Yemeni doctors. Yemenis, he said, would never believe that one of their own kind could excel in medicine. A Yemeni doctor responding to the survey on informing patients described the climate in which he and his compatriots worked: 'The majority of Yemenis believe that medicine and treatment in Yemen are very inadequate. The medical cadre in Yemen has a bad reputation. [People believe that] they don't have high qualifications and enough experience to treat [complicated] cases, and that the medical capabilities in Yemen are limited.' Many doctors responding to the survey attributed the lack of confidence in Yemeni doctors to the limited diagnostic and therapeutic capabilities in the country. One doctor, the director general of medical services at the Ministry of Public Health in 1997, expressed the frustration of having to treat patients without the medical necessities:

When a patient arrives to the emergency room and you don't have the available facilities – the necessary drugs, emergency drugs – to save him or to help him, you are tied. You can't give him anything. I have worked a lot at al-Thawra Hospital in the emergency room. And I have gone and visited hospitals. The doctor knows he wants to do something, but he can't. What to do? He's gazing at the patient. This is really, you know, it's a horrible situation.

Physicians knew that while medicine itself offered possible treatments, they personally could not offer that treatment within the constraints they faced.

An additional constraint doctors mentioned was overcrowded conditions. For example, in 1993, a Yemeni doctor in the dermatology clinic contrasted conditions in al-Thawra Hospital with those he had seen in the Russian hospitals where he trained: 'In the waiting rooms in Russia, patients wait and read until they are called. They don't knock on the doors like they do here. Here, there might be a patient on the bed, another on the chair, one standing over the desk speaking, and one knocking on the door.' Given the sheer number of patients waiting to be seen, another doctor in 1993 said, an accurate diagnosis was impossible to perform. In this situation, with only four or five minutes per patient, he could simply prescribe a variety of ineffective drugs or tests.

Foreign physicians inside the country and complete medical systems outside offered hope, while Yemen could not. As one survey respondent stated, the modern diagnostic methods, high skills and therapeutic equipment available abroad provided patients and family members the hope of a cure. Many people, another respondent noted, 'think that medical techniques in Western countries can save or prolong the patient's life'. However, as we will see, international medical travel often entailed tiring arrangements and high costs, and not always actual cures.

Following medical travellers

Uncovering the myriad decisions, procedures and experiences that can occur from the time people perceive the need to go abroad until they return from their foreign medical care requires research both in Yemen and in the various treatment destinations. Accordingly, this chapter draws on research in Sana'a, Amman and Bombay.[4] Amman was chosen as it was the most common destination for Yemenis seeking medical care. Bombay, not a facilitating Arabic-speaking country, was to serve as a contrast to Amman (see Appendix A for interview questions used).

To gain the most representative results for this broad study I opted to follow the process of treatment abroad rather than the people. Following a specific set of medical travellers through the whole treatment process from Yemen to, for instance, Jordan and back would have resulted in a sample size of only four or five patients at best because of the variation in departures, returns and lengths of time spent abroad.

Over the month of July 1997 I interviewed 25 Yemeni medical travellers in Bombay, locating them usually in hotel rooms where they were waiting for treatment or convalescing. Unlike in Jordan, these patients were almost entirely from the southern areas of Yemen (see Appendix B for summaries of Bombay interviewees). Many suffered from cancer or accident-related conditions like paralysis and severe orthopaedic complaints. In contrast to their Gulf counterparts there, Yemeni patients in Bombay were mainly from lower-income categories, having made major sacrifices, such as selling their houses, to receive their medical care. Statistical information on Yemeni patients was almost impossible to locate since all non-Indian patients were simply listed as 'alien'. Interestingly, when asked why they had selected India as a treatment destination, these patients, mainly from former South Yemen (which had once been administered from Bombay during the time of the British), said it was because it was close. Patients in Jordan, mainly from former North Yemen, said they had not chosen India primarily for one reason: it was far away. Historical connections with a place can influence its perceived proximity.

In August 1997 I made my second research trip to Amman, the first visit having been made for a Master's research thesis on the same subject (Kangas, 1996). In a three-week period I interviewed 46 Yemeni patients, almost all in hospital rooms where they sought treatment for cancer, kidney, heart and various other conditions (see Appendix C for summaries of Amman interviewees). To put these interviews into a larger numerical perspective, I gathered statistical information from the major facilities visited by Yemenis (see Table 14.2).

TABLE 14.2
Numbers available for Yemeni patients treated
at Amman's major facilities, 1992–7

Hospital	1992	1993	1994	1995	1996	1997
University	n/a	n/a	n/a	n/a	n/a	n/a
Islamic	n/a	n/a	958	924	829	476
Khalidi	868	575	514	671	986	697
King Hussein	n/a	388	223	190	121	72
Bashir (radiation)	n/a	115	122	114	134	n/a
Arab Centre			n/a	61	448	294
Jordan					*237	**433
Ibn Al-Haytham					*47	146
Available totals	868	1,078	1,817	1,960	2,802	2,118

Notes: *1996 totals for Jordan Hospital begin in August; 1996 totals for Ibn Al-Haytham hospital begin in October. **The 1997 total number of patients for Jordan Hospital is significantly less than the total computer entries for the hospital (606). Related admissions and multiple symptoms were combined here, leaving a total of 433. n/a.: not available. Blank fields indicate not applicable, new hospital.
Source: Compiled by the author from administrative records.

However, these available figures only hint at the large numbers missing: they do not show, for example, the many small private clinics used by patients. Also, the University Hospital kept no separate records for Yemenis since, according to the director, they were not distinguished from Jordanian patients. Numbers provided for 1997 only cover the period until August, shortly before I left Amman; the additional four months would bring a higher total. The increasing numbers of Yemeni patients shown here over the years are, however, in part a result of improved computerised record-keeping capabilities.

As in Yemen, Jordan recently experienced a remarkable growth in private hospitals. The Arab Centre, Jordan Hospital and Ibn Al-Haytham Hospital all opened in the late 1990s and feature an amazing amount of the latest medical technology for a domestic population of about four million. To be sustainable, Jordan's private facilities need to attract a foreign market, as they were already attempting to do.

Arranging medical care abroad
In going abroad, patients and their family members face various logistical arrangements. For very weak or paralysed patients, these included a stretcher ride in the aeroplane. A stretcher was placed across or on top of

three seats; the patient was then carried up into the aircraft and transferred on to the stretcher. Oxygen could also be made available. As the flight attendants on our Yemenia flight to Amman remarked, flights to Jordan all too frequently had stretcher cases. There were two on this flight: a 23-year-old man who had become paralysed after a fall, and who planned to travel the additional 18 hours by road to Iraq for medical care that was less expensive than in Jordan; and an elderly weak-to-comatose woman who was to undergo treatment for cancer and paralysis, having earlier sought care in Egypt, and who died two weeks after arriving in Jordan.

Medical travellers needed to locate an appropriate doctor or medical facility in their treatment destination. Occasionally time was lost in searching for a compatible specialist or in waiting until the specialist was available for consultation or surgery. In addition, suitable accommodation was needed for companions and convalescing patients. In Bombay, for example, almost all Yemeni medical travellers stayed in hotels, mainly in a Muslim section of the city (off Muhammad Ali Road). In Amman, most people rented furnished apartments, finding them to be less expensive than hotels. Accommodation added to the cost of treatment abroad.

Medical travellers depended on various sources for information on doctors, hospitals, lodgings and transportation. Arrangements could be made through several of the offices that had opened in Yemen. However, the primary source of information relied upon by the patients and family members whom I interviewed were Yemenis who had already been treated abroad. Much information on treatment destinations circulated in qat-chewing sessions, where a returning medical traveller gave an account of his or her experience abroad. Almost every patient or companion in Bombay carried in his shirt pocket cards giving the names of doctors or hotels to use that he or she had received back in Yemen.

Another source of logistical information was the medical attaché in the Yemeni consulate or embassy, at least in Bombay and Amman (and in the Jordanian embassy in Sana'a). These officials were ready to provide information on which doctors to use and which to avoid, and to receive faxed medical records in advance to begin preparations. However, many medical travellers tended not to begin at the embassy, going there mainly at the end of their treatment to have their leave from work certified.

Taxi drivers were another source of information, giving advice on lodgings as well as medical facilities. These were a common source for medical travellers who had heard only that they should go, for instance, to Jordan for medical treatment but not what they should do once they had arrived. In many treatment destinations, however, taxi drivers were said to be interested mainly in the commission they would receive upon the arrival of the patient at the doctor's surgery or at the hotel.

Yemeni medical travellers also consulted Yemenis studying in universities in the various treatment destinations. Additionally, patients and their companions exchanged details of medical conditions and advice on getting around with other medical travellers. An office set up in the Islamic Hospital in Amman to meet the needs of non-Jordanian patients provided a good place to meet compatriots, as did two popular hotels in Bombay.

Financing medical travel
A quick look at the approximate treatment costs listed in Appendix C for Yemeni patients in Jordan shows almost unfathomable amounts, especially when one compares them with the cost of medical care within Yemen or with the cost of living in general (Yemen's 1995 gross national product per capita was $260). The smallest estimated amount spent was around US$1,000; this was for a businessman's check-up in which, happily, everything was found to be fine. The second smallest amount listed was US$1,700; this trio from Al-Qatn (Hadhramawt) had sold their animals to provide medical care for the tumour behind the wife's eye. Unfortunately, because of the unanticipated high costs, they returned to Yemen after completing the initial diagnostic tests only.

Other amounts listed are tremendous: US$5,000 to remove a woman's kidney that had stopped working and was likely to harm the remaining one (a procedure that could have been carried out in Yemen but had not been properly diagnosed); US$4,500 for a butcher's appendicitis that the family had tried desperately to treat in Yemen but which had been diagnosed once as a stroke and once as cancer ('He was about to die!' his wife kept shrieking during our interview); US$6,000 for a farmer's cardiac valve replacement. One family had spent an almost unimaginable US$50,000–$60,000 in Germany simply to begin the analyses to choose the related donor for the mother's kidney transplantation; they then went to Jordan to complete the process at much lower cost. While patients' medical expenses were generally lower in Bombay than in Jordan (see Appendix B), medical travellers in Bombay tended to have fewer financial resources of their own with which to cover costs.

Treatment costs and time needed for a patient with cancer were particularly enormous: US$7,800 to treat a high school director's cancer of the tongue over two months (I later saw him at al-Thawra Hospital's medical committee; the cancer had returned and he, in anguish, was on his way to Germany); US$14,000 for two visits to treat a woman's breast cancer – US$9,000 for a five-month visit the first time and US$5,000 for a three-and-a-half month visit two years later; and US$40,000 for three treatment visits over four years for lymphoma cancer (this 40-year-old man, an artist, died later in Jordan at the radiation department of a governmental hospital where he had been receiving chemotherapy).

Financing a patient's medical care abroad was especially challenging because of the uncertainty about treatment durations and costs. The school director, for example, had travelled alone, thinking that his medical condition was simple, to be easily and quickly treated; only in Jordan did they discover that he had cancer, would need to stay away for several months, and would have to transfer additional money from Yemen. Another family of four did not know how much time would be involved in treating their 11-year-old son's leg cancer; they travelled hastily in February without any winter clothes and ended up staying seven months, spending altogether US$12,000 and missing out on the busy Eid shopping season's earnings from their clothing shop.

Moreover, many of the amounts listed in Appendix B and C were incomplete estimates. Several patients and family members did not know at the time of our interview how much their costs would be since they were only beginning their treatment or had not yet been required to pay their bills. Some gave estimates of how much they had spent so far, not knowing how much remained, including the possible need for return visits.

Assistance via the Central Bank

Given Yemen's 1995 GNP per capita rate of US$260 (UNICEF, 1998), one must wonder how patients and family members are able to pay the exorbitant treatment costs abroad. One place to go to for financial assistance is the government. Since shortly after the 1962 revolution in former North Yemen, the state made a commitment to sending needy patients, though not all, for treatment abroad.[5] In former South Yemen, with its socialist system of medicine, this commitment was even greater.[6] However, unification had embittering results for the former South's medical system. With the reliance on the private sector and decreasing state involvement, patients suddenly had to pay large sums for what was once free, often including life-saving treatments outside the country. Patients and family members whom I interviewed in Bombay criticised these changes.

An official report estimated that in 1995, the government spent US$200 million on subsidising medical care outside the country (*Al-Hayat* newspaper, 11 April 1996). The actual amount of hard currency spent abroad was much higher, however, since except in cases sent by the Ministry of Defence, the government contributed only a fraction of the costs. Moreover, the need and the demand for financial assistance far exceeded allotted resources. Patients and family members often travelled somehow at their own expense, or stayed in the country without treatment.

Both the numbers and amounts of government treatment subsidies decreased steadily during the 1990s. Table 14.3 lists numbers of recipients by month and year from 1993 to 1996, based on statistics I obtained from the Central Bank. These figures should be seen as only suggestive, however, since the Central Bank originally compiled them in order to ensure recipients did not receive more than one subsidy rather than to derive an exact number of total patients. The figures do clearly show the decreases in assistance that occurred over the four years.

As the table indicates, the number of people receiving allotted funds decreased dramatically (3,995 in 1993; 3,459 in 1994; 1,349 in 1995; and 426 in 1996). The amount of the subsidies was reduced as well. Until mid-January of 1993, government employees received US$2,500, while non-governmental employees received US$2,000 (in addition to two return air tickets); these amounts were then reduced to US$1,750 and US$1,400, where they remained for 1994. In 1995, patients continued to receive these amounts until mid-April's economic reforms reduced them to US$850 and US$700. In August 1996 recipients began to receive only US$525. At the beginning of 1998 the amounts were due to increase to about US$900 for government employees, and a little over US$600 for non-governmental employees; the number of recipients were, however, to be reduced.

TABLE 14.3
Number of recipients of subsidies from the Central Bank, 1993–6

	1993	1994	1995	1996	Total
January	236	133	304	16	689
February	151	186	317	16	670
March	273	179	193	58	703
April	250	382	68	59	759
May	470	53	48	45	616
June	187	352	42	98	679
July	410	366	43	31	850
August	445	392	61	32	930
September	359	326	48	28	761
October	418	384	66	24	892
November	339	350	92	8	789
December	457	356	67	11	891
Total	3,995	3,459	1,349	426	9,229

Regarding the 1998 decision on amounts allotted for treatment abroad, the prime minister limited subsidies to 2,400 patients a year (Al-Haruji, 1998).[7] With each person receiving either YR120,000 (around US$900) or YR80,000 (around US$600) depending on his/her work status, and two round-trip tickets, the government would spend approximately YR200,000 (US$1,500) per person, or YR480,000,000 (US$3,636,364) for the 2,400 patients. As one newspaper article pointed out (Al-Haruji, 1998), this amount, albeit large, was not even enough to cover 10 per cent of what patients and family members would end up spending abroad.

The role of the medical committees

A discrepancy exists between the Central Bank total of 426 recipients for 1996, and the total of 1,018 patients selected by Sana‘a's medical committee to receive money from the Finance Ministry in the same year (see Table 14.4). Following the 1991 governmental decree regarding treatment abroad,[8] medical committees in the central hospital of each of the five governorates in unified Yemen – Sana‘a, Aden, Ta‘izz, Hadhramawt and Hodeidah – assessed the need for treatment outside the country in light of the large number of requests for governmental assistance. At the time of writing, Sana‘a's medical committee, based at al-Thawra Hospital, included (among other hospital personnel) the department heads of surgery, paediatrics, internal medicine, and obstetrics/gynaecology. They met once or twice a month to review a tragic parade of patients all needing treatment abroad.[9] While there was often a delay of several months between presenting a case to the main medical committee and receiving money from the Central Bank through the Ministry of Finance, this alone is unlikely to account for the 600 extra cases due to receive assistance that did not show in the Central Bank figures. Further verification is needed, particularly as Sana'a's medical committee is only one of five; this would bring the total of recipients to a much higher number.

TABLE 14.4

Cases selected by al-Thawra Hospital medical committee (Sana'a) to receive financial assistance for treatment abroad, 1996

Department	Finance Ministry			Employer			Total		
	Other	Cancer	Total	Other	Cancer	Total	Other	Cancer	Total
Heart	442	–	442	47	–	47	489	–	489
Neurosurgery	88	24	112	22	1	23	110	25	135
Kidney	115	2	117	10	–	10	125	2	127
General surgery	21	50	71	1	–	1	22	50	72
Internal medicine	21	37	57	4	6	10	24	43	67
Eye surgery	47	6	53	8	–	8	55	6	61
Orthopaedic surgery	25	17	42	4	–	4	29	17	46
Urinary Tract	31	7	38	3	–	3	34	7	41
Ear Nose Throat (ENT)	5	33	38	2	–	2	7	33	40
Obstetrics/Gynaecology	5	14	19	3	6	9	8	20	28
Maxillofacial	4	20	24	1	3	4	5	23	28
Psychiatry/neurology	1	–	1	2	–	2	3	–	3
Dermatology/STD	1	1	2	–	–	–	1	1	2
Others	2	–	2	–	–	–	2	–	2
Total	807	211	1,018	107	16	123	914	227	1,141

Source: Data taken from al-Thawra Hospital, 1996: 18.

For further comparison, Table 14.5 indicates that in 1993 a total of 2,977 cases (compared to 1,018 in 1996) were selected to receive financial assistance from the Finance Ministry for treatment abroad. This table also lists cases that were self-financed ('Bank') but were eligible to change a specified amount of money at the then official exchange rate of 12 riyals rather than at the market rate of 40, giving them access to many more dollars for their riyals. Because of this financial opportunity,

TABLE 14.5
Cases selected by al-Thawra Hospital medical committee (Sanaʿa) to receive financial assistance for treatment abroad, 1993

Department	Finance Ministry			Bank			Employer			Total		
	Other	Cancer	Total	Other	Cancer	Total	Other	Cancer	Total	Other	Cancer	Total
Heart	951	–	951	67	–	67	52	–	52	1,070	–	1,070
General surgery	168	196	364	8	23	31	30	6	36	206	225	431
Eye surgery	274	26	300	33	–	33	23	–	23	330	26	356
Kidney	268	9	277	31	–	31	20	–	20	319	9	328
Orthopaedic surgery	164	37	201	77	1	78	34	–	34	275	38	313
Internal medical	109	104	213	56	5	61	27	3	30	192	112	304
Neuro-surgery	161	38	199	36	3	39	48	–	48	245	41	286
Ear Nose Throat (ENT)	53	77	130	25	1	26	17	–	17	95	78	173
Psychiatry/neurology	57	–	57	60	–	60	9	–	9	126	–	126
Obstetrics/gynaecology	25	54	79	28	7	35	9	–	9	62	61	123
Urinary tract	43	36	79	13	6	19	2	2	4	58	44	102
Dental surgery	6	50	56	–	–	–	2	–	2	8	50	58
Dermatology/STD	19	13	32	4	–	4	8	–	8	31	13	44
Paediatrics	21	–	21	5	–	5	7	–	7	33	–	33
Other	18	–	18	5	–	5	7	–	7	30	–	30
Total	2,337	640	2,977	448	46	494	295	11	306	3,080	697	3,777

Source: Data drawn from al-Thawra Hospital, 1993: 8.

people were said to be using the medical committee for the lower exchange rate, not necessarily for their medical care. This suspicion was fuelled by the fact that there was no follow-up of the use of the money by recipients.

When trying to estimate the amount of money that Yemenis (whether the government or individuals) spent on treatment abroad, it is important to remember that most of the medical travellers with whom I spoke in Bombay and Amman had not received money either from the medical committee in their governorate or from the government in general. Most said they had not applied for assistance because of the long bureaucratic process involved only to receive two plane tickets and about US$500, which would in no way cover their medical costs. At the time of writing, the medical committee at al-Thawra Hospital in Sana'a was limited to selecting sixty cases a month for financial assistance through the Finance Ministry, divided among cancer patients, heart, paediatrics, kidney failure, and perhaps a maxillofacial, ENT, neurological, orthopaedic, obstetric/gynaecological or ophthalmology case. Severe cases such as cancer simply could not wait, especially when they would not receive sufficient funds even to cover the beginning of their medical care abroad.

For return visits abroad for additional treatment, qualifying patients were eligible for half the money allotted per case. In the case of one companion I interviewed in Amman, his brother had several years previously received US$2,500 for a heart valve replacement. However, after arriving in Jordan he learned that this was not enough to cover the surgery, and he had to return to Yemen without completing the treatment. In the ensuing years that it took the family to raise extra money to pay for the surgery, the young man's condition worsened; he then needed an additional valve replacement, had access to even less government assistance at half the amount, and had already spent an initial large sum for his first trip to Jordan. At the time I talked to the family they had already spent a total amount of US$8,000 for the second trip.

Other financial sources

Occasionally patients and family members received partial or full financial assistance from their employer. The Aden Refinery was particularly generous to its employees and their ailing family members. In 1997, for example, it spent US$500,000 on medical treatment abroad for its employees (*Al-Tajammu'* newspaper, 5 January 1998). For these patients almost everything was taken care of: they were met at the airport, taken to an apartment, provided with money for housing, taken to a hospital chosen by the Refinery's representative in Jordan, and treated without ever seeing the bills. When I suggested to Refinery patients that someone could opt to stay in a very simple hotel and pocket the extra money that they received automatically for lodging they replied: 'Yes, but we came here to be treated, not to make money. People are unlikely to jeopardise their recovery by staying in a less than adequate place just to make money.' Even with this beneficence, though, there was still apprehension. One woman being treated for breast cancer worried about how long her Refinery engineer husband would be granted leave from work; she feared that they would be called back before the treatment had finished.

Access to income from *qat* production was another way of financing medical care abroad. A son who was accompanying his father to Amman to receive radiotherapy for throat cancer remarked ironically: 'We use our money from the *qat* to pay for the diseases of the *qat*.' Indeed, there often appeared to be a self-consciousness among Yemenis at the Radiation Department of Bashir Hospital in Amman when discussing any connection that they had to *qat*. When I asked what their land produced, they would begin with wheat and coffee and mention *qat* if I asked specifically. Cancer patients seemed to have been made aware of the deleterious effect on one's health of the chemicals used in *qat* production. Cardiac patients did not have the same hesitancy to discuss their *qat* production.

Several patients and family members with whom I spoke in Amman and Bombay had sold whatever assets were available – their car, gold jewellery or land – to receive the necessary medical care abroad (see Appendices B and C for specified listings of payment sources). If families needed to travel in a hurry for immediate medical care, they would be forced to sell their best land. Buyers knowing of the need for money would frequently offer a price much below the real value of the land. One family had sold their house to try to finance in Bombay treatment of the mother's cancer. At the time I met them, the mother was receiving radiotherapy only for the psychological reassurance that something was being done for her; the doctor told me, as he had told her son, that her cancer had spread too far to be curable.

Occasionally people had received charitable donations from business-men. Here, they often used the medical report granted from a medical committee to attest to the validity of their need for treatment outside the country. In this way the bureaucratic process of reaching a medical committee could be more worthwhile than the initial US$500–$900 they would receive.

Numerous patients and family members had borrowed money to pay for their necessary medical care abroad (see Appendices B and C). One man waiting for his wife to be seen by al-Thawra's medical committee for her heart condition said that the financing of treatment abroad reflected social differences in Yemeni society: 'He who is wealthy will treat his patient [abroad] himself; he who is a high-ranking government employee will travel at the government's expense; and he who is from a low social background has to depend on social solidarity. Someone gives a thousand dollars, someone else gives five hundred dollars, from among the *mughtarabin* [migrants] for instance. [We rely on] social mercy.' Social mercy alone was, however, rarely enough.

Alternatives to medical travel

To reduce the massive amount of hard currency that medical travellers spent abroad and the hardships they encountered, plans were underway at the beginning of 1998 to establish specialised medical centres inside Yemen.[10] It was planned that Jumhori Hospital in Sana'a would maintain facilities for radiotherapy and al-Thawra Hospital would house kidney transplantation and cardiac surgeries. Indeed, the first kidney trans-plantation took place in the country in May 1998 at al-Thawra Hospital with the assistance of a team from Egypt.

If, based on UNICEF (1998) figures for 1996, we look statistically at Yemen and common treatment destinations (see Table 14.6), we find that Yemen had a high infant mortality rate (78 per thousand for under one year of age, 105 per thousand for under five) due to diarrhoeal dehydration, malnutrition, birth-related problems, and parasitic infections (such as malaria) – the types of problems targeted by primary health care programmes. Although it improved in recent years, the country also had a low level of access to health services, particularly in the rural areas where the majority of the population live (81 per cent of those living in urban areas could gain access to health services within an hour or less, compared to only 32 per cent of those living in rural areas). Additionally, Yemen had a low gross national product (GNP) per capita (US$260 in 1995). Within this context, people criticised the amount of government money going into high-technology treatments that benefited relatively few individuals and only to a limited degree. This criticism would also be true of the money spent on establishing and maintaining new, specialised centres.

Indeed, preventive primary health care programmes should not be neglected, since they play a vital role in helping reduce the number of people going abroad for medical care. For example, many of the heart patients travelling for valve replacement suffered from rheumatic heart disease. These cases could have been prevented through the early diagnosis and effective treatment of streptococcal pharyngitis ('strep throat') when they were children (Alwan, 1995: 38–9).

One solution to providing expensive, high-tech treatments would be to turn over their responsibility to the private sector, while the government would concentrate on primary health care.[12] More regulating of private medical facilities would, however, need to be instituted before this could be seen as a viable possibility. For example, listings that I obtained in 1997 from the Ministry of Public Health indicated that 24 hospitals, 55 polyclinics and five specialised centres had opened in the previous five years in the city of Sana'a alone. Private medical facilities were seen as a good investment for businessmen. Indeed, according to a UNDP report for 1995 (1996: 17), private-sector investment in health services rose from YR100 million in 1993 to about YR15 billion in 1995, reflecting a growth rate of 3,000 per cent.

While the private sector might have the capital needed to establish the requisite services, it does not guarantee better care for patients inside the country. Private hospitals were often criticised for bringing in unqualified foreign physicians and being more interested in making money than in treating patients. Indeed, in our 1997 interview the Minister of Public Health recognised that private hospitals and clinics needed further scrutiny as they had been allowed to operate almost without any control. The quality of physicians and services offered needed to be regulated and certified. No matter how technologically advanced and staffed by foreign physicians private facilities might be, they were likely only to perpetuate the mistrust that Yemenis had for local facilities if seen as responsible for errors and focused on money.

TABLE 14.6

Statistical profiles for Yemen and common treatment destinations, 1996

	Under-5 mortality rate	Infant mortality rate (under 1)	Total population (thousands)	Annual no. of births (thousands)	Annual under-5 deaths (thousands)	GNP per capita (US$) 1995	Life expectancy at birth (years)	% of population with access to health services (within 1 hour or less), 1990–5		
								Total	Urban	Rural
Yemen	105	78	15,678	756	79	260	57	38	81	32
Iraq	122	94	20,607	770	94	*1,036	61	*93	*97	*78
India	111	73	944,580	24,381	2,706	340	62	85	100	80
Egypt	78	57	63,271	1,690	132	790	65	99	100	99
Saudi Arabia	30	25	18,836	657	20	7,040	71	*97	*100	*88
Russian Federation	25	20	148,126	1,427	36	2,240	65	–	–	–
Jordan	25	21	5,581	211	5	1,510	69	*97	*98	*95
United States	8	8	269,444	3,827	32	26,980	76	–	–	–
United Kingdom	7	6	58,144	706	5	18,700	77	–	–	–
Germany	6	5	81,922	774	4	27,510	76	–	–	–

Note: *Indicates data that refer to years or periods other than those specified in the column heading that differ from the standard definition, or that refer to only part of a country.

Source: UNICEF, 1997 and 1998.[11]

Another development that could reduce the large number of Yemeni patients leaving the country for treatment abroad is telemedicine. Here, x-rays and CT scans could be digitised and transmitted along with other patient data in a matter of minutes to centres in Jordan as well as to the Massachusetts General Hospital, the Cleveland Clinic, Duke University Hospital, and the Johns Hopkins Medical Centre.[13] Patients could stay in Yemen and receive diagnoses and treatment plans from specialists in other countries and continents. They could also receive second opinions that might help legitimate the skills of Yemeni physicians and facilities. As an example of possibilities, a project linking the King Faisal Specialist Hospital and Research Centre in Riyadh to five American university hospitals was said to have reduced the expenditure for treatment of Saudi liver patients from US$60 million to US$9 million, since patients could be treated in Riyadh instead of in the United States.[14] Telemedicine supported the observation of a surgical oncologist in Bombay who had treated Yemeni patients for years: 'You don't need to move patients as much as you need to move information.' Telemedicine facilities arrived in Yemen in 1997, although few Yemenis had yet to utilise this service.

Conclusion

A challenge for Yemen's social, economic and democratic development is the question of how to provide extensive health care for the country's population – the urban and rural, rich and poor, those just born and those suffering from the degenerative diseases of modern society and old age. This chapter explored two interconnected problems facing Yemen's medical system, both of which motivated international medical travel. One was that the country lacked many advanced diagnostic and therapeutic devices and procedures. Therefore, patients with complicated medical conditions, such as cancer, heart disease, kidney failure, and complex orthopaedic cases, had to seek treatment elsewhere. The second problem was that many people considered the medical options that were available locally to be inadequate. People suspected that local medical facilities and practitioners would produce inaccurate diagnoses, unsuitable treatment plans, and/or debilitating mistakes. Medical services outside the country appeared more capable of producing desirable results than those inside. Many people opted to pursue medical care abroad, even if it meant borrowing substantial sums of money to do so. In addition, international medical travel was furthered by information exchanged in daily social gatherings, where people reiterated the perceived inadequacies of their own medical system as well as the (at times seemingly miraculous) possibilities of those abroad.

To reduce the cost and burden of utilising medical facilities abroad, Yemen would need to develop sophisticated medical capabilities inside the country as well as improve its current offerings. Gaining and maintaining people's confidence in local services will require continual resources and effort. Primary health care programmes are also needed to reduce the country's high infant, child and maternal mortality rates, as well as illnesses that can lead to more complicated conditions later on. Health care planners must strive to find all-encompassing solutions rather than rely on such 'either/or' decisions as: providing either costly high-tech care or less costly and more widely benefiting care for communicable diseases; addressing either medical conditions of the poor or of more well-to-do individuals; seeing health care as being the responsibility of either the public or the private sector. Medicine today cannot be neatly divided into First World (or wealthy) and Third World (or poor) diseases and treatments. As medicine continues to advance, countries, governments, facilities and families worldwide will face pressure to provide the latest devices and procedures to match growing expectations that life should be prolonged/death should be postponed. Yemen, we hope, will be at the forefront of coming up with solutions that others can follow.

APPENDIX A

Questions for Medical Travellers Receiving Treatment in Jordan and India

1. How old are you? (How old is the patient?)
2. Where are you from in Yemen?
3. Where do you reside in Yemen?
4. What is your occupation? Any additional income?
5. What is your medical condition?
6. When did it begin?
7. How did you first know something was wrong?
8. Were you treated in Yemen? What kind of treatment did you receive? Where?
9. Why didn't you stay in Yemen for treatment?
10. Why did you prefer to go to Jordan (India) for treatment?
11. Why didn't you go to any other country, such as Egypt, Iraq, Saudi Arabia, India (Jordan), or Germany?
12 When did you arrive in Amman (Bombay)?
13. Which airline did you travel on?
14. Who accompanied you? Why that person?
15. Where did you go first from the airport? How did you go there?
16. Where are you being treated in Amman (Bombay)?
17. How did you choose that medical facility?
18. Did you visit any other medical facility?
19. What medical care have you received here?
20. What remains in your treatment?
21. Is this your first trip to Jordan (India)?
22. Is this your first time to travel outside Yemen?
23. Where are you staying in Amman (Bombay)?
24. Have you travelled on your own expense or on the expense of any other source?
25. Prior to travelling to Jordan (India), did you visit the medical committee in the hospital in your area?
    No: Why not?
26. Prior to travelling to Jordan (India), what was the information you had on hospitals and doctors in Jordan (India)? How did you learn this information?

27. Did you visit the medical attaché in the Yemeni embassy (consulate)?
Yes: What assistance did you receive?
No: Why not?
28. What do you think of the medical services in Jordan (India)?
29. How much has your treatment, travel, and stay cost so far? Did you have an idea of how much the treatment costs would be when you were in Yemen? Have you received any discount on the cost? How did you obtain the discount? How have you been able to cover the costs for the travel, treatment, and stay?
30. What has the impact of your treatment abroad been on your family and your work?
31. Have any of your other family members gone abroad for treatment? Yes: To where? For what medical condition?
32. Have you met any other Yemenis here? Have you given any information or advice to them or have they to you?
33. What advice would you give Yemenis who are coming to Jordan (India) for medical treatment?

Table 14.7
Summary of interviewees (Bombay, July 1997) – 25 medical travellers

No.	Patient (age)	Medical condition	Companion	Place of residence	Occupation of patient (p) or companion (c)	Source of payment	Approximate costs at time of interview (US$)	Time spent in Bombay†
1	Male (42)*	Paralysed arm from stab wound	Friend from his area	Bayda	Farmer (p)	Own – brothers in the Gulf	Over $4,500	24 days
2	Female (27)*	Kidney stone, abscess, heart	Brother*	Abyan	Military (c)	Own – borrowed, pawned and sold land	Unknown	3 weeks
3	Male (55)	Cancer	Sister's son*	Amran and Saudi Arabia	Working in Gulf (p)	Own – from working in Gulf	Unknown	2 weeks‡
4	Male (40)*	Kidney and slipped disc follow-up	Alone	Bayda	Carpenter (p)	Own – from God	Only beginning	1 day
5	Female (28)	Infertility	Husband*	Shabwa	Clerk in government hospital (c)	Own – borrowed	$2,700	over 1 month‡
6	Female (15)*	Incontinence from car accident	Brother* and mother*	Aden	Government employee in telecommunications (c)	Own – sold car, family assistance, borrowed from work	$3,000 this time (1st time $4,000; 2nd time $2,000)	1 month‡
7	Female (20)*	Epilepsy	Father* and mother*	Shabwa	Inventory clerk in government hospital (c)	Government ($500); own – borrowed	$800	1 week
8	Male (11)	Eye	Father,* mother and brother	Near Mukalla	Driver in Saudi Arabia (c)	Own – from income (from Saudi Arabia)	$200	8 days

No.	Patient (age)	Medical condition	Companion	Place of residence	Occupation of patient (p) or companion (c)	Source of payment	Approximate costs at time of interview (US$)	Time spent in Bombay[†]
9	Female (52)*	Cancer	Husband* and daughter	Aden	Government employee in telecommunications (c)	Own – sold two cars and gold, borrowed	$3,000	1 month
10	Female (55+)*	Cancer	Son* and daughter	Lahej	Military officer in hospital (c)	Own – sold house and women's gold, savings	$2,000	3 weeks
11	Female (56)*	Told was cancer but wasn't	Son	Aden	Municipal employee (c)	Own – family assistance, charity, daughters sold gold	Over $1,600	1 month
12	Female (40)*	Condition following removed lymph gland	Husband*	Hodaidah	Carpenter (c)*	Government ($525); own (a little): unspecified	$600	2 weeks
13	Male (39)*	Bullet injury in leg	Brother	Shibam	Teacher (p)	Own – assistance from friends, borrowed	$3,000 in India ($4,000 and $3,000 in Jordan)	40 days
14	Male (16)*	Ankle injury from motorcycle	Paternal uncle	Qatn	Has shop (p)	Own – relatives in Saudi Arabia	$1,300	40 days
15	Male (15½)*	Blockage in brain	Father*	Yafaa	Farmer	Own – assistance from uncle in Abu Dhabi and relatives; operation was free in government hospital	Unclear	2 months
16	Male (14)	Unclear head injury	Father*	Bayda	Policeman in Bahrain (c)	Own – available (from work in Bahrain)	Unknown	2 days

17	Male (35)*	Brain condition	Brother*	Abyan	Labourer (p); agriculturalist (c)	Government ($525); own – assistance from people in village	$600 [needs $2,800 more]	2 weeks
18	Female (50)*	Breast cancer	Husband*	Aden	Housewife (p); none (c)	Government ($500); own – sold gold	$1,100	8 days
19	Male (16)*	Tuberculosis	Mother* and grandmother	Aden	Teacher (c)	Own – salaries, sold gold	$500	13 days
20	Female (36)*	Kidney infection from medicine	Husband and daughter	Aden	Nurse (p); Hospital administrator (c)	Own – sold gold, Jam'aiyya	$1,700	8 days
21	Male (33)*	Slipped disc	Father* (brother also stayed 3 months)	Outside Sana'a	Farmer (p) (c)	Own – available from *qat* production and from previous work in Saudi Arabia	$16,000 (including small amount for treatment in Iraq and Syria)	8 months
22	Male (55)	Paralysis	Neighbour*	Aden	Building supervisor (p); 'free' work (c)	Own – charity, pawned half his house	Only beginning	2 weeks
23	Male (35)*	Dislocated spine from car accident	Brother and acquaintance	Yafaa	General labourer (p)	Own – relatives	$2,250	2 weeks‡
24	Male (92)	Neurological	Son*	Seiyun	Works in Saudi Arabia (c)	Own – son in Emirates	Unknown	1 day
25	Male (50)*	Cancer	Someone from his village initially, then alone	Hodaidah	Buying and selling (p)	Own – sold store	$1,500	40 days

Notes: *Person interviewed; †At time of interview; ‡Departure was imminent.

Table 14.8

Summary of interviewees (Jordan, August 1997) – 46 medical travellers

No.	Patient (age)	Medical condition	Companion	Place of residence	Occupation of patient (p) or companion (c)	Source of payment	Approximate costs at time of interview (US$)	Time spent in Jordan†
1	Male (23)	Spinal injury	Brother* and mother	Marawʿa (Hodaidah)	Butcher (p); carpenter (c)	Own – borrowed; businessmen's charity	Only beginning	On plane, Iraq-bound
2	Female (65+)	Cancer, paralysis	Two grandsons* and male relative	Taʿizz	Students (c); doctor (c)	Government ($500); own – unspecified	Only beginning	On plane; later died
3	Male (60)*	Appendicitis	Son,* wife,* daughter, daughter's husband	Sanaʿa	Butcher (p)	Own – borrowed	Over $4,500	1 week
4	Adult male*	Throat cancer	Son*	Khowlan	Farmer (p and c)	Government ($500); own – qat production	$5,000	2 months in Iraq, weeks in Jordan
5	Male (35)*	Cancer	Cousin	Mukayras (Bayda)	Postal worker (p)	Own – sold car; borrowed from maternal uncle	$11,000	Over 2 months
6	Male (42)*	Oral cancer	Alone	Bani Hashash	School director (p)	Own – small savings; borrowed	$7,800	2 months
7	Male (20)*	Nasal-pharyngeal cancer	Wife	Bani Hashash	Farmer (p)	Own – available (qat production)	$5,000	Over 1 month
8	Female (36)*	Kidney	Brother	Rawda	At home (p)	Government assistance pending; own – borrowed	Unknown	1 week

#	Sex (age)	Condition	Companions	Place	Occupation	Funding	Cost	Duration
9	Female (38)*	Ulcer and check-up	Husband's sister	Sana'a	Housewife (p)	Own – husband is prominent businessman	$5,000	1 week
10	Male (12)	Chest infection, possibly heart	Father,* mother, grandfather, uncle's two wives and his daughter	Mahbsha (Hajja)	Farmer (c)	Own – borrowed	Unknown	2 days
11	Male (60)*	Dislocated shoulder	Son,* daughter, daughter's husband	Yaf'a and Aden	Retired airport employee (p)	Own – sons working in Saudi Arabia	Unknown	10 days
12	Male (40)*	Bone calcification	Wife, daughter (came for wife's varicose veins)	Ta'izz governorate	Truck mechanic (p)	Own – from earnings	Unknown	1 month
13	Male (50)*	Hip replacement	Alone	Riyadh (orig. Ta'izz)	Labourer (c)	Own – works in Saudi Arabia	Unclear	12 days
14	Male (45)*	Cancer	Son*	Mokha	Was driver (p); student (c)	Employer: Yemen petroleum	Over $3,500	2 weeks
15	Male (57)*	Stomach condition	Son*	Zaydiyah (Hodaidah)	Farmer (p); student (c)	Own – available (unspecified)	Unknown	20 days
16	Male (3½)	Leukemia	Father* and grandmother	Muhbsha (Hajja)	Government hospital employee (c)	Government ($400); own – borrowed	$4,000	3 weeks
17	Female (55)	Kidney	Husband* and son*	Sana'a & Amran	Businessman (c)	Own – available: from private business	$5,000	10 days
18	Female (55)	Breast cancer	Husband's son from different mother	Outside Sana'a	Teacher (c)	Own – sold her land and gold; donation of $2,000	$14,000 ($9,000 first trip, then $5,000)	3½ months, 5 first time

No.	Patient (age)	Medical condition	Companion	Place of residence	Occupation of patient (p) or companion (c)	Source of payment	Approximate costs at time of interview (US$)	Time spent in Jordan†
19	Male (45)	Check-up	Three other businessmen for treatment	Yarim	Businessman (p)	Own – available: businessman	$1,000–1,200	12 days
20	Male (45)	Back problem post-accident	Three other businessmen (see #19)	Yarim and village	Businessman and farmer (p)	Own – borrowed	$2,000	12 days
21	Male (37)	Tests for ENT/gland	Male relative*	Mukalla	Teacher (p); government employee (c)	Own – from relatives in Saudi Arabia and Kuwait	Only beginning	1 day
22	Female (35)	Throat lump	Husband* and other relatives for treatment	Mukalla	Works in Saudi (c)	Own – from work in Saudi Arabia	Only beginning	1 day
23	Male (65)*	Eye	Son	Little Aden	Retired from Aden Refinery (p)	Employer – Aden Refinery	Unknown – employer's expense	2 days
24	Male (31)*	Liver	Alone	Aden	Customs office (p)	Employer ($150 and tickets); own – collected money from family, especially brother-in-law; sold gold	$3,500	40 days
25	Female (59)	Heart	Son* and daughter	Little Aden	Aden Refinery (c)	Employer – Aden Refinery	Unknown – employer's expense	2 weeks
26	Female (50)	Kidney (towel forgotten post operation)	Husband,* son* and daughter	Bani Hashash	Farmer (c)	Own – sold land	$3,500	3 days

No.	Sex (Age)	Illness	Companion	Location	Occupation	Source of funds	Cost	Duration
27	Male (40)*	Lymphoma cancer	Brother	Ta'izz	Artist/painter (p)	Government (tickets); own – savings; selling things	$40,000 for 3 visits over 4 years	5 months; later died
28	Male (65)	Heart	Son*	Hamdan & Sana'a	Farmer (p)	Own – from qat production	$6,000	1 week
29	Male (40)	Dislocated vertebrae	Brother*	Sana'a	Government employee (p); Ministry of Education (c)	Government ($500); own – certain amount available (unspecified); borrowed	$3,000	1½ months
30	Male (20)	Heart	Brother*	Sana'a	Student (p); army (c)	Government ($700); own – salary; savings; money set aside for wedding	$8,000	2 weeks
31	Male (50)*	Kidney	Son* and brother*	Bayhan (Shabwa)	Worker (p)	Own – borrowed	$10,000	1 month
32	Female (41)*	Heart	Husband, son, and daughter	Little Aden	Nurse (p); hospital employee (c)	Employer – Aden Refinery; family assistance for children's airfare	Unknown – employer's expense	1 week
33	Female (42)*	Breast cancer	Husband*	Little Aden	Teacher (p); engineer (c)	Employer – Aden Refinery	Unknown – employer's expense	26 days
34	Male (52)*	Dislocated joints, then brain problem from injection	Alone	Little Aden	Driver (p)	Employer – Aden Refinery	Unknown – employer's expense	1½ months
35	Female (20)	Liver tumour	Brother,* mother, father, uncle (males, in shifts)	Sana'a	University instructor (p)	Own – available: job and commercial work	$30,000	4 months

No.	Patient (age)	Medical condition	Companion	Place of residence	Occupation of patient (p) or companion (c)	Source of payment	Approximate costs at time of interview (US$)	Time spent in Jordan†
36	Female (44)*	Benign brain tumour	Brother and niece*	Sana'a and Ibb	Housewife (p); doctor (c–fem)	Own – family assistance	$4,500	2½ weeks
37	Female (40)*	Brain tumour	Daughter,* brother and sister	Sana'a	Was nurse (p); student (c)	Own – insurance from husband's death; family assistance	Paid $3,500 deposit	2 months
38	Male (45+)*	Bullet wounds in leg	Friend* and brother (who then returned)	Benood (Dhamar)	Farmer (p)	Government (President's Office); own – unspecified	$7,000	17 days
39	Female (42)	Brain cyst	Husband,* son,* daughter	Sana'a	Farmer (c); student (c)	Own – some available (unspecified); relatives in America	Unknown	2 weeks
40	Mother (52); son (37)*	Kidney failure; donor	Husband and daughters	Sana'a	Technical engineer (son)	Own – patient's inheritance from her father; husband's savings	Jordan: unknown; Germany: $50–60,000	2½ weeks
41	Female (50)	Tumour behind eye	Husband* and son*	al-Qatn	No work (c)	Own – borrowed; sold animals	$1,700	1 week
42	Male (80)	Kidney	Daughter and grandson*	Sana'a	Retired from army (p); student (c)	Own – brothers	$3,500	1 month
43	Male (26)	Electrical burn	Brother*	Sana'a	Carpenter (p); university student (c)	Own – borrowed a third; assistance	Unknown	1 month

44	Male (11)*	Leg cancer	Father,* mother and sister	Bayda	Shopowner (c); student (p)	Own – earnings from clothing store; borrowed	$12,000	7 months
45	Male (45)*	Cancer	Nephew*	Hajja	Businessmen (p and c)	Own – available: from commercial work	$3,000	10 days
46	Female (23)	Brain cancer	Sister*	Sana'a and Ta'izz	Was housewife (p); teacher (c)	Treatment scholarship from Yemen for Bashir Hospital; own – borrowed	$11,500	9 months

Notes: *Person interviewed; †At time of interview; ‡Departure was imminent.

NOTES

1 Yemenia is the name of Yemen's national airline.
2 Details of Shaikh 'Abdallah's welcoming reception are drawn from *Al-Sahwa*, Vol. 617, 5 March 1998, pp. 1–3; *Al-Quds al-'Arabi*, Vol. 9, No. 2,740, 4 March 1998; and *Al-Shurawi*, No. 36, 16 March 1998, p. 29.
3 During my interview with him in 1995 the Jordanian medical attaché in Yemen cited estimates of airport departures indicating that approximately 60,000 Yemenis in 1993 and 40,000 in 1994 went abroad for medical care. He also estimated that each patient spent an average of US$3,000. This amount is repeated in the first of the series in *Al-Thawra* newspaper on treatment abroad (Al-Haruji, 1998: 3) as being the minimum for very simple medical cases: more complicated cases were said to cost more than $10,000. The estimate of 200,000 Yemenis each year appeared in a 1994 article in the *Yemen Times* entitled 'Rising Investments in the Health Sector', 24 October 1994, p. 4.
4 The research upon which this chapter is based was generously supported by grants from Fulbright and the American Institute for Yemeni Studies. I would like to thank these institutions for their support and the Yemeni Centre for Studies and Research for granting research clearance. Special thanks go to the many patients and family members, government officials and hospital administrators who shared their time with me.
5 A president's decision concerning 'Rules for Treatment Outside the Yemen Arab Republic' appeared in the *Official Gazette*, Number 8, issued on 3 July 1963, pp. 85–6. A 1975 decree appeared in the publication of the Legislation of the Yemen Arab Republic 1975, Office of Legal Affairs of the Supreme Council and the Cabinet, p. 370. A 1991 decree was published in the *Official Gazette* of the Ministry of Legal Affairs, No. 17, 15 September 1991, pp. 17–21. A new decree was expected to be published in the *Official Gazette* during 1998.
6 At the time of writing I had not located official documents concerning the former South Yemen's provision of resources for medical treatment abroad.
7 This total may appear to be more than the 426 recipients listed in the Central Bank statistics. However, as will be seen, the 426 figure is most likely inaccurately small.
8 See footnote 5.
9 When I began sitting in to observe the medical committee in September 1997, it met twice a month. Around May 1998, because of reduced numbers of patients to be selected for assistance, the committee began to meet once a month. At the time of my departure in August 1998, plans were being made to move Sana'a's medical committee out of Al-Thawra Hospital and into a separate office where specialists from several medical facilities would meet to review patients' cases. The objective was to relieve an already overburdened Al-Thawra Hospital of the time and responsibility involved in administering the committee.
10 Interview with the Minister of Health, 15 October 1997.
11 Figures for access to health services are from UNICEF, 1997. All other data are from UNICEF, 1998.
12 The Minister of Health mentioned this intention during our interview (cf. fn. 9), as does the second part of *Al-Thawra* newspaper's series on treatment abroad (quoted in Al-Haruji, 1998: 3). [Al-Haruji is the author of the two-part series.]
13 Interview with Dr Abdul Rahman Ishak, 24 November 1997.
14 'KFSH linked to US hospitals', *Arab News*, 20 (283), 7 September 1995: 2.

15

Islam, Custom and Revolution in Aden: Reconsidering the Background to the Changes of the Early 1990s

Susanne Dahlgren

Introduction

The question of state-level institutional changes in a country like Yemen is problematic, since there is no unitary nationwide context that can be investigated without considering the variations that prevail in different areas of the nation. Historically, centralised rule has never been very successful from the point of view of assessing social changes, so in order to obtain an idea of what is happening in the country, one should approach from the local level towards the national, not the other way around.

Nor, historically, have state-level changes, including institutional changes, been of immediate importance to the masses. Naturally I am not arguing that legislation does not matter, because it does; rather, I am suggesting that such questions should be addressed when studying legal changes. My point is that it is not enough to study laws as legislation without also investigating the processes that lead to a particular legal change, as well as the signals these laws give to society at large. Of course the state level, too, should be analysed, but when a state-level analysis is suggested to cover society as well, this becomes more problematic, as has particularly been the case in studies dealing with the former People's Democratic Republic of Yemen or South Yemen (PDRY). In this chapter, I will examine Adeni society of the late 1980s – the period preceding Yemeni unification – and will suggest an outline for a more complex analysis of social life in the former capital city of South Yemen than is usually offered. This will not, of course, attempt to suggest anything about the PDRY in general, since what happens outside Aden has always been a case by itself.

Studies that have considered South Yemen as 'Marxist' (Ghanem, 1976: 194), 'a Marxist state' (Kostiner, 1996: 7) and 'a full member of the socialist camp' (Amin, 1987: 87) have produced a somewhat ahistorical and homogeneous image of a society which was not nearly as uniform as they suggest. Concentrating on state-level policies, they establish an image of a society transformed by legal changes. A more complex analysis is needed if, for instance, one wants to understand the process by which the Adeni ruling élite rapidly reoriented its ideological premises and reorganised its positions in the process of Yemeni unification, both processes being reflected in the post-unification legislation of the new republic. I will make my point, on the one hand by examining social practice as I documented it during my initial stay in Aden in the late 1980s, and on the other, by investigating the prevailing discourses of that time: as I will argue, there were three of these, rather than one ('Marxist' or 'Socialist') as the studies noted above suggest.

Legislation in practice: the case of who should organise a marriage

To begin with, let us consider two different views on how a marriage should be organised.[1] In the neighbourhood in Khormaksar[2] where I lived in Aden, characterised by tall blocks of flats surrounded by colonial-era spacious villas, I got to know Zainab and Soha, two women in their early twenties.[3] I met them for the first time at Zainab's wedding. She was about to start a new life in the house of her new husband, whom she had barely met. Her father had arranged the marriage with the groom's father, a colleague who came from the same village as Zainab's family. Judging from the joy and happiness of the wedding guests, an assembly of women of all ages, this was supposed to be a highlight of some kind in Zainab's life, but her face, which showed a mix of embarrassment and confusion, told a different story. Zainab was from a family where girls were instructed from an early age to perform what are considered women's tasks at home, and to be ready for marriage and giving birth to sons.

The parents of Zainab's friend Soha came from the same village, but Soha's expectations were quite different. She was about to graduate from university and become a teacher, and after graduation would marry her fiancé, whom she had met at the university and who was also a teacher. Her father had given his consent to their marriage. 'It is the children who should find their own spouses', he had said. It would be *'ayb* (disgraceful) for the parents to arrange marriage for them.

Soha's family background was similar to Zainab's. Both families were former *qaba'il* (tribal people), who had moved to the capital after the revolution.[4] Even in the city the two families enjoyed similar socio-economic status. Both girls lived in extended family households where the father was a government employee and the mother was in charge of the household with other female members helping her. Nevertheless the ideas of the two families as to what was disgraceful (*'ayb*) in relation to the marriage arrangements of their offspring were quite different.

How can one explain these opposing ideas among families whose socioeconomic and sociohierarchical position was similar? Why did these two families define what is *adab* ('proper comportment'; the opposite of *'ayb*, 'disgraceful') so differently?[5]

The cases of Zainab and Soha seem to imply that there were several sets of social values in Adeni society in the late 1980s. Zainab's family adhered to the way her father's ancestors were said always to have followed, i.e. 'the truly traditional way' that is often described as the 'Yemeni way' – the 'customs and traditions' (*adat wa taqalid*) that are transferred from generation to generation. Soha's family, by contrast, had acquired ideas about marriage, introduced by the Yemeni revolution in the South – that it was a contract between a man and a woman who were equal in rights and duties. As women were in the habit at that time of reading the 1974 Family Law, they knew it gave them the right to choose their husbands, too.

At that time a third set of values existed in Aden, one which used religious, 'Islamic', rationalisations in discussing social practice. This was not as well institutionalised as the other two, but it did not disappear during the years of revolution. Together, these three appeared to be the main frameworks that people used when trying to make some meaning out of their existence. An example of how they were used in everyday talk is a letter received from a female reader during a heated debate in the official daily newspaper *Al-Thawra* in winter 1991 on the desirability of marrying an educated or uneducated bride:

> Many Yemeni men seem to think the oriental man is governed
> by *customs, traditions* and *religion*. But what about the oriental

woman? By what is she governed? The oriental woman and the Yemeni woman in particular is governed by *religion* before she is governed by *tradition*. (. . .) We Yemenis know *good manners* . . . The chaste woman who goes out takes her chastity wherever she goes.[6]

These three frameworks can be called *adat wa taqalid* (customs and traditions), *din* (religion) and *thawra* (revolution). It should be emphasised, however, that *din* alone does not stand for Islam, since custom and revolution are influenced by it, too, contributing to the local variations of Islam. Rather, *din* is a specific understanding of Islam that presents this particular religious discourse as the only rightful way of life.

Each of these three sets of social values, giving guidelines as to how a person should ideally present her/himself in front of others, constitutes an understanding of what is proper comportment (*adab*). The primary place of socialisation into each set of values varies and each has its own mediators. To start with customs and traditions, the idea of a shared honour passed from one generation to the next is primarily mediated in the family by senior members, both male and female. Men and women have different roles in life according to this representation. Thus the upbringing of girls and boys begins to follow different lines in early childhood.

During the period of the PDRY, religious knowledge was spread basically within the family. The reading of religious texts formed part of the daily routine among pious people. For illiterate housewives, their more literate family members were important: they recited the Qur'an and discussed religious matters. Mosques were maintained by the government and religious instruction given in the mosques followed lines that did not contradict the goals of the revolution. Since religious programmes were not transmitted by Adeni television and radio during that period, North Yemeni radio and television, as well as radio broadcasts from neighbouring countries (most notably Saudi Arabia), provided channels for religious knowledge and contributed to the mediation of a particular kind of religious understanding, referred to here as *din*. This was in some contrast to the way religious knowledge was transmitted through state-controlled methods (cf. Molyneux, 1995: 425). As part of the latter, schoolchildren received two hours of religious teaching a week (Al-Hubaishi, 1988: 186). Islamic holidays were observed as public holidays and local *ziara*s (visiting the shrine of a saint) were allowed to take place,[7] but increasingly in a mode of folk festivals.

In addition to these, one should not forget the role of migration in transmitting both 'customary' and 'religious' ideas. Many Adeni families had members working in another Peninsular country where the role of such ideas was more apparent than in Aden, both among the migrant community and society at large (see Lackner, 1985: 3).

The revolution took root by using many of the same mediating channels as the two above representations. Even in the revolutionary discourse, the family was the basic place of socialisation – hence the role of women as mothers was also acclaimed. The comprehensive coeducational school system and adult education were important tools in transmitting what was called 'knowledge' (*ma'rifa*), as was the labour market. People who were illiterate and those who were outside the fields of state intervention were also given the opportunity to 'improve themselves', as it was called, through radio and television broadcasts that transmitted the new ideas in a variety of forms.

Each of the three frameworks presented here has its explicit gender ideal and constitutes an ideology[8] or understanding of the 'larger propositions of the universe' (Ortner, 1989: 60) in which people seek legitimisation for their aspirations. All three frameworks, including 'religion' (*din*), can be studied as *practical ideologies*, sets of beliefs that are constituted mainly by implicit shared assumptions on such basic aspects of the social order as notions of tribe, kinship, family, person, sexuality, nation, religion and worldview, as defined by Eickelman (1981: 86). Practical ideology does not mean that people share a common level of consciousness in their actions; quite the contrary. Studying these frameworks as practical ideologies leaves space for various particular relationships established in everyday practice, as will be shown later. Ideology is an ideal representation of society, a medium in which social actors make sense of their world. Implicit in the idea of ideology is contradiction and conflict (Eagleton, 1994). Ideologies can structure practice, but they do not transform social reality without human intervention.

Aden in the late 1980s

After independence in 1967, a revolutionary government took over. However, much of the old society survived the process of social transformation introduced by the new rule. This involved in particular the family, as I will later show. Even during the British colonial period

(1839–1967), the declared policy of the British was not to touch 'custom and religion', where the family in particular was considered to belong.[9] Additionally, families, and especially women, were barely influenced by the occupiers' way of living either (Ingrams, 1970: 125, 127).

From the perspective of gender relations and family, two particular state interventionist policies were relevant after independence. The first was the call directed to women to join the labour market and the educational field. The second was the new family legislation (Family Law, Law No. 1 for 1974), which aimed at transforming family relations and establishing new relations between a man and a woman 'equal in rights and duties', as the law states.[10] However, as my field material shows, this legislation failed to transform gender relations inside the family, establishing instead a new type of marriage, especially popular among young professional people, that emerged alongside the old form of marriage. Even though the revolutionary discourse contributed to the formation of social fields that were guided by revolutionary ideas (for instance, the cross-sex labour market), fields that were influenced by customary thinking prevailed (as, in particular, did the family).

The difference between the two discourses in marriage has many manifestations, including, *inter alia*, the common thinking that the revolution brought about a 'free-choice marriage' – in other words, the woman could now choose her husband. According to local communication, 'free-choice marriage' was distinguished from the old type of marriage, understood as the 'customary marriage', (i.e. arranged marriage), by being called 'love before marriage', whereas the latter is referred to as 'love after marriage'. After Yemeni unification, when the religious discourse became more evident, a third type of marriage spread in Aden. This was the 'Islamic' way of contracting a marriage, and was characterised by modesty in spending and festivity and stripped of other 'non-Islamic' customs in organising a wedding.

During the colonial period, Islamic scholars were excluded from participating in the legal regulation of family matters that took place during that period. The role of the *qadi* was limited to that of a mere marriage registrar (*madhun*). A corrupted version of Islamic law, known in other areas of the British Empire as Anglo-Mohammedan law, prevailed in Aden as well. A variety of Islamic practices existed side-by-side, including veneration of local saints, holding of *dhikr* sessions in specific mosques, and Wahhabism (which centred round the famous Islamic scholar al-Bayhani); there were also various Sufist movements and the customs of different Shi'i communities. Alongside these, Aden was also an active centre for such spiritual practices as *zar* and *tambura* (see Kapteijns and Spaulding, 1994; also Makris, 1994).

After independence, Islam was made a state religion and mosque *imams* and other religious functionaries were now nominated by the Ministry of Justice and Waqf. Islam gained an official status in the new constitution, and 'non-orthodox' practices had to give way to 'proper' Islamic practices.[11] Religious adherence became increasingly a personal matter. The state policies with regard to Islam contributed to the continued exclusion of Islamic scholars from the fields where family relations were regulated.

A new discourse on family

When the new government introduced changes after independence,[12] it had to take both Islamic and customary traditions into consideration, though in different ways. In fighting the old customs and practices that were considered backward (*takhalluf*), the new rulers turned to Islam to find legitimisation for discrediting them. Thus the new ideas were sometimes made to look as if they had been taken from Islamic holy writings. For example, the new family legislation was prepared with reference to Islamic jurisprudence, but in the spirit of the revolution. Thus the principles of free-choice marriage, bridal money (*mahr*), religious interpretations as to the limits to polygamy, and the period women had to wait before remarriage (*'iddat*) were all introduced in public discussions as being taken from *hadith* (Ghanem, 1976: 191; Molyneux, 1982: 9, and 1991: 247).[13] The process of public consultations in the early 1970s, when the draft law was discussed, was described thus:

> For four months a committee of experts visited the main cities, the large villages, the souqs where the Bedouin congregated, and islands such as Socotra. During these meetings, which drew large crowds, for instance 14000 people in Shihr . . . the official representatives were at pains to defend the new law within the context of Islam.
>
> 'We researched the old books of Hadith . . . to show that we had not created anything; everything is in Islam. We only gave vitamins to old ideas, to have them triumph', says one former member of the committee. (*The Middle East*, February 1983)

Legislation on women's inheritance rights also followed *shari'a*: basically it allowed a woman to inherit only half the share of a man (cf. Molyneux, 1991: 261). Not surprisingly there was a lot of discussion as to whether these stipulations really followed *shari'a*, and whether the whole of the South's Family Law was in accordance with Islam in the first place (Molyneux, 1995: 428). Here the point is to show that the new rulers made deliberate efforts to use Islam in legitimising their policies. According to the new revolutionary government, a radical change in society was expected to take place slowly, in step with changing attitudes among the population. A good example is a speech by the country's second president, Salim Rubayya 'Ali, given at the first congress of the General Union of Yemeni Women (GUYW) in 1974:

> The freedom of the woman does not lie in the fact of taking off the 'veil' and unveiledness as has happened in certain governorates where it [has] caused a lot of errors [that have] obliged the Organization to make great efforts for dealing with [them] . . . The freedom of the woman lies in the fact that we are to prepare her fully in the sphere of knowledge and education and to inculcate in her mind new traditions that lie in the secret of her love of work and production and to consider work a holy thing which should be respected and adhered to.[14]

In this authoritative speech, an illuminating example of government rhetoric, it is interesting how concepts linked both to customs and traditions ('new *traditions*') and to religion ('work as *a holy thing*') were used in seeking legitimation for new ideas. Manipulation of the vocabulary identified with these two discourses was not only typical of the new rulers, but was also an important element in daily practice, where ideological statements were used to give motivation for a variety of actions and deeds.

One of the basic characteristics of Adeni society in the late 1980s and early 1990s was that the three discourses to a large extent prevailed in contradiction to each other, revealing thereby a struggle of ideologies. However, while the opposing discourses existed contemporaneously, they could not simultaneously occupy the same space. The coexistence of contesting ideologies was manifested in everyday practice by a division of social space into fields controlled by one set of rules – guidelines that were presented in a particular ideology also as proper behaviour (*adab*).

My field notes offer an example of how this division organised everyday life.

Moving between different *adabs*

When I returned to Aden to do additional fieldwork in the spring of 1991 the atmosphere had totally changed as a result of the confusion and irregularity of the transitional period that followed Yemeni unification in May 1990. In the anomalous atmosphere, the following incident occurred.

I was supposed to meet a young woman, called here Nafisa, in a local clubhouse belonging to the Adeni Women's Union. As I approached the gate of the building in my car, a young man I had not met previously waved at me to show me where to stop. As I stopped the car, Nafisa stepped out from behind the gate and got in. After saying hello, she explained that the young man was her brother, whom she had asked to stand in the road to inform her of my arrival so that she herself could avoid waiting in the street. I was surprised. I had met Nafisa a couple of times before at Aden University where she was a third-year student, and had formed a very different idea of her, seeing her as an active, independent young woman who did not mind what others around her thought about her activities.

While driving to her house, to which she had invited me for the first time, I had a second surprise. As we approached she suddenly pulled down her *khunna* (the old type of face veil). Of course this was not the first time I had had the unpleasant feeling of speaking to someone whose eyes or facial expressions I was unable to see, but I was confused because I had no idea that Nafisa was in the habit of wearing a veil. When I had met her earlier at the university she, like 90 per cent of the other unmarried young women in the early 1990s, wore a neck-to-ankle robe, *balto*, with a head scarf, which some women named *hijab* (the 'religious headwear') though most simply called it *mandil* (scarf).

Inside the house, an elegant four-storied building which her father shared with his third wife (who was not Nafisa's mother) and nine of Nafisa's full and half-siblings, she explained why she had put on her veil in the car. As the house was situated next to a mosque and was in the mosque area, she did not want to upset those going in to pray. Another, apparently more personal, reason was that nobody in her neighbourhood had yet seen her face since the family had moved back from Saudi Arabia (where she had spent her school years). She explained that she was not yet ready to marry, even though, at the age of 22 being already quite 'old' to be married as well as being a beautiful young woman, she knew that there were pressures to marry her off. Her father had in fact given his support to her finishing her studies first, but as she pointed out, one never knew – any father might change his mind if a good offer appeared.

It seemed to me, however, that a more obvious reason for avoiding marriage proposals was the fact that Nafisa had already secretly chosen the man she wanted to marry – a fellow student called Mohammed, about whom her father knew nothing. Using, as I had learned, the most cunning tactic mastered by Adeni women, she had made the approach to this man look as though it was he who had made the running. She explained that this was necessary because men did not usually like women to take the initiative.

At the women's club, Nafisa helped me to conduct interviews among women who came there to learn various skills that ranged from reading and writing to sewing and typing and acquiring 'knowledge' (*ma'rifa*) necessary for life outside the home. This particular club was an especially interesting place to meet women from less fortunate social backgrounds. It was situated in the crowded northern area of the town, where the old shanty town and the elegant villas of the well-to-do were linked by the refugee camps that housed people who had been pushed into Aden in the early 1990s by the wars in the Gulf and the Horn of Africa.

The club was homosocial, for women only, except at particular times of the week when the club secretary offered counselling for couples in marriage disputes. Being in the club was like being in any ordinary house. Women removed their outdoor clothes and relaxed as if they were in their own home. This was an intentional move on the part of the Women's Union to persuade families to consent to housewives and unmarried girls who observed sexual segregation going to the club.

I realised when conducting the interviews, that Nafisa acted somewhat arrogantly towards the poor, illiterate young women, many of whom came from the refugee camps and lived in extremely difficult conditions without electricity and running water. It was interesting to observe her in her elegant expensive outfit, sitting upright and showing her high ancestry in such a direct and, in my view, impolite way, and to see how socially inferior women expressed deference in front of this woman with high *karama* (respect in the eyes of the others). The hierarchy was embodied in their submissive postures, and manifest in the cheap material of their clothes. It was a game where everybody acted according to their *adab*, proper conduct which, according to customs and traditions, varies according to gender and social estate.

As I got to know Nafisa, I began to feel that I knew three different Nafisas, each of whom acted according to a different but internally consistent set of rules. First I had met Nafisa of the university, the one who had told me about the boyfriend whom nobody except her younger sister knew about. She was an independent young woman who knew what she wanted of life and how to obtain it. This Nafisa was the best student in her class and far more intelligent than many of her peers, including her boyfriend, a fact she herself was conscious of (but which she concealed from him).

The second Nafisa was the one who acted piously in the vicinity of the mosque, communicating to the neighbourhood that she was the dutiful daughter of a proper Muslim. This was the behaviour expected of her by her father, a merchant who had spent many years in Saudi Arabia promoting the family's business interests. Even this she did without artificiality, as did many other women whom I had come to know and in whose lives religious practices formed a central part.

The third Nafisa was the status-conscious young woman of high social standing, whose family were élite *mashaykh* people who could claim descent from Qahtan, the mythical forefather of the people of South Arabia. This Nafisa showed her superiority to the poor and socially low women in the women's club. A traditionally minded family like Nafisa's followed the old rule of equal social standing in marriage arrangements (*kafa'a*). This was one of the reasons why she had to wait, to play for time, in order to try to find a way to get her father's consent to a marriage with a man of her choice, one step lower in the old social hierarchy.

Nafisa's behaviour seemed to shift from one code to another as she moved from one audience to another. Thinking about this I realised that many other women and men I knew acted the same way. What was acceptable and normal in one situation was not acceptable in another. This shifting code-policy seemed to form a natural part of everyday practice. Not only were clothes changed when moving from one social space to another, for instance when going home from work, but the pattern of behaviour also changed. A male friend of mine, who was an accountant in a government office, and who was an even-handed workmate and comrade to his female colleagues during the working day, turned when at home into a traditional head of the family who expected his wife to serve him. And the wife did serve him, even though she would never have accepted a man treating her in that way at her own workplace.

I found this same phenomenon in many homes. 'That's how the Yemeni man is,' explained one housewife with five children, when I asked her why women did not bring up their sons to help at home. 'Even if you try to teach your son, his father will discourage him. And if not the father, then his peers.' The state of gender relations at work was thus not the same as at home, and different rules often governed these two places.

Adopting different rules when changing social settings did not seem to trouble Nafisa; on the contrary, she appeared to enjoy mastering her *adab* in different social fields. For her, coasting between contradictory rules was a natural part of managing her everyday life. The only visible conflict was her preference for marrying on romantic grounds ('love before marriage') and against her family's adherence to the customary ways of arranging the marriage for her.

The fact that different social fields have their own rules and that accordingly people can make smooth changes in their behaviour is not something unique. Naturally this happens everywhere. Rather, the point here is to show how everyday practice is structured by social dynamics, and how tensions between contradictory social norms are manifested in practice. Of course, not everybody in Aden had the same attitude to the contradictions of daily life, or had the opportunities for manoeuvring with available resources in the way that Nafisa did. Her situation was quite the opposite from that of a lower-stratum woman, who might not have had many choices in her life. For such people life itself is a heavy load, since they drift among the imperatives of a difficult life where one option provides only a slightly better outcome than another. It is a situation in which the framework of hopelessness rarely changes the vision of life as a big misery.

'I hope that my children's life will be easier than my life has ever been,' said Noor, a working woman in her mid-fifties, when I asked about her expectations for the future. Since the death of her husband 15 years earlier, she had worked as a factory messenger, making tea and running errands inside the plant, in the lowest paid and least respected of jobs. Her 'choice' was between living off distant relatives or accepting work that she did not like since she preferred to stay in her own home.

Old and new ideas

How do the three ideologies occupy social space? To start with the revolutionary ideology, gender relations were considered to be among the basic social relations that would have to be changed during the course of the revolution. As presented in the revolutionary discourse, new gender relations needed to be created to fight the old, negative customs (*takhalluf*). The revolution therefore introduced a policy called women's emancipation (*tahrir al-mar'a*) (cf. Shamiry, 1984: 9–10).

Most women I met during my two years in Aden[15] seemed to approve of the new role and opportunities given to women by the revolution. It was understood that not everyone could benefit from the new resources, such as education, but it was considered positive that these things had become available for women, too. Even though the policies of the 'new Yemeni woman' had been introduced from above as a government measure, they were widely welcomed among women and among many men, too. If anything was open to criticism, it was the problems involved in implementing these rights, such as housing shortages, child-care problems, and women's double burden with the household chores. Rather typically, a 35-year-old woman who worked as a secretary described the changes to me in this way: 'After independence the woman could take up work outside the home and improve herself. She now has a role in society. Earlier, the woman lived like a prisoner inside four walls.'

The egalitarian gender roles appeared to have taken hold in workplaces and educational establishments and remained so even after Yemeni unification, when official state support for this policy was withdrawn. However, within the home the old patriarchal rule still largely prevails, manifested in everyday life as the submission of women and younger family members to the elder and the male.

If the home was structured by old customary ideas and if new social spheres such as the unsegregated labour market were influenced by revolutionary ideas, where did religious ideology come into the picture? As we saw in Nafisa's case, the surroundings of mosques were considered to be areas of pious behaviour. During the era of the PDRY, religion was not so much suppressed as not particularly encouraged. People tended to regard religion as a private matter and the devout hid their piety behind the walls of their homes even though public religious practice was not banned. The number of pious families in Aden increased after the Gulf War. These were people who had become manifestly religious while living in Saudi Arabia and other Gulf countries, where religiosity was strongly encouraged and even imposed by particular militant elements in society. In such families, leisure time was differently organised from that in other homes, and included religious contemplation and study of the Qur'an and other holy writings. A preference for sex segregation was also evident among these families.

By the early 1990s, a manifest religiosity had started to gain a foothold in other fields, too, and had become popular among many young people. An unmarried 18-year-old typist wearing *hijab* explained her wishes for the future: 'I hope I will become an ideal mother and a good housewife.' She indicated that this was the principal way for her, as a woman, to become a proper Muslim. Another 16-year-old girl, unemployed and living in a shanty town in the northern part of Aden, explained the attitudes among young people: 'The influence comes from the North [of Yemen] and in the same way they become influenced by us.'

Gender ideals

The suggestion of three coexisting main gender ideologies was discussed above with reference to what people say and do, and how those ideologies serve to structure social space. We now look at what kind of ideals these ideologies represent for women, as the 'woman question' always tends to surface during periods of insecurity and change. The following ideals are only roughly outlined – naturally there are different ideas of what is really the ideal and what implications it has. Male and female understandings may, for example, be very different from each other.

As Table 15.1 indicates, the ideal woman is based on two very different ideas of 'woman', according to custom and to religion respectively; therefore these two ideas should not be mixed. One of the most striking differences between the two has to do with rationalisations used in explaining the segregation of sexes. Based on the idea of woman as an irresponsible being, customary ideology maintains that women should be isolated from the opposite sex so that they cannot cause harm to their male guardians. Religious discourse does not present women as being without responsibility, but explains that the sexes should be separated from each other so that the divinely established order is not shaken. What is common to both custom and religion is that women and men are thought to have separate, complementary roles, but even in this respect the two are different. While religious ideology allows woman an active role, customary discourse objectifies her and presents her from the point of view of the male. In contrast to both of them, revolutionary ideology is based on equality between the sexes and invites women to participate in building the society alongside men.

TABLE 15.1
Female ideals

Ideology	Discourses	Activities and practices (limitations and resources)
'Customs and traditions' (*adat wa taqalid*) 'Women have no '*aql*'	Women need to be protected; 'The chaste woman does not frequently leave her house'; women should not be in professions which require rational judgement	Veiling and seclusion; calling women bad names; prestige system; male guardianship; giving birth to sons
'Religion' (*din*) 'A woman can gain '*aql* through learning but her basic task is to serve her family'	There are clearly marked areas where women are supposed to limit their activities; a woman should study to become a good Muslim and mother	Religious and general education; work in certain fields; martyrdom through motherhood; segregation; the 'Islamic dress'
'Revolution' (*thawra*) 'Everyone can improve him/herself through learning'	Women should participate alongside men in building up the society; women and men are equal in marriage; everybody's duty is to study; women's emancipation (*tahrir al-mar'a*)	Education and work outside the home; occupational and political career; Family Law (1974) and marriage counselling[16]

According to customs and traditions, women obtain their public recognition through membership in the male lineage. As Dresch puts it, 'the idiom of shared honour through shared male descent is the starting point for most social accountancy; the map, if you like, on which bearings of all sorts are laid. By itself it says nothing about females' (1989: 44).

In this representation women are identified as daughters, sisters, wives and mothers to a male, whose honour depends on them. A woman's proper behaviour is a concern of her entire family.

In the religious discourse, women are considered to be different from men due to their basic role as providers of offspring to the Muslim community (*umma*). Women are directed specifically to this role as the means by which they can climb the hierarchical ladder of religious striving for a share of paradise. Woman's function in society is therefore limited to areas that enhance her role as a good mother. Her *'ilm* (learning) is needed to give the best possible education to her children, whereas men's *'ilm* is there to guide and to take responsibility for the family.

The revolutionary discourse is in clear contradiction to both the above. As women become economically independent from men, the divinely legitimated order of man above woman comes into question. Similarly, the equality of women and men in marriage unsettles the customary order, reinforced by ancestral lineage and according to which women are under the guardianship of men because they are weaker in moral strength.

In Table 15.1, 'Activities and practices' can be seen both as resources and limitations. What is a resource in one situation can be a limiting factor in another. Take for instance the veil: irrespective of their ideas as to whether veiling should be practised or not, women acknowledge the benefits of being able to *have* a presence without having *to act* that presence. In other words, the veil provides a woman with space to move on her own terms in the presence of other people. A young woman who normally wore no head covering told me that when she went in secret to meet her boyfriend, she considered putting on a veil.

Nafisa used the resources that belong to the religious discourse in her behaviour near the mosque. Similarly, she used the old social hierarchy – her superior lineage and the respect she could expect from women of lower status – that is part of the customs and traditions. At the university, she took advantage of the resources provided by the revolution – the right to education and the right for a woman to choose her husband.

Conclusions

In this chapter, I have argued that Adeni society in the late 1980s was not transformed in the manner that has been described in some earlier literature. Instead I suggest that if we look at actual social practice, a multiplicity of social formations prevailed. In everyday practice, this was manifest in social fields organised by mutually contrasting rules of behaviour. Behind those rules of behaviour I outlined three main ideological representations that I called 'customs and traditions', 'revolution', and 'religion'. I also emphasised that 'religion' alone does not stand for Islam, but that Islam as a religion is present in all three, contributing to the local varieties of Islam. In this light, I would not consider the legislative changes that affected the family after the Yemeni unification to be so dramatic. Before unification, demands to curb the 'too many rights' of women had already been raised in the circles of power.[17] Unification provided a good excuse to adjust the situation without the need to have a public discussion on these difficult and emotionally charged questions.

It was common in Aden in the early 1990s to refer to 'pressure from the North' when discussing matters that raised strong feelings.[18] Even so, whether the actual pressure really came from the North is open to question. Changes in male–female relations and the new atmosphere in Aden that was hostile to 'uncontrolled' women resulted from an internal process in which existing power relations were readjusted.

Since unification, the 'religious' discourse has become particularly strong. Such issues as women's new veiling, termination of coeducation for children reaching puberty and the need for limiting women's movement outside the home have all been motivated by people whose arguments are characteristic of the 'religious' discourse. Even in this new situation, the three major ideologies discussed here have continued to exist side by side. This time however the circumstances are dramatically different, as some ideologies are also promoted with the firing of guns, and a wave of intolerance has swept over Aden.

NOTES

1 This contribution is based on field research in Aden, People's Democratic Republic of Yemen, between October 1988 and November 1989 and, following unification, in Aden, Republic of Yemen, between June and December 1991, and April and June 1992, two years in all. Research for this and for my PhD thesis was made possible by funding from the Academy of Finland.

2 Khormaksar is a former cantonment area built by the British in the 1950s, and connects mainland Aden to the peninsula, the oldest parts of the town. At the time when this all happened (1989), Aden was capital of the People's Democratic Republic of Yemen (PDRY).

3 Names of the individuals mentioned here have been changed.

4 Tribal people or tribesmen (*qabā'il*, sing. *qabili*) denotes here that section of the rural population whose descent, occupation and political organisation is referred to in those terms both by themselves and by others. In addition to that, being tribal is, as Adra (1985: 279) states, a value-laden concept and an earned title.

5 The concept of *adab* has many meanings in Arabic and in reference to Islam (cf. Metcalf, 1984). This contribution deals with *adab* in the sense of a corpus of correct behaviour. According to Metcalf (1984: 2–3), *adab* refers to 'a high valuation of the employment of the will in proper discrimination of correct order, behaviour, and taste. The plural *ādāb* defines rules or codes of behaviour.' Dresch describes *adab* as 'good manners' (1989: 40).

6 *Al-Thawra*, Winter 1991 issue, as quoted in *Middle East Times*/Yemen Edition, February 1991; emphasis added.

7 During colonial times, the most notable *ziara*, the al-Aidrus festival, was a public holiday (Colony of Aden, 1941, Ordinance No. 14).

8 By 'ideologies' I mean those views of the surrounding world that act to organise and link the particular into the general and, in this way, give relevant motivations to existence. When ideologies are seen from the point of view of the actors and their relationship to the structures, it becomes irrelevant to speculate whether it is a question of 'false' or 'non-false' consciousness.

9 Even though this was the declared policy, the British in actual terms did intervene in the family regulation, for example by excluding the Islamic *ulama* from all court practice. This point is dealt with more fully in my PhD dissertation.

10 *Family Law* (People's Democratic Republic of Yemen 1976, part I, chapter I, section 2).

11 Adeni people have always been divided on the question whether *ziaras*, *dhikr*s or Sufist movements really belong to Islam or not.

12 Changes that affected the position of women began only after June 1969 (the so-called Corrective Movement), when the left wing of the ruling National Liberation Front took power.

13 This point is discussed in more detail in my PhD dissertation.

14 *Documents of the General Union of Yemeni Women* (People's Democratic Republic of Yemen, 1977: 7), original English translation, emphasis added.

15 In my field data, 75 per cent of the working women said they had taken a job outside the home for economic reasons. A minority gave other reasons, including the wish to make a professional career. The structured part of my field data

consisted of 57 women at home and 254 women working outside the home in all main fields. I met these people in homes, offices, shops, factories, cooperatives, hospitals and clinics, construction sites, court houses, agricultural farms, the Aden television building, nurseries, schools, institutes, the Aden University and the Women's Union Clubs. The choice of people in my data was random, and data was collected with no attempt to represent a sample.

16 Women's Union and Local Defence Committees were involved in legal arbitration for solving marriage disputes. See *Family Law*, [People's Democratic Republic 1976: Part II, § 25(b)], Molyneux, 1989: 207 and Shamiry, 1984: 53.

17 Personal communication with a leading member of the PDRY judiciary in 1989. See also Molyneux, 1995: 425.

18 During the transitional period, terrorist actions were occasionally directed against places that served, produced or stored alcohol. However, it was widely believed in Aden that those who were behind these violent actions were beer importers who wanted to take the market from the popular local Seera beer, rather than any militant religious forces. Both were still assumed to come from the North.

16

Land Distribution after Unification and its Consequences for Urban Development in Hadhramawt[1]

Thomas Pritzkat

Introduction

Urban development in the Third World has been extensively discussed. Issues on which research has focused have been land- and property-markets, urban sprawl, lack of institutions as well as mismanagement and corruption, to name but a few.[2] Why then another case study? Simply because, after Yemeni unification in 1990, the unique opportunity has arisen in the formerly socialist South Yemen to study urban development *in statu nascendi*. With the political and economic thawing in the South, new, external forces have come to bear and impinge upon the local situation. Changes, among other factors introduced by unification into Yemen's political and economic superstructure, have manifested themselves in frenetic construction activities in most of the urban centres in the Southern Governorates.[3] A specific case in point is the coastal town of al-Mukalla,[4] the capital of Hadhramawt province, which witnessed a construction boom that is unique in its history.

One of the most important factors underlying this development was the decision of the government after unification to hand out state land at no cost, for indemnification as well as for investment purposes. This chapter analyses the post-unification juridical measures governing land tenure and control over land, and also traces the repercussions and consequences of these measures for urban development in the Southern Governorates, using the case of Mukalla as an example.

The legal framework

Ironically, the basis for the handing out of government land in united Yemen was established by the last law to be issued in the People's

Democratic Republic of Yemen (PDRY). A week before official unification took place in May 1990, and in anticipation of privatisation measures in the unification process that would be beyond its control, the regime in Aden passed a law (No. 18 of 1990; *Qanun tamlik al-masakin*; PDRY, 1990) that would address this issue. This law transformed into ownership titles the usufruct rights that had formerly been held by the beneficiaries of the nationalisation measures introduced by the 1972 Housing Law (No. 23 of 1972; *qanun al-iskan*).[5] On the basis of usufruct documents issued by the PDRY authorities to the beneficiaries (*al-muntafi'un*) of nationalised building property, every holder of such property could now apply to have his usufruct title to nationalised property transferred to a title of personal ownership.

At the same time, Law No. 18 for 1990 also called for the indemnification of the former proprietors. A policy for determining the value of assets was loosely defined and the new owners were required to pay a certain percentage of this value to the previous owners, either in a lump sum or in instalments. For the loss of their residence, the former owners were to be additionally compensated by the government with state land, i.e. with an 'equally sized plot of land for the construction of a residence' and additionally a 'plot of land that equals the value of the old building' (PDRY 1990, Section 9, Article 1).[6] With the ratification of this law, the *status quo ante unificationem* had effectively been cemented by the ruling élites in Aden, the corollary being that the holders of the new documents were now legally protected from any claims by the previous owners.

With the unification of the two Yemeni states, a new constitution was ratified (RoY, 1991a). In Article 6, it guarantees the inviolability of private ownership. However, no new law was passed that revoked the former nationalisation laws passed by the régime in Aden. Instead, the political will to protect private property and to return formerly nationalised property to its previous owners is merely reflected in various presidential decrees and 'general directives' (*ittijahat al-'amma*). However, these new presidential decrees (issued by a special committee within the Prime Minister's Office, and signed by the president) or prime ministerial decrees do not operate on the same juridical level as laws passed by parliament. In fact, in Yemen, decrees do not have the juridical power to revoke laws: in order to declare a law, which was passed by parliament null and void, a new law to that effect needs to be passed. The result was that de jure the former PDRY nationalisation laws continued to enjoy the force of law in united Yemen, at least in the transition period.

Confronted with often complex ownership structures, and finding the issues involved too highly politicised, the Yemeni government has apparently been unable to settle the ensuing 'land question' on a general and definitive level. Rather, it has preferred to deal with each claim for restitution or indemnification individually on an ad hoc basis, leaving the entire matter in an exceedingly ambiguous state. Consequently, the only regulation that addresses the return of formerly nationalised building property is rather vaguely worded, and makes no precise specifications as to the process of restitution of the formerly nationalised housing properties. Since unification, all problems pertaining to the regulation of property questions in the urban sphere in the Southern Governorates have been addressed by a decree issued by the prime minister dating from 12 September 1991 (decree concerning directives to deal with land questions in the Southern Governorates; in the following: September decree). This decree forms the basis upon which the property questions resulting from PDRY Law No. 23 for 1972 (*qanun al-iskan*) are dealt with.

In its preamble, the decree refers directly to PDRY Law No. 18 for 1990 mentioned above. It states that this law would represent an initial reform measure (*khutuwat islahiyya*) of the PDRY nationalisation approach, that envisaged compensation for the former owners. Faced with a problematic situation in respect of land in the Southern Governorates, the government of the Republic of Yemen would now consider how to 'strengthen and broaden the regulations envisaged in law No. 18 for 1990' and 'grant the right to compensation to all those whose properties have been nationalized' or, at least, 'return what is possible to return without causing social problems' (RoY, 1991b; preamble).

The September decree considers all commercially used premises (*mahallat tijariyya*), as well as premises occupied by foreign embassies or institutions of the Yemeni government (provided the latter had not been transformed into residential apartments) as being 'possible to return without causing social problems'. The former beneficiaries of commercial premises were to be allowed a two-year period to leave their hitherto occupied buildings; after this period the previous owner was entitled to take possession of his property (RoY, 1991b, Section 4, Articles a, b and d).

Regarding residentially used building property (*masakin*), the main regulations of Law No. 18 were restated and the principle that 'indemnification has precedence over restitution' was applied. Should the owner and the former beneficiary not reach a mutually acceptable agreement (*taradhi*), the decree aims to compensate the initial owner with an adequate piece of government land. According to paragraph 2: 'All Yemeni owners are to be [. . .] indemnified for residential buildings for which usufruct documents ['*uqud intifa*'] or ownership documents ['*uqud tamlik*] have been issued to its occupants.' As compensation, the former owner would receive a plot of building-land which 'shall be equal [*mu'adila*] in value to the value of his building' (Section 2, Articles a and c).[7] In addition, the one-time owner was to receive a certain amount of money, based on the estimated value for his property. The new owner had to pay a certain percentage of this estimated value to the original owner (Section 2, Article c).

Along with promises of the return of formerly nationalised lands, Yemeni unification also brought to the country an economy that was close to accepting free-market principles. Liberalisation of the economy was reflected in the ratification of a new Investment Law (No. 22 for 1991) which in theory facilitated private investment in the country by, for example, allowing tax-free importation and re-exportation of foreign investment capital and the exportation of foreign currency profits out of the country (RoY, 1991c; Section 17 and 19).

To administer the new law and overcome bureaucratic and regulatory obstacles, the Law called for the establishment of a powerful autonomous organisation – the General Investment Authority (GIA; *al-hay'a al-'amma li-l istithmar*). The president of the GIA was appointed in February 1992 and given the rank of deputy prime minister, thereby reaffirming the significance attached by the government to the organisation. The organisation's headquarters are situated in Sana'a, with branches located in the country's major population centres, i.e. Hodeidah, Ta'izz, Aden and Mukalla.

However, where town development in the Southern Governorates was concerned, the most important innovation of Law No. 22 for 1991 was the fact that the GIA was empowered to distribute state land for the establishment of investment projects: 'The Authority may [. . .] allot land needed to establish projects and sign relevant contracts on behalf of the agencies concerned. Such agencies are obliged to furnish the

Authority with all maps and information concerning land available for such purposes . . .' (Article 34/6). Furthermore, the GIA will 'have the competence to purchase or lease land for the purpose of establishing projects. It may also [. . .] reserve land and expropriate land that it deems necessary to achieve this end against fair compensation' (Article 34/14d). However, for the potential investor there are certain limitations imposed as to receiving land from the GIA: 'investors and project sponsors shall desist from disposing of land owned or leased to the project by the Authority for purposes other than those for which licensed [. . .] In case of violation, the contract signed with the investor or project in this regard shall be deemed to be cancelled and all relevant rights shall revert to the Authority . . .' (Article 74 b/5).

Land distribution

In Hadhramawt province, the guiding principle of the September directive – i.e. that 'indemnification has precedence over restitution' – was reinterpreted and reversed by the provincial authorities. Here (as in some of the other Southern Provinces) the principle of 'restitution has precedence over indemnification' applied and, as a result, it was the beneficiaries of the PDRY nationalisation measures who were to be indemnified with state land, while the original proprietors were given back their property. This reinterpretation of the September directive was based on a decision by the governor of Hadhramawt province. His decision met with the approval of the president of the Republic, but was not formalised in writing.[8]

In Hadhramawt at the time of writing previously nationalised building property can be reclaimed on grounds of official ownership documents – usually dating back to the days of the Qu'ayti-Sultanate – or of traditional documents.[9] In the absence of these, a claimant may present two witnesses to substantiate his claim. The witnesses will either testify to a former de facto ownership, acquisition or inheritance of a given plot. The petitions in question are verified and authenticated by a committee consisting of local notables and representatives from the local branches of the the Ministry of Housing, Planning and Urban Development (MCHUP) and the Ministry of Justice, and a representative of the provincial governor. Once a claim has been approved by the committee, the former beneficiaries were given a five-year period (as of

1992) to leave their hitherto occupied premises[10] During this period, they were expected to have built a new residence or to have made other living arrangements.[11]

The one-time beneficiaries of the now-returned building properties are compensated with two plots of government land, each measuring between 100 and 200 m². As voiced in an argument by the provincial government, one of these plots could be meant for residential construction, the other could be sold to finance the new necessary building structure. The plot of allotted land has the legal status of leasehold (*hikr*), and the new beneficiaries are given the right of usufruct (*haqq al-intifa'*) for a (renewable) period of 99 years.

The provincial government's reinterpretation of the September directive is understood to be a 'confidence-building measure', aimed at promoting confidence in the political and economic stability of the Hadhramawt among both potential investors and former landlords. Furthermore, it is intended to transmit a positive signal towards members of the expatriate Hadhrami community who are considered *ergo ipso* by the provincial government as powerful investors, on grounds of their general affluence.[12]

However, the distribution of land for private building purposes is not a new phenomenon in Hadhramawt, since it was an already established practice in the time of the Qu'ayti-Sultanate and also during the period of socialist rule. Like today, the legal status of state land distributed for private building purposes was that of leasehold, and documents were issued by the *maliyya*, the Sultanate's treasury department. Under the socialists, usufruct documents were initially not issued, until the authorities finally decided to supply them at the beginning of the 1980s.

In the time of the PDRY, however, the application procedure was extremely complicated. Requests were minutely scrutinised and the 'political correctness' of the applicants was checked and double-checked. The slow procedures resulted in the government issuing a relatively low number of land plots. Between 1982 and 1989[13] only 3,534 land plots were distributed in the whole of the Mukalla *mudiriyya*,[14] even though actual demand was much higher (cf. Table 16.1). By 1995, a backlog of some 30,000 applications dating back from the 1980s had accumulated in the archives, and applicants were still waiting to be allotted a plot of land.

TABLE 16.1
Building concessions handed out in the
Mudiriyya al-Mukalla (1967–94)

Pre-unification		Post-unification	
Year	Number	Year	Number
1967	185	1990	1,341
1968	257	1991	1,119
1969	–	1992	2,395
1970	60	1993	1,381
1971	286	1994	314
1972	289		
1973	73		
1974	58		
1975	92		
1976	111		
1977	49		
1978–86	**		
1987	258		
1988	281		
1989	796		
Yearly average 1967–89: 215		Yearly average 1990–4: 1,310	

Note: **no data available.
Source: RoY / *Wizarat al insha'at wa-l iskan wa-tatwir al-hadari / Idarat al-iskan*, (1995a) Mukalla.

With Yemeni unification and the ensuing endeavours to return the nationalised property and to process the seemingly insurmountable backlog of applications, chaos was inevitable. The demand for land was insatiable. The main institution in charge of land distribution, the local branch of the MCHUP (*Idarat al-iskan*; henceforth *Iskan*) started distributing land on an historically unprecedented level. Land was given on an unrestricted basis to former beneficiaries of the nationalised properties, investors, would-be investors and people who had applied for a plot of land back in the 1980s. However, not only were individuals eligible on grounds of compensation or investment purposes catered for by the land-issuing authorities: anyone with 'friendly relations' to the authorities in charge could also expect to gain a plot of land. If such 'relations' did not exist, they could be established by monetary means (see below).

Until the beginning of 1995, 56,209 plots of land had been distributed in the district of Mukalla, of which 7,350 (i.e. 13 per cent) were used for indemnification purposes (*ta'widh*), as Table 16.2 indicates. Government land was handed out virtually free of charge. The only (official) fees charged were a 'one-off payment' to the *Iskan* of YR10,000 (US$77), plus an additional annual amount of YR0.65 per square metre.[15]

TABLE 16.2
Number of plots of state land distributed in the
Mudiriyya al-Mukalla (1982–95)

Pre-unification		Post-unification	
Year	Number	Year	Number
1982	2	1990	1,606
1983	166	1991	4,099
1984	199	1992	12,112
1985	406	1993	9,167
1986	227	1994	20,043
1987	257	1995	182*
1988	1,268		
1989	1,010		
Total 3,354		Total 56,209**	
Yearly average 442		Yearly average 9,368	

Notes: * = from 1 January 1995 to 31 March 1995; ** = of which 7,350 plots for indemnification.
Source: RoY / *Maslahat al-aradi w'al 'aqarat al-dawla* (1995b), Mukalla.

The *Iskan*, however, is not the only government institution responsible for handing out land. The GIA also distributes government land – for investment purposes – and is herewith further assisted by yet another institution, which acts on the Investment Authority's behalf by handing out state land to agricultural investment projects. It is referred to as the *Idarat al-zira'a* (henceforth *Zira'a*), the local branch of the Ministry of Agriculture and Water Resources. Plots of land distributed by the two latter institutions greatly exceed, in terms of size, the ones given out by the *Iskan*: land given out for investment purposes can measure up to several hundred hectares, according to the land requirements of the project applied for.

With regard to ownership documents, the latter institutions will in theory only give out documents setting aside plots of land for investment projects which have received prior approval by the GIA. With such a document (*wathiqat hajz ard*), the would-be investor would then go to the *Iskan* to have a proper leasehold document issued.

The handing out of state land required a general land survey and land registration, something that had not previously been attempted either by the Sultans or the socialists since there were no obvious reasons for doing so at the time. However, local engineers and technicians of the *Idarat al-iskan* have been vigorously engaged in this activity since the beginning of the 1990s: the entire coastal belt of the Mukalla *mudiriyya* is being partitioned into building blocks (leaving spaces for streets and necessary communal purposes). These in turn have been subdivided into individually numbered plots and are being distributed plot by plot to applicants and other groups alike.

The evolving land market

One corollary of the government's decision to hand out land free of charge on a large scale was the establishment of a Wild West type of real-estate market in Mukalla.[16] As the word spread that, in comparison to the Northern Governorates where most lands are privately owned, state land in Hadhramawt was to be had at relatively low prices, a 'land hysteria' set in. The easiest way to acquire a large plot of land was to submit an 'investment' project to the GIA. Many 'investors' thus simply handed in an application without ever having any intention of implementing it. In 1996, out of 1,300 'investment' projects in Hadhramawt, only 70 were actually implemented; the rest are regarded by the Director General of the General Investment Authority in Sana'a as 'mirage-projects' (see *Al-Thawra*, 7 April 1996: 2).

As a result, real-estate agencies (*makatib al-'iqarat*) began to spring up in the town.[17] The local Chamber of Commerce speaks of over one hundred agencies that started business in 1993 alone. These dealt with the preliminary documents handed out by the GIA, in land that had been handed out to the former beneficiaries of the nationalisation measures as indemnification land (*aradi li-ta'widh*), as well as ownership titles (*mulk-*titles). This agitated real-estate market became increasingly overheated in 1994 when oil discoveries were made 150 km north of Mukalla, triggering high expectations as to the town's future development.

Another important factor in the development of the land market and the subsequent construction boom has been the demand for real estate from abroad. Members of the expatriate Hadhrami community in Saudi Arabia and the Emirates (referred to as *mughtaribin* in Yemeni Arabic, i.e. 'someone who lives abroad') buy land plots by the dozen (some up to a hundred) in a frenzy, either through their respective agents in town (*wakil*, sing., *wukala*, pl.) or, more often, through specialised real-estate agencies. According to information obtained from some of the latter, *émigré* Hadhramis residing in Saudi Arabia and the Emirates purchased between 90 and 95 per cent of all land sold on the market. Transactions between Mukalla and the countries of residence of the *mughtaribin* are made speedily via fax and negotiations are carried out via mobile phone.

The huge demand for land has resulted in soaring land prices. In the heady days of 1993, prime plots of approximately 100 m^2 in downtown Mukalla fetched up to YR40 million (equivalent to around US$3,000 per square metre, at an exchange rate of YR130 to the US dollar), while a similar plot along the tarmacked roads on the outskirts of Mukalla still fetched up to US$1,000/m^2 in prime locations.[18]

The three government institutions in Mukalla in charge of land distribution (*Iskan*, GIA and *Zira'a*) have begun to resemble a gold mine for those who are in the right position to exploit a situation brought about by the high stakes involved, as well as by the fact that virtually everyone in and out of town has tried either to gain access to land or to sell an acquired plot at a profit. The directors of the three institutions have found themselves in fortunate circumstances: from 1990 onwards their positions offered the possibility of personal enrichment which provincial governors in the Roman Empire would have enjoyed. In the uncertain years that followed unification, some of the later directors of these institutions (and other officials as well) seemed to regard state land as a kind of private resource. They took the opportunity to misappropriate government land through irregular documentation, thereby allowing relatives, selected clientele, and financially well-endowed individuals to gain access to choice land.

In order to acquire a select plot of land, extraordinarily high 'administrative fees' had to be paid to the authorities. These 'fees' could reach astronomical heights. One investor, for example, reports having paid YR30 million 'acceleration money' for the issuing of a plot of prime land in the outskirts of Mukalla (US$230,000; the equivalent of the annual budget of Hadhramawt province), and this incident is by no means exceptional. The same procedure was followed for gaining access to plots of indemnification land in areas well suited for residential purposes. Anyone not complying with the unwritten rules was likely eventually to be allotted a plot in a rugged, undesirable and isolated area far away from the nearest settlement.

To give an example: the Director General (*mudir al-'amm*) of the *Idarat al-iskan* in Mukalla was ousted from his position in 1996 for 'irregularities' that occurred during his tenure of office. His alleged delinquencies included issuing multiple documents for the same plot of land; levying additional fees (for which no receipt was given) for services provided by his authority to claimants of land; selling on his personal account open spaces that had previously been designated in the planning brief for communal and government purposes; and, lastly, establishing a position for his juvenile son in the *Iskan* administration (cf. *Al-Ayyam*, 28 January 1996: 4).

Similarly,[19] an individual who was a director of the GIA in Mukalla before 1994 (now reported to be affluent and residing in exile in Saudi Arabia) gave out ownership documents for investment land, instead of the normal 'reservation document'. The corollary was that in these cases stipulations made in the Investment Law with regard to investment land would no longer apply. Instead, land handed out in such a way had henceforth to be considered as private property.

In yet another instance, high-ranking officials in Mukalla (who are often army officers as well) personally appropriated state land or gained control over the land-issuing procedures (in fact, some of the most valuable estates in Mukalla today are reputed to be owned by these officials). If these 'power brokers' did not appropriate the real estate directly, they were at least able to turn their 'intervention' in land-issuing procedures into financial profit.

Impelled by the high stakes involved, virtually every means to gain access to land seems to have been exercised in the region. In 1995, members of an armoured brigade of the Yemeni Armed Forces, stationed in Al-'Abr (a desert outpost close the Saudi-Yemeni border), occupied the *Idarat al-iskan* in Say'un[20] by force. The soldiers made its director an offer that he found somewhat hard to refuse: land in exchange for his life. Some time later, the same 'technique' was applied in the town of Shibam, some 30 km to the west of Say'un. Here, however, the 'offer' was less compelling since the organisation's director had good relations with the tribesmen in and around the town. A group of heavily armed Say'ar bedouins, backed by some equally well-armed town-dwellers, helped the director to thwart the soldiers' attempt.

Town development under new conditions

As was to be expected, the circumstances noted above have had repercussions that affected the development of the town of Mukalla itself. Between 1990 and 1995 Mukalla witnessed a construction boom triggered off by the land distributions, the ensuing demand for real estate from abroad, and the oil discoveries in the region.

In its dynamics as well as in its extent, this building boom (often linked to speculation) has been singular in the town's history and displays certain similarities to the 'Californian Gold Rush' of the nineteenth century. Mukalla's built-up surface tripled in the years between 1990 and 1995, and wide areas around the town are dotted with newly erected buildings, construction sites and 'staked claims'. The latter take the form of concrete poles jammed into the ground or walls erected to declare a claim to a specific property.

Expressed in statistical terms, the construction boom is reflected in the growing amount of building material that is handled through the port of Mukalla. Whereas 15,352 tons of timber had been handled in 1989, this figure reached 20,827 and 30,083 tons in 1992 and 1993 respectively. As for commodities like cement, the ratio is even more striking. While 49,289 tons had been traded in 1989, as indicated in Table 16.3, the numbers rose to 139,962 and 209,378 tons in 1992 and 1993 respectively (RoY / Mukalla Port Authority, 1994). However, these computations must be regarded only as the tip of the iceberg, since massive amounts of construction material are being transported overland as well. Furthermore, the number of building concessions handed out by the *Iskan* can attest to the dynamics involved. Between 1967 and 1977 a total of 133 concessions per annum was given out, while in the three year period from 1990 to 1993, an annual total of 1,559 concessions was reached, an appreciable percentage increase (again see Table 16.3).[21]

Since 1990 the town has expanded rapidly, mainly along a drawn-out axis running from east to west. In the process of this 'ribbon-type' of development (which principally follows the asphalted roads), two main growth centres can be distinguished. In the west of Mukalla, the former bedouin settlement of Fuwwa, around 12 km from the town centre, has evolved into a booming settlement where areas measuring square kilometres have recently been built up to include residential as well as commercial premises.[22]

TABLE 16.3
Building materials handled via the port of Makalla (in tons)

Timber		Cement	
Year	Amount	Year	Amount
1989	15,352	1989	49,289
1992	20,827	1992	139,962
1993	30,083	1993	209,378

Source: RoY / Mukalla Port Authority (1994).

The eastern growth area lies approximately 10 km to the east of Mukalla's centre, in and around the settlements of Rawqab and Bawish. Formerly a fishing village and an agricultural settlement respectively, these settlements have now evolved into another focal point for the recent town development. As with Fuwwa, there are areas of several square kilometres in size that have been covered with new buildings or construction sites, especially along the paved road leading from Mukalla proper towards the airport of Riyyan (and from there into the interior of the province).

But the recent development of Mukalla is not confined solely to these two areas. In Mukalla itself, open spaces have been built up, especially in the northern quarter of Dis ('*Hayy Oktober*' in socialist parlance), and in uninhabited areas like *wadi* beds and mountainous terrain. And along the coast, 'tourist projects' are lined up one after the other. The majority of sites consist of a compound containing a number of bungalows, shopping facilities, restaurants and a swimming pool. Most of these projects (which in 1996 were still under construction and in different phases of completion) are owned and run by *émigré* Hadhramis, in most cases being a copy of existing similar recreation projects that they owned in Saudi Arabia or the Gulf States. As Mukalla is perceived to be 'virgin territory' in terms of tourism, this kind of investment strategy seems to be the proper one to which to adhere.[23]

Another investment activity in the developing growth poles involves the setting up of shopping centres (*marakiz tijariyya*), chalets and apartment blocks – irrespective of economic return or of market demand. In 1996, around 75 per cent of the *marakiz tijariyya* were empty, and the same was true for most of the houses recently constructed by the *mughtaribin*.[24]

Problems of urban development after 1990

In view of the above, and given the meagre financial resources of the provincial government (the 1995 budget did not exceed US$230,000), it will not be surprising to learn that most of the town's newly developed areas are in dire need of basic infrastructure facilities. These are practically non-existent, since land distribution and the booming construction have outpaced any attempts by the state to cater for such services.[25]

Fresh water can in most cases only be obtained via water trucks furnished by the town's municipality (*baladiyya*), while wastewater management is left to individual households. In the centre of Mukalla, the disposal of wastewater also poses a problem. Although a new sewage system was installed in socialist times, it did not meet the entire requirements of the town. Today, the quarter of Dis has to manage without an effective sewage system, and thus drains its unfiltered wastewater directly into the *wadi al-'ayqa* (the town's main, and periodically dry, river-bed) that runs through the town. Here, large ponds filled with sewage abound, representing a serious sanitary problem and a potential hazard to the population's health.

The situation with regard to electricity is similarly grave. In 1995, the actual capacity of the town's two power plants was calculated at a combined 7 MW (nominally 16.7 MW). According to official sources, however, the actual demand averages around 50 MW, due to the increase in construction and the constantly growing numbers of electric appliances installed in commercial as well as in residential premises (such as air-conditioning, etc.).

At the time of unification, 30 per cent of households in Mukalla's western expansion zone of Fuwwa, and almost 60 per cent of households in Rawqab and Bawish in the east, were supplied with electricity. However, in 1995 only 5 per cent of all households in these regions received regular electricity deliveries. Most households today are either forced to use private, gasoline-powered generators or to tap into the municipal electricity net wherever possible. The Public Corporation for Electricity (a government department in charge of the power supply) can only meet this demand by alternating the supply of electricity to different town quarters over a 24-hour period. This results in recurring power-cuts that regularly paralyse the town for hours.[26]

Another major drawback of urban development – alongside the lack of basic infrastructural services – is the lack of land management by the state, which is reflected in erratic land distribution procedures. Until 1996, there was no apparent sign of cooperation among the three land-distributing institutions, *Iskan*, GIA and *Zira'a*. On the contrary: all three vied with each other over who would be first to allot land – and to profit from the unofficial 'fees'. This fierce competition reverberates in a chaotic apportionment of land plots. At the beginning of the surveying measures, the GIA and the *Idarat al-zira'a* handed out land in regions that had not yet been surveyed by the technicians of the *Iskan*. Even after the completion of the surveying procedures, GIA and *Zira'a* continued to allot holdings of thousands of hectares, in blatant breach of the existing plan and the projected land zoning.

This lack of coordination, added to the fact that at times multiple documents for a single plot were handed out deliberately (see above), has produced an array of claims over who actually is to be the owner or beneficiary of the plots concerned. As a result, the municipal courts are choked with a flood of pending cases concerning conflicting claims to land.[27] As legal procedures are time-consuming and their outcomes uncertain, claimants tend to take matters into their own hands by pulling out each other's 'staked claims' (sing. *rakn*, pl. *arkan*) and replacing them with new, 'proper' ones. As a consequence, the already existing confusion simply worsens.

In addition, illegal occupations and/or illegal construction (*bina' 'ashwa'i*) on state land become the rule rather than the exception. To make matters worse, the provincial government has been handing out usufruct documents for these illegally occupied lands, thus providing a further incentive to circumvent existing regulations. Furthermore, the general climate of legal fluidity and ambiguity gives rise to individual interpretations of the delimitation of allotted building plots. Thus even individuals who have been allocated land through official channels are often spurred on to redefine the size of their assigned plots as they see fit, while others apply for a second allotment of indemnification land under a different name. This is done without remorse, since some of the state's authorities are perceived to be at the forefront of irregularities pertaining to these matters.

Nor are the surveying procedures of the state without their share of shortcomings. Irregularities within the higher levels of the institutions involved continue on a smaller scale as well: some of the rank-and-file employees measure out land plots at their whim. Thus, newly drawn maps of recently surveyed areas do not always correspond with the actual size of the region surveyed. For example, areas that in reality measure 1,200 hectares are shown on the map as having a size of only 1,100 hectares.[28]

Conclusion

The first years after unification have been difficult ones. The authorities had a plethora of difficult issues to deal with, partly resulting from the socialist heritage in the Southern Governorates. In the urban space, one of the central questions that had to be dealt with was the topic of nationalised housing property. In Hadhramawt province, an attempt to resolve the issue was made by restoring properties to their former owners, and by subsequently distributing state land for indemnification to the erstwhile beneficiaries.

With the coming of a market economy and the ensuing laws of supply and demand, the resource 'land' suddenly turned into a valuable commodity in Southern Yemen and was vigorously sought after. Given the state's decision about how the land distribution was to be dealt with, namely the system of handing out land free of charge to virtually everyone who applied, a valuable resource that could have been directed towards financing the region's infrastructure was lost.

The de facto relinquishment of government control over the resource 'land' has thrown the door wide open to speculation and mis-management. Because ample space was found within the often-confused situation after Yemeni unification to profit from the existing juridical limbo, land distribution in the Southern Governorates has been a mixed blessing.

For those who took advantage of the situation, the benefits of the government's decision are obvious, but in terms of town development, the handling of the land-distributing procedures produced catastrophic results. Planning procedures and attempts to direct the booming town growth became virtually impossible since no central state agency was able to stop the dynamics set in motion by the government's decision to distribute state land on a large scale at no cost. The practice of handing out land free of charge has led to the above-mentioned loss of a potential source of state revenue.

Within the last few years, this situation seems to have altered and a more sound approach appears to have gained the upper hand. Since mid-1996, state land in Mukalla has been auctioned off to the highest bidder. This type of commercialisation might finally help to finance the infrastructural services of which most towns in the Southern Governorates are in dire need. However, given the vast land transactions of the past, the question arises as to whether there is any valuable state land left to be sold at all.

NOTES

1 Research in Hadhramawt Province, Republic of Yemen, was conducted for 12 months between 1994 and 1996. Data in this article stem either from the author's personal investigations in the Hadhramaut (where not otherwise indicated) or from mostly unpublished Arabic documents, which were obtained during field research. Arabic documents have been translated by the author.

2 For further reading refer – amongst others – to Davie (1994), Rakodi (1997), UNCHS (1996), World Bank (2000).

3 These comprise the territory of the former People's Democratic Republic of Yemen (PDRY) and include (from west to east) the provinces of Aden, Lahej, Abyan, Shabwa, Hadhramawt and Mahra.

4 Mukalla is located approximately 600 km to the east of Aden and 300 km west of the Yemeni-Omani border.

5 This law nationalised the housing property of absentee landlords and properties not personally inhabited by their respective owners.

6 Buildings used for commercial purposes (*masakin al-murtabita bi-l 'amal*) and buildings within military compounds are exempt from this regulation.

7 See footnote 1.

8 Oral communication, governor of Hadhramawt province; 4/1995.

9 These consist of a meticulous description of the location or building, usually signed by dozens of witnesses. The author has seen documents describing plots in the above-mentioned manner with his very eyes.

10 This arrangement does not apply for commercially used premises. In 1994 a resolution by the provincial government, worked out in cooperation with the local Chamber of Commerce, yielded for the erstwhile tenants a one-year period (starting from the beginning of 1995) during which the rent for each shop (*fatha*) in the Mukalla Suq was fixed at YR5,000 a month. After this period, the one-time owner was entitled to take possession of his property or to demand any rent that he deemed fit (cf. Republic of Yemen, 1994).

11 A mass dislocation has, however, not taken place. In most cases, owner and tenant struck an agreement that allowed the latter to stay – albeit with a new contract. Data obtained from the *idarat al-iskan* in Mukalla (1995, unpublished document) confirm this tendency. Out of a total of 3,265 contracts 2,598 had been renewed by 1995. In case of conflict, the matter is addressed to a committee consisting of the Aqil al-hara (Sheikh of the quarter) and government officials.

12 Personal communication from the governor of Hadhramawt province, 1995. According to this source, the availability of the resource 'land' in and more particularly around the town of Mukalla is a significant factor in having made this decision possible.

13 Data referring to the period between 1967 and 1981 are not available.

14 Administrative district, including the city's neighbouring towns Ghayl Ba Wazir, Shihr and Burum and its respective hinterlands.

15 For the size of a land plot of, say, 400 m², the beneficiary has to pay the amount of YR260 per year, the equivalent of roughly US$2 (exchange rate at the time of field research: YR130 – to the US$).

16 A similar development can be found in the larger towns of the interior of the province like Say'un or al-Qatn.

17 At least one agency that deals in land plots from Hadhramawt has also opened up in Sana'a.

18 However, the price level had dwindled to some extent by 1996.

19 The following accounts are based upon information gathered during field research in Hadhramawt.

20 Say'un lies in the interior of the province, some 250 km north of Mukalla in the Wadi Hadhramawt, the main agricultural area of the province.

21 Numbers are aggregated. Data for the period between 1978 and 1986 are not available; in 1987 and 1988, 270 building concessions were handed out annually; in 1989 the figure was 796. The latter figure can be explained by the expanding liberalisation of the economy in the wake of Yemeni unification which resulted in less strict issuing procedures.

22 At the time of the PDRY, a study commissioned by the Ministry of Housing had selected the settlement of Fuwwa as the potential expansion zone for Greater Mukalla and worked out a detailed building and zoning scheme. However, due to administrative shortcomings and financial constraints, only parts of this plan were put into practice. At the beginning of the 1980s, some residential blocks were constructed, in addition to a hospital. With Yemeni unification, the old Master Plan that had been gathering dust in officials' desks was relaunched. Land was parcelled out more or less according to the specifications of the plan, and Fuwwa rose to become a residential quarter for some of the better-off Mukallawis.

23 As tourists usually pass through Mukalla in *quantités négligeables* only, this kind of investment prompts the question as to who is ever to use the facilities.

24 For the rationale behind these investments, see Pritzkat (1999, pp. 399–418).

25 In this respect, however, Mukalla does not seem to be an exception in the Middle Eastern context. In Muscat, after the takeover by Sultan Qabous and the ensuing development, wide areas of the town were similarly left without any infrastructural services (cf. Scholz, 1990).

26 In the summer of 1995, for example, each quarter was supplied with electricity for only two hours daily.

27 This is especially the case in Aden, the former capital (cf. Mercier, 1996, p. 64f.).

28 Placed in the context of the above, the utilisation of the 'surplus' land is fairly easy to imagine.

17

Housing and Health Care in the City of Hodeidah

Marina de Regt and Ali M. Ghailan

Introduction

The city of Hodeidah has changed dramatically since the early 1990s. In August 1990, a few months after unification and as a result of the Gulf crisis, nearly a million returnees came back to Yemen. From the outset the new government had to deal with a number of immense and urgent problems, among which was the settlement of the returnees. Many of them stayed in and around the city of Hodeidah, since this was the first sizeable Yemeni city beyond the Saudi border, and there was land there that could be settled on. The availability of government land attracted not only the returnees but also rural migrants and others who had been living elsewhere in the city, with the result that four new slum areas appeared on the outskirts of town. The adverse living conditions in these areas called for strong (government) intervention, but only some of these efforts were successful.

This chapter examines two development projects which were established in the mid-1980s with the aim of improving the living conditions of poor urban dwellers in Hodeidah, since housing and health care are two of the most important sectors in the development of poor urban areas. Both projects – the Hodeidah Urban Development Project (HUDP) and the Hodeidah Urban Primary Health Care project (HUPHC) – started in the slum area of Ghulail, and were implemented by the Yemeni government in cooperation with foreign donors. They were intended in due course to extend their services to other parts of the city, and as such could have contributed to better living conditions in the new slums. In 1990 both projects were affected by the influx of returnees. This called for an appropriate response, combined with the need for new policies and administrative arrangements in both projects. However, the achievements of the two projects were very different. While

HUDP failed to improve the living conditions of the new slum dwellers, HUPHC addressed the problems of the new poor with relative success.[1]

In this chapter, a brief account of Hodeidah's history and a description of the two projects will be followed by an explanation and analysis of the different developments in both projects and the reasons behind these differences. The intention is to show that although the influx of returnees hampered the development of the city, it was not the main reason why certain social policies met with failure.

A short history of the city

Contacts between Yemen and other countries (African as well as Asian) date back many centuries and, as a typical port city, Hodeidah has a very diverse population. Forty years ago the city was a small town with an old Turkish quarter – a reminder of the days when the Ottomans had attempted to make it an efficient port. Because of recurrent wars, Hodeidah had never previously been able to develop, and only after the September 1962 revolution did the city began to grow. The opening up of the Yemen Arab Republic in 1970 attracted many foreign companies to the country. Moreover, the first years of the new Republic coincided with the oil boom in Saudi Arabia and the Gulf States, and many Yemenis migrated to work abroad. Remittances became the main source of income for the state, as well as for many (rural) families. As a result of the availability of foreign currency the import sector grew enormously, and Hodeidah, which developed as North Yemen's main port, even became a major international port.

Because of the growing importance of the city during the 1970s the government paid much attention to developing the city's infrastructure. Water and sewerage systems were installed, main roads were surfaced, and schools were built. These activities were financed by the government or financially supported by other Arab countries. People from various other Yemeni towns (e.g. Ta'izz and Aden) settled in the city in order to benefit from the improved facilities.[2] Many of them were merchants and educated people who found work in trade and industry. The government sold land to anyone who was interested in buying, and a commercial area (*hayy al-tijari*) was developed close to the port. The increased job opportunities as well as the improved facilities also attracted many rural migrants, mainly from the Tihama region, where deprivation in the villages pushed many to leave for Saudi Arabia or for the city of Hodeidah. When the government stopped selling land in the late 1970s, people started to occupy certain areas without permission, thereby creating slum conditions. South of Hodeidah, on the empty land where small villages had been the only settlements, the large slum area called Ghulail came into being, inhabited mainly by rural migrants (see map).

Around the time of the rural migration to Hodeidah, a group of expatriate migrants also came to live in the city. During the 1950s the economic and political situation of North Yemen was unsettled as a result of continuous conflicts between the Imam and revolutionary forces, and many Yemenis left the country at this time. Some went to the US, Vietnam or the Gulf States, but the majority migrated to East African countries (including Ethiopia, Eritrea, Kenya, Tanzania, Chad and Sudan), where they found work and established families, often by marrying an African wife.

In the mid-1970s many of these expatriates decided to return to Yemen, encouraged by the favourable policies of President Al-Hamdi[3] whose promise to returning migrants of a better future included, among other inducements, access to free land, housing and job opportunities. The area of Al-Mughtaribin in the north of Hodeidah was assigned specifically to these returnees,[4] most of whom found employment in the wood wholesale business of Al-'Aswadī and in other companies. Unfortunately the benefits of these policies did not last long, since the area was deprived of any further infrastructural development after Al-Hamdi's murder in 1977. Even today the population of this area still consists mainly of return migrants and *muwallidin* (people of mixed descent, often having a Yemeni father and an African mother).

The squatter area of Ghulail

At the end of the 1970s, many inhabitants of Hodeidah regarded Ghulail as a remote area outside the city, and very few of them had even been there. However, when the government started to condone squatting, increasing numbers of people moved into the area, and migrants from outside the city, as well as individuals who had previously lived in other parts of Hodeidah, started to settle there. A female health worker tells how she came to live in Ghulail:[5]

My mother was born in Al-Zuhrah, a village north of Hodeidah, but she came to Hodeidah when she was a young girl. My father was born in Al-Marawi'ah, south of Hodeidah, although he is originally from Zabid. He moved to Hodeidah when his parents died. When my parents got married they first lived in the inner city and when my oldest sister was born they moved to another house. They were always moving houses. I was born in 1971 in the area of Al-Mitraq, the area close to the *suq*. We moved to Ghulail when 'Alī 'Abdullāh Salih became president. The area was empty at that time and the land belonged to the government. There used to be a village. When we heard that people were occupying land without permission, my parents decided to occupy a piece of land as well. We had problems with our landlord at that time and instead of renting another house they decided to squat. We had never heard of Ghulail before; the area was called al-Khabt[6] at that time. When we heard that people from the city had started to live there, we moved there too.

The fact that Ghulail grew into a slum area can be explained in a number of ways. As a result of the infrastructural improvements carried out in the 1970s, the prices of land and houses in older areas of the city, such as Al-Hali and Al-Duhmiyya, increased as better-off people began to buy houses and land from the poor. The poor then moved to more remote areas where land was cheaper or even free. While most of the land in other cities in Yemen is in private hands, the land in and around Hodeidah is owned by the government, having previously been in the hands of the Imam and then confiscated after the revolution (Wenner, 1991: 81–2). Since most of the plots were not registered they could therefore easily be occupied when the government allowed it. Many people were attracted by this situation, including poor migrants who were in need of land, and the powerful who tried to benefit from the availability of land by selling it to those in need. Ghulail was one of the main areas into which these people moved.

Buringa (1986: 23) estimated that in 1981 the total population of Ghulail stood at 11,846. When a baseline study was carried out by the Hodeidah Urban Primary Health Care project, a population figure of 17,000 was used for the year 1986, based on an average growth percentage of 7.5 per cent. It is clear from this study that more than 75 per cent of the inhabitants of Ghulail originated from the Hodeidah Governorate, including Hodeidah City. The rest came mainly from the Dhamar Governorate (Wusab and Al-Rayma) and from the Sana'a Governorate.

Around 32 per cent had lived in the area for six to ten years, and this correlates with the fact that in 1978 the new government under President 'Ali 'Abdullah Salih condoned squatting. Twenty-eight per cent of the inhabitants had lived in the area from one to five years, and 16 per cent had lived there from 11 to 15 years (Buringa, 1986: 19).

Buringa's baseline study describes living conditions in Ghulail in 1986–7. Although the situation in Ghulail has improved a lot over the last 15 years, as will become clear in the following paragraphs, her description continues to fit the situation prevailing in a number of new slum areas in Hodeidah City. In general, conditions in the slums resemble the way people used to live in their home villages. The compounds are big, surrounded by fences of straw or corrugated iron, and one or two huts of straw or wood are built on each compound. The financial situation of the household determines the material from which the houses are made. Very poor families have only a hut made of straw, but those who are a little better off build a wooden dwelling (called a *sandaqa*).

When the family's financial situation improves, a concrete block wall is built around the compound for security, after which the wooden hut might be replaced by a small room made of stone. The huts and the stone rooms are used mainly for storing personal belongings and for sleeping in at night during the winter. Daily living, however, is carried on outside on the compound, where a number of typical Tihama couches and beds[7] are placed. A corner of the compound is often separated by a piece of corrugated iron for use as a kitchen. Cooking is usually done on kerosene or sometimes on calor-gas stoves. The bathroom consists of a fenced-off part of the compound where a concrete hole in the ground serves as a toilet. Water flows into the ground through a short pipeline, four to six metres long. Most people have a well on their compound and use this water for cleaning.[8] The distance between well and toilet is often minimal and even when the water is used only for cleaning, there is a risk that it is contaminated and will spread contagious diseases. Water for cooking and for drinking is obtained from the nearest public tap or is purchased in jerry cans from delivery trucks. In most cases electricity is not available: kerosene lamps are used for lighting and car batteries are rigged up for watching television. As there is no regular rubbish collection in the slums, mountains of refuse accumulate, in which animals scavenge for something edible.

The poor living conditions in Ghulail came to the attention of several donor organisations in the early 1980s. The Hodeidah Urban Development Project (HUDP) and the Hodeidah Urban Primary Health Care project (HUPHC), both of which were carried out in close cooperation with Yemeni ministries, were independently identified for support and started their activities in 1985.

The Hodeidah Urban Development Project (HUDP)[9]

In the early 1980s the World Bank decided to make Ghulail a pilot area for urban development. In order to improve the living conditions of the inhabitants of slum areas throughout the whole country the World Bank had proposed a national urban development project (UDP), based on initial studies that had identified the needs and objectives of urban sector development in the Yemen Arab Republic. The UDP was designed to be the first in a series of urban development activities that would receive continuing support from the World Bank (Yemen Ministry of Municipalities and Housing, 1981: 1). Two pilot areas were chosen for upgrading and were officially handed over by the Yemeni cabinet to the Ministry of Municipalities and Housing: one was the slum area of Al-Musaik in the north of Sana'a, and the other was the slum area of Ghulail in Hodeidah. In addition, a site and services project was planned in the area of Sawad Sa'wan, also in the Al-Musaik area of Sana'a (Yemen Arab Republic, Ministry of Municipalities and Housing, 1981: 1). Other urban areas were to be upgraded on the basis of the results of these projects.

Following a feasibility study made in 1982, the actual implementation of the Hodeidah Urban Development Project began in Ghulail in 1985. The aim was to secure people's housing by giving them legal access to land, and as such to encourage people to improve their living situation themselves. Initially the total area of Ghulail (250 hectares) was to be handed over to the project, but, based on cost projections, a smaller area of 105 hectares was chosen, some 65 hectares of which were populated while around 40 hectares remained vacant. The inhabited parts of the area were to be upgraded, and the vacant parts would be assigned to people whose houses had been sacrificed to the construction of new streets, as well as being opened up for the provision of public services such as schools, clinics, gardens, police stations, etc. In addition, a further

1,500 empty plots were intended for employees with limited incomes. Around 2,240 households would benefit from the project.

The management and implementation of the project were entirely in Yemeni hands, with regular advice and supervision from the World Bank. The World Bank also covered the implementation costs of the project, but the running costs of the basic facilities were to be paid by the community via a cost-recovery system.[10] Following the initial period of the project[11] the Ministry of Municipalities and Housing would become responsible for financing its extension. Initially the idea was to extend the project to other poor parts of the city through the selling of vacant plots of land in Ghulail to salaried workers who would pay a monthly mortgage. With this money, activities could be started in a second area, the part of Ghulail that had been put at the ministry's disposal but not yet included in the project. The areas of Al-Rabasa, Al-Sana'i and Al-Zaid were planned as future project areas (see map).

The first period of the HUDP was fairly successful. The area was upgraded by opening up the roads to facilitate traffic flows, thereby improving mobility and trade between the city and the slum. The area was mapped, in order to divide the land equitably, and new roads were planned. Main roads were paved, and the project provided for basic facilities such as a water supply, sanitation, electricity and street lighting.

In some cases, however, the costs of the new services were too high for the poor, who were tempted to sell their plots to richer people. Initially the project was able to prevent this with explicit rules forbidding the sale of land, but in the long run this situation could not be controlled and, as will be explained below, this led to the failure of the HUDP.

The Hodeidah Urban Primary Health Care project (HUPHC)[12]

As a result of the poor living conditions in Ghulail, severe health problems were encountered, particularly among mothers and children. A high infant and child mortality rate (around 130/1,000 in 1986) and a high prevalence of infant malnutrition were the main reasons behind the primary health care project set up by the Dutch government in conjunction with the Yemeni Ministry of Public Health. Primary health care (PHC) has been part of national health policy since 1977, but concrete PHC activities started only with the setting up of a national primary health care project in 1981, in cooperation with WHO and

UNICEF. This focused on rural areas and aimed at supplying the entire rural population with appropriate health services by the year 2000 (Stephen, 1992: 208). Urban PHC services were not included in the project, since medical staff and facilities are often overrepresented in urban areas (Hodeidah Health Improvement and Waste Disposal Project, 1986: 41).

During the mid-1980s it became clear that PHC services were also needed in urban areas. On the one hand, not all inhabitants of urban areas have equal access to health services in the city. Poor people often have no money to visit health clinics and hospitals, even when services are given free of charge, and the costs of transportation and drugs are even more significant in preventing them from attending clinics (de Regt and Exterkate, 1996). On the other hand, most urban health services are curative-oriented and as such do not solve the immediate problems of the urban poor, for whom preventive mother and child health (MCH) services, health education, clean drinking water, sanitation, and the availability of food are basic needs. Curative services do not address such needs.

Although the Yemeni government had not planned any urban PHC units, the Dutch government initiated the first urban PHC project in Yemen, based in the city of Hodeidah. The project was centred initially on the slum area of Ghulail. According to results achieved there, the intention was to extend the scheme to the poor area of Al-Mughtaribin, the area occupied mainly by *muwallidin* (people of mixed descent, often having a Yemeni father and an African mother), and gradually to expand to other parts of the city.

Health care activities started in Ghulail in 1985 when the governmental health centre in the area, which had until then offered only curative services, was assigned to the project. Following a year of training, a number of female primary health care workers (*murshidat*; sing. *murshida*) were employed in the centre. Even though there was a serious lack of female health staff (such as nurses and midwives) in the cities, no *murshidat* had ever previously been trained in an urban area, one of the main reasons being the low level of female education in Yemen. Thus the training as a *murshida* offered women with a primary school certificate an opportunity to continue their studies and to obtain a job.

In the following years a primary health care system was developed that focused particularly on mother and child health care (MCH), and the Ghulail health centre started to offer MCH services, such as the weighing and vaccination of children, pre- and post-natal care, family planning, and health education. Simple curative services were available for the treatment of minor common diseases. A major part of the work of the *murshidat* involved making home visits in the area, getting to know mothers and their children, and educating them in their houses. A special health information system was designed for the follow-up of families at particular risk, such as malnourished children and young mothers.[13] In order to improve the position of women, literacy and sewing classes were started in cooperation with the Yemeni Women's Union. Management of the project was undertaken by a Yemeni and a Dutch co-director, and the team included two Dutch expatriates.[14]

The primary health care approach in Ghulail seemed to have fruitful results since coverage rates, for example of child vaccinations, clearly increased. People reacted positively to the home visits of the *murshidat*, and showed willingness to visit the health centre for needed services (Hodeidah Health Improvement and Waste Disposal Project, 1986: 47). Inhabitants of other areas as well as those from Ghulail itself visited the health centre. The presence of the Urban Development Project also helped to improve the impact of the health care activities. The fact that housing was legally secured and that basic facilities, such as clean water and sanitation, were supplied through the UDP made people receptive to (preventive) health messages. The two projects worked closely together, for example in the mapping of the area, and the UDP benefited from the work of the *murshidat* as extension agents.

The impact of both projects encouraged other slum dwellers to request the same kind of improvements. A second training course for *murshidat* was organised in 1988, and in 1989 a second health centre on the other side of the city, in the area of Al-Mughtaribin, was included in the Hodeidah Urban Primary Health Care project. In 1990 some 80 to 90 per cent of the MCH needs in the two areas were covered by the project and the two health centres were visited by many people from other areas (cf. Hodeidah Health Office, 1993: 4).

The arrival of the returnees in 1990

The year 1990 is important in the history of Yemen. The reunification of North and South Yemen on 22 May 1990 came as a surprise, but was enthusiastically received by most Yemenis as well as by the international community. However, the newly formed state had to deal with serious economic and political problems at both national and international level. The main international problem was Iraq's invasion of Kuwait in August 1990, a few months after unification. The position taken by Yemen in the Gulf crisis, condemning the invasion but requesting an Arab solution to the problem, resulted in almost a million Yemenis being forced to leave Saudi Arabia, the Saudi government having suddenly changed its policy towards Yemeni guest workers. Only those workers who had a Saudi *kafil* (sponsor) were allowed to stay.

Most of the migrants returned home to Yemen via Hodeidah, the nearest city beyond the Saudi border. Those with relatives in other parts of Yemen, especially single men, went back to their birthplaces and were rapidly reintegrated into society (UNICEF, 1993: 37). However, those who had been away for a long time and many who had been born in Saudi Arabia and had never been in Yemen at all settled in camps around the main cities (Sana'a, Ta'izz, Ibb and Hodeidah). Having lived for years in urban environments, they were unwilling to return to the countryside, where there was no work for them (Stevenson, 1993: 17).

Hodeidah went through rapid changes after the outbreak of the Gulf crisis, and by 1990–1 the population of the city had grown by approximately a third to 300,000 inhabitants (Nientied and Öry, 1991: 1). While the camps in other cities gradually disappeared, those of Hodeidah have endured, and large squatter settlements have developed on the outskirts of town (e.g. Al-Salakhana, Al-Rabasa, Al-Baydha). A female health worker tells how she came to live in a new slum:

> My father comes from a village in the Tihama but he moved with his family to Saudi Arabia when he was still young. He got married to my mother who was from a Saudi family. At that time it was quite normal for Yemeni men to get married to Saudi women. I was born in Jeddah in 1970. I finished my primary school but I left school when I got married. I was 15 years old. My husband was born in Saudi Arabia but his family comes from a village in the north of the Tihama. He worked and I stayed home with the children. When the problems started in August 1990 my husband decided to leave. My parents could stay because they have Saudi nationality, and we could also have stayed because one of my relatives could have been our *kafil*. But my husband wanted to go to Yemen although neither of us had ever been there. We arrived in

Hodeidah and we rented an apartment in Al-Mitraq area, in the inner city. But when we heard that people were occupying land in Al-Salakhana, on the northern outskirts of town, we decided to move there as well. Because we were among the last migrants who moved there we only found a bad piece of land close to the main road.

The low standard of living in the new squatter areas called for significant (government) intervention. During the first six months following the arrival of the returnees, food and water were distributed through the Emergency Recovery Project, a national programme designed to improve their situation, and financed largely by foreign donors. Public water taps were installed, and two new health centres were built, also with donor support. The government made many other promises but little materialised from these (Stevenson, 1993: 17). However, although the HUPHC project was able in 1993 to extend its activities to all governmental health centres in the city, and as such contributed to a better health status of the slum dwellers, the HUDP did not succeed in extending its services. The reasons for the failure of the HUDP and the relative success of the HUPHC are discussed below.

Conflicts of interest in the housing sector

At the time the Hodeidah Urban Development Project started it was agreed that the improvements in the Ghulail area were meant for poor people living there as squatters. Since it could be foreseen that poor people would be tempted to sell their land to richer people interested in the improved facilities, a precondition of the project was that people were not permitted to sell their plots to other people (Nientied and Öry, 1991: 10). The Ministry of Municipalities and Housing endorsed this view.

However, it became clear from an impact study of the activities of the health care project, carried out by an external research team in 1990 (Abdulghani et al., 1991), that the population of Ghulail had changed rapidly. In 1986 only 9 per cent of the population had settled in the area during the previous 12 months, but this percentage had increased to 20 per cent for the UDP area and 37 per cent for the non-UDP area in 1990. Ghulail's population had increased from 18,000 in 1986 to 25,000 in 1991 (Abdulghani et al., 1991: 13).

Not only had more people settled in the area, but the composition of the population had also changed. The UDP had successfully improved living conditions in Ghulail, but despite its stated policy the project was not able to prevent the purchase and sale of land. Merchants and land brokers started to purchase the plots and the houses of the poor and to occupy empty land in the project area. In some cases they wanted to build houses for themselves, and in other cases they were only interested in making money out of buying and selling. In the latter case, poor people were hired to occupy large plots of land by claiming that they were in need of a dwelling place. They would settle on these lands for a certain period and then move, for the benefit of the people who had hired them. The main problem was that this happened openly and was condoned by the government: senior government officials obviously had their own interests in this strategy. Enforceable laws that could have prevented these practices were lacking, because those in power often benefited from the situation.

One of the reasons why poor people preferred to sell their houses was that they could not afford the costs of the new services (Abdulghani *et al.*, 1991: 27). Most of those who sold their plots moved from Ghulail to the adjacent area of Al-Rabasa, another slum area south of Hodeidah. Preparations had already been made for the UDP's second project area (i.e. the remaining 145 hectares) but it was impossible for project staff to prevent these changes from happening. Several people claimed ownership of the land, and this obstructed implementation of the second phase. The area developed under its own momentum, but to the benefit of the rich instead of the poor.

The housing situation in Hodeidah deteriorated even more with the arrival of thousands of returnees from Saudi Arabia. These people were in need of land and were willing to buy land from anyone. Most came back from Saudi Arabia with their savings and all their belongings, and initially had money to spend, although they became increasingly impoverished with time. The UDP system in Ghulail could no longer be controlled when richer people, including many of the returnees, started to buy land and to build. Land tenure became a fertile black market among individual citizens and the official authorities (Qassim, 1994: 15).[15] Land was being occupied everywhere, not only for housing but also for the building of workshops, factories and the like. There were no policies or guidelines to be followed for overseeing the integration of the returnees into the city (Nientied and Öry, 1991: 7–9). The government had hoped that the returnees would stay only temporarily and that the settlements would gradually disappear, as had been the case in other cities.

Structural development of the areas began only in 1994, with the slums still in existence. Roads were opened and the land was secured. Financed by Dutch development aid, the drinking water system was extended to the new slum areas. In addition, money from the Emergency Recovery Project was used to set up a site and services project in the east of Hodeidah, next to Al-Salakhana and Al-Sana'i. Initially this project was intended for returnees, but later on applied to anyone who was able to pay the project's required monthly service costs (Nientied and Öry, 1991: 10). As a result, not many poor people benefited from this new urban development project either. Planning of the areas had started suddenly and far too late. Many houses were demolished and their inhabitants were moved to unsuitable places.

A common interest in primary health care (PHC)

While problems in land tenure and housing led to an uncontrolled situation, different developments occurred in health care. The influx of an estimated number of 60,000 returnees[16] who had settled mainly in the squatter areas and who were in great need of good health services, attracted many donors. Oxfam built a health centre in Al-Salakhana, ICD (International Cooperation for Development)[17] supported a health clinic in Al-Rabasa, and USAID, Oxfam, ICD and HUPHC financed courses for *murshidat*. The lack of coordination among the many donor organisations working in the same field led to the realisation that it would be more fruitful to work together in conducting these activities. In May 1993 the Ministry of Public Health decided, in conjunction with all donors involved, to bring urban PHC activities together under the umbrella of the HUPHC. The PHC system developed in Ghulail and Al-Mughtaribin would be implemented in all 13 governmental health centres in the city of Hodeidah.

Although the HUPHC had initially aimed to extend its activities gradually, first to the poor areas on the outskirts of town and possibly to the rest of town later on, it decided that it was better to include all health centres in its programme straight away. This was to prevent the uncontrolled growth of activities.

With the extension of the project to all governmental health centres the HUPHC became an integral part of the Ministry of Public Health. A special department for urban primary health care was created in the Hodeidah Health Office.[18] The Yemeni co-director of the HUPHC became head of this department and the Dutch (and later British) co-director became his adviser. The urban PHC department came under the authority of the Director General, who thus got a bigger say in the implementation of project activities. Links with other departments of the Hodeidah Health Office became closer, which was seen as important for the sustainability of these activities.

Murshidat who were trained in Ghulail and al-Mughtaribin were dispersed throughout the health centres in town and some were appointed as heads of clinics. The new areas were mapped, family cards were distributed to all families via home visits, and health centres that lacked the requirements of a primary health care centre were upgraded. All these extra activities were paid for by Dutch development aid, while the Yemeni Ministry of Public Health paid (most of) the salaries and the costs of electricity, water and telephones. The ministry's limited budget was insufficient to continue the same level of care that the health centres had achieved. This heavy reliance on foreign assistance was the main reason why the national ministry was working towards cost recovery in the form of small fees for services. After several studies and discussions, cost recovery started in Hodeidah in 1995.

In order to involve the local community in managing the recovered money, local health committees were formed at each health centre and given the task of deciding how this money was to be used. It was needed primarily for the running costs of the health centre, such as the purchase of consumables and cleaning materials and the costs of maintenance and repairs, but it was also intended for community activities such as garbage disposal programmes. Although they are part of the current national health policy, local health committees are established only infrequently, and if they are formed at all, have tended to consist mainly of high-ranking officials and health staff. They are therefore often unrepresentative of the communities who use the services. In Hodeidah, however, 13 local health committees were formed as the result of an intensive process of group discussions and of home visits by *murshidat* aimed at identifying and selecting well-known community individuals, both male and female.

Community participation programmes have often been criticised for assuming that communities are homogeneous entities and consequently for neglecting the differences within communities. They pretend to defend the interests of communities while community members may have very different and conflicting interests (see, for example, the contributions in Guijt, 1999). In Hodeidah the heterogeneity of the communities was taken into account in the selection of community representatives. The five members of the local health committee had as far as possible to reflect the composition of the community: women and men, educated and uneducated, young and old, rich and poor. In areas with a high percentage of returnees, most of the members would be returnees; in old areas of the city centre, the length of time that individuals had been living there was a more important criterion.

The selection of local health committees in Hodeidah took almost 10 months and resulted in 13 committees all over the city, each consisting of 4 or 5 community members. More than a third of the total of 63 community members were female: most of them were teachers, students or housewives, but there were also a few traditional birth attendants and seamstresses on the committee. In most cases the men were government employees or teachers, but students and shopkeepers were also included.[19]

After the start of the cost-recovery system in September 1995, the committees met monthly to discuss the spending of the money, as well as to initiate various community activities such as rubbish disposal. Although local authorities or other political powers were expected to claim part of the recovered money in order to decide upon its use, this did not happen during the time that the project was still supported by foreign donors. Both national and local officials in the Ministry of Public Health supported the HUPHC's cost-recovery and community participation programme. Where the planning, implementation and utilisation of health activities in Yemen had previously been the exclusive preserve of the government, a real dialogue was established between the state and local communities, and the latter even had a say in the financial management of health care.

However, since September 1999 foreign donor support (both technical and financial) to the primary health care activities in urban Hodeidah has come to an end, and a number of changes have taken place. Although the local health committees do still exist, their power has gradually declined to approving requests put forward by the head of the health centre while being unable to choose what they would like to do with the money. The income from the cost-recovery programme goes directly to the financial department of the Hodeidah Health Office, which decides how the money will be used. Community participation has gradually become synonymous with cost recovery: the community participates by paying fees for services and by purchasing medicines, which both used to be free of charge, without having a real say in how their contributions are spent. Participation is reduced to making financial contributions, and has thus lost its democratic dimension.

The changes that have taken place in Hodeidah are remarkable in view of the new health sector reform policies that were launched in 1998 (Republic of Yemen, Ministry of Public Health, 1998) and which maintained that community participation and cost recovery were central elements of the national policy. Furthermore, giving significant management roles to community members was regarded as necessary to ensure the responsiveness of the health system to the needs of the population, to secure transparency of financial dealings, and to enable the health system to pull in additional resources (Ministry of Public Health, 1998: 24). However, bringing these objectives into practice has proved to be a difficult process.

Conclusions

This chapter has described two development projects in the fields of housing and health care in order to analyse the successes and failures of certain social policies in Hodeidah. The lack of a good housing policy in the 1980s had consequences for the development of the city during the 1990s. The private interests of government officials and other people in power resulted in a fertile black market for land and houses, which in turn hampered the implementation of activities that were aimed at securing land for the poor. The influx from Saudi Arabia and the Gulf States of returnees who were in need of land reinforced the ongoing process of the sale and purchase of land, but was not the real reason for a failing housing policy. The fact that there was no housing policy or that the existing policy was not controlled is the main reason why urban development in Hodeidah got out of hand. However, the situation began to improve from 1994, and a start was made on infrastructural development in the new slum areas.

The health care situation in Hodeidah, on the other hand, shows a different picture. The influx of thousands of returnees in 1990 also put enormous pressure on the Ministry of Public Health, and implementation of existing health policies was not easy as the situation demanded a great deal of attention. In 1993 the HUPHC project extended its activities to the rest of the city and became the umbrella organisation for all urban PHC activities. This in itself was a positive result of the Gulf crisis. A cost-recovery and community participation programme was put into practice, and until recently there was no inappropriate use of power and money by the authorities.

In order to explain the HUDP's failing housing policy and the HUPHC's successful health policy, it is necessary to look at the different relationships in the two projects between the government, donor organisations, and community members. Both projects were planned and implemented by the Yemeni government and a foreign donor. The World Bank was the foreign donor for the HUDP, while the activities of the HUPHC were initiated and funded by the Dutch government. However, management of the HUDP was completely in Yemeni hands. The Ministry of Municipalities and Housing was authorised to implement and manage the project, and to take financial responsibility, and all the project employees were Yemeni. In the HUPHC management was in the hands of two co-directors, one a European[20] and the other a Yemeni who was also an employee of the Ministry of Public Health. Two other Dutch team members were involved in implementing the project. The fact that the donor was represented at field level could be one of the reasons for the HUPHC's success in extending its services. Through such an arrangement, the donor can forestall any misuse of power as well as misuse of funds and can also initiate activities. On the other hand, this can also hamper sustainability since it creates a dependency relationship in which people do not learn to rely on themselves. Expatriate involvement in the HUPHC gradually disappeared, and from 1999 onwards the ministry became fully responsible for the project activities.[21]

A second and very different relationship in both projects was that between the project and community members. In the HUPHC community members were involved from the outset, first via the *murshidat* who were part of the target group and secondly through local health committees which gained authority over the spending of the cost-recovery money. Although the donor organisation initiated the training of *murshidat* and the forming of local health committees, both these steps were taken seriously by the national Ministry of Public Health and were included in the new health sector reform policy. In the HUDP, community members were never formally involved. In the short term, community members and the authorities benefited from the uncontrolled situation, since both were able to buy and sell land. However, in the long term, the interests of community members were harmed because the recipients did not benefit from the new services and their housing conditions remained the same. One solution might have been to register land tenureship via a committee consisting, among others, of representatives from the Ministry of Municipality and Housing and from within the community. This committee might even have been able to prevent the sale and purchase of land. The new housing policy mentions 'a more action-oriented planning system which facilitates public participation' (Republic of Yemen Ministry of Housing and Urban Planning, 1997), but clear community participation guidelines are still lacking.

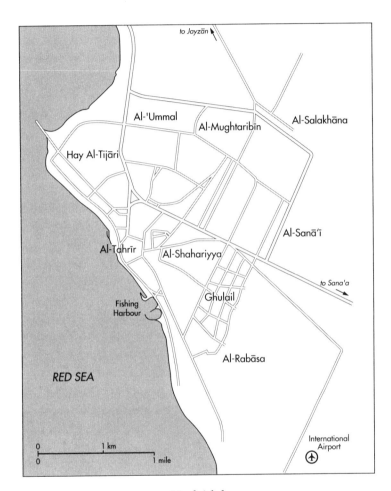

to Jayzān

Al-'Ummal

Al-Mughtaribīn

Al-Salakhāna

Hay Al-Tijāri

Al-Sanā'ī

Al-Tahrīr

Al-Shahariyya

to Sana'a

Ghulail

Fishing
Harbour

Al-Rabāsa

RED SEA

0   1 km
0   1 mile

International
Airport

Hodeidah

NOTES

1 The 'new poor' were identified in a Standards of Living survey carried out among the inhabitants of Hodeidah City by an independent team of researchers in 1993, on request of the Dutch Ministry of Development Cooperation. As it was observed that income was a rather weak indicator to study poverty, due to its variability and reliability, an alternative multidimensional approach was used. Twenty selected variables – among others, household size and composition, type of dwelling unit, availability of water and electricity, educational standard of household members, fertility rates, infant and child mortality rates, health care experiences, main sources of income, approximate income and expenditures – were used. Four relatively homogeneous groups of households were identified: the established poor, the new poor, the middle class and the upper class. The established poor are characterised by relatively small households, often incomplete (female-headed households, one-person households), living in simple dwelling units built of stone or blocks. This group can be found all over the city and has lived on average 11 years or more in the same place. The new poor consist mainly of squatters, living in huts, tents or shacks on the outskirts of the city, with an average duration of residence of four and a half years (in 1993). The annual household income of the new poor was relatively high, and their poverty status is mainly based on their residential characteristics (Jongstra, 1996: 164). The middle class is geographically spread throughout most of the neighbourhoods, and lives in houses built of blocks or in apartments with piped water, public electricity and sewerage. Household sizes are average, as are income and expenditures. Fertility rates are remarkably high among the middle class. The upper class is concentrated in two areas of the city, occupies houses of good quality with water, electricity and sewerage, and possesses various household assets that are indicative of wealth. Household expenditures and incomes are significantly higher than those in the other groups.

2 By 1967, when the People's Democratic Republic of Yemen was established in former South Yemen, a number of people originally from Aden had already moved to Hodeidah where they foresaw better trading possibilities than under the new socialist regime.

3 President Al-Hamdi governed the Yemen Arab Republic from 1974 to 1977. He became famous for his fight against corruption, his promotion of economic development and for the centralisation of political control. He was assassinated in October 1997, and was succeeded by Colonel Ahmad Al-Ghashmi.

4 The term *mughtaribin* means literally those who live away from home, or emigrants. The term is used for people with a Yemeni background who have lived for a considerable period abroad and who have eventually come back to Yemen. Originally it was the returnees from East African countries who were called *mughtaribin*. However, after the Gulf crisis the term started to be applied to returnees from Saudi Arabia and the Gulf States, although they themselves prefer to be called *'a'idin* (which literally means returnees) because this emphasises that Yemen is their home country.

5 This information is based on interviews conducted by Marina de Regt as part of her PhD research on female primary health care workers (*murshidat*) trained and employed in Hodeidah in the period 1985–2000 (de Regt, 2003).

6 *Al-khabt* literally means the desert or 'the badlands' (Stone 1985: 13).

7 A typical Tihāmah couch (*qa'adah*) and bed (*sarir*) consist of a wooden frame and a hemp-strung seat.

8 The wells are around 20 metres deep, dug into the ground and surrounded by car tyres or concrete rings. The saltiness of the well-water normally prevents people from drinking it but if no other water is available people will do so, even though this can cause them severe health problems.

9 The information about HUDP is based mainly on the experiences of Ali M. Ghailan who worked as an engineer on the project from 1986 till 1994.

10 The allocated budget for this project was YR22 million (in 1985 the rate was 1 US dollar = 5 Yemeni riyals).

11 The first project phase was planned for the period from 1984 till 1989.

12 Most of the information on HUPHC is based on the experiences of Marina de Regt who worked as an anthropologist on the project from 1993 till 1998.

13 Mothers under 16 years of age were considered young mothers.

14 The Dutch expatriates who worked in the HUPHC were a public health nurse and a midwife (in the period 1984–93), and a public health nurse and an anthropologist (in the period 1993–8).

15 As Qasim notes, the central government declared that the land to which new settlers moved was government property and prohibited its sale and purchase. However, this declaration aggravated the situation and created even more confusion and disorder.

16 Exact data on the total number of returnees who settled in Hodeidah are not available since no registration took place at the time of the crisis.

17 ICD used to be known in Yemen as the British Organization for Community Development (BOCD), but it changed its name in 1992.

18 The Hodeidah Health Office is the governmental branch office of the Ministry of Public Health.

19 For a more detailed description of the selection process of local health committee members, see de Regt, 1997: 124–38.

20 The first two team leaders of the project were Dutch; the third was British.

21 For details on the state of affairs after the end of Dutch funding, see de Regt (2003).

18

The Education Sector in Yemen:
Challenges and Policy Options

---

*Mutahar A. Al-Abbasi**

Introduction

Yemen needs to build a sound education and training system able to face the double challenge of globalisation and information technology, and to deliver a relevant education to the country's students.

Yemen's constitution guarantees all Yemeni citizens the right of education, and the government's commitment to education is reflected in its spending on the education sector as a proportion of public expenditure and GDP. In 1997 education expenditure was 16 per cent of total government spending and accounted for 5.3 per cent of GDP (CSO, 1998). Despite the high priority given to education, the sector faces many challenges including: (1) high population growth rates and consequently the increasing school-age population; (2) the low quality and coverage of education; and (3) financial unsustainability.

This chapter analyses and assesses the challenges facing the education system in Yemen, and in particular the many constraints on education finance that have resulted from the ongoing economic reforms and government restructuring. It also examines certain education indicators, such as enrolments and dropouts, at the national level, and suggests improvements to the system.

Socioeconomic conditions

Population patterns

Yemen's population pattern has changed drastically over the recent period, and according to the 1994 population census, the country had around 16 million inhabitants. Rapid population growth combined

---

* Associate Professor, Department of Economics, Sana'a University, Yemen.

with stagnant growth in the economy will lead to a rapid increase in demand for food and in the need for job opportunities. Based on the continued high fertility rate (about 7.7 children per woman), the population will continue to grow, and will have doubled by the year 2013 (base year 1994).

The age group 0–14 represents more than half of the population (around 50.3 per cent), and the age structure of the population is unlikely to change substantially over the next decade. The burden of educating this age group will therefore be a major challenge to Yemeni society. The majority of the population still resides in rural areas, and depends basically upon agricultural activities. In 1994, the rural population was estimated to be 77 per cent of the national total. However, the urban population (23 per cent of the total) is expected to grow faster than the rural population, because of opportunities for higher-paid jobs outside the agricultural sector and the availability of services in the cities (UNDP, 1997b).

The labour market

The labour market in Yemen is characterised by a surplus of unskilled and semi-skilled workers, and by a shortage of qualified personnel with professional and technical skills. The return in 1990 of more than 800,000 migrants from the Gulf States during the Gulf crisis was a major shock for the labour market, the structure of which was severely affected by the flow of returnees. Because of this increasing supply of labour with limited opportunities for work, real wages as well as overall standards of living were declining.

Official statistics show that the population of 10 years old and over involved in economic activities is 3.3 million, around 22 per cent of the total population (CSO, 1998). Fifty-three per cent of this working population is employed in agriculture and fishing, 16 per cent in the public sector including defence and education, 15 per cent in trade and other services, 6 per cent in construction, and 4 per cent in industry. Such a distribution accounts for the limited productivity of workers and the resulting low income and welfare levels.

The effectiveness of a labour force in the development process can be measured by the level of knowledge, professional expertise and technical skills acquired at schools, vocational centres and universities. For Yemen, labour force data reveal the lack of training and education for the population over 10 years old. Illiteracy is the dominant phenomenon in all the age groups, and has a negative effect on the productivity levels of workers in the economy. Data from the 1994 census indicated that male residents aged 10 years and above could be categorised according to education status as follows: 37 per cent were illiterate (unable to read and write), 37 per cent were literate, and 18 per cent had obtained basic education. Six per cent had secondary education and fewer than 2 per cent were university graduates. For females, the situation was much worse than for males: illiteracy among women was 76 per cent while only 16 per cent were literate.

The government is the largest employer of university graduates, whose qualifications and performance are not, however, properly assessed or challenged since monitoring and evaluation systems are lacking or absent. Official data show that there were more than 400,000 civil servants (excluding military personnel), of whom 75 per cent had educational training that ranged from primary school to postgraduate programmes. Data disaggregated by gender are not properly documented, but it is estimated that the female share of the civil labour force was approximately 15 per cent (CSO, 1998).

FIGURE 18.1
Percentage distribution of population (10 years and above) by educational status

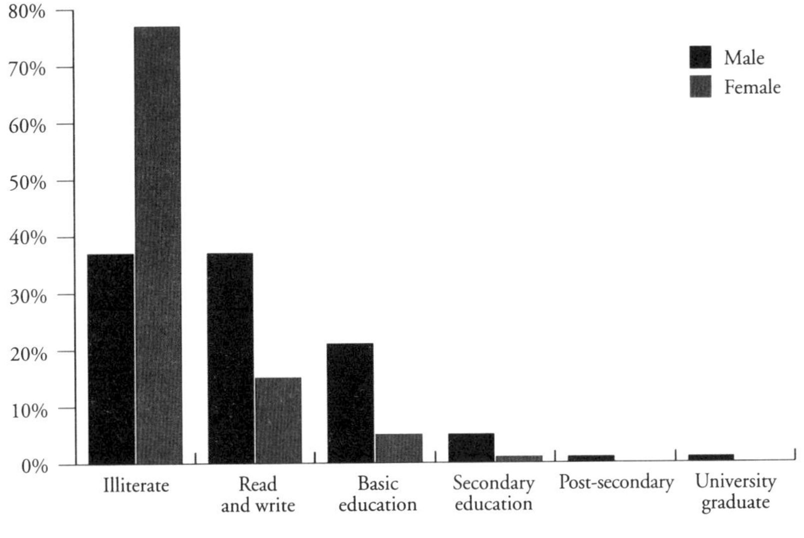

Source: Central Statistical Organisation, 1996.

The government is currently unable to employ additional university graduates, due to the low absorptive capacity of official institutions and to the clear recognition of the need for a major reform of both public administration and the civil services. Such reform might well include freezing overall gross recruitment into government employment, removing ghost employees from the payroll, and enforcing the retirement laws (World Bank, 1995a).

Moreover, the official projection for government labour force requirements till the end of the 1990s already showed that government needs for graduates from universities, vocational and technical institutes at home and abroad was falling short of the expected supply. It was projected that for the year 1997 the government would require only 10 per cent of the expected graduates from faculties of agriculture, humanities and law. Around 50 per cent of the available supply of business graduates would be needed. On the other hand the projection showed that the supply of teachers in basic and secondary schools would fall short of demand by about 10 per cent (Al-Abbasi, 1997).

The role of educational institutions

Yemen's education system should play a vital role in correcting distortions in the labour market. However, concern is growing, especially in the business community, about the qualifications of graduates from public schools and universities and their ability to perform their duties to the level of expectations. Some private enterprises, for example, are particularly concerned about two essential skills – fluency in English, and computer literacy – which are not available in general public schools or public universities.

Educational planning has not been well matched with the planning of manpower needs, due to the lack of communication and coordination between the relevant institutions in the public sector on the one hand, and between them and the private sector on the other. In addition, statistics and forecasts of supply from the educational institutions as well as the necessary data about labour market needs are missing.

The education sector: situation and trends

National objectives for education

The government developed national objectives for the education system that were to be achieved as part of the 1996–2000 five-year plan. They aimed to (1) provide education opportunities for all school-age boys and girls; (2) encourage enrolment in vocational and technical education for students aged 15 to 17; (3) promote and support female education, especially in rural areas; (4) increase the number of first-grade pupils by 30 per cent by the year 2000; (5) build 3,551 classrooms for secondary schools; and (6) improve teacher training programmes.

Objectives for higher education were more general and less well defined, but emphasised the need for (1) setting admissions criteria to take account of national development needs and the capacity of the universities; (2) starting the first phase of construction of the universities of Ta'izz, Ibb and Hadhramawt; and (3) for increasing student enrolment in applied sciences by 60 per cent (MPD, 1997a).

Given those objectives, the demand for more resources has obviously increased and will continue to do so over the coming decade, given high population growth rates and a consequent increase in school-age populations, higher enrolment rates for girls in basic and secondary education, and high student enrolment at public universities.

Unfortunately, however, government spending on education is constrained by limited budget resources.

General education

Student enrolment

The Yemeni government regards basic education as obligatory for all school-age children. Enrolment in general education has grown phenomenally over the last 20 years, and over 3.5 million Yemenis were enrolled in pre-university education and training schools in 1996. However, gross enrolment ratios (GER) for basic and secondary education are estimated to be 51 per cent of the population in the 6- to 17-year-old age group, which is considered relatively low even compared to standards in developing countries (CSO, 1998).

Statistics show that with regard to GER there are significant variations between, and considerable gender disparity within, governorates. Aden governorate ranks first with an average GER of 91 per cent, while

Aljawf comes last with a GER of 24 per cent. In general, remote governorates (e.g. Aljawf, Sa'ada, Marib, Hajja) have high numbers of school-age children outside the education system, possibly exceeding 70 per cent (Al-Abbasi and Almutawakel, 1998).

FIGURE 18.2
Gross enrolment ratios by governorates, 1996

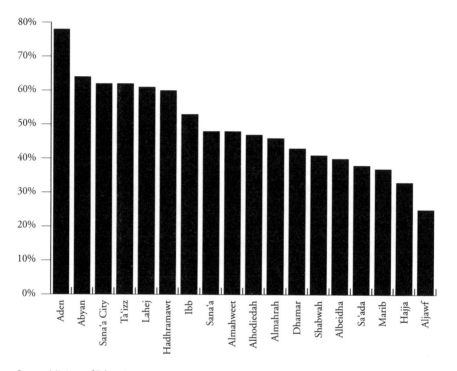

Source: Ministry of Education.

Enrolment in technical education and vocational training is low compared with secondary education. In 1996, enrolment totalled 3,000 students and accounted for only 2 per cent of secondary education. Female enrolment in vocational education was non-existent. From the experience of many developed as well as developing countries it is evident that vocational and technical education plays a central role in reducing pressures on universities, and in meeting growing demands for skilled labour. In the case of RoY, however, vocational education is facing major problems, including limited capacity, low quality and total dependence on the government budget.

Gender disparity
One of the greatest challenges that the government will face in coming years is the education of women. Female enrolment and dropout rates are high, especially in rural areas. Only 39 per cent of girls are enrolled in primary schools compared with 80 per cent of boys, and the disparity is even greater at later educational stages. Only 11 per cent of girls are enrolled in secondary schools, compared with 42 per cent of boys, and in universities only 3 per cent of women are enrolled. The low levels of education and high illiteracy rates make it difficult for women to enter the workforce, especially in urban areas where skilled labour is in greater demand.

The gender gap is due not only to low female enrolment in rural areas, but also to high female dropout rates, particularly after completion of basic education. Data on male and female enrolments across governorates indicate wider gender disparity at secondary education level compared with basic education. The exception is in the governorate of Aden where male–female disparity in basic education is only 9 per cent, and in secondary education a mere 1 per cent, while the overall GERs in both levels are 91 per cent and 41 per cent respectively. The percentage of females outside basic education is reaching alarming levels in most of the governorates.

The government is supporting efforts to encourage more female enrolment in basic and secondary education, but the mechanisms to implement such a policy in rural areas are still not well organised. Consequently, high illiteracy among females will continue to be a critical issue in the future, and this raises questions of equality, coverage and access to education.

FIGURE 18.3
Gross enrolment ratios by gender and level of education, 1995–6

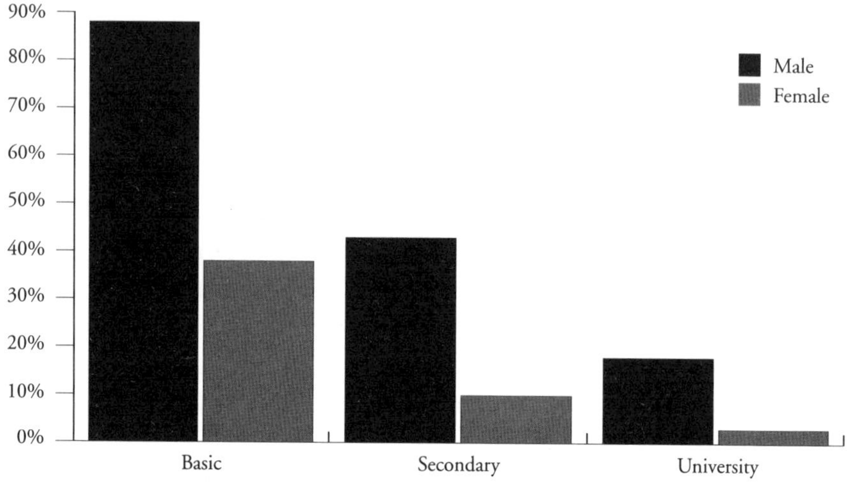

Source: Ministry of Education.

Rural-urban disparity
Although the majority of the population lives in rural areas (77 per cent), over half of all enrolments in general education are urban. As noted above, the overall GER in basic education reached 91 per cent in Aden governorate in the school year 1997, but was only 24 per cent in Aljawf. Furthermore, female enrolment in rural areas is very low relative to that of urban areas. In Aden, for instance, the female enrolment rate in basic education is 86 per cent while in Wusab-Alsafil (Dhammar) it is around 10 per cent (Al-Abbasi and Almutawakel, 1997). Clearly the wide gap between urban and rural enrolment rates requires urgent action to encourage more rural students – particularly female – to enrol in the education system.

Dropout rates
Dropout in education is a major source of wastage. The level can be estimated by tracing trends in educational flows from one grade to another. A UNICEF study (Meharotra and Thet, 1996) shows that Yemen heads the list of Arab countries with the highest rate of primary school children who are unable to complete the grade in which they were originally enrolled.

Dropout rates differ from one governorate to another, and depend on the level of urbanisation and the level of literacy. The fact that fourth-grade dropouts are unlikely to obtain sufficient skills to stay literate indicates that the level of education inefficiency is alarming. By fourth grade, dropout rates range between 10 and 23 per cent. The data also show gender disparity in dropout rates. Most governorates exhibit higher dropout rates among females. The several reasons for this are related more to the educational environment than to cultural traditions or to societal biases against female education. They include a preference for segregated schools, especially when girls reach the age of 15; shortage of female teachers and female administrators; long distances between students' homes and schools, especially in rural areas; and lack of sanitation facilities (toilets).

In general, it is evident that the majority of school-age children remain outside the education system, and this implies that illiteracy will remain a dominant feature for many years to come. The many explanations for this problem include the socioeconomic conditions in which children live, lack of school buildings and facilities, shortage of coeducational schools, and absence of female teachers.

Teaching staff

Employment of teachers is the responsibility of the Education Office in the individual governorates. The expansion of student enrolment matched with numbers of teachers has resulted in a high student–teacher ratio (STR) in basic and secondary education, and the overall ratios were 32 and 21 respectively. However, the student–teacher ratios differ considerably across governorates and between rural and urban areas. For basic education schools, STR reached 45 in Sana'a city, while it was only 14 in Almaharah, the remotest area in the country (CSO, 1998). These numbers could be deceptive when one considers the field of specialisation and the level of training of the teachers, and the distribution of teachers between rural and urban areas.

School buildings and classrooms

One of the major problems in the education sector is deteriorating school buildings. Many existing schools in urban areas and the overwhelming number in rural areas lack the basic requirements of convenient classrooms, water supply, electricity, sanitary facilities, etc.

Student–classroom ratios differ widely across governorates. However, this indicator should be taken cautiously, as the concept of a classroom does not always mean a soundly built room with a roof, a door, windows, student desks, etc. It is sometimes simply a gathering of students grouped in the same grade. This group of students can have their lessons under trees, in a tent or just in the open, which is a very common practice in rural areas.

Higher education

Higher education in Yemen started thirty or so years ago with the establishment of Sana'a and Aden universities. The aims at that time were to help the two states, to foster modernisation, and to provide the highly skilled human resources required to manage public and private institutions all over the country. Since then, the two main Yemeni universities have partially succeeded in absorbing a high proportion of secondary school graduates and in establishing different principal disciplines, but have fallen short in developing relevant curricula to reflect labour market needs, and in improving the educational quality of their outputs.

From the early 1980s, both universities started to establish branches of the College of Education in several of the governorates to meet the country's increasing demand for basic and secondary school teachers. By 1998, there were five more public universities located in the governorates of Ta'izz, Ibb, Hadhramawt, Dhamar and Hodeidah, and there were also twelve Education Colleges, affiliated to Sana'a and Aden universities, which are located in small towns in different regions and rural areas. However, the expansion of universities and colleges all over the country is not matched by an increase in academic staff, libraries, laboratories and other educational facilities. On the contrary, such expansion has continuously led to management inefficiency, financial bottlenecks and deteriorating quality of outputs. At the same time, the public universities are facing many challenges such as financial unsustainability, over-enrolments, low educational quality, and lack of relevance to national development needs (Al-Abbasi, 1997).

University enrolment

The rapid increase in enrolment rates in basic and secondary schools is raising the demand for education at university level because of the absence of attractive post-secondary training programmes, such as community colleges or polytechnic institutions. As a result, university enrolment increased from 114 students in 1970 to more than 140,000 students in 1997. Most of this growth has been in the social sciences and humanities, whereas enrolment in applied sciences accounts for only 9 per cent of the student population. Despite the significant increase in student numbers, female enrolments are still low. For every 100 male university students there are on average only 20 female students in each university, which is less than one fourth of the international figure (CSO, 1998).

FIGURE 18.4
Enrolment at public universities, 1997

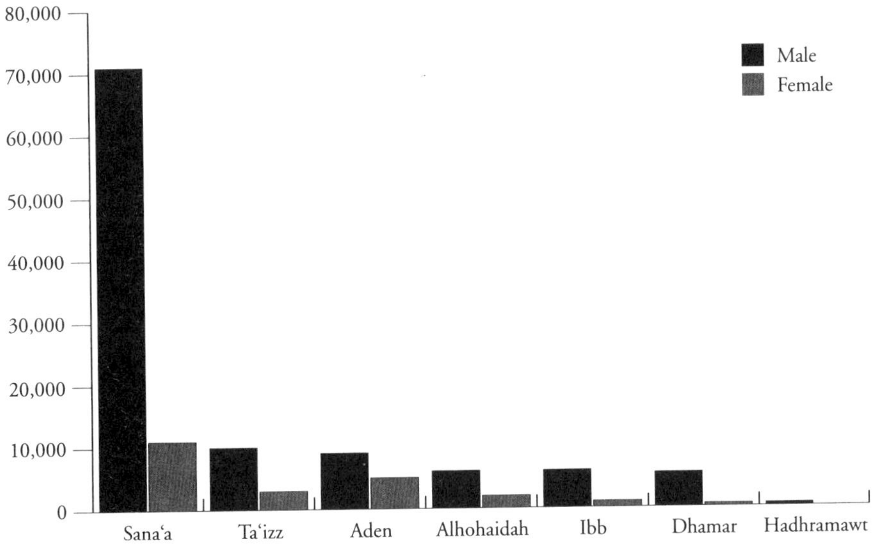

Source: Mottahar, 1998.

Admission to the universities is based on secondary-school-grade averages and on the quota determined by the university council. Most of the public universities have been having difficulties in setting firm criteria and conditions for admission, due to political pressures and to the lack of planning. The annual growth rate of enrolments at public universities is increasing by an average of 20 per cent, and if the annual rate of admission continues to grow as it has done over the past few years, the university population could well double within three to five years. This means that more financial and human resources are going to be needed to manage and educate these masses in the foreseeable future. Generally speaking, firm measures should be taken so that admission to public universities will coincide with the availability of resources and with market needs.

Teaching staff

The traditional dependence of public universities on foreign teaching staff is beginning to decline, due to the implementation of a government programme designed to make university teaching more attractive for Yemenis. However, reliance on a certain number of foreign teaching staff will continue as universities expand into many governorates that lack Yemeni staff trained to meet instructional and research personnel needs. During the past few years the level of female teaching staff has remained as low as 5 per cent.

TABLE 18.1
Staff–student ratios in the public universities, 1996

University	Ratio
Sana'a	1:142
Aden	1:36
Ta'izz	1:119
Hadhramawt	1:31
Dhamar	1:191
Ibb	1:175

Source: Central Statistical Organisation, *Statistical Year Book*, 1998.

Funding for graduate programmes in various disciplines to enable Yemeni staff to study abroad used to be provided by sources such as USAID, IDA and some EU countries, as well as Arab states (e.g. Egypt). This funding ceased in 1990, and such programmes are now funded by the Yemen government in less expensive countries such as Iraq, Sudan, India and Egypt (Al-Abbasi, 1997). Additionally, Sana'a and Aden universities now provide masters and doctoral programmes in human sciences and in a few other disciplines related to university teaching.

Faculty retention is a major problem for Yemen's universities. University teaching is not attractive to many Yemenis because of the low salaries, which contrast sharply with those of foreign faculty members. Monthly salaries of non-Yemeni staff are approximately US$1,800 for professors, US$1,600 for associate professors, and US$1,400 for assistant professors. Non-Yemeni staff also receive a full housing allowance. For Yemeni staff, monthly salaries are US$400 for professors, US$338 for associate professors, and US$266 for assistant professors. Combined with the lack of facilities and equipment, this disparity makes opportunities in the private sector more rewarding. Most Yemeni staff have at least one additional job in order to supplement their income, a practice which is on the increase and which has an adverse effect on the quality of higher education in Yemen (Al-Abbasi, 1997).

Private education

In general, education is the responsibility of the government. However, private investment in general and higher education is starting to emerge in Yemen, and recently there has been a substantial increase in the number of private schools, especially in Sana'a city. Most governorates, however, still lack these facilities. Poor economic conditions and low incomes constitute the main barrier to the spread of private schools. In higher education, there were in 1998 seven private universities, five of which are in Sana'a. They generally offer arts and social science education, such as business administration and law. Data are not available on enrolment at private schools and universities, and their share is obviously low compared with enrolment in the public education system although demand continues to increase. However, all parties concerned with improving the country's educational standards are critical of certain private institutions that are viewed more as profit seekers than as providers of good quality education.

Private institutions are considered as supplementary to the public schools and universities, and in terms of teaching and management are heavily dependent on the staff working in public institutions. In fact, some of the private institutions were established and funded by professionals who work in public education. These institutions were set up in the absence of any laws or clearly defined criteria and conditions for establishing and operating private schools and universities. The government has ceased to issue permits for new private education institutions and is attempting to regulate the existing ones.

Financing education

The macroeconomic context

Over the period 1990–4 Yemen experienced a number of shocks that adversely affected the situation and performance of the economy. The disappointing economic performance was reflected in stagnating real non-oil economic activities and a rise in unemployment. Fiscal deficits were sizeable and financed essentially by the domestic banking system; monetary growth was rapid, inflation accelerated sharply, and the free market exchange rate depreciated significantly.

In late 1994, the government responded to the deteriorating economic situation by embarking on a comprehensive Economic, Financial and Administrative Reform Programme (EFARP) which had the following objectives: (1) to implement a comprehensive national programme for administrative, functional and legal reform; (2) to achieve economic, fiscal and monetary reform; (3) to review education policy with the aim of improving effective and efficient human resources; (4) to develop and strengthen the social safety net; and (5) to accelerate efforts to establish an effective and sustainable water management system. To achieve these aims, the government committed itself to implementing policy and institutional reforms and to increasing investment and maintaining the physical and social infrastructures (Prime Minister's Office, 1997).

The IMF, World Bank, United Nations and other multilateral and bilateral donors supported this initiative with financial resources, policy advice and technical assistance, and the programme was further strengthened in 1996 with a series of fiscal and monetary measures that yielded markedly positive results. From mid-1997, the government started to implement a new phase of the economic reform programme under the Enhanced Structural Adjustment Facility (ESAF).

Initially, the EFARP aimed to mobilise revenues and to contain expenditures (particularly the wage bill and subsidy outlays) through adjustment in domestic prices. The restrictive fiscal measures reduced the fiscal deficit and cut government borrowing from the local bank to zero. The budget deficit was reduced to 5.4 per cent of GDP in 1997, down from the 1994 level of 17 per cent.

During 1997, the government followed a tight credit policy, which led to a considerable reduction of its domestic debt. This resulted in the decline of monetary expansion to around 10 per cent down from its 1995 level of 49 per cent. To strengthen monetary management, the foreign exchange market was reformed, and in mid-1996 multiple exchange rates were eliminated and a unified floating exchange rate was adopted, leading to stability in the exchange market (IMF, 1997).

Thus, inflation declined from approximately 105 per cent in 1994 to around 10 per cent in 1997.

Figure 18.5
Selected economic indicators, 1997

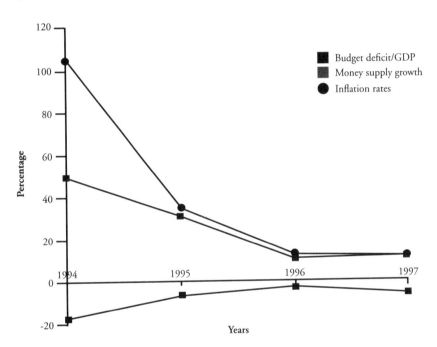

Sources: Ministry of Finance, Central Bank of Yemen and researcher estimates.

In the external sector, oil exports constitute more than 90 per cent of total export earnings. However, because of the decline in oil prices in the second half of 1997, oil revenues fell short of what was expected. This caused some disturbance in both the government budget and the balance of payments. Another major source of balance of payments disequilibrium is the huge external debt. This reached more than 180 per cent of GDP in 1996, and was estimated to be around US$9.7 billion, a substantial share of which was owed to Russia (66 per cent).

However, in late 1997 the government reached an agreement at the Paris Club for 80 per cent relief of the Russian debt with the remainder put for rescheduling on Naples Terms, thereby reducing Yemen's external debt to $2.47 billion (which accounted for 43 per cent of GDP) (Prime Minister's Office, 1997).

It is anticipated that the consequence of structural adjustment will be to foster economic growth, but that this will have different impacts on the various sectors of the economy. Certainly the provision of social services is still far below international standards, illiteracy is prevalent in all age groups, and there is a chronic shortage of health services which makes infant and maternal mortality rates among the highest in the world. The social sectors, particularly education and health, will also be considerably affected by the fiscal and monetary measures.

Budget structure

Low spending on basic social services is explained by macroeconomic factors. A combination of the low level of aggregate public expenditure, a bias against the social sectors, and/or a bias against basic social services within the social sectors produces a low level of public expenditure on basic social services.

One of the objectives of examining the structure of government expenditure is to determine how the share of education has fared relative to other sectors. Another is to assess the fiscal priority given to social spending in the context of other pressures and priorities on government spending. Over the period 1991–6 the share of education in total government expenditure was fairly constant (around 19 per cent). By and large, education represents the largest part of government expenditure on social services, and it is often the second largest category of the entire budget (see Table 18.2).

The other characteristic of the budget structure is the increasing share of both government-provided economic services and the public debt. The share of servicing the public debt increased from 11 per cent of total government expenditure in 1991 to 14 per cent in 1996, and expenditure on economic services increased by the same percentage over the same period (see Table 6.2). To alter this trend, certain measures have to be taken to redefine the role of the public sector. Spending should be directed to the most important sectors, mainly education and health. Public resources are heavily burdened by a substantial subsidisation of certain key commodities: wheat and flour, petroleum products, electricity and other services.

TABLE 18.2
Government expenditures by sector, 1991–6
(as % of total expenditures)

	91	92	93	94	95	96	97*	98*
Public administration	12	14	11	10	9	10	13	18
Security and order	9	10	9	9	9	6	6	6
Defence	30	29	29	35	30	19	17	15
Education	19	19	20	19	19	16	16	17
Health	4	4	4	3	4	4	3	4
Social services	3	3	3	3	3	2	2	3
Economic services	11	12	12	8	12	15	11	12
Public debt	11	10	12	13	14	10	11	10
Government subsidy						17	23	14
Government expenditures as % of GDP	30	31	31	32	27	28	43	42

Note: * = provisional.
Source: Ministry of Finance, *State Budget of 1998*, Sana'a, Yemen.

Apart from debt servicing, military and security expenditure has also been a constraint on public expenditure for human development. In 1996, 25 per cent of government expenditure was allocated to military and security spending, compared with 20 per cent for education and health. The government is, nonetheless, committed to increasing spending on the social sector, mainly education, while reducing spending on other sectors (IMF, 1997).

Financing general education

The share of education in the total public budget and the structure of the education budget have had a marked effect on the overall performance and efficiency of the sector and in particular on coverage, quality and equality. The public budget is the major source of financing for basic, secondary and higher education. The government's commitment to education is reflected in education expenditure as a proportion of both public expenditures and GDP. Over the period 1990–6, public spending on education fluctuated and accounted on average for 19 per cent of total spending, while the share of education expenditures to GDP declined from 7.6 per cent to 5.3 per cent. In 1998, the allocated budget for education remained constant at 16 per cent of the total government budget.

Recurrent versus investment expenditures
Analysis of the government budget begins with the distinction between recurrent and investment expenditures. Figure 18.6 shows that, at around 10 per cent, the share of investment expenditure in total expenditure is rather low. It was mostly below 10 per cent throughout the 1990s, which is below the average for developing countries. However, the major part of donor assistance does not appear in the budget. Only since 1996 has there been a move to incorporate donor funds in the budget. Therefore the low share of investment expenditure is a fallacy.

FIGURE 18.6
Recurrent and investment expenditures on education, 1991–6

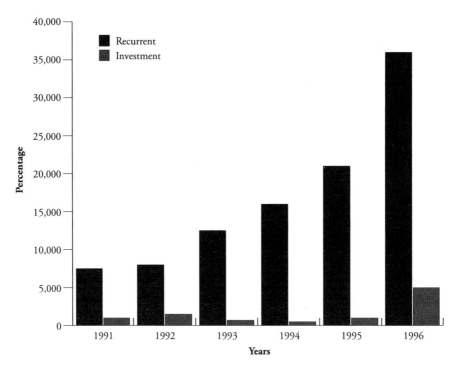

Source: Ministry of Finance.

Recurrent expenditure occupies the bulk of the general education budget, in 1996 making up 92 per cent of total spending on pre-university education (amounting to YR31 billion). About 73 per cent of Ministry of Education (MOE) expenditures went to salaries and wages, while 17 per cent was allocated to goods and services. Despite the high proportion of spending by education on goods and services, only 2 per cent was allocated for maintenance, which explains the deteriorating situation in most schools of the country.

Resources among governorates are unevenly distributed. Although differences in population density and the gross enrolment rate are major factors that should influence the allocation of resources, in practice there is no correlation between these two concerns and resource allocation. The crucial element in obtaining resources, especially for investment expenditures, are the political element and the level of influence that can be exerted on the MOE and the Ministry of Finance (MOF).

On the other hand, statistics point to the extremely high share of recurrent expenditure compared to investment expenditure in each governorate. On the whole, the share of recurrent expenditures exceeds 95 per cent of total expenditure in most governorates, and such allocation of funds leads to the downsizing of investment expenditure.

Nominal versus real expenditures

Although student enrolment increased by 28 per cent during the period 1990–6, education expenditure declined significantly in real terms. Using 1990 prices, education expenditure in 1995 dropped to almost one-third of its nominal value, and the gap between nominal and real expenditures widened during the same period.

The significant decline in financial resources has had a considerable impact on the quality of public education and services, at national as well as at governorate levels. Since wages and salaries accounted for more than 80 per cent of the total education budget, real wages for Yemeni teachers declined between 1990 and 1997 by more than 85 per cent, using the Consumer Price Index (CPI). This had an adverse effect on the performance of the teaching staff at all levels. From field visits, it was found that 10–20 per cent of appointed teachers were reported absent ('ghost' staff). This percentage varied from one governorate to another, and was much higher in rural areas. Some school heads and teachers justified this phenomenon by pointing out that the low remuneration received hardly covered an individual's daily expenses. Many teachers tended, as a result, to seek a second job, while school principals would, because of weak monitoring, turn a blind eye.

FIGURE 18.7

Nominal and real expenditure on education, 1990–6

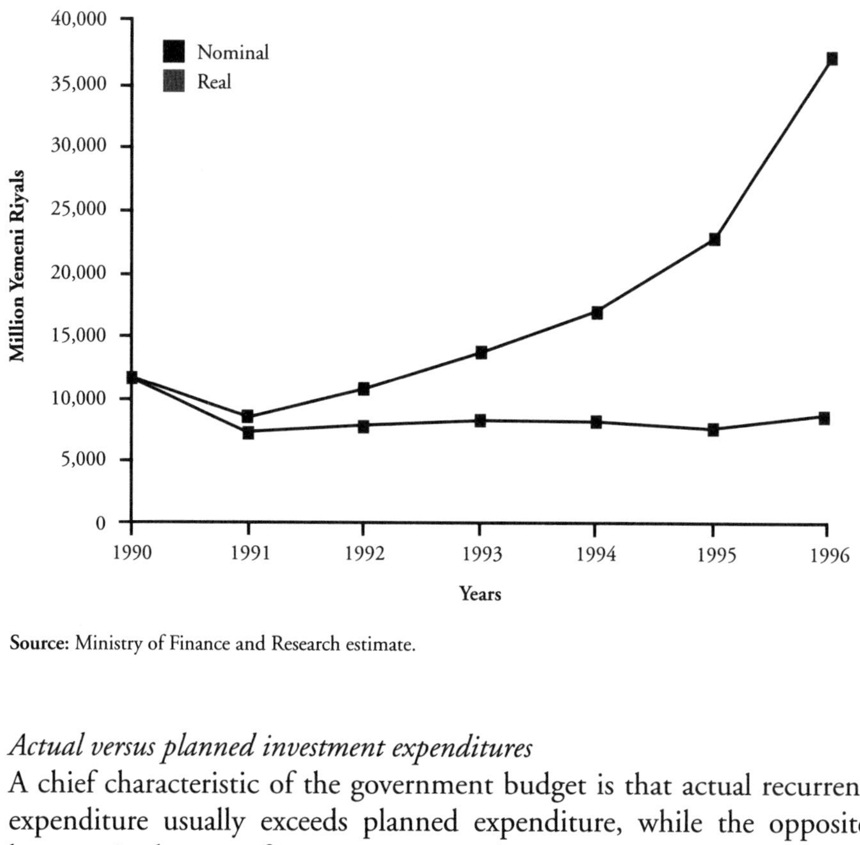

Source: Ministry of Finance and Research estimate.

Actual versus planned investment expenditures

A chief characteristic of the government budget is that actual recurrent expenditure usually exceeds planned expenditure, while the opposite happens in the case of investment expenditures.

Planned allocations in education vary widely compared with implementation. In 1995, the share of investment expenditure in the total education budget was small (less than 10 per cent). Nonetheless, in 1996 and 1997, the MOE did not allocate even the projected shares. In return, actual recurrent expenditure exceeded planned expenditure by 86 per cent. Given weak and indeed absent financial and administrative supervision and control, there is a strong motive to transfer funds from capital use to allocations relating to vested interests such as travel expenses, overtime, and other bonuses. In 1995, actual investment expenditure accounted for only 32 per cent of that planned, while actual recurrent expenditure exceeded that planned by 87 per cent. The situation improved in 1996 with a close match between actual and planned expenditure in wages and O&M (Operation and Maintenance) but actual investment expenditure accounted for half of what had been planned (Ministry of Finance, 1997a).

TABLE 18.3
Actual as a percentage of planned expenditure
on education, 1995 and 1996

	1996	1995
Wages and salaries	114%	187%
Goods and services	106%	190%
Investment	51%	32%

Source: Ministry of Finance, *Final Accounts for Government Budget*, Sana'a, Yemen, 1997.

Education expenditure projections

A World Bank study (1996) on public expenditures in Yemen projected that government expenditure would grow by 20 per cent annually between 1996 and 2000 and at a decreasing rate each year. Increases in recurrent expenditure for pre-university education were projected to be significantly less than investment expenditure. For university education, equal growth rates of recurrent and investment expenditure were projected to reach YR64.7 billion in 2000. Total spending on education was assumed to be a fairly constant proportion of both the public budget and GDP.

Review of the government plan demographics indicate that enrolment in basic and secondary education was to expand beyond the projections by 2002, with more emphasis on the education of girls in rural areas and more focus on improved quality in secondary education. Due to the absence of post-secondary institutes or community colleges, pressure will continue to mount on public universities to admit more students. The government has already decided to establish new universities which will require heavy investment spending, and the Ministry of Education is establishing two community colleges in Sana'a and Aden. Planning for higher education growth usually occurs as a result of political pressure rather than labour market needs, as reflected in government decisions to open more public universities without thorough preparation with regard to staffing and facilities (building, libraries, laboratories, etc.). This policy has enormous financial implications (Al-Abbasi, 1997).

Enrolment scenarios

Two possible enrolment scenarios are utilised, based on the following assumptions: (1) a constant population growth at 3.5 per cent per annum for all ages, for the period 1994–2004; (2) total recurrent expenditure for the period 1997–2002 was projected to increase with the gross enrolment ratio for basic and secondary students; and (3) the cost of constructing a new classroom amounts to US$14,000.

SCENARIO 1: HIGH GROWTH IN ENROLMENT

The high-growth scenario assumes that the MOE planned to intensify efforts to encourage female students to enrol in basic and secondary education, with the overall student per classroom ratio remaining stable at 28:1. It is also assumed that admission policies at public universities were not to change significantly between 1998 and 2002.

General education

- Recurrent expenditure was to increase from the 1996 figure of YR30.9 billion to YR92.3 billion in 2002 (see Table 18.4). This expenditure could increase further if the government were to raise teacher salaries. These budget projections assume that government operation and maintenance (O&M) funding would continue at the pre-existing level and assumes at least some private-sector funding.
- Because of the high percentage of unfinished school buildings in the country and high enrolment, investment was projected to increase from the 1996 level of about YR2.2 billion to approximately YR11 billion in 2002.

Total general education expenditures was to increase from the 1996 figure of YR33.1 billion to YR103.2 billion in 2002.

Higher education

- Recurrent expenditure was to increase from YR3.1 billion in 1996 to YR27.2 billion in 2002 especially if the government had increased teachers' salaries. These budget projections assume that government O&M funding continue at the same level.

- Significant investment for construction of new campuses and substantial improvements were required to accommodate the growing enrolment.

- Investment expenditure was to increase from its 1996 level of about YR1.5 billion to about YR37.5 billion in 2002.

- Spending on higher education was to increase from its 1996 level of around YR4.6 billion to YR64.7 billion in 2002.

According to scenario 1, total expenditure on education was expected to increase from YR37.8 billion in 1996 to YR111.2 billion in 2002. The percentage of GDP spent on education was projected to rise from 5.7 per cent in 1996 to 8.4 per cent in 2002.

TABLE 18.4

Projected state budget expenditure, fiscal years 1998–2002 (YR bn): Scenario 1

	1996 Actual	1997 Estimated	1998 Projected	1999 Projected	2000 Projected	2001 Projected	2002 Projected
MOE expenditures							
Recurrent	30.973	35.188	44.153	54.483	66.096	78.807	92.321
Investment	2.165	8.877	9.051	9.482	9.934	10.409	10.907
Total	33.138	44.065	53.204	63.965	76.030	89.216	103.228
Higher education expenditures							
Recurrent	3.074	3.925	6.244	10.044	15.844	20.877	27.236
Investment	1.538	4.218	9.914	17.802	24.768	30.797	37.466
Total	4.612	8.143	16.159	27.847	40.612	51.674	64.702
Total expenditures on education							
Recurrent	34.047	39.113	50.397	64.528	81.940	99.683	119.557
Investment	3.703	13.095	18.965	27.284	34.702	41.206	48.373
Total	37.750	52.208	69.363	91.812	116.642	140.890	167.930
GDP at market prices							
Expenditures on education	665.0	758.1	864.2	976.6	1093.8	1214.1	1323.4
(as % of GDP)	5.7%	6.9%	8.0%	9.4%	10.7%	11.6%	12.7%

Source: (1) Ministry of Finance, 1997, *Final Accounts*, Sana'a, Yemen; (2) Researcher's estimate.

SCENARIO 2: LOW GROWTH IN ENROLMENT

Under the low-growth scenario, a significant change was assumed in admission policies at public universities between 1997 and 2002. Community participation to finance school O&M expenses was to be encouraged and jointly managed by local governments through the newly established School Maintenance Fund.

TABLE 18.5

Projected state budget expenditure, fiscal years 1997–2002 (YR bn): Scenario 2

	1996 Actual	1997 Estimated	1998 Projected	1999 Projected	2000 Projected	2001 Projected	2002 Projected
MOE expenditures							
Recurrent	30.973	35.188	40.474	44.441	48.800	53.592	58.858
Investment	2.165	8.877	8.792	9.211	9.650	10.111	10.596
Total	33.138	44.065	49.266	53.652	58.451	63.703	69.454
Higher education expenditures							
Recurrent	3.074	3.925	6.244	8.137	10.205	12.293	14.750
Investment	1.538	4.218	9.914	15.341	18.622	22.453	26.968
Total	4.612	8.143	16.159	23.478	28.827	34.746	41.718
Total expenditures on education							
Recurrent	34.047	39.113	46.718	52.578	59.005	65.885	73.608
Investment	3.703	13.095	18.707	24.552	28.272	32.564	37.564
Total	37.75	52.208	65.425	77.130	87.277	98.449	111.172
GDP at market prices							
Expenditures on education	665	758.1	864.23	976.58	1093.8	1214.1	1323.4
(as % of GDP)	5.7%	6.9%	7.6%	7.9%	8.0%	8.1%	8.4%

Source: (1) Ministry of Finance, 1997, *Final Accounts*, Sana'a, Yemen; (2) Researcher's estimate.

General education

- Recurrent expenditure was to increase from the 1996 figure of YR30.9 billion to YR58.9 billion in 2002. This expenditure could increase if the government increases teacher salaries.
- Given the deterioration of school buildings and the expansion of schools in remote areas, the projection for investment expenditure was estimated to be at the same level as that in scenario 1.

- Assuming implementation of administrative reform and improvements in financial management, expenditure on general education was set to almost double from YR33.1 billion in 1996 to YR69.5 billion in 2002.

Higher education

- Recurrent expenditure was to increase from YR3.1 billion in 1996 to YR27.2 billion in 2002.
- Some investment for improvements to existing facilities would have been required to accommodate even this rate of growth.
- Investment expenditure was to increase from YR1.5 billion in 1996 to YR27 billion in 2002.
- Spending on higher education was to increase from its 1996 level of YR4.6 billion to YR41.7 billion in 2002.

Sources of education revenues

The main source of education revenues is the government budget. Historically, external sources played a key role in funding education. Before 1990, many Arab countries (e.g. Saudi Arabia, Kuwait) contributed heavily to the education sector through the construction of many school buildings, payments for teaching staff, funding for scholarships abroad, etc.). Other international donors (e.g. US, IDA, UAE) contributed by constructing building and other facilities. After 1990, and because of the Gulf War, external support declined sharply, apart from a limited loan provided by the World Bank.

Education revenues are minimal, and constitute only 3 per cent of the education expenditure. There are three sources of revenue in the education budget:

(1) the contribution of parents for cost recovery, which include symbolic fees for textbooks, registration, examinations and certificates. The relative importance of these items in the total revenues declined by 50 per cent between 1991 and 1995;

(2) revenues from state properties which come mainly from what is called 'exceptional revenues' (i.e. penalties, charges, undisbursed and transferred funds from previous years);

(3) cash credit and cash assistance which have formed an increasing share in education revenues since 1994, and which represent the

bilateral and multilateral contribution to the Yemeni education system.

The support of the private sector for education has taken different forms. From the mid-1970s until the late 1980s community participation in education was widely mobilised through cooperative associations for development and through local councils, particularly in the northern governorates. Community participation came either in the form of cash donations or through provision of building materials and labour for constructing schools. Many rural schools were built in this way, and the MOE had only to provide teachers, textbooks and other educational equipment. It is estimated that many rural schools in areas were initiated and built by cooperative associations. Such mobilisation has, however, become marginal since the late 1980s.

More recently, well-known businessmen have emerged as major providers of funds to build new schools in various parts of the country. Oil companies operating in Yemen have also entered this field, committing themselves to providing school furniture and equipment to many schools in some governorates. Data on the size and magnitude of such contributions are not well recorded at the MOE. The role of parents of students is limited to raising funds needed for maintenance and repair works; in some cases, and in rural areas, they would also provide housing and a monthly allowance for expatriate teachers.

Given the huge financial requirements of the education sector, it is extremely important to mobilise non-conventional resources such as *zakat* (obligatory almsgiving) and *awqaf* (religiously endowed property). Historically, such resources were utilised as a significant source of finance for basic social services, especially education. Although *zakat* yields a very small proportion (2.6 per cent) of total tax revenues, it has considerable potential and could, if properly exploited through the religious dimension, increase the current level of *zakat* receipts. According to the Qur'an, *zakat* is a religious obligation that should be directed to specific purposes. Though nowadays it is usually administered through specific government institutions, it should perhaps be managed by the people themselves or by non-governmental organisations, as a way strengthening community participation. In a decentralised system, each region would collect and distribute its own *zakat* receipts.

Conclusions and policy options

Few sectors in Yemen show as much promise, yet suffer as much pressure, as education. The education system is in deep crisis, with a deterioration in quality because of underfinancing, government budget constraints and competing priorities, misallocation of funds, and widespread mismanagement. The system is unable to meet the huge demand for qualified teachers, provides an insufficient number of schools and classrooms, fails to supply adequate facilities and teaching materials; and is grappling with the administrative complexities of unifying and reforming what were formerly two very different and inefficient systems.

Pre-university education

Enrolment

A sound education policy should contain the solid objective of increasing enrolment in basic education with priority given to female recruitment and rural areas. Simply expanding enrolment is, of course, not enough. The quality of education also matters. The end product of the present system of basic education is often low-level learning and high dropout rates, particularly for rural girls, the poor, and children in remote areas. There needs to be a clear recognition by national policy that without sustained and systematic efforts to improve the quality of basic education – including teacher training, curriculum development and upgrading of facilities – more enrolment will simply lead to a larger, more inefficient system. Thus, investment to improve basic education will need to be cost-effective.

To make the education system more relevant to development needs, vocational and technical education (VTE) needs to be strengthened and expanded. Surveys of manpower needs in Yemen reveal the urgent need for semi-professional manpower in the field of management and accountancy, as well as for technicians in civil and electrical engineering, automotive and computer technology, refrigeration and air-conditioning technology. According to government policy stated in the first five-year plan for 1996-2000, enrolment in VTE was expected to reach 12 per cent of the total enrolment at secondary school level by the year 2000, suggesting that the total number of students in VTE might be around 80,000 by the same year. In 1995/6 enrolment in VTE amounted to 3,000 students which constituted only 1 per cent of total enrolment in secondary education.

Financing

Given the increase in the share of education in the public budget and other recent upward trends, Yemen appears to be moving in the right direction. The rapid increase in total public expenditure, combined with a fairly constant social budget share, has made it possible to raise education expenditure. Admittedly, the period and the extent of this achievement have been relatively brief, and the changes have so far been inadequate compared with existing needs. Additionally, it is in the education sector that the case for cost recovery at the higher levels is the strongest. Yemen is so far from achieving universal schooling that the subsidising of higher education is highly inequitable. Given the substantial differences in social return between basic and higher education, it is even economically inefficient. However, the constraints on such cross-subsidisation are often considerable.

Political economy reasons represent by far the most significant constraint on budget restructuring in favour of basic education. Governments that restructure expenditure will face the active and passive resistance of the beneficiaries of the pre-existing expenditure pattern, even if it is neither cost-effective nor equitable. Governments will also face the politically difficult issue of introducing a cost-recovery mechanism at higher levels of education, and, for that matter, any social service. Apart from this major hurdle, even the most politically committed executive branch of government will face other constraints. Nonetheless, and given the macroeconomic constraints on intersectoral restructuring, most governorates will need to introduce or increase user fees at secondary and higher education, although user fees should not under any circumstances be applied without providing for exemptions for those unable to pay. Besides, and in general, basic social services (including education) must be free, and cost recovery should take place only for non-basic services.

In brief, the public budget for basic and secondary education needs to be restructured along the following broad lines:

- Actual investment spending on education has been falling far below budgeted allocations. While there was a slight improvement in this divergence in 1996, the issue should be resolved in relation to proper policies regarding the transfer of funds to local authorities.
- Any additional resources for the education sector should give priority to improving the current situation of existing schools rather than

building new ones. In addition, the MOE would be more efficient if it provided the full cost of a smaller number of projects each year, rather than allocating a portion of funds necessary to build a larger number of projects that will not be made operative in one year.

- More resources should be allocated to O&M at all levels to sustain an acceptable level of operation, while responsibility for maintenance could accrue to local authorities.
- Salary structure should be reconsidered in order to attract qualified people into the profession, taking into account that raising allowances is no longer a convincing policy measure.
- For the near future, the government budget remains the major source of education financing, but additional resources will be required both to maintain and increase capacity, and to improve the quality of education. These needs will have to be met in part from local revenues which must be considered in the broader context of administrative decentralisation and changing centre-local fiscal relations.
- *Zakat* would be administered by non-governmental organisations and in the context of a decentralised system where every region would collect and distribute its own *zakat* receipts.
- In order to reduce the wage bill, overstaffing and underemployment, a long-established feature of the government apparatus, should be curtailed in the wake of the adoption of the government's Economic, Financial and Administrative Reform Programme in 1994.

Higher education

The opportunity for entry into higher education now exists in Yemen and any attempt to limit access will be seen as a threat to the students and their families. As a result, containing growth and introducing cost sharing may meet serious resistance from students, and on some issues the faculty may support them. How might these issues be managed to bring about the necessary changes to Yemen's higher education system? The following discussion outlines areas of policy development that should be considered.

Managing demand

Overall enrolment in Yemen's public universities is increasing faster than the planning and funding needed to accommodate this growth. The most recent growth took place with inadequate planning and insufficient funding. This has resulted in a serious decline in educational quality. Moreover, a part of the increasing demand for higher education could be other schools and institutes.

One way of addressing the problem is for each University Council to establish the overall enrolment level of the university, which should relate directly to the overall funds that will be available from the government budget. Individual councils can then establish the maximum enrolment for each programme with the various faculties of each university, and ensure that these limits are rigidly enforced.

Financial diversification

Public universities currently possess the autonomy to collect and manage their income, a process which is considered to be the fundamental requirement for implementing cost-recovery programmes. Given this status, universities could find different ways of raising funds; for example, through consultancy, research, short-term training, renting facilities, etc. Less than 5 per cent of the overall revenue received by the universities from government is generated from fees, such as registration, library and laboratory use, and breakage. Revenue from these fees is currently allocated to the central administration and the various faculties of each university. It is possible for these and similar fees to be increased to cover 10 per cent of the overall budget over a few years and to act as a base for a gradual increase so that higher education can become cost-effective. All fee income that is allocated to the faculties should remain with the faculty, and not be transferred elsewhere.

Private higher education

The newly developing system of private universities can be expanded to become an important component of higher education. In addition to providing educational opportunity, the private universities are implementing new and relevant programmes.

It is advisable that the MOE should be given the responsibility for developing and implementing a programme that will provide oversight of private higher education. It will also ensure that the private programmes continue to make a positive contribution to Yemen's development, rather than being viewed strictly as a business venture.

University programmes

The relevance of the universities to national needs should be a common concern for the university community, the government and the citizens. This chapter indicates that a large part of the education provided at the universities is failing to prepare graduates successfully to enter employment, a concern that was voiced by employers as well as students and graduates. The reasons are many and diverse. Most are directly related to the decline in the limited financial resources allocated to the university system. Measures must be taken to transform the system into an important national educational resource.

Educational planning ought to match manpower planning. This can be achieved by improving communication and coordination between the responsible institutions and the private sector, and it should be reflected in the type of programmes and curricula provided by public and private universities.

The Role of the State in a Traditional Society

Dr Abdul-Kareem Al-Iryani
(Minister of Foreign Affairs)[1]

The role of the state is a dynamic process. It is directly linked to social traditions, economic changes and technological innovations. To take the history of Europe as an example, the renaissance and the Industrial Revolution brought about radical changes in the role of the state. Before that, the role of the state was essentially simple, whether it was a city state or an empire.

By the end of the First World War, the role of the state began to take on what might be called an international character. During the last quarter of the nineteenth century, the Ottoman Empire, and Imperial China and Japan were trying to adjust to the new role of the state which originated in nineteenth-century Europe.

After the First World War, the Russian revolution created a new role for the state under the ideological thesis of scientific socialism, democratic centralism and centrally planned economies. This was in sharp contrast to democratic liberalism, freedom of the press, free and fair elections and a free market economic system. The great struggle between these two roles began in earnest after the Second World War and lasted from 1950 to 1991 when the great failure predicted by Zbigniew Brzezniski (in his book *The Grand Failure: The Birth and Death of Communism in the 20th Century*) occurred earlier than he had predicted. The USSR began to disintegrate in 1992.

It is worth noting that most of the states in the so-called Third World which emerged during the 1950s and 1970s had adopted the Russian style in various degrees, particularly the one-party system and centrally planned economy. In today's world, the role of the state is steadily becoming almost universal. The socioeconomic goals are dominated by liberalisation, privatisation, globalisation and freely floating national currencies. The political role of the state is now dominated by democratisation, free and fair elections, good governance and the protection of human rights.

So the universal role of the state at the advent of the twenty-first century can be summarised as follows:

- Fostering the rule of law and individual as well as collective security of its citizens.
- Maintaining an independent judiciary.
- Adopting a stable economic policy, freeing the economy from distortions and combating corruption.
- Enhancing democracy or democratisation and popular participation in free and fair elections.
- Judicious use of national wealth with special attention to disadvantaged groups in society.
- Directing state resources to investment in social services (health, education and welfare) and infrastructure projects.
- Protection of the environment.
- Protection of human rights.

Of course we all know that these functions will not be applied in a vacuum nor are they applied with the same yardstick in all our societies. The nature of the society, its heritage, demographic constitution, level of economic development and prevalence of state institutions, all greatly affect the role of the state, assuming that such a state wishes to adhere to the above principles.

Now let us look at the most important aspects of Yemeni society, which make up the milieu in which economic, social and political developments take place.

First, we can all agree that Yemen has a traditional society. We may not agree on the aspects of traditionalism and their relative impact on economic and political developments. In my view, the most important aspects of Yemeni society are:

- legacies
- statehood
- settlement
- religious values

- tribalism
- demographic homogeneity
- minimal social stratification and general social mobility

These aspects all affect development. Let me dwell on each character-istic, as follows:

Legacies

The legacy of Yemen's ancient civilisation has its influence in Yemeni society even today. The earliest records of Yemeni civilisation date back to the second millennium BC. Meanwhile, extensive records of prehistoric human activities are being discovered at several historic sites. These records may prove that ancient Yemeni civilisation represents a continuum of human existence of the same ethnic origin until today. It is now well established that Yemeni civilisation flourished in parallel with those of the Nile Valley and Mesopotamia. However, the advent of Islam in Yemen did not lead to lingual and cultural substitution as it did in the Nile Valley and Mesopotamia. Therefore, traditional continuity is a hallmark of Yemeni society.

Nationhood

This aspect of Yemeni tradition is very important in maintaining Yemeni territorial integrity during the weakness of central authority. The traditional feeling of nationhood or statehood has protected Yemen from disintegration during periods of internal conflict. One hundred and thirty years of British colonialism did not lead to diversion among Yemeni social and tribal links or to the evolution of two distinct states. The institution of statehood is deeply rooted in Yemeni history. Pre-Islamic states of Saba, Qataban, Hadhramawt and Himyar created a deep-rooted tradition of statehood. Yemen was the first country to regain its statehood during the early Abbasyd period of Islamic caliphs who ruled the entire Islamic world, except Andalusia.

Sedentary population

The settled nature of Yemeni society plays an important role in all aspects of Yemeni development. Unlike the situation which existed in Northern

Arabia or even in the neighbouring African states, Yemenis are neither nomadic nor pastoral. Ninety per cent of the population live in permanent dwellings and the majority are still subsistence farmers.

Religious values

Like most developing Muslim societies, religious values are extremely important in the state's efforts towards modernisation. The impact of religious values is most stark regarding the role of women. The woman's share in education, employment and public life is one of the lowest in the world.

Tribalism

Tribalism in Yemen is as old as Yemeni civilisation. It is, in fact, an institution with its rules and regulations. Tribes are divided on a genealogical basis. Yemen's modern history has been dominated by the activity of northern tribes, whether during resistance to the Ottoman rule or the war between the republicans and the royalists. However, it is my view that tribalism is a rural institution. It is being weakened by education, modernisation and urbanisation.

Demographic homogeneity

Yemeni society, ancient as it is, is demographically homogeneous. There are no ethnic divisions. In fact, the people in Yemen are claimed to be descendants of Qahtan, while people of North Arabia are claimed to be descendants of Adnan. Uncertain as these divisions may be, demographic homogeneity remains a notable fact of Yemeni society.

Minimal stratification and high social mobility

Many ancient societies are characterised by a high degree of stratification (India is the strongest example). It is my view that despite its long history of human settlement that dates back to at least the Bronze Age, Yemeni society did not evolve the institution of social stratification. Similarly, Yemeni society is characterised by unimpeded social mobility compared with ancient Asian societies. Perhaps the dominant role of trade and migration in Yemen's history is the reason for this phenomenon.

I shall summarise very briefly my own assessment of the impact of the traditional aspects of Yemeni society on economic and political development. Traditional as it is, Yemeni society is characterised by openness, i.e. it is an extroverted society, if that is the right phrase. I believe that the mercantile heritage and migration have fostered this character. Therefore, modern development and modern means of production are readily accepted and quickly learned and adopted. I hope that those of you who have dealt with rural development in Yemen would agree.

Nevertheless, one cannot easily dismiss the constraints that these traditional aspects put on economic development. It is clear that religious values and tribalism have affected the role of women. Women are the most deprived group in our society. However, my general conclusion is that traditionalism has not really been a serious barrier to economic development.

Now, let me go to the second topic of this important symposium, namely democracy. Yemen is a country committed to democracy and is undergoing a democratisation process, i.e. it is a nascent democracy. This commitment to democracy was a very important catalyst in realising Yemen's unity. It was also a unifying factor in fighting the secessionist effort of 1994.

Despite Yemen's commitment to democracy, Yemen, like all emerging democratic states, is faced with real challenges that must be overcome in order to become a fully fledged constitutional democracy.

These challenges are:

- A low standard of living. The per capita income is less than US$400.
- A weak economic system. This is now undergoing a radical restructuring.
- Weak constitutionality. Education is going to be an important factor in this regard.
- The conflict between traditional and modern legal systems. A modern legal system is a prerequisite for the evolution of a civil society.
- Weak parliamentary traditions. Parliament has not yet established its own traditions of being a regulatory and inspecting institution. This role is still very weak.
- Lack of continued voter interest. This is especially visible following an enthusiastic participation in voting.

- Lack of participatory tradition in public life. One can see this from the weak interest in protection of shared (public) property.
- Sparse existence of state institutions relative to the size of the population. Yemen has one of the lowest numbers of law-enforcement officers and supporting judiciary in the world. In a dictatorial regime, these institutions are a means of oppression. However, in an emerging democracy, they are needed for fostering human rights and creating a civil society.

With regard to constraints that may be imposed by various aspects of Yemeni traditions on democratisation, I may surprise you by claiming that at this stage of democratic development, these traditional aspects have not constrained either men's or women's participation during elections. However, there are only 2 women in the 301 members of parliament. Such a result is not unique to traditional societies. We all know the limited role of women in European democracies up until the fourth quarter of this century.

My final comment about the above-listed challenges to Yemen's democratisation is that we all know it is an evolutionary process. The most important factor is continuity of commitment to democratisation. An emerging democracy may be plagued with many shortcomings, it may not be fully free and fair, and it may even be corrupt. However, democracy is endowed with a self-repair system.

We must admit that several democratisation processes were abolished in the Arab world under the pretext of corrupt practices. Some have come back and some are still absent. To cite an example, I asked a Jordanian friend in 1989 how the parliamentary elections were going after more than 20 years of absence. He expressed surprise that the candidates didn't seem to change any of their improper campaign practices. They are doing the same as they did before. In my view this proves that only continuity will correct these shortcomings.

NOTE

1 This chapter was originally the opening speech at the conference on 'Yemen: The Challenge of Social, Economic and Democratic Development', organised by the Centre for Arab Gulf Studies at the University of Exeter, Exeter, UK, 1–4 April 1998.

Contributors

Mutahar A. Al-Abbasi is Deputy Minister for Development Plans at the Ministry of Planning and International Cooperation, Yemen; he is also Associate Professor, Department of Economics, Sana'a University.

Yahya Almutawakel is Associate Professor of Economics at Sana'a University. He holds a Ph.D. from the University of East Anglia, specializing in industrial economics and international trade. He has held several senior posts in the Yemeni Ministry of Planning and International Cooperation and published in regional academic journals.

Nora Ann Colton is Professor of International Economics at Drew University. She received her Ph.D. from St Antony's College, Oxford University. She is a specialist in Middle Eastern economics and speaks Arabic fluently. Her publications include a forthcoming book on the Yemeni economy.

Susanne Dahlgren Ph.D., studied anthropology at the University of Edinburgh, the London School of Economics and Political Science and the University of Helsinki. The chapter in this volume received the *Association for Middle East Women's Studies* Junior Scholar's Prize in 2001.

Nader Fergany is Director of the Almishkat Centre for Research in Cairo and Lead Author, Arab Human Development Report. He has taught and undertaken research at numerous institutions in Egypt and elsewhere, and published widely on demography, international migration, labour markets, education and development.

Ali M. Ghailan is a civil engineer who lives and works in Hodeidah.

Mouna H. Hashem is a social development consultant and researcher. Her experience includes project planning, and research in poverty alleviation, social exclusion, education, gender and community participation. She holds a Ph.D. from the University of Michigan in Urban, Technological and Environmental Planning.

Hussein Al-Hubaishi was educated in Aden, Egypt, Britain and the USA. Formerly a Legal Advisor of the President and Council of Ministers, Head of the Legal Office of the State, 1967–88, he chaired the Joint Committees for the Delimitation of the Maritime Boundaries (Yemen/Saudi Arabia, Yemen/Oman): 1996–2004; and has published widely in English and Arabic.

Abdul-Kareem Al-Iryani is a senior Yemeni statesman and former Prime Minister and Minister of Foreign Affairs.

Beth Kangas is currently a lecturer in the anthropology department at Wayne State University in Detroit, Michigan. She received her Ph.D. in cultural and medical anthropology from the University of Arizona.

Helen Lackner is an Honorary Fellow at the Institute of Arab and Islamic Studies, University of Exeter and a research associate of CEFAS (Centre français d'archaeologie et de sciences sociales de Sana'a) in Sana'a, Yemen. She also works as an international consultant in social aspects of rural development.

Kamil Mahdi is Lecturer in Economics of the Middle East and the Director of Gulf and Arabian Studies at the Institute of Arab and Islamic Studies, University of Exeter. His other Ithaca Press publications include *State and Agriculture in Iraq*, and two edited books: *Water in the Arabian Peninsula* and *Iraq's Economic Predicament*.

Thomas Pritzkat studied Islamic Sciences, Ethnography and Geography in Berlin, Cairo and London, taking an M.A. from the School of Oriental and African Studies, and a Ph.D. from the Free University, Berlin. Currently, he is Chief Technical Advisor with the German Development Co-operation (GTZ) in Sana'a.

Marina de Regt is an anthropologist who has worked for six years on development projects in Yemen. In 2003 she received her Ph.D. from the University of Amsterdam for her dissertation on women health workers in Hodeidah. She is currently doing research on migrant domestic workers in Yemen.

M. Mosleh Al-Sanabani is Assistance Professor in the Faculty of Agriculture, University of Sana'a. He obtained his Ph.D. in soil and water science from the University of Arizona in 1991. His research focuses on management of water and soil in dry lands.

Charles Schmitz is Associate Professor in the Department of Geography at Towson University, Baltimore, Maryland. His recent research interests include transnational politics and identity in Yemen and the legal battle for human rights in Guantánamo Bay, Cuba.

Nageeb A. R. Shamiry is a member of the Supreme Judicial Council of the Republic of Yemen, and was previously president of the Supreme Court of the PDRY (South Yemen). He is author of numerous publications on legal issues.

Richard N. Tutwiler is Research Professor and Director of the Desert Development Center at the American University in Cairo. An applied anthropologist, he formerly led the Natural Resource Management Program at ICARDA in Aleppo. Dr Tutwiler has over twenty years of experience in the agricultural and rural development sectors in Yemen.

Christopher Ward is an Honorary Fellow of the University of Exeter. He studied at Oxford University, and worked for the World Bank 1980–2004, largely in Africa and the Middle East. His publications include Bank papers on agriculture and the environment in Madagascar, Iran, Jordan and Yemen.

Ilse Worm (M.A. in Islamic Sciences, M.Sc. in Public Health) is a freelance consultant in health and development. She lived and worked in Yemen between 1994 and 1997, and contributed to the development of mother and child health services through several Yemeni–German cooperation projects.

Anna Würth studied anthropology and Middle Eastern studies at the Free University of Berlin, where she earned her Ph.D. in 1998. Her research interests are Islamic law, judicial reform, gender and human rights. Her publications include *Ash-Shari'a fi Bab al-Yaman* (in German). She currently teaches at the Free University of Berlin and is an advisor to the German Institute for Human Rights in Berlin.

Bibliography

Statistics obtained from the Authorities in Mukalla (Idarat al-iskan; Maslahat al aradi/Authority for State Property etc.) stem – literally – from big, worm-infested and dusty tomes in which unmotivated and underpaid civil servants engrave bits of information they deem worthwhile to be communicated to posterity.

Al-Abbasi, Mutahar (1997), 'Higher Education in Yemen: Structural Adjustment, and Labour Market Needs', study submitted to Sanaʿa University and the World Bank.

Al-Abbasi, Mutahar (1998), 'Public Expenditures on Social Services: A Review of Education and Health Sectors'. Proceedings of The Second Yemeni Economic Conference, May 1998, Sanaʿa, Yemen.

Al-Abbasi, Mutahar and Yahya Almutawakel (1998), 'Decentralization and Education Expenditures in Yemen: Financial and Economic Analysis', study submitted to the World Bank Resident Mission in Sanaʿa, Yemen.

Al-Abdin, al-Tayib Zein (1975), *The Role of Islam in the State, Yemen Arab Republic (1940–1972)*, unpublished PhD thesis, Cambridge University.

Abdulghani, N., R. van Dijk, F. Muller and J. Velema (1991), *Hodeidah Urban PHC Project: Results of an Impact Study*, Hodeidah (Yemen).

Abdulghani, Nagiba (1993), 'Legislation and Health Care for Yemeni Women', paper presented at the Conference on *Yemeni Women and Legislation*, 28–9 November 1993, Sanaʿa (Arabic).

Adra, N. (1985), 'The Tribal Concept in the Central Highlands of the Yemen Arab Republic', in N. S. Hopkins and S. E. Ibrahim (eds.), *Arab Society*, Cairo: The American University in Cairo Press.

Al-Agbari, T. and M. Al-Hebshi (1993), 'Policy and Social Background', in Deutsche Gesellschaft für Technisch Zusammenarbeit (GTZ), *Innovation Development in the Agricultural Sector: Open Orientation Phase, Appraisal Report, Annex 1*, Eschborn: GTZ.

Agricultural Research and Extension Authority (AREA) and SURDP (Southern Upland Rural Development Project), 1993.

Al-Akwa', Isma'il (1986), *Al-madaris al-islamiyya fi al-yaman*, Sana'a: Maktabat al-Jil al-Jadid.

Al-Akwa', Isma'il (1995), *Hijar al-'ilm wa ma'aqiluhu fi al-yaman*, 5 vols (1903, 1905, 1918), Beirut: Dar al-Fikr al-Mu'asir.

Albar, A. (1993), 'Poultry Production in Yemen', in Deutsche Gesellschaft für Technisch Zusammenarbeit (GTZ), *Innovation Development in the Agricultural Sector: Open Orientation Phase, Appraisal Report, Annex 2*, Eschborn: GTZ.

Al-'Alimi, Rashad (1989), *Al-taqlidiyya w'al-hadatha fi al-nizam al-qanuni al-yaman*, Sana'a: Dar al-Kalima.

Almutawakel, Y. (1992), *Import Substitution as an Industrial Strategy in the Yemen Arab Republic*, unpublished PhD thesis, University of East Anglia, England.

Alsanabani, M. M. (1997), 'Land Management Options under Various Land Tenure Systems', *Regional Workshop on Natural Resources Management*, Cairo.

Alsanabani, M., A. Aw-Hassan and A. Bamatraf (1997), 'Impact of Land Tenure on Mountain Terrace Maintenance in Yemen', paper presented at workshop on 'Property Rights, Collective Action and Technology Adoption', 22–6 November 1997, Aleppo: ICARDA.

Alwan, Ala'din (1995), *Prevention and Control of Cardiovascular Diseases*, EMRO Technical Publications, World Health Organisation, Eastern Mediterranean Series 22, Alexandria, Egypt.

Amin, S. H. (1987), *Law and Justice in Contemporary Yemen*, Glasgow: Royston Ltd.

Al-'Amrani, Muhammad (1984), *Nizam al-qada' fi al-islam*, Sana'a: Ma'had al-'Ali li'l-Qada'.

AREA (1997), *Agricultural Research Strategy*, jointly developed by AREA, ASMSP (Agricultural Sector Management Support Project) and ICARDA (International Center for Agricultural Research in the Dry Areas), Agricultural Research and Extension Authority (AREA), Dhamar, Republic of Yemen.

Assa'edi, Abdullah Saleh (1996), *Baseline Data Survey for Family Health Project in Ibb and Abyan Governorates*, GTZ, Ibb and Abyan.

Bahobeishi, Nageia *et al.*, 1992, 'Towards Safe Motherhood Policies and Strategies in the Republic of Yemen', in Central Statistical

Organisation, Ministry of Planning and Development, Republic of Yemen, 1992, *Population and Health in the Republic of Yemen*, Proceedings of the First National Population Policy Conference, 26–9 October 1991, Sana'a, pp. 91–135.

Botiveau, Bernard (1986), 'L'exception et la règle; la justice vue par les magistrats', *Bulletin du CEDEJ*, Vol. 20, No. 2.

Botiveau, Bernard (1996/7), 'Yémen: politiques législatives et mutations de la culture juridique', *Chroniques Yéménites*, Sana'a: CFEY.

Bowen, Donna Lee (1997), 'Abortion, Islam and the 1994 Cairo Population Conference', *International Journal of Middle East Studies*, Vol. 29, No. 2, pp. 161–84.

Brown, William (1963), 'The Yemeni Dilemma', *Middle East Journal*, Vol. 17, Autumn: pp. 349–67.

Bundesinstitut für Bevölkerungsforschung (ed.) (1994), *Internationale Konferenz über Bevölkerung und Entwicklung* (ICPD), Wiesbaden.

Bujra, A. (1971), *The Politics of Stratification: A Study of Political Change in a South Arabian Town*, Oxford: Clarendon Press.

Buringa, J. (1986), *The Inhabitants of al-Ghulayl: Some Background Data*, Hodeidah: Hodeidah Health Improvement and Waste Disposal Project.

Burrowes, Robert (1987), *The Yemen Arab Republic; the Politics of Development 1962–1986*, Boulder, CO.: Westview Press.

Bury, Wyman (1915), *Arabia Infelix*, London, Macmillan.

Carapico, Sheila (1993), 'The Economic Dimensions of Yemeni Unity', *Middle East Report* (September–October).

Carapico, Sheila (1998), *Civil Society in Yemen: The Political Economy of Activism in Modern Arabia*, Cambridge: Cambridge University Press.

Central Bank of Yemen (1973), *Annual Report 1972–1973*, Sana'a.

Central Bank of Yemen (1986), *Annual Report 1986*, Sana'a.

Central Bank of Yemen (1992, 1994, 1996), *Annual Books*, Sana'a: CBY.

Central Bank of Yemen (1997), *Yemen's Foreign Debt: Expectations for the Paris Club*, report prepared by a CBY team (in Arabic).

Central Planning Organisation (CPO) (1977), *Statistical Yearbook 1977*, Sana'a.

Central Planning Organisation (CPO) (1983), *Evaluation and Analysis of 1975 Population and Housing Census concerning Population Distribution and Internal Migration in the YAR*, Sana'a, Statistical Department, May.

Central Planning Organisation (CPO) (1987), *Statistical Yearbook 1987,* Sana'a.

Central Planning Organisation (CPO) (1988), *Statistical Yearbook 1988,* Sana'a.

Central Planning Organisation (CPO) (various) *Statistical Yearbooks,* Sana'a.

Central Statistical Organisation (CSO) (1990), *The Emigrants,* Sana'a: Centre for Statistical Organisation [in Arabic].

Central Statistical Organisation (CSO) (1991), *Migrants: The Results of the Survey Administered after 2 August 1990,* Sana'a, Government Printing Office (in Arabic).

Central Statistical Organisation (CSO) (1991), *Population and Development in the Yemen Arab Republic,* Sana'a: Central Statistical Organisation.

Central Statistical Organisation (CSO) (1994), *Poverty and Monitoring Information System: Short Report on Poverty Indicators in Yemen Based on the Population and Housing Census 1994,* Sana'a: Central Statistical Organisation.

Central Statistical Organisation (CSO) (1996), *Primary Results of the Population Census, 1994,* Sana'a, Yemen.

Central Statistical Organisation (CSO) (1996), *Statistical Yearbook 1995,* Sana'a.

Central Statistical Organisation (CSO) (1996a), *Final Results of the 1994 Population, Housing and Establishments Census: General Report,* Sana'a: CSO.

Central Statistical Organisation (CSO) (1996b), *Statistical Yearbook,* Sana'a: CSO.

Central Statistical Organisation (CSO) (1998), *Statistical Year Book,* Sana'a, Yemen.

Central Statistical Organisation (CSO) (1998), *Yemen Demographic and Maternal and Child Health Survey 1997,* Sana'a: Central Statistical Organisation.

Central Statistical Organisation (CSO) (various) *Statistical Yearbooks,* Aden.

Central Statistical Organisation (CSO), Ministry of Planning and Development, Republic of Yemen (1992a), *Yemen Demographic and Maternal and Child Health Survey,* Sana'a.

Central Statistical Organisation (CSO) (1992b), *Population and Health in the Republic of Yemen,* Proceedings of the First National Population Policy Conference, 26–9 October, 1991, Sana'a.

Central Statistical Organisation (CSO) (1992c), *National Population Strategy 1990–2000* and *Population Action Plan*, endorsed by the Ministerial Cabinet, 1991, Sana'a.

Central Statistical Organisation (CSO) (1994), *Statistical Year Book 1993*, Ministry of Planning and Development, Sana'a, Yemen.

Central Statistical Organisation (CSO) (1997), *Statistical Year Book 1996*, Ministry of Planning and Development, Sana'a, Yemen.

Chaudhry, Kiren (1997), *The Price of Wealth: Economics and Institutions in the Middle East*, Ithaca, NY: Cornell University Press.

Chaudhry, M. A. *et al.* (1992), *Water Resources Management Options in the Sana'a Basin*, Sana'a: High Water Council/UNDP.

Chelhod, J. (1985), *L'Arabie du Sud*, Vol. 3, *Culture et institutions du Yemen*, Paris: Maisonneuve and Larose.

Chenery H. B. and L. Taylor (1968), 'Development Patterns: Among Countries and Over Time', *Review of Economics and Statistics*, Vol. 50 (4): pp. 391–416.

Christman, Henry M. (ed.) (1996), *The Public Papers of Chief Justice Earl Warren*, New York: Capricorn Books.

Colony of Aden (1941), *Ordinances Enacted during the Year 1941*, Aden: Cowasjee Dinshaw & Bros.

Colton, Nora Ann (1992), *International Labour Migration: The Case of the Yemen Arab Republic*, Oxford University, unpublished doctoral dissertation.

Colton, Nora Ann (1993), Interviews with officials at the Aden branch of the Ministry of Migration, August.

Comisso, Ellen (1991), 'Property Rights, Liberalism, and the Transition from "Actually Existing" Socialism', *East European Politics and Society*, Vol. 5, No. 1, 162–88.

Cosgrove, W. *et al.* (1996), *Yemen: Rural Water Supply Sector Study*, Washington DC, World Bank.

Coulson, Noel (1969), *Conflict and Tensions in Islamic Jurisprudence*, Chicago: Chicago University Press.

Dameem, A. (1993), 'Plant Protection and the Use of Pesticides', in Deutsche Gesellschaft für Technisch Zusammenarbeit (GTZ), *Innovation Development in the Agricultural Sector: Open Orientation Phase, Appraisal Report, Annex 2*, Eschborn: GTZ.

Davie, Michael (1994), 'Guerres, idéologies et territoires: Urbanisation récente de la côte libanaise entre Jbayl et Sayda', in *Annales Géographie* (Paris), Vol. 575, pp. 57–73.

De Soto, Hernando (1988), 'Constraints on People: The Origins of Underground Economies and Limits to their Growth', in Jerry Jenkins (ed.), *Beyond the Informal Sector*, San Francisco: Sequoia Institute.

Detalle, Renaud (1993), 'The Yemeni Elections Up Close', *Middle East Report*, No. 185, November–December 1993, pp. 8–12.

Deutsche Gesellschaft für Technisch Zusammenarbeit (GTZ), (1993), *Innovation Development in the Agricultural Sector: Open Orientation Phase*, Appraisal Report, Eschborn: GTZ.

Doriye, Joshua (1992), 'Public Office and Private Gain: An Interpretation of the Tanzanian Experience', in M. Wuyts, M. Mackintosh and T. Hewitt (eds.), *Development Policy and Public Action*, London: Oxford University Press and the Open University.

Dresch, Paul (1989), *Tribes, Government and History in Yemen*, Oxford: Clarendon Press.

Eagleton, Terry (1994), *Ideology; An Introduction*, London and New York: Verso.

Economic and Social Commission for West Asia (ESCWA) (1990), *Promoting Industries based on Local Resources in Yemen and Democratic Yemen*, Amman: UNESCWA.

Economic and Social Commission for Western Asia (ESCWA) (1992), *The Impact of the Gulf Crisis on the Economies of Western Asia*, Beirut.

Economic and Social Commission for Western Asia (ESCWA) (2003), *Statistical Abstract of the ESCWA Region*, Issue 22, New York: United Nations.

Economist Intelligence Unit (EIU) (1995), *Country Report: Oman, Yemen, 1994–1995*, London: Economist Intelligence Unit.

Economist Intelligence Unit (EIU), *Country Profile – Yemen and Oman*, London: EIU, various years.

Eickelman, Dale, (1981), *The Middle East: An Anthropological Approach*, Englewood Cliffs, NJ: Prentice Hall.

El Mallakh, Ragei (1986) *The Economic Development of the Yemen Arab Republic*, London: Croom Helm.

Fadel, Muhammad (1996), 'The Social Logic of Taqlid and the Rise of the Mukhtasar', *Islamic Law and Society*, Vol. 3, No. 2.

Al-Fadli, Muhammad (ed.), (n.d.), *Watha'iq dimuqratiyya fi al-yaman*, No. 3, Sana'a: YAR, Majlis al-sha'b al-ta'sisi.

FAOSTAT-PC (1996), *Agricultural Statistics*, Rome: FAO.

Faria, V. (1995), 'Social Exclusion and Latin American Analyses of Poverty and Deprivation', in G. Rodgers *et al* (eds.), *Social Exclusion: Rhetoric, Reality, Responses*, Geneva: International Institute for Labour Studies.

Al-Fatesh, I. and E. de Nooy (1993), 'Water Management and Tubewell Irrigation in the Central Highlands', in Deutsche Gesellschaft für Technisch Zusammenarbeit (GTZ), *Innovation Development in the Agricultural Sector: Open Orientation Phase, Appraisal Report, Annex 3*, Eschborn: GTZ.

Fergany, Nader (1994), 'Construction of Quality of Life Indices for Arab Countries in an International Context', *International Statistical Review*, 1994.

FIAS (World Bank, Foreign Investment Advisory Service), 1997,

Food and Agriculture Organisation (FAO) (1989), *Spate Irrigation: Proceedings of the Subregional Expert Consultation on Wadi Development for Agriculture in the Natural Yemen*, Rome: FAO.

Food and Agriculture Organisation of the United Nations (1996), *Yemen, World Food Summit Follow-up Draft Strategy for National Agriculture Development Horizon 2010*, 13–17 November 1996.

Fox, Jonathan (1995), 'Governance and Rural Development in Mexico: State Intervention and Public Accountability', *Journal of Development Studies*, Vol. 32, No. 1, October, pp. 1–30.

Franz, Erhard (1995), 'Die Kontroversen um die Internationale Konferenz für Bevölkerung und Entwicklung im arabisch-islamischen Raum', in Deutsches Orient-Institut (ed.), *Nahost Jahrbuch 1994*, Opladen, pp. 195–200.

Gandy, Christopher (1971), 'The Yemen Revisited', *Asian Affairs*, Vol. 58: pp. 295–304.

Gargousi, M. (1997), *Investment Programming and Preparation of Annual Plans, UNDP Project in Support of the Five-Year Plan*, Sana'a, August (in Arabic).

Gatliff v. Dunn, 1738, and Johnson v. Lathman, 1850.

Ghanem, I. (1976), 'A Note on Law No. 1 of 1974 Concerning the Family, People's Democratic Republic of Yemen', in R. B. Serjeant and R. Bidwell (eds.), *Arabian Studies* III, London: Hurst.

Globovaskaya, Elena (trans. by M. A. Bahr) (1981), *Hawl Mas'alat fiat al-dunya fi al-yaman* [The Issue of Marginal Groups in Yemen], Beirut: Dar Al-Hana.

Glosemeyer, Iris (1995), *Liberalisierung und Demokratisierung in der Republik Jemen 1990–1994*, Hamburg: Deutsches Orient Institut.

Government of the Republic of Yemen, UNICEF and Programme of Cooperation, 1999–2001 (1997), *Making a Difference: Joint Strategy to Achieve the Well-Being of Children and Women in the Republic of Yemen*, November.

Government of Yemen and UNDP – Yemen Country Office (1997), *Poverty Alleviation & Employment Generation*, UNDP Programme Support Document, June.

Graham, Wendy J. and Oona M. R. Campbell (1992), 'Maternal Health and the Measurement Trap', *Social Science and Medicine*, Vol. 35, No. 8, pp. 967–77.

Guijt, Irene and Meera Kaul Shah (eds.) (1999), *The Myth of Continuity: Gender Issues in Participatory Development*, London: Intermediate Technology Publications.

Hagendoorn, L. (1993), 'Ethnic Categorization and Outgroup Exclusion', in *Ethnic and Racial Studies*, Vol. 16, No. 1, pp. 26–51.

Halliday, Fred (1974), *Arabia Without Sultans*, Middlesex: Penguin Books.

Halliday, Fred (2002), *Revolution and Foreign Policy: The Case of South Yemen 1967–1987*, Cambridge: Cambridge University Press.

Al-Haruji, Khalid (1998), two part series on 'Treatment Abroad', *Al-Thawra*, 16 February: 3; 17 February: 3.

Hashem, M. (1996), *Goals for Social Integration and Realities of Social Exclusion*, Geneva: International Institute for Labour Studies.

Haykel, Bernard (1997), *Order and Righteousness: Muhammad 'Ali al-Shawkani and the Nature of the Islamic State in Yemen*, unpublished PhD thesis, University of Oxford.

Hill, Enid (1987), *Al-Sanhuri and Islamic Law*, Cairo: AUC Press.

Hodeidah Health Improvement and Waste Disposal Project (1986), *Evaluation Report*, Hodeidah.

Hodeidah Health Office (1993), *Urban Health Development Plan*, Hodeidah.

Al-Hubaishi, H. A. (1988), *Legal System and Basic Law in Yemen*, Worcester, Billing and Sons Ltd.

Al-Hubaishi, H. (1997a), 'Arbitration in Yemen', paper presented at seminar of Yemeni Judges, Sana'a, 7 December 1997.

Al-Hubaishi, H. (1997b), 'Commercial courts in Yemen'.

Human Rights Watch Middle East (HRW) (1992), *Yemen: Steps Toward Civil Society*, New York, HRW/Middle East, Vol. 4, No. 10.

Ingrams, Doreen (1970), *A Time in Arabia*, London: John Murray.

International Fund for Agricultural Development (IFAD) (1985), *Report of the Special Programming Mission to People's Democratic Republic of Yemen*, Rome: IFAD.

International Institute for Labour Studies (1996), *Social Exclusion and Anti Poverty Reduction Strategies*, Geneva: International Institute for Labour Studies.

International Labour Office (ILO) (1972), *Employment, Incomes and Equality: A Strategy for Increasing Productive Employment in Kenya*, Geneva: ILO.

International Labour Office (ILO) (1989), *Year Book of Labour Statistics*, Geneva: ILO.

International Monetary Fund (IMF) (various years), *Balance of Payments Statistics Yearbook*, Washington DC: IMF.

International Monetary Fund (IMF) (1990), *International Financial Statistics Yearbook*, Washington DC: IMF.

International Monetary Fund (IMF) (1997), 'Republic of Yemen: Enhanced Structural Adjustment Facility', draft proposal prepared by the Yemeni Government in collaboration with staff of the IMF and the World Bank, Washington DC, US.

International Monetary Fund (IMF) (1997), *Republic of Yemen, Enhanced Structural Adjustment Facility, Medium-Term Economic and Financial Policy Framework, 1997–2000*, prepared by Yemeni Authorities in Collaboration with the Staffs of the International Monetary Fund and the World Bank, August.

International Monetary Fund (IMF) (1997), *Republic of Yemen: Recent Economic Developments*, report prepared by an IMF mission.

Jazairy, I., M. Alamgir and T. Panuccio (1992), *The State of World Rural Poverty*, New York: New York University Press.

Jenkins, Jerry (1988), 'Informal Economies Emerging from Underground', in Jerry Jenkins (ed.), *Beyond the Informal Sector*, San Francisco: Sequoia Institute.

Jongstra, Eduard (1996), *The Return Migrants of Hodeidah City, Yemen*, paper presented at the Arab Regional Population Conference, Cairo, December 1996.

Kangas, Beth (1996), *Therapeutic Itineraries in a Global World: Yemeni Biomedical Treatment Abroad*, unpublished Master's thesis, Department of Anthropology, University of Arizona, Tucson.

Kapteijns, Lidwien and Jay Spaulding (1994), 'Women of the Zar and Middle-class Sensibilities in Colonial Aden', *Sudanic Africa*, Vol. 5, Bergen: Centre for Middle Eastern Studies, University of Bergen.

Kempe, Annica *et al.* (1994), *The Quality of Maternal and Neonatal Health Services in Yemen – Seen Through Women's Eyes*, Stockholm: Radda Barnen.

Kennedy, John (1987), *Flower of Paradise*, Netherlands: D. Reidel Publishing Company.

Khalid, Z. (1996), *Characterization of Land Use and Elements of Farming Systems*, Dhamar, Yemen: AREA.

Khalid, Z. and A. Johaish (1997), *Crop and Farm Budgets, Land Utilization Aspects and Possibilities for Farming Systems Improvements*, Dhamar, Yemen: AREA.

Al-Khawlani, M. (1993), 'The Impact of Seed Multiplication on the Environment', in Deutsche Gesellschaft für Technisch Zusammenarbeit (GTZ), *Innovation Development in the Agricultural Sector: Open Orientation Phase, Appraisal Report, Annex 2*, Eschborn: GTZ.

Köhler, Damaris, (1996), 'Du bist ledig und schwanger? Geh woanders hin', Deutscher Entwicklungsdienst (Ded) Brief, No.1, 1996, pp. 20–1.

Kostiner, J. (1996), *Yemen: The Tortuous Quest for Unity, 1990–1994*, London: Pinter.

Kruseman, G. P. (1996), *Sources for Sana'a Water Supply (SAWAS Project)*, Sana'a: NWSA/TNO.

Lackner, Helen (1985), *PDRY: Outpost of Socialist Development in Arabia*, London: Ithaca Press.

Lackner, Helen (1985), *The PDRY*, Boulder, CO: Westview Press.

Leftwich, Adrian (1995), 'Bringing Politics Back In: Towards a Model of the Developmental State', *Journal of Development Studies*, Vol. 31, No. 3, pp. 400–27.

Leveau, Rémy *et al.* (eds.) (1999), *Le Yémen contemporain*, Paris: Karthala.

Lichtenthaler, G. (2003), *Political Ecology and the Role of Water: Environment, Society and Economy in Northern Yemen*, Aldershot: Ashgate Publishing Limited.

Lightwood, J. M. (ed.), *The Encyclopaedia of Forms and Precedents*, 3rd edn., London: Butterworths.

Llewellyn N. and Hoebel F. A. (1941), *Conflict and Case Law in Primitive Jurisprudence*, Norman University of Oklahoma Press.

Al-Maitami, M. (1997), 'Azmat al-'Umla al-Yamaniyya', Monthly Monograph Series of the Arab Center for Strategic Studies, Damascus.

Makhlouf Obermeyer, Carla (1992), 'Islam, Women and Politics: The Demography of Arab Countries', *Population and Development Review* (New York), Vol. 18, No. 1, pp. 33–60.

Makris, G. (1994), 'Creating History: A Case from the Sudan', *Sudanic Africa*, Vol. 5, Bergen: Centre for Middle Eastern Studies, University of Bergen.

Mallat, Chibli (1995), 'Three Recent Decisions of the Yemeni Supreme Court', *Islamic Law and Society*, Vol. 2, No. 1.

al-Mani', Ilham Muhammad (1994), *al-Ahzab wa-al-tanzimat al-siyasiyah fi al-Yaman (1984–1993): dirasah tahliliyah*, Sana'a: Mayallat al-Thawabit.

Mann, Michael (1988), *States, War and Capitalism*, New York and Oxford: Basil Blackwell.

Marshall, Enid A. (ed.) (1973), *Gill, The Law of Arbitration*, 3rd edn, London: Sweet and Maxwell.

Al-Masodi, 'Abd al-'Aziz (1987), *The Yemen Opposition Movement 1918–1948*, Georgetown University, unpublished PhD thesis.

Mayer, Heinz (1991), *Funktion und Grenzen der Gerichtsbarkeit im Rechtsstaat*, Wien: Manzsche Verlagsbuchhandlung.

Meharotra, Santosh and Aung Tun Thet (1996), *Public Expenditures on Basic Social Services*, UNICEF Staff Working Paper, No.1, New York, US: UNICEF.

Mehrah, Golnar (1995), *Girls' Drop-out from Primary Schooling in the Middle East and North Africa: Challenges and Alternatives*, Amman, Jordan: UNICEF.

Meneley, Anne (1996), *Tournaments of Value: Sociability and Hierarchy in a Yemeni Town*, Toronto, University of Toronto Press.

Mercier, Eric (1997), *Aden, un parcours interrompu* (Collection Villes Monde Arabe; Vol. 3), Tours: URBAMA; Sana'a: CFEY.

Merkin, Robert (1987), *Encyclopaedia of Competition Law*, Vol. II, Ch. 2, London: Sweet and Maxwell.

Messick, Brinkley (1993), *The Calligraphic State: Textual Domination and History in a Muslim Society*, Berkeley, CA: University of California Press.

Metcalf, B. D. (1984), *Moral Conduct and Authority: The Place of* adab *in South Asian Islam*, Berkeley: University of California Press.

Ministry of Agriculture and Irrigation, *Agricultural Statistics Year Book*, 1985 and 1996 edns, Sana'a.

Ministry of Agriculture and Water Resources (MAWR) (1990), *Agricultural Statistics Year Book 1989*, Sana'a: MAWR.

Ministry of Agriculture and Water Resources (MAWR) (1997), *Agriculture Statistics Year Book 1996*, Sana'a: MAWR.

Ministry of Education (1992), *Educational Statistics 1987–1988*, Sana'a: Ministry of Education.

Ministry of Education (1995), *Educational Statistics*, Sana'a, Yemen.

Ministry of Finance (1997a), *Final Accounts for Government Budget*, Sana'a, Yemen.

Ministry of Finance (1997b), *State Budget of 1998*, Sana'a, Yemen.

Ministry of Finance (1997c), *The Financial Statement of the Public Budget Projects for the Fiscal Year 1998*, Sana'a, Yemen.

Ministry of Information (MoI) and CSO (1997), *Final Report and Results of the First Industrial Survey*, Sana'a: CSO.

Ministry of Insurance and Social Affairs (1991), *The Emigrants*, a paper prepared for the Government of the Republic of Yemen [in Arabic].

Ministry of Planning and Development (MPD) (1991), *Population and Development*, Sana'a: Ministry of Planning and Development.

Ministry of Planning and Development (MPD) (1992), *General Economic Memorandum*, Round Table Conference, Geneva.

Ministry of Planning and Development (MPD) (1997a), *The First Five-Year Development Plan, 1996–2000*, Sana'a, Yemen.

Ministry of Planning and Development (MPD) (1997b), 'Republic of Yemen: Facing the Challenge', prepared for the Consultative Group for Yemen, organised by EU Brussels, Belgium.

Ministry of Public Health, Republic of Yemen (1994a), *Forward-looking Policies and Strategies for Health Development in the Republic of Yemen*, draft, Sana'a.

Ministry of Public Health, Republic of Yemen (1994b), *Ministerial Decree*, 17 December 1994, Sana'a (Arabic).

Ministry of Public Health, Republic of Yemen (1995), *First Five Year Plan for Health Development* (1996–2000), Sana'a (Arabic).

Ministry of Public Health, Republic of Yemen (1996a), *National Plan for the Training of 4000 Community Midwives*, Sana'a.

[442]

Ministry of Public Health, Republic of Yemen (1996b), *Shari'a Guidelines for Family Planning Methods*, Sana'a, Minister's Office (Arabic).

Moench, M. (1997), *Local Water Management: Options and Opportunities in Yemen*, Sana'a: World Bank.

Molyneux, M. (1982), 'State Politics and the Position of Women Workers in the People's Democratic Republic of Yemen 1967–77', *Women, Work and Development*, Vol. 3, Geneva: International Labour Office.

Molyneux, M. (1989), 'Legal Reform and Socialist Revolution in South Yemen: Women and the Family', in Sonia Kruks, Rayna Rapp and Marilyn B. Young (eds.), *Promissory Notes: Women in the Transition to Socialism*, New York: Monthly Review Press.

Molyneux, M. (1991), 'The Law, the State and Socialist Policies with Regard to Women: The Case of the People's Democratic Republic of Yemen 1967–1990', in D. Kandiyoti (ed.), *Women, Islam and the State*, London: Macmillan.

Molyneux, M. (1995), 'Women's Rights and Political Contingency: The Case of Yemen, 1990–1994', *The Middle East Journal*, Vol. 49, No. 3.

Moore, Mick (1993), 'Declining to Learn from the East? The World Bank on "Governance and Development"', *IDS Bulletin*, Vol. 24, No. 1.

Mottahar, Mohammed (1998), *Higher Education in the Republic of Yemen: Current Situation and Future Prospects*, report presented to the Arab Regional Conference on Higher Education, Beirut, Lebanon.

Al-Mu'allimi, Ahmad (1954 and 1981), 'Al-Shari'a al-mutawwakiliyya aw al-qada' fi al-yaman', reprinted in *Al-Iklil*, 1981, No. 5.

Al-Muntada al-qada'i (The Judges' Club) (1991), *Al-Nizam al-asasi li-l-muntada al-qada'i*, arts. 1, 2, Sana'a.

Al-Muntada al-qada'i (1992), *Qarar raqm li-l-sanat 1992 bi-sha'n isdar al-l'iha al-dakhiliyya*, arts. 5, 47, Sana'a.

Al Murtadha, A. Y. (1948) (957 AH), *al-Bahr al-zakhkhar*, edited by A. A. al Giraphi, Egypt: Khanki Press.

Mutwali, A. (1975), *Al-Shar'ia Al-ilamiyya*, Alexandria, 1975.

National Committee for Women, Republic of Yemen (1995a), *Report on the Participation of the National Committee in the Fourth World Conference in Beijing, 4–15 September 1995*, Sana'a (Arabic).

National Committee for Women, Republic of Yemen (1995b), *The First Conference on Women after Beijing, 31 October 1995*, Conference Minutes and Summary, Sana'a.

Nientied, Peter and Ferko Öry (1991), *Mission Report of Pre-identification Mission to Hodeidah*, Rotterdam: Institute for Housing and Urban Development Studies.

Ofer, Gur (1967), *The Service Industries in a Developing Economy: Israel as a Case Study*, New York: Praeger.

Oi, J.C. (1992), 'Fiscal Reform and the Economic Foundations of Local State Corporatism in China', *World Politics*, Vol. 45, No. 1.

Oi, J.C. (1995), 'The Role of the Local State in China's Transitional Economy', *China Quarterly*, No. 144.

Ortner, S. B. (1989), *High Religion: A Cultural and Political History of Sherpa Buddhism*, Princeton: Princeton University Press.

Othman. A. (1978), 'Al-akhdam fi al-yaman: asluhum wa taqaliduhum' [Al-Akhdam in Yemen: Their Origins and Traditions], in *Majallat al-Dirasat al-Yamaniyya*, No. 1, pp. 69–77.

People's Democratic Republic of Yemen (1976), *Family Law: Law No. (1) of 1974*, Aden, 14 October.

People's Democratic Republic of Yemen (1977), *Documents of the General Union of Yemeni Women, First General Congress of Yemeni Women in Sa'yun, 15–16 July, 1974*, Aden, 14 October.

People's Democratic Republic of Yemen (1990), *Qanun tamlik al-masakin raqam 18 li-'am 1990* [Law No. 18/1990 concerning the transferal of housing property], Aden.

People's Democratic Republic of Yemen, Central Statistical Organisation (1990), *Statistical Yearbook 1988*, Aden.

Peterson, J. E. (1982), *Yemen: The Search for a Modern State*, Baltimore and London: Johns Hopkins University Press and Croom Helm.

Poverty Information Monitoring Systems (1999), *Short Report on Poverty Indicators in Yemen Based on the Population and Housing Census, 1994*, Sana'a: PIMS – a joint RoY/CSO, World Bank, IMF and UNDP initiative through the Paris 21 Monitoring Group.

Pradhan, Sanjay (1996), *Evaluating Public Spending: A Framework for Public Expenditure Review*, World Bank Discussion Paper No. 323, Washington DC.

Prime Minister's Office (1997), 'The Government Programme', an official document submitted to the Parliament, Sana'a, Yemen.

Pritzkat, Thomas (1999), 'The Hadhrami Community in Saudi Arabia and the Rationale of Investing in the Homeland', in Leveau *et al.* (eds.), pp. 399–418.

Qandil, Nasir (1986), *Hakadha tafajjara al-burkan* ('Adan, 13 Yanayir 1986), Beirut, Al-Haqiqah Bris.

Qassim, Taher Ali (1994), *Ana Shahaat* [I am a Beggar]*: A Report on the Living Standards in Hodeidah City for the Hodeidah Urban PHC Project*, The Hague: Directorate General for International Cooperation, Ministry of Foreign Affairs.

Rais Riasit Majlis al-Wuzara', [President of the Council of Ministers] (1991), *Birnamij al-bina' al-watani w'al-islah al-siyasi w'al-iqtisadi w'al-mali w'al-idari* [Programme for the construction of the nation and political, economic, financial and administrative reform], Sana'a, al-Jumhuriyya al-Yamaniyya.

Rakodi, Carole (ed.) (1997), *The Urban Challenge in Africa: Growth and Management of its Large Cities*, Paris: UN University Press.

Reardon, T. and S. Vosti (1995), 'Links Between Rural Poverty and the Environment in Developing Countries: Asset Categories and Investment Poverty', *World Development*, Vol. 23, pp. 1,495–1,506.

Regt, Marina de, (1997), 'Community Participation in the Squatter Areas of Hodeidah, Yemen', *Sharqiyyât* 9 (2), pp. 124–38.

Regt, Marina de and Marja Exterkate (1996), *Health Attendance of the Poor after the Introduction of Cost-recovery*, Hodeidah Urban Primary Health Care Project, November.

Regt, Marina de (2003), *Pioneers or Pawns? Women Health Workers and the Politics of Development in Yemen*, PhD dissertation, University of Amsterdam.

Republic of Yemen (1991a), *Dustur al-gumhuriyya al-yemeniyya* [Consitution of the Republic of Yemen], Sana'a.

Republic of Yemen, *Qarar ra'is al-wuzara* 12.9.1991 [Prime Minister's Decree dated 12.9.1991] (1991b), *Ittijahat al-camma li-l mucalaja al-shamila li-qada'ya al-iskan fi-l muhafazat al-janubiyya an-natija can tanfid qanun ta'mim al-masakin raqm 23 li-camm 1972m* [General Directives to Address the Housing Issue in the Southern Governorates resulting from the implementation of Law No. 23/1972 Regarding the Nationalisation of Housing Property], Sana'a.

Republic of Yemen (1991c), Investment Law No. 22 of 1991, Sana'a.

Republic of Yemen (1994), Wizarat al-idara al-mahalliyya / maktab muhafiz muhafazat hadhramawt [Ministry of Local Administration / Bureau of the Governor of Hadhramawt]: *Ittijahat al-'amma li-mu'alaja wa hall qada'iyya al-mahallat at-tijariyya* [General directives to

Treat and Solve the Question of Commercial Establishments], Mukalla.

Republic of Yemen, Wizarat al insha'at wa-l iskan wa-tatwir al-hadari/Idarat al-iskan, [Ministry of Construction, Housing and Urban Planning / Housing Administration] (1995a), unpublished document, Mukalla.

Republic of Yemen (1994), *The National Report on Women's Situation in the Republic of Yemen*, issued by the National Preparatory Committee for the Fourth International Conference on Women 1994, Beijing 1995, Sana'a.

Republic of Yemen (1996), *New Population Action Plan (1996–2000)*, Second National Population Policy Conference, 26–9 October 1996, Sana'a (Arabic).

Republic of Yemen, Central Statistical Organisation (1997a), *Statistical Yearbook 1996*, Sana'a.

Republic of Yemen, Court of Appeal Sana'a City (1997b), *Kitab al-ilhsa' al-sanawi al-thani lil-'am 1417*, Sana'a.

Republic of Yemen, *Maslahat al-aradhi wa-'iqarat al-dawla* [Authority for State Properties] (1995b), unpublished document, Mukalla.

Republic of Yemen Ministry of Housing and Urban Planning (1997), *Draft Housing Policy*, March.

Republic of Yemen, Ministry of Justice, High Judicial Institute (1989), *Injazat al-ma'had al-'aliy li-l-qada'*, Sana'a.

Republic of Yemen, Ministry of Justice, High Judicial Institute (1997c), *Al-Khittat al-islah al-qada'i*, Sana'a.

Republic of Yemen, Ministry of Planning and Development (1996), *First Five-Year Plan (1996–2000)*, (in Arabic).

Republic of Yemen, Ministry of Planning and Development (1997), *Republic of Yemen: Facing the Challenge, A Program of Investment Projects and Policy Reforms to Promote Economic Growth and Social Development*, prepared for the Consultative Group for Yemen, Brussels, June.

Republic of Yemen Ministry of Public Health (1994), *Forward-looking Policies and Strategies for Health Development in the Republic of Yemen* (draft), September 1994.

Republic of Yemen Ministry of Public Health (1998), *Health Sector Reform in the Republic of Yemen: First Paper for Discussion*, July 1998.

Republic of Yemen, Mukalla Port Authority (1994), unpublished document, Mukalla.

Rodgers, G. (1994), *Overcoming Social Exclusion: Livelihoods and Rights in Economic and Social Development*, Discussion Paper Series No. 72, Geneva: Institute for Labour Studies.

Rodgers, G., C. Gore and J. Figueiredo (eds.) (1995), *Social Exclusion: Rhetoric, Reality and Responses*, Geneva: International Institute for Labour Studies.

Rodriguez, A. (1997), 'Rural Poverty and Natural Resources in the Dry Areas: The Context of ICARDA's Research', working paper, Aleppo: ICARDA.

Sachs, Jeffery and Wing Thye Woo (1994), 'Understanding the Reform Experiences of China, Eastern Europe and Russia', in C. H. Lee and H. Reisen (eds.), *From Reform to Growth: China and Other Countries in Transition in Asia and Central and Eastern Europe*, Paris: Organisation for Economic Cooperation and Development.

Al-Sa'edi, Abdullah Saleh (1996), *Baseline Data Survey for Family Health Project in Ibb and Abyan Governorates*, GTZ, Ibb and Abyan.

Saint, William (1992), *University Developments in Africa: Strategies for Stabilization and Revitalization*, Technical Paper No. 194, Washington DC: World Bank.

Al-Saqqaf, Mohammed (1993), 'Les projets de révision de la constitution du yémen réunifié', *Cahiers du GREMAMO*, No. 11.

Selvaratnam, Viswanathan and Omporn Regal (1991), 'Higher Education in Yemen: The University of Sana'a', draft working paper, Population and Human Resources Department, Washington DC: World Bank.

Scholz, Fred (1990), *Muscat, Sultanat Oman Geographische Skizze einer einmaligen arabischen Stadt*, Berlin: Das Arabische Buch.

Shaher, K. (1991), 'Al-bunya al-ijtima'iyya al-taqlidiyya fi al-yaman' [Traditional Social Structures in Yemeni Society], in *Majallat al-Dirasat al-Yamaniyya*, No. 43, pp. 211–48.

Shamiry, N. (1984), *Huquq al-mar'a fi tashriy'at al-yaman al-dimuqratiyya (Women's Rights in Legislation in Democratic Yemen)*, Aden: Dar al-Hamdani lil-taba'a w'al-nashr.

Shamiry, Naguib (1985), 'The Judicial System in Democratic Yemen', in Brian R. Pridham (ed.), *Contemporary Yemen: Politics and Historical Background*, London: Croom Helm.

Shamiri, Nageeb (1995), 'Yemen (Country Survey)', *Yearbook of Middle Eastern and Islamic Law*, Vol. 2.

Shapiro, Martin (1981), *Courts: A Comparative and Political Analysis*, Chicago: University of Chicago Press.

Al-Sharjaby, G. (1986), *Al-Shara'ih al-ijtima'iyya al-taqlidiyya fi al-mujtama' al-Yamani* [Social Stratum in Traditional Yemeni Society], Beirut: Dar Al-Hadith.

Social Fund for Development (SFD) (October 1999), *Two Years of Operation Experience and Adaptation*, Report, Sana'a: Social Fund for Development (SFD Yemen).

Steinmo, Sven (1993), *Taxation and Democracy: Swedish, British, and American Approaches to Financing the Modern State*, New Haven: Yale University Press.

Stephen, W. J. (1992), *Primary Health Care in the Arab World*, London: Somerset House.

Stevenson, T. (1993), 'Yemeni Workers Come Home: Reabsorbing One Million Migrants', *Middle East Report*, No. 181, March–April, pp. 15–20.

Stiglitz, Joseph E. (1994), *Whither Socialism?*, Cambridge, Massachusetts: MIT Press.

Stone, Francine (ed.) (1985), *Studies on the Tihamah: The Report of the Tihamah Expedition 1982 and Related Papers*, Harlow: Longman.

Stone, Linda (1989), 'Cultural Crossroads of Community: Participation in Development – A Case from Nepal', *Human Organization*, Vol. 48, No. 3, pp. 206–13.

Swanson, John C. (1979), *Emigration and Economic Development: The Case of the Yemen Arab Republic*, Boulder, CO: Westview Press.

Taïb, Essaïd (1995), 'Le juge algérien et la notion d'indépendence', *Droit et Cultures*, Vol. 30.

Tarbush, Qa'id M. (1993), 'Thawrat 26 sibtimir wa sirat al-tashri' al-dusturi fi al-yaman', in Markaz al-Dirasat w'al-Buhuth al-Yamani (ed.), *Thawrat 26 sibtimir*, Sana'a,

Al-Tayyib, 'Abd al-Malik (1995), *Madlulat al-qada' w'al-qudah*, no publication information available.

Al-Thawra Modern General Hospital (1993), *Annual Statistical Report on Hospital Activities for 1993*, Sana'a, Yemen.

Al-Thawra Modern General Hospital (1996), *Annual Statistical Report on Hospital Activities for 1996*, Sana'a, Yemen.

Thompson, Virginia and Richard Adloff (1968), *Djibouti and the Horn of Africa*, Stanford, CT: Stanford University Press.

Todaro, Michael (1969), 'A Model of Labor Migration and Urban Unemployment in the Less Developed Countries', *American Economic Review*, March: pp. 138–48.

Tutwiler, R. (1990), 'Agricultural Labor and Technological Change in the Yemen Arab Republic', in D. Tully (ed.), *Labor and Rainfed Agriculture in West Asia and North Africa*, Dordrecht: Kluwer, pp. 229–51.

Tutwiler, R. (1995), 'Is Time Worth Money in Sivas and Kayseri?', *ICARDA Caravan*, Vol. 1, pp. 12–13, 19.

Tutwiler, R. and A. Aw-Hassan (1996), 'Trip Report to Wadi Hadramaut, January 1996', Aleppo, Syria: ICARDA.

Tutwiler, R. and E. Bailey (1997), 'Agricultural Growth and Sustainability: Conditions for Their Compatibility in the Rainfed Production Systems of West Asia and North Africa', in S. Vosti and T. Reardon (eds.) *Sustainability, Growth, and Poverty Alleviation: A Policy and Agroecological Perspective*, Baltimore: Johns Hopkins University Press, pp. 278–93.

Tutwiler, R., N. Haddad and E. Thomson (1997), 'Crop-Livestock Integration in the Drier Areas of West Asia and North Africa', in N. Haddad, R. Tutwiler and E. Thomson (eds.), *Improvement of Crop-Livestock Integration Systems in West Asia and North Africa*, Aleppo: ICARDA, pp. 5–23.

Twining, W. and D. Miers (1982), *How To Do Things With Rules*, London: Weidenfeld and Nicolson.

UNDP (1973), *Background Paper for a Country Programme: Yemen Arab Republic*.

UNDP (various years), *Human Development Report*, New York, United Nations.

UNDP (1996), *Development Cooperation Report – 1995, Yemen*, Sana'a, Yemen.

UNDP (1996a), *Development Co-operation Yemen 1993–1994*, report prepared by the Office of the UN Resident Coordinator, UNDP, Sana'a.

UNDP (1996b), *Development Co-operation Yemen, 1995*, report prepared by the Office of the UN Resident Coordinator, UNDP, Sana'a.

UNDP (1997a), *Advisory Note for the Republic of Yemen*, March.

UNDP (1997b), *Preventing and Eradicating Poverty: Main Elements of a Strategy to Eradicate Poverty in the Arab States*, New York, May.

UNDP and Government of Yemen (1997), *Poverty Alleviation and Employment Generation, Programme of the Government of Yemen*, UNDP Programme Support Document, Report No. YEM/97/300/B/01/99, Sana'a.

UNFPA (1997), *Proposed Programme Recommendation by the Executive Director Assistance to Government of Yemen*.

UNFPA, 'The Right to choose: Reproductive Rights and Reproductive Health', *The State of World Population 1997*, New York: United Nations Family Planning Association.

UNICEF (1993), *The Situation of Children and Women in the Republic of Yemen*, Sana'a, Yemen.

UNICEF (1993), *The Situation of Women and Children in the Republic of Yemen 1992*, Sana'a.

UNICEF (1997), *The State of the World's Children, 1997*, Oxford: Oxford University Press.

UNICEF (1998), *The State of the World's Children, 1998*, Oxford: Oxford University Press.

UNICEF, World Bank and Radda Barnen in partnership with the Yemen Government (1997), *To be Seen and Heard: Children and Women in Especially Difficult Circumstances in the Republic of Yemen*.

United Nations (1995), *The Copenhagen Declaration and Programme of Action: World Summit for Social Development*, New York: United Nations.

United Nations (1995), 'Programme of Action adopted at the International Conference on Population and Development: Cairo 5–13 September 1994', *Population and Development*, Vol. 1, New York: United Nations.

United Nations (1996), 'The Beijing Declaration and the Platform for Action', *Fourth World Conference on Women*, Beijing, China, 4–15 September 1995, New York.

United Nations Conference on Housing and Settlement (1996), *An Urbanizing World: Global Report on Urban Settlements*, Oxford: Oxford University Press.

United Nations Development Programme (UNDP) (1997b), *Development Co-operation Report*, Sana'a, Yemen.

United Nations Development Programme (UNDP) (2000), *Human Development Report 2000*, New York: UNDP.

United Nations Education, Scientific and Cultural Office (UNESCO) (1989), 'Yemen Arab Republic: Development Needs of the Education Sector', Education Finance Division, UNESCO, Paris.

United Nations in Yemen (2001), *Yemen: Common Country Assessment*, Sana'a: Horizons Publishing.

United Nations Statistics Division (1992), *Statistical Yearbook*, prepared by the Department of Economic and Social Affairs, New York: United Nations.

United Nations Statistics Division (1995), *Statistical Yearbook CD-ROM (SYB-CD)*, prepared by the Department of Economic and Social Affairs, New York: United Nations.

United Nations Statistics Division (1997), *Statistical Yearbook CD-ROM (SYB-CD)*, prepared by the Department of Economic and Social Affairs, New York: United Nations.

Van der Gun, J. A. M. *et al.*, (1995), *The Water Resources of Yemen*, Report WRAY-35, Sana'a and Delft, Ministry of Oil and Mineral Resources and TNO.

Ward, C. S. (1997), *Yemen: Towards a Water Strategy*, Report No. 15718-YEM, Washington DC: World Bank.

Ward, C. S. and Moench, M. (1999), *Yemen: Local Water Management in Rural Areas – A Case Study*, Sana'a: World Bank.

Weir, Shelagh (1985), 'Economic Aspects of the Qat Industry' in B. R. Pridham (ed.), *Economy, Society and Culture in Contemporary Yemen*, London: Croom Helm.

Weir, Shelagh (1985), *Qat in Yemen*, London, British Museum.

Welchman, Lynn (1988), 'The Development of Islamic Family Law in the Legal System of Jordan', *The International and Comparative Law Quarterly*, No. 37.

Wenner, Manfred W. (1991), *The Yemen Arab Republic: Development and Change in an Ancient Land*, Boulder, Colorado: Westview Press.

Woost, Michael D. (1997), 'Alternative Vocabularies of Development? "Community" and "Participation" in Development Discourse in Sri Lanka', in R. D. Grillo and R. L. Stirrat (eds.), *Discourses of Development: Anthropological Perspectives*, Oxford/New York: Berg, pp. 229–53.

World Bank, *Agriculture Sector Review*, 1993.

World Bank (1976), *Current Economic Position and Prospects of the Yemen Arab Republic*, Washington DC, World Bank.

World Bank (1979a), *Agriculture Sector Memorandum*, Washington DC, World Bank.

World Bank (1979b), *People's Democratic Republic of Yemen; A Review of Economic and Social Development*, Washington DC, World Bank.

World Bank (1986), *Yemen Arab Republic: Current Position and Prospects*, Report No. 5621-YAR, Washington DC.

World Bank (1992), *Republic of Yemen, Human Development: Societal Needs and Human Capital Response*, Report No. 9765-YEM, Population and Human Resources Division, Washington DC.

World Bank (1993), *Implementing the World Bank's Strategy to Reduce Poverty*, Washington DC: The World Bank.

World Bank (1994), *Republic of Yemen, Health Sector Review*, Washington DC.

World Bank (1995a), *Republic of Yemen: Dimensions of Economic Adjustment and Structural Reform*, Report No. 14029-YEM, Country Operation Division, Washington DC.

World Bank (1995b), *Republic of Yemen: Public Expenditure Review*, Report No. 16147-YEM, Country Operation Division, Washington DC.

World Bank (1996), *Republic of Yemen: Poverty Assessment*, Report No. 15158-YEM, Middle East Human Resources Division, Washington DC.

World Bank (1996), *World Development Report 1996: From Plan to Market*, Oxford: Oxford University Press.

World Bank (1996a), *Republic of Yemen: Poverty Assessment*, Report No. 15158-YEM, Washington DC, 26 June.

World Bank (1996a), *Social Indicators of Development 1996*, Washington DC: The World Bank.

World Bank (1996b), *Republic of Yemen: Financial Sector Note*, internal report prepared by a World Bank team.

World Bank (1996b), *Republic of Yemen: Public Expenditure Review*, Report No. 16147-YEM, Country Operation Division, Country Department II and Middle East and North Africa Region, 27 November.

World Bank (1996b), *Republic of Yemen: Poverty Assessment*, Report No. 15158-YEM, Washington DC: The World Bank.

World Bank (1997), *Republic of Yemen Enhancing Policy Options: Human Development Group Middle East and North Africa*, Report No. 16322-Yem., Vol. II, Washington DC.

World Bank (1997), *World Development Report 1997: The State in a Changing World*, Oxford: Oxford University Press.

World Bank (1997), *Yemen: A Population Sector Study*, Report No. 16322-YEM, Washington DC: World Bank.

World Bank (1997a), *Sector Notes: Agriculture, Education, Health, Power, Transport, Water*, prepared for the Consultative Group Meeting for Yemen, Brussels, June.

World Bank (1997b), *Yemen: Towards a Water Strategy, An Agenda for Action*, Report No. 15718-YEM, 13 August.

World Bank (2000), *World Development Report*, Washington: World Bank.

World Bank (2001), *World Development Indicators 2001 – CD-Rom*, Washington DC: The World Bank.

World Bank (2002), *Yemen: Poverty Update*, Report No. 24422-YEM, Washington DC: World Bank.

World Food Programme (1997), *Country Programmes, Executive Board Third Regular Session*, Agenda item 7, Yemen 1998–2001, 8 September 1997.

Würth, Anna, *Al-Shari'a fi Bab al-Yaman: Recht, Richter und Rechtspraxis an der Familienrechtlichen Kammer des Gerichts Süd-Sanaa (Republik Jemen) 1983–1995*, Berlin: Duncker & Humblot.

Yemen Arab Republic, Central Planning Organisation (n.d), *Statistical Yearbook 1975/1976*, Sana'a.

Yemen Arab Republic, Law Office (n.d.)(a), *Tashri'at al-jumhuriyya al-'arabiyya al-yamaniyya min 1.1.1975 hatta 30.6.1976*, Sana'a.

Yemen Arab Republic, Law Office (n.d.)(b), 'Qarar majlis al-qiyada raqm 65 li-sanat 1976 b'il-isdar qanun mahakim amn al-dawla', *Tashri'at al-jumhuriyya al-'arabiyya al-yamaniyya min 1.1.1975 hatta 30.6.1976*, Sana'a.

Yemen Arab Republic, Law Office (n.d.)(c): 'Qanun al-'uqubat al-'askari raqm 15 li-sanat 1975', *Tashri'at al-jumhuriyya al-'arabiyya al-yamaniyya min 1.1.1976 hatta 30.6.1977*, Sana'a, 115–57.

Yemen Arab Republic, Law Office (1979), 'Majmu'at al-ahkam, mahkamat al-isti'naf al-'ulya, al-shu'ba al-tijariyya 1977–1978', *Al-Majalla al-qada'iyya al-yamaniyya*, 1, Sana'a.

Yemen Arab Republic, Ministry of Justice (n.d.), 'Qarar majlis al-qiyada bi'l-qanun raqm 23 li-sanat 1976 bi-tanzim al-sulta al-qada'yya', *Majmu' al-qawanin al-islamiyya*, Sana'a.

Yemen Arab Republic, Ministry of Justice (1980a), *Khittat al-islah al-qada'i al-shami*, Sana'a.

Yemen Arab Republic, Ministry of Justice (1980b), *Majallat al-buhuth w'al-ahkam al-qada'iyya al-yamaniyya*, No. 1, Sana'a.

Yemen Arab Republic, Ministry of Justice (1983), *Kitab al-ihsa' al-sanawi li-l-'am al-qada'i 1982*, Sana'a.

Yemen Arab Republic, Ministry of Municipalities and Housing (1981), *Urban Development Project Hodeidah*, Vol. 7, December 1981.

Younis, Nabil *et al.* (1993), 'A Community Study of Gynaecological and Related Morbidities in Rural Egypt', *Studies in Family Planning*, Vol. 24, No. 3, pp. 175–86.

Zabarah, Ahmad Muhammad (1979), *Nuzhat al-nazar fi rijal al-qarn al-rabi' 'ashar*, Sana'a, Markaz al-Dirasat w'al-Buhuth al-Yamani.

Al-Zaeem, I. (1994), 'Towards Developing an Industrial Strategy in the ROY', paper presented to the seminar on *Developing the Industrial Sector*, Sana'a.

Newspapers
The Middle East, February 1983.
Middle East Times/Yemen edition, February 1991.
14 October (Aden).
26 September (Sana'a).

Magazines
Al-Ayyam, Aden.
Al-Haqq, Sana'a.
Official Gazette, Sana'a.
Al-Sahwa, Sana'a.
Al-Thawra, Sana'a.
Al-Ummal, Sana'a.

Note: Statistics obtained from the Authorities in Mukalla (Idarat al-iskan; Maslahat al aradi/Authority for State Property etc.) stem – literally – from big, warm-infested and dusty tomes in which unmotivated and underpaid civil servants engrave bits of information they deem worthwhile to be communicated to posterity.

Index